CROSSING BOUNDARIES

The Exclusion and Inclusion of Minorities in Germany and the United States

Edited by

Larry Eugene Jones

Berghahn Books
NEW YORK • OXFORD

Published in 2001 by

Berghahn Books

www.berghahnbooks.com

Library of Congress Cataloging-in-Publication Data

Crossing boundaries : the exclusion and inclusion of minorities in Germany and the United States / edited by Larry Eugene Jones
p. cm.
Papers originally delivered at a conference held at the University of Buffalo in the fall of 1998.
Includes bibliographical references.
ISBN 1-57181-285-7 – ISBN 1-57181-306-3 (pbk.) 1. Jews—Germany—History—1933–1945. 2. Jews—Germany—Social conditions—20th century—Congresses. 3. Germany—Social conditions—1933–1945—Congresses. 4. Germany—Ethnic relations—Congresses. 5. Germany—Emigration and immigration—Social aspects—History—20th century—Congresses. 6. African Americans—Social conditions—20th century—Congresses. 7. United States—Social conditions—20th century—Congresses. 8. United States—Ethnic relations—Congresses. 9. Migration, Internal—United States—History—20th century—Congresses. I. Jones, Larry Eugene.

DS135.G3315 C76 2001
796.815–dc21 2001035398

British Library Cataloguing in Publication Data

A catalogue record for this book is available from the British Library.

Contents

ACKNOWLEDGMENTS

The "Crossing Boundaries" conference in Buffalo would not have been possible without generous financial support from the German Academic Exchange Program (DAAD) and the Office of the Vice Provost for International Education, the Dean's Office of the Faculty of Arts and Sciences, the Office of Conferences in Disciplines, the Department of History, and the Graduate Group for German and Austrian Studies at the State University of New York in Buffalo. By the same token, a generous grant from the Lucius N. Littauer Foundation subsidized publication of the conference papers in the volume at hand. The editor and organizers of the conference would like to take this opportunity to express their appreciation for the support they have received from these sources.

INTRODUCTION

"Crossing Boundaries" as Leitmotiv and Metaphor

Larry Eugene Jones

"Crossing Boundaries"—these two words serve not only as the leitmotiv around which the following collection of essays has been organized but also as a metaphor for the life and career of the person who inspired their composition: Georg G. Iggers. Georg Iggers's entire life has been one of crossing boundaries: geographical, racial, and professional. As a young boy, Iggers and his family fled Nazi Germany to resettle in the United States, where he proceeded to launch a promising academic career with a doctorate in French intellectual history at the University of Chicago. As a Jew in Nazi Germany, Iggers had experienced the pain of racial discrimination firsthand and immediately developed a deep and abiding sense of empathy with the plight of African Americans in his adopted land. As a young academic teaching in the segregated South, Iggers became actively involved in the civil rights movement and the struggle for racial equality.[1] As a mature scholar, Iggers continually challenged the ideological and political boundaries that distinguished cold-war academic culture and championed the cause of greater understanding on both sides of the Iron Curtain. And as a historian, Iggers has done his best to break down the professional and disciplinary boundaries that had come to characterize much of modern academic life and to promote a new, more interdisciplinary approach to the study of history.[2]

It is therefore only appropriate that the theme of Crossing Boundaries was chosen as the leitmotiv of a conference held at the University of Buffalo in the fall of 1998 to celebrate Georg Iggers's retirement from the teaching faculty. In true Iggers fashion, the conference was designed to explore from a comparative perspective the ways in which Germany and the United States dealt with the issues of migration, multi-ethnicity, discrimination, and integration. These issues were central to Iggers's life, his

German-Jewish experience as a refugee from Nazi Germany, his engagement in the struggle for racial equality in the United States, and his commitment to German-American scholarly cooperation and German-Jewish reconciliation in the postwar period.

At the core of the conference stood a comparison between the respective fates of the Jew in Germany and the African American in the United States. For while in Nazi Germany the German Jew experienced the progressive revocation of emancipation culminating in expulsion and extermination, the African American was locked in a struggle to realize the full promise of American democracy and had already succeeded in breaking down some, though by no means all, of the barriers that blocked the path to full social, economic, and political equality. Subordinate to this overarching theme were a number of related questions such as public policy toward immigrants and minorities in Germany and the United States, the experience of those who were targets of these policies, the specific forms that the struggle for civic equality took in the two countries, and the way in which the issues of migration, multi-ethnicity, discrimination, and integration have informed historical thinking in the postmodern era.[3]

The following essays have been organized according to the format of the Buffalo conference. In his keynote address on "The Expulsion of Jewish Professors and Students from the University of Berlin during the Third Reich" Konrad H. Jarausch sets the stage for the essays that are to follow by presenting a detailed analysis of the causes, processes, consequences, and implications of the purge of Jewish faculty and students from the University of Berlin. In his concluding remarks Jarausch steps back from the events themselves to ponder what is to be learned from "this paradigmatic self-decapitation of the German university." In venturing a tentative answer, Jarausch not only calls into question "the western cult of the expert, since specialized expertise, however great, does not guard against complicity in acts of inhumanity," but also stresses the need for "a rethinking of the tenuous relationship between scholarship and freedom." For while the German university had developed what Jarausch terms "an admirable ideal of academic freedom" in its conflicts with the church and state throughout the nineteenth century, the betrayal of this ideal by the expulsion of the German Jews after 1933 should remind us—and here Jarausch paraphrases Wilhelm von Humboldt—that "free inquiry ... can never be taken for granted but must be struggled for anew in each generation."

The next three essays expand upon the status and treatment of minorities by focusing on public policy in Germany and the United States. Klaus Bade initiates the discussion with an analysis of the German Citizenship Law of 1913 as an attempt to regulate immigration into Germany from eastern and east central Europe by making citizenship a function of nationality rather than territoriality. In using "ethno-cultural" and "ethnonational" criteria in the definition of German citizenship, the Reichstag set a precedent that not only formed the basis of German immigration policy through the Weimar Republic and Third Reich but was subsequently incorporated into Article 116 of the Grundgesetz of the German Federal Republic. Jochen Oltmer continues this general line of inquiry by focusing on migration policy in Germany from 1918 to 1939. Oltmer, however, places the situation in Germany in a broader European context and examines not merely the government's efforts to regulate immigration into Germany but also its campaign to preserve the sense of Germanness, or *Deutschtum*, of Germans who, for reasons of economic necessity, had emigrated to other parts of the world.

With Ronald Bayor's essay on racism as a determinant of public policy in the American city, however, the focus shifts from Germany to the United States. Here Bayor shows how deeply embedded racism was in the formulation and implementation of urban planning in the United States and documents how municipal authorities in cities as diverse as Chicago, New York, Atlanta, Miami, and Detroit used ordinances, zoning laws, land grants, site and tenant selection for public housing, even physical barriers to ensure the residential segregation of black from white. Here, however, one discovers an interesting reversal of the situation of the Jew in Germany. For whereas in Germany municipal authorities often defied national policy by encouraging Jewish settlement with an eye toward the obvious economic advantages they hoped this would bring, in the United States municipal authorities employed stratagems such as these to discourage the internal migration of African Americans from the South to the cities of the North and to obstruct the policies of a national government committed, though to be sure at times only half-heartedly, to breaking down racial barriers in education and housing.

If the essays by Bade, Oltmer, and Bayor tend to concentrate more upon building boundaries than crossing boundaries, the next set of essays by Werner Angress, Supriya Mukherjee, and Michael Hänel describe the experiences of three German Jews who were forced to leave their homeland in search of more hospitable circumstances. Angress looks back upon his own experiences as a German Jew who left Germany in 1937 to relocate first in London, then in Amsterdam, and finally in the United States. Angress provides real-life texture to the refugee experience by describing what it was like to have lived as a Jewish teenager in Nazi Germany and how one adapted to the new world into which the refugee, most likely without any advance preparation, was suddenly submerged. Angress concludes his memoir by relating what must have seemed like the final irony, his enlistment in the U.S. Army and his return to Germany as a paratrooper in the 82nd Airborne Division. Angress's experience differed significantly from that of the two individuals whom Mukerjee and Hänel have as the topics of their respective essays, William Stern and Ernst Cassirer. Stern and Cassirer were both established academics in pre-Nazi Germany and prominent members of the German-Jewish intelligentsia that the Nazis had vilified so relentlessly in their attacks on the Weimar state. Stern, an eminent psychologist and pedagogue at the University of Breslau, left Germany in 1933 at the height of his career and reputation to emigrate to the United States, where he found a new home at Duke University. But, as Mukerjee explains, Stern's sojourn in the United States was far from happy. Not only did he experience difficulty in learning the English language, but he found himself strangely at odds with the prevailing trends in American psychology. Yet for all of that, Stern never abandoned his faith in the future and steadfastly clung to the intellectual optimism that defined his view of the world right up until his death in 1938.

Like Stern, Ernst Cassirer regarded himself as a spokesman for the rationalist and humanist culture of the eighteenth-century Enlightenment. And like Stern, Cassirer was forced to leave Germany in 1933 in search of a new home that took him first to England, then to Sweden, and finally to the United States, where he taught at Yale and Columbia. Even as a refugee scholar, however, Cassirer refused to recognize any contradiction between the rationalist and humanist values to which he was so deeply committed and those of Germany's national culture as epitomized in the lives and thought of G. E. Lessing, Moses Mendelssohn, Immanuel Kant, and Johann Wolfgang von Goethe. Like Stern, Cassirer regarded Hitler as an aberration of German history, although at the end of his life his faith in the power of philosophy to break the power of myth began to waver.

The next set of essays by Patricia Mazón, Trude Maurer, Tony Freyer, and Manfred Berg focus on the struggle for equal rights in Germany and the United States. Mazón's essay deals in fact with two minorities—Jews and women—and their struggle for equal access to German universities in Imperial Germany. The struggle of the two groups intersected in a particularly interesting way in the case of foreign students from Russia. For not only did the applicant pool from Russia include a disproportionately high number of Jewish applicants, but women applicants were subject to far more rigid admission standards than their male counterparts. Efforts to break down these barriers in the period before the outbreak of World War I were, as Mazón demonstrates, only partly successful. Maurer's essay on the Central Association of German Citizens of the Jewish Faith (Centralverein deutscher Staatsbürger jüdischen Glaubens or CV) focuses more directly on the struggle for civil equality in imperial Germany. As the CV's name suggests, the organization was founded on the premise that there was no contradiction between being Jewish and being German and that the promise of Jewish emancipation was to be realized within a liberal polity in which all citizens, regardless of their race or religion, enjoyed equal rights. Toward the end of her essay Maurer draws some tentative, though nonetheless tantalizing, comparisons between the struggle of German Jews for civil equality in Imperial Germany and the civil rights movement in the United States.

The African American struggle for civil equality provides the background for Tony Freyer's essay on Georg Iggers and the Little Rock School Crisis of 1957 to 1959. Here Freyer shows how Iggers's own experience of persecution as a Jew in Nazi Germany informed his commitment to racial equality and prompted his engagement in the Little Rock desegregation crisis. But in a larger sense, Freyer argues, Iggers's involvement in the struggle for racial equality was a concomitant of his commitment to scholarly integrity. From Iggers's perspective, scholarship and political engagement are necessary and indispensable complements of each other. As a white man, Georg Iggers assumed a conspicuous and often controversial role in the African American struggle for civil equality. As Manfred Berg demonstrates in his essay on the role of whites in the National Association for the Advancement of Colored People (NAACP), by no means was Iggers the only white to become involved in this struggle. For not only was the NAACP founded on the principle of interracialism, but whites played an instrumental role in the NAACP's growth and development as grass-roots activists, leaders, and supporters. This was particularly true in the North, where local chapters with white membership exceeding 10 percent were not uncommon. Moreover, the transfer of leadership from white to black hands at the height of the civil rights conflict was accomplished on a consensual basis without a rupture of ties to white allies in the liberal establishment.

While each of these essays focused on different aspects of the struggle to break down gender, ethnic, and racial boundaries in Germany and the United States, the final set of essays by Tony Freyer, Georg Iggers, and Eckhardt Fuchs explore the ways in which the issues of migration, multiethnicity, discrimination, and integration have impelled historians to cross traditional boundaries in historical writing and thinking. In his essay on the historiography of the civil rights movements, Freyer argues that "civil rights historiography may benefit from a renewed interest in the institutional dynamics of social struggle." This particular aspect of the civil rights conflict, Freyer contends, has been largely overlooked in recent historical writing because of the increased attention focused on "the growth of African American group identity within local organizations or protest organizations from the 1930s to the 1970s, particularly the rise of the civil rights movement identified with Martin Luther King's leadership." The way in which recent historical writing on the civil rights movement has separated activism from litigation has several serious shortcomings that Freyer hopes to correct by reminding us first that King and his followers incorporated a strategy for judicial action into their nonviolent protest campaign, and second that it was the combination of political activism and action in the courts that eventually opened the way to attaining the ideal of equal justice.

In making this argument, Freyer touches briefly upon a question that lies very much at the heart of Iggers's essay on the relationship between objectivity and involvement in writing the history of German historiography. Here Iggers argues that, while history must not be reduced to ideology, "historical scholarship does not operate in a vacuum, but is deeply shaped [both] by the milieu in which it originates and … [by] personal experiences…." This requires an examination of the ideological and philosophical assumptions from which the historian is proceeding and a determined commitment on his or her part to "remain aware of his or her perspective and at the same time remain intellectually honest." Only then, Iggers contends, can the historian escape the uncritical historical objectivism attributed to Leopold von Ranke, the dean of German historians, without at the same time falling into the radical relativism of Hayden White or Frank Ankersmith. Iggers's essay, in turn, serves as the point of departure for a critical examination of the way in which the German historical guild has viewed world or universal history. Like Iggers, Fuchs argues that the German view of world or universal history belies implicit ideological assumptions that all too frequently escape critical examination. Here too German historical writing was informed by a nationalist and Eurocentric bias that prevailed without serious challenge from the time of von Ranke until the 1970s. Fuchs concludes his essay with an appeal for a "transcultural history of historiography" that seeks to overcome the epistemological limits inherent in the very act of writing history through the combination of what he calls "transcultural comparison" and "transcultural transfer." Only then can the historian cross the boundaries that have characterized historical writing in Germany and the rest of the Western world since its emergence as a discrete discipline in the eighteenth and nineteenth centuries.

Taken in their totality, the essays in this volume constitute a challenge to the historical profession as it enters the twenty-first century. In the past historians have played an all too prominent role in constructing the boundaries—whether political, gender, ethnic, racial, or professional—that define modern life. Nowhere is this more apparent than in Germany and the United States, where historians have been actively engaged in the construction of master narratives that relegate minorities of whatever kind to a status of inferiority and that make them targets of discrimination, repression, expulsion, and ultimately extermination. To be sure, much of this has changed with the emergence of a more critical historiography that has sought "to deconstruct" these narratives and the exclusionary models of state, culture, and society implicit in them. The task historians face in the twenty-first century will be to build new models of inclusion capable of transcending the boundaries that their predecessors have helped construct and to search for new paradigms of historical understanding that no longer privilege one sector of society, one culture, or one national tradition at the expense of another. Therein lie the challenge of this book and the enduring legacy of Georg Iggers.

Notes

1. For a more detailed overview of Iggers's life and work, see the essay by D. A. Gerber, "From Hamburg to Little Rock and Beyond: The Origins of Georg Iggers's Civil Rights Activism," in *Geschichtswissenschaft vor 2000. Perspektiven der Historiographiegeschichte, Geschichtstheorie, Sozial- und Kulturgeschichte. Festschrift für Georg G. Iggers zum 65. Geburtstag*, ed. K. H. Jarausch, J. Rüsen, and H. Schleier (Hagen, 1991), 509–22.
2. In this respect, see above all else G. G. Iggers, *New Directions in European Historiography*, 2nd ed. (Middletown, Conn., 1984), and idem, *Historiography in the Twentieth Century: From Scientific Objectivity to the Postmodern Challenge* (Hanover, N.H., 1997).
3. For a report on the conference, see U. Schneckener, "'Crossing Boundaries: German and American Experiences with the Exclusion and Inclusion of Minorities': Konferenz an der State University of New York, Buffalo, USA, 17.–19. September 1998," *Comparativ* 6 (1998): 103–7.

KEYNOTE ADDRESS

The Expulsion of Jewish Professors and Students from the University of Berlin during the Third Reich

Konrad H. Jarausch

The "flight of the muses," as it has been euphemistically called, is one of those catastrophic moments of the twentieth century that connect European with American history. On the artistic level, the expulsion of Jewish intellectuals from Nazi Germany marked the brutal end to the experimentation of Weimar culture, transferring many of its creative impulses across the Atlantic. On the social level, the academic purge meant the destruction of an innovative subgroup that had expanded the frontiers of Central European *Wissenschaft* and human knowledge in general. And on the human level, the forced departure and reluctant transplantation of about 4,600 creative people involved as many broken careers or disappointed hopes as it did successful new beginnings. Since many traces of this exodus have already vanished, an act of critical remembrance is needed in order to keep this exemplary debasement of scholarship from being forgotten.[1]

The politicization of public memory complicates the recovery of the complexities of this academic drama. In the Anglo-American world, the recent framing of the outcome of this persecution as the "Holocaust," symbolized by the Washington museum of that name, serves both as a necessary reminder against forgetting and sometimes as a barrier to critical understanding. In the media, the emotional appeal of Daniel Goldhagen's blanket indictment seems to overpower the more differentiated rational arguments of his critics. In West Germany public rituals of guilt have created a private desire for a *Schlußstrich*, for letting bygones be bygones, while the "mandated anti-Fascism" of the German Democratic Republic (GDR) has left Easterners unprepared to deal with the legacy of racism. And now the debate about communist crimes, sparked by Courtois's controversial *The Black Book of Communism*, threatens to overshadow recollections of the Nazi atrocities.[2]

The destruction of crucial sources and a lack of sustained scholarly attention to the issue also make an analysis of the expulsion of Jewish professors and students difficult. Celebratory anniversary volumes of individual universities have understandably been reluctant to confront the darkest pages of their institutional past. Moreover, the split between history of science studies of academic disciplines and social histories of student movements has also kept the two strands of research from cooperating.[3] In the particular case of the leading German institution in Berlin, Western scholars were long kept out of the university archives and the Marxist-Leninist administration was reluctant to deal with earlier anti-Semitism, postponing the publication of the pioneering study by Rudolf Schottlaender by two decades. Only in the 1980s did the intellectual and political climate shift toward more critical analyses of the betrayal of academic freedom by the universities.[4]

Since time constraints prevent a comprehensive analysis, the following remarks can only sketch some outlines of the removal of Jewish students and professors from the Friedrich-Wilhelms-Universität.[5] But newly accessible archival materials, more exact statistical information, and a perusal of Jewish periodicals will make it possible to rethink some of the central questions. The subsequent comments will start with national developments in order to determine to what degree developments in the German capital were representative or peculiar. In contrast to the faculty-centered literature, they will also treat students and professors equally so as to probe their multiple interactions. Finally, they will try to reconstruct causes, processes and consequences of this "unprecedented event" which "initiated the demise of Berlin's bourgeois university in a moral and largely also in a scholarly sense."[6]

Causes

The reason for the expulsion of Jewish students and professors from German universities was a fateful interaction of long-range anti-Semitic prejudice with a short-range social crisis of the academic professions. While the purge of the universities was part of a wider upheaval that the Nazis termed a "national revolution," it was also prepared by appalling collaboration from within academe. Only an extraordinary combination of factors could produce a fundamental departure from the neohumanist tradition of higher learning that had pioneered the concept of academic freedom, however imperfectly realized. Why did the distinguished representatives of German *Wissenschaft*, world leaders around the turn of the century, prove so wanting in political foresight and ethical commitment?[7]

The answer to this is indeed complex. In the first place, the modern version of academic anti-Semitism originated during the late 1870s in Berlin. With his call to cultural assimilation, phrased misleadingly as "the Jews are our misfortune," the nationalist historian Heinrich von Treitschke provoked the infamous anti-Semitism dispute *(Antisemitismusstreit)* in 1879. Although the classicist Theodor Mommsen defended tolerance with liberal arguments, *völkisch* outsiders like Julius Langbehn and Paul de Lagarde transformed cultural resentment in their seemingly scientific tracts into a biological anti-Semitism, thereby making it inescapable for the victims and acceptable in conservative and Protestant circles of the faculty.[8]

Students compounded the situation by founding the so-called Association of German Students (Verein Deutscher Studenten or VDSt), in order to propagate Christian, patriotic and imperialist ideas, centered around anti-Semitism. Protected by the aged founder of the Reich, Prince Otto von Bismarck, the VDSt captured institutions of student self-government through ingenious agitation and forced most prestigious organizations like the *Burschenschaften* to accept anti-Semitism into their programs.[9] Within one generation the spread of social and racial hostility against the Jews among the faculty and the students transformed the outlook of academics and professionals, laying the ideological foundation for later intolerance.

Second, severe overcrowding created an instructional and professional crisis for academics during the Weimar Republic. After World War I, veterans, refugees and women increased university enrollment by 50 percent from 79,304 students in 1914 to 125,104 in 1923. At the same time, the hyperinflation of the early 1920s impoverished students of modest means, not only forcing them to take odd jobs but also threatening their very survival through starvation and disease. The recovery of the mid-1920s—by 1925 there were 89,469 students—proved short-lived, and during the Great Depression student numbers once again rose to record heights with a total of 138,010 in 1931 as more and more young people stayed in college to avoid unemployment. As a result of overcrowding, student politics fiercely polarized between leftist and rightist ideologies.[10]

The masses of new graduates blocked entry into a shrinking set of academic professions. Teachers had to wait up to ten years for a secure position, three-fourths of the engineering graduates remained unemployed, and in other careers a ruthless struggle for placement developed. Governments tried to balance the budget with dismissals or hiring freezes and thereby shut out the younger generation, making the slogan of the "academic proletariat" a grim reality. The job crisis led to a fundamental breach of trust, since frustrated graduates blamed the Weimar Republic for their troubles and looked for convenient scapegoats, such as the Jews.[11]

Only to established professors did the situation seem somewhat less threatening. The *Ordinarien*, or professors with permanent chairs, complained instead about the dictated peace of Versailles and the institutional shortages of German science due to outmoded laboratories and declining libraries. But during the agony of the Republic Chancellor Heinrich Brüning's salary cuts also affected them, reducing their real incomes by about one-third. In spite of their relative security, professors therefore also feared rapid impoverishment, such as a loss of servants, which they construed as decline of culture. Although the older generation was less directly threatened, the crisis weakened their tenuous bonds to the Republic even further.[12]

Third, during the overcrowding crisis a limited, but important number of academics openly embraced the movement of National Socialism. Among men, neither liberal remedies that stressed increased competition nor socialist slogans that would spread the pain evenly could compete with rightist promises of removing all newcomers such as women, leftists or Jews as competitors. Weimar's prolonged academic crisis allowed racists to activate the underlying imperial anti-Semitism and to make it popular as a patent remedy for all problems even among erstwhile skeptics.[13]

As a result some disoriented students, led by Baldur von Schirach, founded the National Socialist German Student League (Nationalsozialistischer Deutscher Studentenbund or NSDStB) in the mid-1920s.[14] With its radical program of cleansing the universities of alien influences, the sectarian NSDStB scored phenomenal successes in the student elections during the World Economic Crisis:

TABLE 1: Results of Student Elections at the University of Berlin, 1927–1929[15]

Berlin	**1927**	**1928**	**1929**
NSDStB	118=2%	749=15%	1,377=19%
Entire	5,195=100%	5,134=100%	7,162=100%

In Berlin, the NSDStB increased its votes tenfold within two years and began to intimidate Jewish students physically. "All at once the caps were torn off our heads and countless fists pummeled us," a victim recalled. Shouting "Death to the Jews," Nazi students also beat up Republicans and Communists, smashing the bulletin boards of the Left.[16] As a result of persuading dueling fraternities and nationalist corporations to cooperate, the NSDStB captured the Berlin student government and had already seized power on the national level in 1931. These offices allowed the Nazis to pour out a propaganda stream and to persecute individual democratic professors who were mostly Jewish as "un-German."[17]

In contrast, professors were not so taken by National Socialism, since it seemed too plebeian and anti-intellectual. Only a minority of the mandarins, organized in the Weimarer Kreis, was liberal, democratic, or socialist; the great majority remained apolitical and at best tolerated the Republic;

finally a strong minority of nationalists either looked back to the lost monarchy or searched for new forms of authority.[18] Among the latter, eighty-seven professors signed election appeals for the Nazis during the 1932 elections, especially among the humanists and engineers. In Berlin eight faculty members, like the ethnologist Fischer, ignored Friedrich Meinecke's warnings and joined an appeal in February 1933 that called Hitler's seizure of power "the right path." But younger instructors showed more interest in the Nazis, joined the Storm Troops (Sturm-Abteilungen or SA) in droves and eventually formed their own National Socialist Docent League (Nationalsozialistischer Dozenten-Bund or NSDB).[19]

This evidence suggests that the expulsion was less forced upon the universities from the outside than prepared by a growing minority of activists from the inside. The overcrowding, unemployment and pay cuts of the Depression activated the festering poison of anti-Semitism, leading the majority of the politicized students and a small minority of nationalist professors into the Nazi camp. In this fateful development, the university of Berlin played a key role, serving as seedbed of modern anti-Semitism during the Empire, and becoming a stronghold of NSDStB intimidation during the late Weimar Republic. Though most professors remained more restrained in their criticism of the Republic, they did not publicly oppose the student radicals, since many practiced a traditional form of silent social discrimination toward the Jews.[20]

Processes

The Nazi seizure of power gave right-wing activists the opportunity to act out their prejudices. On 13 April 1933 the Berlin student government published "Twelve Theses against the Un-German Spirit" which warned: "Our most dangerous enemy is the Jew and whoever supports him." These racial nationalists wanted to reverse assimilation by insisting on "the will and ability to overcome Jewish intellectualism and the liberal tendencies of decadence associated with it." To achieve this aim, the flyer called for an anti-Semitic purge: "We demand the selection of students and professors on the basis of proof that they think in a German spirit." Though the nationalist rector Kohlrausch distanced himself from the crudity of this assault, he did not denounce the demand simply because "it is an injustice."[21]

The ostensible reason for the anti-Semitic agitation was the charge of Jewish overrepresentation in German intellectual life. Ironically, this phenomenon was a by-product of anti-Semitic restrictions which made the learned or free professions one of the few alternatives to commerce so that about one-third of doctors and lawyers came from Jewish backgrounds.[22] Anti-Semitic propaganda fastened upon the discrepancy between the Jewish share of less than 1 percent in the population and the several times higher proportion among students, ignoring the steep decline from a high of 9.4 percent during 1894/95 to a low of 4.7 percent in 1931/32 in Prussia.[23] Nonetheless, there were some characteristic clusters that racists could cite:

1. Jews concentrated in urban institutions like Berlin (the most Jewish with 931 or 11.5 percent in 1926), Frankfurt, Breslau, or Cologne.
2. Some disciplines like medicine (22.2 percent in 1911/12), or law (11.1 percent) attracted more Jewish students than others like the arts and sciences (3.5 percent), or Christian theology (none).
3. Specific departments at some institutions were known to be particularly "Jewish." The most dramatic case was Berlin, where 37 percent of the medical, 20.2 percent of the law, and 7.5 percent of the arts and science students were Jewish in 1911/12.[24]

Not only sheer numbers but different social behavior also aroused prejudice, since Jews were known to be hard-working and East European or poor students did not always follow the norms of the *Bildungsbürgertum*. Excluded from prestigious corporations, they were forced to found their own associations which set them apart from the rest. For example, in 1923 Berlin had one corporation for German Jews (Sprevia), one Zionist corporation (Kadimah), a sport and rowing club and an association for Jewish history and literature.[25]

A professorial career, nonetheless, remained difficult for Jewish academics, since social prejudices hindered their advancement. According to imperfect statistical evidence, compiled by Ferber, about 7 percent of all appointments between 1864 and 1938 which indicated religious affiliation were Jewish, to which one could add about the same percentage of converted or secular Jews. The number of Jewish scholars was highest in the junior ranks, indicating a gap between relatively free entry and restricted advancement due to informal barriers which demanded higher performance of minority candidates. Though the data are too fragmentary to indicate field distribution, the memoir literature suggests that Jewish academics favored innovative specialties such as social medicine, physics, psychology or the social sciences, since the chances of success were higher in less entrenched fields.[26] As newcomers, Jewish academics often triggered envy among gentile competitors through their unusual behavior and willingness to take risks.

The expulsion rested on two laws, passed in April 1933, that channeled the anti-Semitic agitation among students from below into legal codes from above.[27] The first measure was the "Law for the Restoration of the Professional Civil Service," which cynically suggested that the radical repeal of established rights would restore bureaucratic professionalism for those patriotic Germans who were not dismissed. In effect, the vaguely phrased provisions provided a carte blanche for a thorough Nazi purge of the civil service. While paragraph two mentioned "improper training" in order to get rid of Social Democratic appointees, paragraph three focused on non-Aryan descent, defined as one of four grandparents. The only exceptions, included on President Hindenburg's request, covered those appointed before 1914 or having served at the front during World War I. Since paragraph four stipulated "political unreliability" and paragraphs five and six referred to "simplification of administration,"[28] they provided a broad pretext to get rid of political enemies, whether they were democratic or communist. Nonetheless, this civil service purge was primarily directed at Jewish targets, among them university faculty of all ranks, and when their number turned out to be limited, its exclusionary spirit was extended to the professions as well.[29]

In regard to students, the Nazis proceeded similarly, promulgating a law "against the overcrowding of German universities" that hid its anti-Semitic purpose behind broader enrollment restrictions.[30] Its stipulations confined annual enrollments to 15,000 high school graduates, set a ceiling for women at 10 percent of the student body and limited Jewish matriculations to 1.5 percent with the pretext of bringing them in line with the Jewish proportion of the general population. At the same time the law restricted the Jewish share of any institution to 5 percent, which required a de facto reduction of "non-Aryan Germans," only cushioned by exceptions for children of war veterans or of mixed marriages.[31]

Since these legal restrictions encouraged anti-Semitic rowdies as well as prejudiced instructors to intensify their discrimination, some discouraged Jewish students simply dropped out, thereby stopping many a budding scholarly career. In Berlin 111 communist, social democratic or republican students were relegated and altogether about six hundred students, most of whom were Jewish, were expelled during the summer of 1933.[32] While one may argue about the effectiveness of the enrollment reductions, these admission curbs were devastating for Jewish students.

Due to various exceptions, the brutal implementation of these measures took several years, suggesting that the expulsion must be understood as a drawn-out process. By 13 April the first sixteen Berlin professors were already pensioned off, while the Ministry of Culture demanded the completion of a questionnaire that included a question about the grandparents' religion and ethnicity in order to identify earlier converts. The NSDStB boycott of classes with the slogan "Jews Cannot Be Leaders of Students" forced other prominent scholars like the chemist Fritz Haber to give up their posts.[33] Before the beginning of the winter semester of 1933 about two hundred faculty members, including some staff, were dismissed or retired with pensions reduced by one quarter.

Two years later the Hindenburg exceptions were canceled through the Nuremberg racial laws and previously dismissed scholars barred from laboratories, libraries and archives, making the continuation of their intellectual work impossible. This appalling breach of academic ethics provoked individual protests among only a few honest scientists like Max Planck who defended his colleague Liese Meitner. To the shame of the Berlin university, it must be clearly stated that there was no collective resistance and that even those nationalist academics who disliked the brutal style accepted the substance of the purge.[34]

Jewish students were also expelled from the university incrementally by legal prohibition as well as by discriminatory practice. After filling out a similar questionnaire, all "non-Aryans" were excluded from the mandatory Union of German Students on 22 June 1933, thereby degrading them to second-class status. On all levels, Nazi students and professors systematically made their lives miserable: For instance, the names of the dismissed were published in blacklists, all forms of financial aid canceled, and Jewish students limited to working on Jewish patients or topics. A crucial blow was their exclusion from state examination during 1935, and the interdiction of receiving doctorates in 1937, since the prohibition of academic degrees barred access to professional careers. Finally, from 1938 on enrollment was only possible with proof of Aryan ancestry.[35] The few remaining exceptions concerned children of mixed marriages, which were increasingly discriminated against and most were ultimately excluded as well. In April 1933 the *CV-Zeitung* commented sadly on the "loss of equality of German Jews" through legalized discrimination: "We feel like the banned who are allowed to live in their own homes."[36]

In retrospect this shameful self-decapitation of the German universities remains difficult to understand. It is astounding how successful a large minority of radicalized students and a smaller group of nationalist faculty members were in promoting this exclusion in the misguided hope of a national rebirth that would wipe out the shame of Versailles and overcome the crises of Weimar. But even more scandalous is the compliance of the silent majority of professors and students which forsook the neohumanist legacy of academic freedom by failing to resist.

Many plausible reasons have been advanced to explain this academic lapse: Perhaps the prior social isolation of the victims made it easier not to feel solidarity; perhaps the noisy agitation of radical students kept timid academics from speaking out; perhaps the illusion of national rebirth led respected scholars like Eduard Spranger to pardon Nazi measures as youthful excesses. Nonetheless the ease with which racist zealots overturned humanistic traditions continues to puzzle. The blindness of those who did not realize that they sacrificed their scientific ethics by looking away remains a shocking betrayal.[37]

Consequences

The result of the anti-Semitic purge was the forced de-assimilation of Jewish academics. While Aryan nationalists gloated over the removal of "parasites" from the university, disconsolate Jews complained that their expulsion created "a social problem of incomprehensible magnitude." The reversal of centuries of integration inspired the construction of "a kind of German-Jewish sector" in which the majority of Jews clustered around the Central Association of German Citizens of the German Faith (Centralverein deutscher Staatsbürger jüdischen Glaubens) tried to remain loyal Germans, in hopes of future improvement. In contrast, Zionists saw the purge as proof of the necessity of separate existence: "Our own salvation is our Jewish being."[38] The establishment of a separate "teaching institute" for Jewish scholarship (Wissenschaft des Judentums) in Berlin could only be a temporary measure, since the Nazis would not stop with mere exclusion.

The statistical balance sheet of the expulsion is appalling enough. One foreign office report of December 1934 shows 136 names from Berlin (of whom 115 were Jews, 8 Communists and 16 administrative removals) among the 612 German faculty expelled. Various other Berlin lists contain between 193 and 242 names, indicating that roughly 250 scholars were expelled from institutions in the German capital. Since nine-tenths of the dismissed faculty were Jewish, the anti-Semitic intent of the purge is obvious.[39]

A more detailed analysis of 221 individuals listed in *Verfolgte Berliner Wissenschaft* indicates that 178 of them were from the university, 26 the technical university, 17 from other institutions and 10 independent scholars. Among the expelled, 43 percent were from the medical and 33 percent from the philosophical faculties, but only 5 percent came from the law school and there were no theologians. Since merely 12 percent were full professors, dismissals fell most heavily on the associate professor (47 percent *Extraordinarien*) or assistant professor (25 percent *Privatdozenten*) ranks, i.e., on less established scholars.[40] Even if the mixture of "voluntary retirement" and involuntary removal is difficult to sort out, this distribution suggests that the purge fortuitously eliminated precisely those Jews who were competitors of struggling younger German scholars.

Among students the expulsion had equally drastic effects. The CV advised advanced students to finish up quickly, and beginners to change into other careers or to study abroad, if one could afford it.[41] Though they break off in the winter semester of 1934/35, the official German university statistics show a drastic decline:

TABLE 2: Numbers and Percentages of Jewish Students at German Universities, 1932/33–1934/35[42]

	Jewish Students	Total Enrollment	Jewish %
1932/33	3,336	88,235	3.78
1933	1,908	110,238	1.73
1933/34	812	102,007	0.80
1934	656	91,480	0.72
1934/35	538	84,629	0.64

This time series is confirmed and continued in the compilation by Charlotte Lorenz under the heading "Germans of Alien Ethnicity," which is more inclusive than the above, but shows the same trend.

TABLE 3: Numbers and Percentages of Students of Alien Ethnicity at German Universities, 1932/33–1938/39[43]

	Ethnically Alien Students	Total Enrollment	Alien %
1932/33	3,616	119,702	3.0
1933/34	1,955	104,409	1.9
1934/35	1,110	84,704	1.3
1935/36	776	75,305	1.0
1936/37	441	62,810	0.7
1937/38	185	56,395	0.3
1938/39	51	55,944	0.1

Berlin data amplify this general picture of collapse with additional details. During the winter 1933/34 only 542 Jewish students were still listed by the student union, indicating a reduction by one-half during a single year.[44] One year later a similar list contained merely 248 names (half studying medicine), almost half of whom were only partly Jewish.[45] During the summer of 1937, there were merely 57 Jews left and during summer 1939 only 17 remained.[46] These dry figures for professors and students provide a chilling record of the destruction of a grand tradition of German Jewish learning.

The terrible human tragedies produced by this callous expulsion can be summed up in only a few words. Its many victims suffered the loss of their profession, income and self-respect, thereby cutting off social relations and overturning life plans. As the captivating diary of the Dresden philologist Victor Klemperer indicates, this rejection by the German intellectual community shattered established self-definitions and forced a rediscovery of Jewishness, especially among assimilated Jews.[47]

The expelled reacted in a variety of ways to the threat: A few committed suicide from grief or died prematurely from disappointment. Younger academics and prominent scientists emigrated to more hospitable environments, principally in the United States and England, but also some of the neighboring European countries. Optimistic German patriots remained in the hope that the terror would turn out to be a mistake and be over soon. Yet others, especially in the older generation, simply ignored the danger and carried on more or less normally. Finally, a few courageous individuals actively resisted, defending Jewish rights, fighting for emigration and the like.[48]

A moving letter from the psychologist Kurt Lewin to his mentor Wolfgang Köhler, one of the few non-Jews to protest against the purge, exemplifies this tortured soul-searching. In spite of his love for Germany, he believed he had "no choice but emigration," not because "of revulsion against ugly incidents or fear of personal suffering ... but due to the social realities." Based on repeated experiences of discrimination in his profession and the military during the recent war, he predicted that "Jewish rights" would continue to be diminished in the future and that restrictions on Jewish life would "be implemented ruthlessly in the schematic manner typical of the Germans." Revealing the depth of his frustration, Lewin added: "It is clear that a Jew must feel deeply cheated if that legal equality, on which he has based his entire work, is suddenly taken away." Clairvoyantly, he attributed anti-Semitism to "the lack of pride, quiet matter-of-fact confidence, or self-esteem that exists even without a uniform" and to the inability of "the leading stratum of the *Kleinbürgertum* to acknowledge the achievements of the Jews." From these anguished thoughts he concluded, "I cannot imagine how one can live at present as a Jew in Germany in a manner that satisfies even the most primitive demands of truthfulness."[49]

Emigration was easier if one was young or in a field like the sciences where cultural capital was transportable. For the humanities or social sciences, linguistic barriers were higher and doctors as well as lawyers often had to retake their professional examinations. The younger one's age, the quicker one could assimilate to a new culture and reformulate career plans, whereas older people often faced a devastating loss of social esteem. Nothing was more pathetic than a world-famous professor forced to survive on odd jobs.

Seeking shelter just across the German frontier in Vienna, Prague, or Paris was initially easier, but in the end turned into a greater tragedy. The overcrowding of the professions made obtaining visas difficult, forcing migration to Latin America or the Far East, if one could not get into favored destinations like the U.S. or Great Britain. It was a bitter irony that many expelled academics thought of themselves as Germans and were often identified with the Nazi system which they had barely escaped. Only a small minority emphatically reasserted its Jewishness and went on to Palestine.[50]

This exodus led to a fundamental weakening of higher education in Germany. Even if its precise amount is still disputed among historians of science, the actual and potential loss of academic quality was enormous. In the six years from 1933 to 1939 about 45 percent of all university positions turned over, a much higher rate than normal, which suggests that this exchange of personnel was largely due to the anti-Semitic purge. Since in many disciplines academic life went on without interruption, Klaus Fischer argues convincingly that only 14 to 17 percent of the professors really emigrated, but ignores in his calculation that another substantial percentage was pushed out, but stayed on in Germany.[51] If one wants to get a more precise picture of the impact, three aspects are particularly important.

First, the impact on scientific research was considerable, since four of eight German Nobel prize winners in chemistry were reputed to be Jewish, as were six of twelve in medicine. Though the exact figures are in dispute, the expulsion drastically reduced potential for innovation, something which plebeian Nazi leaders were unable to comprehend. When the liberal industrialist Bosch tried to explain the loss to Hitler, the latter answered with disarming ignorance: "Then we will work for a hundred years without physics or chemistry!"[52]

Second, the university was weakened institutionally, since its autonomy was seriously diminished. The introduction of the Führer principle in Berlin destroyed academic self-government and left scholarly decisions to the whim of uninformed Nazi zealots in the NSDStB or the NSDB.[53] Finally, there was also considerable political damage, since Jewish professors tended to be more liberal, democratic and socialist. Their purge removed much critical potential which has sometimes been described with the German metaphor of "intellectual yeast."[54]

Since the example of physics with Albert Einstein is well known, it needs to be emphasized that other disciplines such as history were strongly affected as well. Eleven Berlin historians were expelled as Jews, including famous names like the Prussian scholar Otto Hintze (due to his Jewish wife), the Marxist historian Gustav Mayer, the archivist Ernst Perels, and the ancient specialist Arthur Rosenberg. Among the younger cohort Elias Bickermann, Hans Baron, Gerhard Masur, Dietrich Gerhard and indirectly Felix Gilbert (who was on scholarship in Rome) were involved as well.

Some non-Jewish colleagues such as the liberal intellectual historian Friedrich Meinecke and the conservative Russian specialist Otto Hoetzsch also had conflicts with the regime. Moreover the promising assistants Eckhart Kehr and Hajo Holborn emigrated to the U.S.[55] Since these were some of the most interesting Weimar minds, Arthur Rosenberg concluded: "A later time will have to state that after 1938 lively and critical historical research did and could no longer exist in the German Reich and that after 1933 a critical German historiography therefore only lived on in emigration."[56]

All hopes for a restoration of the traditional *Ordinarienuniversität* or for a new kind of *völkisch* higher learning turned out to be illusory. Even if some fields like biological or ethnological research profited and new specialties like racial or military science were established by the Nazis, the Third Reich did not lead to a re- but rather a de-professionalization of German scholarship. While the anti-Semitic purge initially created career chances for younger scholars, the consequences of their collaboration with the NSDAP were simply disastrous: The general havoc wreaked by World War II ultimately also brought ruination for all areas of "German science."

The involvement of some historians like Theodor Schieder, Werner Conze, or Franz Petri in the Nazi domination of Europe that has recently come to light is a troubling reminder of the vulnerability of one's own profession.[57] Moreover, the well-known participation of numerous medical doctors and technical experts in the implementation of the Holocaust is the darkest chapter of German scholarship. The expulsion of the Jews therefore marks the beginning of a process of academic self-abdication which in the end threatened to annihilate the very science it purported to serve.[58]

Implications

Two generations after these events, individual memories are beginning to fade and to give way to public memorialization in speeches, monuments and media retrospectives. Virtually all participants of the academic expulsion have passed away and only those who were children at the time can still dimly remember the upheaval. In the repeated retelling, the disturbing memories of the participants have started to diverge, with Jewish recollections focusing on the grievous injustice and individual survival, emplotting the purge as yet another tale of suffering by gentile hands.

Gradually, guilt-ridden German remembrances, focused on commission or omission, have also come out into the open, since those responsible no longer dared contradict self-criticism. For instance, the semi-invisible memorial to the book-burning of 1933 in front of the Humboldt University library has attempted a critical memorialization through the emptiness of glass shelves under ground. The endless debate about the construction of an abstract holocaust memorial in the new/old capital of Berlin or a greater focus on the actual sites of suffering are another case in point.[59]

Though laudable, these attempts at critical understanding are themselves somewhat problematic because they script the story as a morality play with fixed roles. Jewish professors and students are stage-cast as victims, evoking much polite sympathy for their suffering, but they are treated largely as passive and bereft of agency. No doubt, the victim role has distinct advantages, since it assures the concern of others, but it has proven deeply unsatisfactory for fostering a sense of pride and constructing a Jewish state. Moreover, the cloying philo-Semitism that this perspective has triggered among many well-meaning but sometimes uninformed Germans is embarrassing in its excesses.[60]

Instead, the case of the academic expulsion challenges historians to recover a multitude of Jewish actions and reactions to their "social death," ranging all the way from compliance to resistance. Whether in staying on or in emigrating, the core of the struggle was to recapture that normality which the Nazis had so brutally torn away. Kurt Lewin concluded his letter with the plea: "I hope that you will understand and approve that I have to try, even if I know that my life will be torn in two by it, to find a place for my children and myself where one can live with dignity."[61]

In this moral drama the Germans, all too few of whom could be counted among the "just" who helped the persecuted, are largely left with the thankless role as perpetrators. Since Nazi thugs no longer boast of their deeds in public, the expulsion, along with other unspeakable acts, has almost become a crime without a villain—nobody wants to be held responsible for all the suffering. More interested in explaining Hitler's rise to power, older historians commented only reluctantly and in impersonal terms on the annihilation of the European Jews. Only in the last years has a younger generation of scholars started to insist on exact descriptions of the process and on investigating personal responsibility.[62]

In the example of the academic expulsion, the record is quite clear that a rapidly growing group of Nazi students and a much smaller number of nationalist professors promoted the purge of Jewish influence in the universities. Did these racist intellectuals act from a deep-seated "eliminationist anti-Semitism" or from a cluster of other motives?[63] The above remarks have tried to suggest that the shift to a racial anti-Semitism during the 1880s was a crucial precondition, but that only through the social crisis of the Weimar Republic did a fanatic fringe metamorphose into a political mass movement with a largely youthful following.

What of the countless so-called bystanders who watched without protesting and by doing their duty aided and abetted Nazi crimes? In fastening upon the bombing, the dying at the front, the flight from the East and the subsequent division, Germans have in their recollections tried to claim the role of victims for themselves.[64] But historians of everyday life have started to ask embarrassing questions about the complicity of "ordinary Germans" in a daily persecution which they have largely erased from their own memory.[65] Can their actions be conflated with the crimes of perpetrators or must their complicity be explained with a different set of factors?

In the academic purge, the bystander category especially fits the corporation students who allied themselves with the NSDStB in taking over student government and the nationalist professors who went along with the purge of their colleagues in spite of some legal misgivings. It was not just indifference but social prejudice against Jews, to pick up Hannah Arendt's distinction, which facilitated their cooperation in the exclusion of their competitors, since they did not mind having the brash newcomers curbed. Beyond undoubted opportunism and authoritarianism, a sweeping sense of national renewal, projected by the Nazis, also silenced the occasional pangs of conscience regarding the cruelty of their methods.[66]

What lessons can be learned from this paradigmatic self-decapitation of the German university? A first consequence ought to be a questioning of the Western cult of the expert, since specialized expertise, however great, does not guard against complicity in acts of inhumanity. In the pinch, some scholars will always be interested in performing an experiment that has never been done before, no matter how great the pain in the subjects and how strong the moral strictures against it. Perhaps the most appalling facet of the Holocaust was the participation of an entire generation of personally decent but politically murderous academic specialists and legal administrators in its planning and implementation.[67]

Another conclusion should be a rethinking of the tenuous relationship between scholarship and freedom. Though academics aim to be "objective" and above politics, this stance is woefully inadequate in situations when the preconditions for scientific research crumble and it is abused for ideological ends. In countless conflicts with the meddling church and the bureaucratic state, the German university had developed an admirable ideal of academic freedom in the nineteenth century. The shocking betrayal of this tradition by the expulsion of German Jews after 1933 should remind later audiences that free inquiry, to modify Wilhelm von Humboldt's phrase, can never be taken for granted but must be struggled for anew in each generation.[68]

Notes

1. K. H. Jarausch, "Removing the Nazi Stain? The Quarrel of the German Historians," *German Studies Review* 11 (1988): 185–201. See also M. Ash, ed., *Forced Migration and Scientific Change: Emigré German-Speaking Scientists and Scholars after 1933* (Cambridge, 1996).
2. A. Lüdtke, "'Coming to Terms with the Past': Illusions of Remembering, Ways of Forgetting Nazism in West Germany," *Journal of Modern History* 65 (1993): 542–72; K. Sühl, ed., *Vergangenheitsbewältigung 1945–1989. Ein unmöglicher Vergleich?* (Berlin, 1994). See also P. Novick, *The Holocaust in American Life* (Boston, 1999), and S. Courtois, ed., *The Black Book of Communism: Crimes, Terror, Repression* (Cambridge, 1999).
3. R. Berthold et al., eds., *Die Humboldt-Universität. Gestern–Heute–Morgen* (Berlin, 1960), and H. Klein, ed., *Humboldt Universität zu Berlin. Überblick 1810–1985* (Berlin, 1985).
4. Foreword to R. Schottlaender, *Verfolgte Berliner Wissenschaft* (Berlin, 1988). See also "Vertreibung jüdischer Mitglieder der Humboldt Universität zur Zeit des Faschismus," exhibition of the Humboldt University library in 1987, documented in *Humboldt-Universität* 32 (1987/8), nos. 10, 20, 35–36, 38–39, 40.
5. H. Bernhardt, "Dem Andenken jüdischer Studenten unserer Universität," *Beiträge zur Geschichte der Humboldt-Universität zu Berlin* 23 (1989): 68–76; and K. Düwell, "Berliner Wissenschaftler in der Emigration," in *Wissenschaft in Berlin* (Berlin, 1987). See also M. Grüttner, *Studenten im Dritten Reich* (Paderborn, 1995).
6. A. Rüger et al., "Die Universität als Instrument und Opfer der faschistischen Herrschaft," *Überblick*, 81. See also W. Fläschendräger and G. Steiger, *Magister und Scholaren. Professoren und Studenten und Hochschulen im Überblick* (Leipzig, 1981).
7. F. Paulsen, *Die deutschen Universitäten und das Universitätsstudium* (Berlin, 1902); and C. E. McClelland, *State, Society and University in Germany, 1700–1914* (Cambridge, 1980).
8. H. Berding, *Moderner Antisemitismus in Deutschland* (Frankfurt, 1988), 113ff.; R. vom Bruch, *Wissenschaft, Politik und öffentliche Meinung. Gelehrtenpolitik im wilhelminischen Deutschland 1890–1914* (Husum, 1980).
9. K. H. Jarausch, *Students, Society and Politics in Imperial Germany: The Rise of Academic Illiberalism* (Princeton, N.J., 1983); and N. Kampe, *Studenten und 'Judenfrage' im Deutschen Kaiserreich* (Göttingen, 1988).
10. M. H. Kater, *Studentenschaft und Rechtsradikalismus in Deutschland, 1918–1933* (Hamburg, 1975); and K. H. Jarausch, *Deutsche Studenten 1800–1950* (Frankfurt, 1984), 141ff.

11. Citations in K. H. Jarausch, "Die Not der geistigen Arbeiter. Akademiker in der Berufskrise, 1918–1933," in *Die Weimarer Republik als Wohlfahrtsstaat*, ed. W. Abelshauser (Wiesbaden, 1987), 280ff.
12. F. K. Ringer, *Die Gelehrten. Der Niedergang der deutschen Mandarine 1890–1933* (Stuttgart, 1983), 220ff.
13. K. H. Jarausch, "Die Krise des deutschen Bildungsbürgertums im ersten Drittel des 20. Jahrhunderts," in *Bildungsbürgertum im 19. Jahrhundert*, ed. J. Kocka, 4 vols. (Stuttgart, 1989), 4:180ff.; and idem, *The Unfree Professions: German Lawyers, Teachers and Engineers, 1900–1950* (New York, 1990), 78ff.
14. See A. Faust, *Der Nationalsozialistische Deutsche Studentenbund*, 2 vols. (Düsseldorf, 1972); M. H. Kater, "Der NS-Studentenbund," *Vierteljahrshefte für Zeitgeschichte* 22 (1974): 148ff.; and P. Chroust, *Gießener Universität und Faschismus. Studenten und Hochschullehrer 1918–1945* (Münster, 1994), 135f.
15. "Die Berliner Universitätskrawalle," *CV-Zeitung*, 29 Jan. 1932. See also Rektoratsbericht an Minister, 22 July 1931, and other material in the Humboldt-Universitäts-Archiv (hereafter cited as HUA), Rektor Nr. 21, as well as the file on "Disziplin und Exzesse an der Berliner Universität," in Bundesarchiv Berlin-Lichterfelde, 49.01, Nr. 1581.
16. H. Klein, ed., *Humboldt Universität zu Berlin. Dokumente 1810–1985* (Berlin, 1985), 53.
17. G. Giles, *Students and National Socialism in Germany* (Princeton, N.J., 1985), 44ff.
18. H. Döring, *Der Weimarer Kreis. Studien zum politischen Bewußtsein verfassungstreuer Hochschullehrer in der Weimarer Republik* (Meisenheim, 1975); not always reliable, H. P. Bleuel, *Deutschlands Bekenner. Professoren zwischen Kaiserreich und Diktatur* (Bern, 1968); empirically more exact Chroust, *Gießener Universität*, 168ff.
19. Appeal of 25 Feb. 1933, HUA, Rektor Nr. 21/1. See also A. Faust, "Professoren für die NSDAP. Zum politischen Verhalten der Hochschullehrer 1932/33," in *Erziehung und Schulung um Dritten Reich*, ed. M. Heinemann, 2 vols. (Stuttgart, 1980), 2:31ff., and G. Leaman, *Heidegger im Kontext. Gesamtübersicht zum NS Engagement der Universitätsphilosophen* (Heidelberg, 1993).
20. Giles, *Students and National Socialism*, 73ff.; and M. H. Kater, "Die nationalsozialistische Machtergreifung an den deutschen Hochschulen. Zum politischen Verhalten der akademischen Lehrer bis 1939," in *Die Freiheit des Anderen*, ed. H.-J. Vogel et al. (Baden-Baden, 1981), 49ff.
21. Published in L. Poliakov and J. Wulf, eds., *Das Dritte Reich und Seine Denker* (Berlin, 1959), 117ff.; "Die Studenten-Thesen 'gegen den undeutschen Geist,'" *Jüdische Rundschau*, 28 Apr. 1933; Schottlaender, *Verfolgte Berliner Wissenschaft*, 35.
22. M. H. Kater, *Doctors Under Hitler* (Chapel Hill, N.C., 1989), 177ff.; and Jarausch, *Unfree Professions*, 128ff.
23. Exact figures in H. Titze et al., *Das Hochschulstudium in Preußen und Deutschland 1820–1944* (Göttingen, 1987), 225ff.
24. Preußisches Statistisches Landesamt, *Preußische Statistik*, vols. 279, 281, 285, 353; *Statistik der Landesuniversitäten und Hochschulen* (Berlin, 1925–28), 2ff.; Deutsche Hochschulverwaltungen, *Deutsche Hochschulstatistik*, vols. 8 and 9 (Berlin, 1932 and 1933), 46ff., 56ff. See also Kampe, *Studenten*, 79ff.
25. HUA, Rektor Nr. 801, 869, 884, and 1005; N. Balk and P. Kersten, eds., *Berliner Hochschul-Taschenbuch* (Berlin, 1923), 1: 123ff. Cf. Glenn R. Sharfman, "The Jewish Youth Movement in Germany, 1900–1936" (Ph.D. diss., University of North Carolina, 1989).
26. C. v. Ferber, *Die Entwicklung des Lehrkörpers der deutschen Universitäten 1864–1945* (Göttingen, 1956); and F. K. Ringer, "The German Academic Community, 1864–1938," *Central European History* 25 (1993): 251–80.
27. NSDStB flyer of 30 Jan. 1933, HUA, Rektor Nr. 21/1. Cf. "Zwischenfälle an der Berliner Universität," *Börsen-Courier*, 1 Feb. 1933. For further information, see Rüger, "Die Universität als Instrument und Opfer," 79ff.
28. HUA, Kurator Nr. 1110 and 1111, text and implementation orders for the law on the restoration of professional public service.

29. For the background, see J. Caplan, *Government Without Administration: State and Civil Service in Weimar and Nazi Germany* (Oxford, 1988); and Jarausch, *Unfree Professions*, 130ff.
30. A. Götz von Olenhusen, "Die 'Nichtarischen' Studenten an den deutschen Hochschulen. Zur nationalsozialistischen Rassenpolitik," *Vierteljahrshefte für Zeitgeschichte* 14 (1966): 175–206, and N. Wenning, "Das Gesetz gegen die Überfüllung der deutschen Schulen und Hochschulen vom 25. 4. 33," *Die deutsche Schule* 78 (1986): 141ff.
31. Jarausch, *Studenten*, 176ff.; Giles, *Students*, 107f; and C. Huerkamp, "Jüdische Akademikerinnen in Deutschland 1900–1938," *Geschichte und Gesellschaft* 19 (1993): 326ff.
32. "Wegen staatsfeindlicher Gesinnung von den Hochschulen gewiesene Studenten 1933–34," with a list of about six hundred names of students expelled from all German universities on the basis of "antinational attitude," HUA, Richter. Figuring out an exact number is difficult, since the relegations took place in several waves and a few students were later rehabilitated as erroneously expelled. Cf. Klein, *Dokumente*, 57.
33. Schottlaender, *Verfolgte Berliner Wissenschaft*, 27, 61ff.; Rüger, "Die Universität als Instrument und Opfer," 81ff.
34. Schottlaender, *Verfolgte Berliner Wissenschaft*, 85ff. See also Planck an Vahlen, 30 Aug. 1933, in Klein, *Dokumente*, 58, and E. Spranger, *Mein Konflikt mit der Hitler-Regierung 1933* (als Manuskript gedruckt, 1955), 2–6. Somewhat apologetic is H. Heiber, *Der Professor im Dritten Reich. Bilder aus der akademischen Provinz* (Munich, 1991).
35. "Das neue Studentenrecht," *CV-Zeitung*, 20 Apr. 1933; material on implementation in BA Po, 49.01, Nr. 796; Olenhusen, "Nichtarier," 181ff.
36. "Deutsch-jüdische Wirklichkeit," *CV-Zeitung*, 13 Apr. 1933; W. Benz, *Die Juden in Deutschland 1933–1945. Leben unter nationalsozialistischer Herrschaft* (Munich, 1988).
37. D. U. Adam, *Judenpolitik im Dritten Reich* (Düsseldorf, 1972); and H. Becker, H.-J. Dahms, and C. Wegeler, eds., *Die Universität Göttingen unter dem Nationalsozialismus* (Munich, 1987).
38. "Jüdische Zwischenbilanz," *Jüdische Rundschau*, 13 Apr. 1933; "Unsere Pflicht!" *CV-Zeitung*, 27 Apr. 1933. See also Benz, *Juden in Deutschland*, 314ff.
39. I would like to thank Professor Mitchell Ash for making this document available to me. See also Klein, *Dokumente*, 60ff.; Rüger, "Die Universität als Instrument und Opfer," 84; and E. Y. Hartshorne, *The German Universities and National Socialism* (London, 1937), 94ff.
40. Schottlaender, *Verfolgte Berliner Wissenschaft*, 123–30. Chroust, *Gießener Universität*, 225ff., has calculated a dismissal quota of 20.9 percent for Giessen.
41. "Die Studentenhilfe," *CV-Zeitung*, 4 May 1933, and "Erschwerter Bildungsweg," ibid., 6 July 1933. See also Chroust, *Universität Gießen*, 235 f.
42. Figures from Hochschulverwaltungen, ed., *Deutsche Hochschulstatistik*, 9 (1932): 4ff.; 11 (1933): 14ff.; 12 (1933/34): 46ff.; 13 (1934): 46ff.; 14 (1934/35): 46ff. The Jewish proportion among foreigners declined more slowly, since anti-Semitic restrictions were not applied quite as sharply to them.
43. C. Lorenz, *Zehnjahres-Statistik des Hochschulbesuchs und der Abschlußprüfungen* (Berlin, 1943), 1: 106ff., in contrast to Huerkamp, "Jüdische Akademikerinnen," 327.
44. Non-Aryans as stamped on 9 November 1933 in a membership list of the *Deutsche Studentenschaft*, HUA, Richter Nr. 3016.
45. "Stammrolle für reichsdeutsche Nichtarier der Universität Berlin vom WS 1935/36," HUA.
46. Ibid., and Verzeichnis der Studenten, SS 1937 and SS 1939, HUA. Most of the remaining Jewish students were enrolled in medicine.
47. V. Klemperer, *Ich will Zeugnis ablegen bis zum letzten. Tagebücher*, 2 vols. (Berlin, 1995). See also M. Kaplan, *Between Dignity and Despair: Jewish Life in Nazi Germany* (New York, 1998), and T. Tegelow's forthcoming dissertation on the linguistic separation of Jews and Germans (Chapel Hill, N.C., 2001).
48. Moving descriptions can be found in H. Göppinger, *Juristen jüdischer Abstammung im 'Dritten Reich'. Entrechtung und Verfolgung*, 2nd ed. (Beck, 1990), 219ff.
49. Departure letter of Lewin to Köhler, 20 May 1933, reprinted in H. A. Strauss et al., ed., *Emigration. Deutsche Wissenschaftler nach 1933. Entlassung und Vertreibung* (Berlin, 1987) with lists of 1936, 1937 and 1941.

50. Cf. Kater, *Doctors Under Hitler*, 206 and W. Mock, *Technische Intelligenz im Exil 1933–1945* (Düsseldorf, 1986), 150ff. Eric Kohler is currently working on a big study, concerning the fate of doctors who emigrated to the U.S.
51. K. Fischer, "Die Emigration von Wissenschaftlern nach 1933. Möglichkeiten und Grenzen einer Bilanzierung," *Vierteljahrshefte für Zeitgeschichte* 39 (1991): 535–49; Ringer, "German Academic Community," 278f.
52. "Jüdische Nobelpreisträger," *CV-Zeitung*, 14 May 1993; A. Beyerchen, *Scientists under Hitler: Politics and the Physics Community in the Third Reich* (New Haven, Conn., 1977); and K. L. Pfeiffer, "Vertreibung des Geistes—Deutsche Fallstudien zur Selbstdemontage Alteuropas," in *Wissenschaft und Nationalsozialismus*, ed. R. Geißler and W. Popp (Essen, 1988), 79ff.
53. Schottlaender, *Verfolgte Berliner Wissenschaft*, 30, 133ff.; Rüger, "Die Universität als Instrument und Opfer," 82ff.
54. H.-H. Knütter, *Die Juden und die deutsche Linke in der Weimarer Republik* (Düsseldorf, 1971), 222ff.
55. Schottlaender, *Verfolgte Berliner Wissenschaft*, 121ff. Only Hintze, Perels, Meinecke, and Hoetzsch appear in the list of the historical guild, compiled by W. Weber, *Priester der Clio* (Frankfurt, 1984). Cf. J. J. Sheehan, ed., *An Interrupted Past: German-Speaking Refugee Historians in the US after 1933* (Cambridge, 1991).
56. A. Rosenberg, "Die Aufgabe des Historikers in der Emigration," in *Freie Wissenschaft. Ein Sammelband aus der deutschen Emigration*, ed. E. J. Gumbel (Strasbourg, 1938). See also R. Jütte, *Die Auswanderung jüdischer Historiker nach Palästina 1933–1945* (Stuttgart, 1991).
57. M. Burleigh, *Germany Turns Eastwards: A Study of Ostforschung in the Third Reich* (Cambridge, 1988); P. Schöttler, ed., *Geschichtsschreibung als Legitimationswissenschaft 1918–1945* (Frankfurt, 1997). See also R. Hohls and K. H. Jarausch, eds., *Versäumte Fragen. Deutsche Historiker im Schatten des Nationalsozialismus* (Munich, 2000).
58. K. H. Jarausch, "Die unfreien Professionen. Überlegeungen zu den Wandlungsprozessen im deutschen Bildungsbürgertum 1900–1955," in *Bürgertum im 19. Jahrhundert*, ed. J. Kocka, 3 vols. (Munich, 1988), 2:136ff.
59. J. Kramer, "The Politics of Memory," *The New Yorker*, 14 August 1995; and M. Fisher, *After the Wall: Germany, the Germans and the Burdens of History* (New York, 1995).
60. J. Peck, M. Ash, and C. Lemke, "Natives, Strangers and Foreigners: Constituting Germans by Constructing Others," in *After Unity: Reconfiguring German Identities*, ed. K. H. Jarausch (Providence, 1997), 61ff.
61. Lewin letter, cited in n. 42. See also Kaplan, *Between Dignity and Despair*, 229ff.
62. H. Marcuse, *Legacies of Dachau: The Uses and Abuses of a Concentration Camp, 1933–2000* (New York, 1998). Cf. U. Herbert, "Der Judenmord war das Kernereignis des Jahrhunderts," reprint from *Welt im Gespräch*, Sept. 1998.
63. D. J. Goldhagen, *Hitler's Willing Executioners: Ordinary Germans and the Holocaust* (New York, 1986). See also S. Friedlander, *Nazi Germany and the Jews: The Years of Persecution, 1933–1939* (New York, 1997), vol. 1.
64. L. Heineman, "The Hour of the Women: Memories of Germany's Crisis Years and West German National Identity," *American Historical Review* 101 (1996): 354–95.
65. C. Browning, *Ordinary Men: Reserve Police Batallion 101 and the Final Solution in Poland* (New York, 1992).
66. See the preface on anti-Semitism in H. Arendt, *The Origins of Totalitarianism* (New York, 1973). See R.-J. Baum, "Wir wollen Männer, wir wollen Taten!" *Deutsche Corpsstudenten 1848 bis heute* (Berlin, 1998), 135ff., 180ff.
67. U. Herbert, *Best. Biografische Studien über Radikalismus, Weltanschauung und Vernunft 1903–1989* (Bonn, 1996); and G. Aly and S. Heim, *Vordenker der Vernichtung. Auschwitz und die deutschen Pläne für eine neue europäische Ordnung* (Hamburg, 1991).
68. Jarausch, *Unfree Professions*, 226f. See also P. Lundgreen, ed., *Wissenschaft im Dritten Reich* (Frankfurt, 1985).

PART ONE

MIGRATION, ETHNICITY, AND MINORITIES IN PUBLIC POLICY IN GERMANY AND THE UNITED STATES

Chapter 1

IMMIGRATION, NATURALIZATION, AND ETHNO-NATIONAL TRADITIONS IN GERMANY

From the Citizenship Law of 1913 to the Law of 1999

Klaus J. Bade

In the past, Germans abroad and foreigners in Germany have experienced all imaginable forms of cross-border migration: emigration, immigration, and transit movements; labor migration of Germans across the German borders as well as the influx of foreign labor into Germany; refuge and forced migration of Germans into foreign countries and of foreigners to Germany, of Germans as victims and as offenders within and outside German national borders. In addition to the movement of people across borders, German history has also witnessed the movement of borders across people and within German borders the exclusion of minorities, such as Jews, ethnic Poles, Sinti, and Roma. In this context there is a direct line of continuity from the nationally-romantically (*völkisch-romantisch*) inspired dissociation of the "other" (*Fremde*) in the early nineteenth century, to the ethno-nationalistic agitation against "strangeness" (*Fremdartige*) in the late nineteenth and early twentieth centuries, to the systematic destruction of "alien races" (*Fremdrassige*) in Nazi Germany and German-occupied Europe.

The horrible end of this path casts a long-lasting shadow of mass crimes against ethnic, cultural, religious, and other minorities. The memory of the fact that in Nazi Germany and in German-occupied Europe millions of Jews and other victims were deprived of their rights, persecuted, and murdered complicates the discussion of minority issues, quota regulations, and the inevitably resulting problems of inclusion and exclusion well into the 1990s. Whenever the decision-making process regarding potential immigrants' applications has been compared in public discourse to the "selection" at the ramps of Nazi concentration camps, the shadows of the past has continued to darken the present.[1]

From a Country of Emigration to a Country of Immigration

In the long-term development of Germany from a nineteenth-century country of emigration to a country of immigration in the late twentieth century,[2] there was for a time an intrinsic coherence and interdependence in the development of ethno-national thinking and migration policies. In spite of many differences of opinion evident at the governmental level as well as in legislation and administration of the individual German states, general intentions and tendencies regarding transnational migration in Germany were twofold: to protect German transatlantic emigrants leaving home in a mass movement heading to the west and mainly to the United States until the early 1890s, and to protect Germany from a continental mass immigration expected from eastern Europe. The linkage of both ideas—that is, of safeguarding emigration and controlling immigration—was not a uniquely German way of thinking in transnational migration affairs but rather a basic element of migration policy in interventionist nation states from World War I until the age of liberal migration policy in the Atlantic economy. However, a peculiarity of Germany's historical development was the huge importance of ethno-national thinking and defensive attitudes against immigration from eastern Europe in public debates on migration policy, citizenship law, and naturalization—unlike the United States' overall posture against the "new immigration" from eastern and southern Europe.[3]

With respect to the question of transnational migration and the respective policies and attitudes in Germany, the focus of this essay will be mainly on immigration. What I would like to analyze here is the general development of legislation and the political debate on immigration and naturalization and the influences that ethno-national thinking had on both of these issues in Germany from the Reich Citizenship Law (*Reichs- und Staatsangehörigkeitsgesetz*) of 1913 to its reform in 1999. To place these issues in the broader context of Germany's historical development, I will begin by discussing aspects of nineteenth-century Germany and end with a brief review of the current debate in united Germany.

Since transatlantic emigration became a social mass movement[4] in the first half of the nineteenth century, public and governmental activities concerning the emigration question have been shaped by two main issues: on the one hand, humanitarian and charitable motives, and on the other hand, ideological and manipulative intentions. Both perspectives were highly complex with often overlapping argumentation. The public discussion of these issues climaxed in the 1840s and 1880s. Part of the argumentation regarding humanity and charity in the middle of the century[5] included private advising efforts for prospective emigrants and appeals for governmental protection of the emigrants. The emigration law passed by the Frankfurt National Assembly in 1849 represented the climax of endeavors for governmental commitment.[6] In the field of the ideological and manipulative discussion of migration issues at mid-century, most efforts were aimed at influencing, controlling, "organizing," i.e., taking advantage of migration, especially for socio-economic purposes. The principal arguments focused on cultural "bleeding" (*Aderlaß*), the loss of human capital, and persons avoiding conscription. At the same time, emigration was favored as a means to balance social problems by using transatlantic emigration as a "social safety valve" against the danger of a social revolution.[7]

In the second half of the nineteenth century, the concern with emigration reached another plateau as it coincided with the discussions on colonial expansion in the late 1870s and early 1880s. Emigration was still considered to be a "socio-political necessity" (F. Fabri) in order to reduce social tensions. However, there was the simultaneous desire to preserve the "Germanness," or *Deutschtum*, of the emigrants and to avoid the loss of human capital, especially to the competing power of the U.S. economy, on the world market. Therefore, emigration was to be "directed" from North to South America or to German colonies still to be founded.[8] All of these plans remained essentially unfulfilled. Emigration on the whole could not be controlled or even "directed" to South America.[9] The German colonies in Africa and the Pacific that had been founded in 1884–85 and were subsequently lost during World War I were absolutely unsuited for mass immigration. Moreover, already in the early 1890s, German transatlantic emigration as a social mass movement had come to an end and did not increase again until the 1920s.[10] As was the case in the public debate of the 1840s, the discussion on emigration during the late 1870s and the early 1880s again brought about the demand for emigration legislation. However, the mass movement was mostly left to itself.

During the Bismarckian period, there was no chance for emigration legislation. This seems very odd given the general shift from liberalism to protectionism and state intervention that took place, for example, in the areas of welfare legislation, protective tariffs against foreign trade competition, and overseas protectorates. Bismarck and the agrarian-conservative political elite of the German Reich, however, refused to consider an emigration law. This refusal stemmed from the belief that a legislative pursuit of emigration issues would mean official acknowledgment of the problem and might intensify a mass phenomenon that was already unpopular, especially among agrarian employers in the Prussian East. The predominant contingent of the mass emigration of the 1880s, after all, had come from the largely agrarian northeast regions of the Reich, where there was a growing labor shortage.[11] More than a quarter of a century after the founding of the German Empire, the first "Imperial Emigration Law" (*Reichsauswanderungsgesetz*) became effective in 1897, years after mass emigration had ceased to be a major problem. The law concentrated largely on the protection of German emigrants and contained only a few indirect possibilities to "control" the emigration by counseling emigrants and granting licenses to emigration agencies and shipping lines.[12]

Toward an Ethno-national Understanding of Citizenship Rights

While there was a clear lack of interest from the German nation state on questions of emigration, there had been from the outset a strong commitment to continental immigration, which was subject to the policies of the individual German federal states. This interest was of Prussian origin inasmuch as the largest contingents of continental labor migration crossed Prussia's eastern borders, growing steadily from the 1890s and increasing to a mass movement with annual fluctuations in both direction in the decade before the outbreak of World War I.[13] Moreover, as discussed first by Rogers Brubaker,[14] defensive attitudes toward immigration can be related to the path from ethno-cultural to ethno-national self-consciousness and the consequent strengthening of the jus sanguinis tradition based upon the principle of ethnic heritage. As A. Fahrmeir has shown, however, it was not until the late nineteenth and early twentieth centuries that ethno-national thinking, on the one hand, and jus sanguinis traditions, on the other, merged to create an ethno-national understanding of citizenship rights. By the mid-nineteenth century, the German states had come to agree upon the general validity of the jus sanguinis principle in lieu of the jus soli tradition that was based upon the principle of territoriality and that had been valid in citizenship regulations until then. This decision, however, had little to with subsequent ethno-national perspectives and conceptions but was the product of pragmatic legal considerations that stood in the background. "Germany," after all, was not a centralized state like France, but a patchwork of several large and medium-sized and numerous small and tiny territories. Had citizenship been defined by place of birth, i.e., by jus soli as in France, this would have caused a juridical chaos that would have worsened with the growing mobility that accompanied the process of industrialization. For this reason, Germany clung to the Romantic political concept, namely the affiliation to a unique German culture and ethno-cultural tradition, and derived children's nationality exclusively from that of their parents (jus sanguinis). The corresponding regulations of the Prussian Subjects' Law (*Untertanengesetz*) became part of the regulations for the whole Reich in 1871 and formed the basis of the Reich Citizenship Law of 1913.[15]

Under the "belated nation's" public law, neither an immediate "German" citizenship nor a German "nationality" existed before 1913. Until that time, one was a subject of the Prussian or Bavarian Kingdom, or of the Grand Duchy of Baden; it was only through this federal link that one became a German. This changed only with the Reich Citizenship Law of 1913, where Paragraph 1 defined a German as follows: "A German is a person who is a citizen of a Federal State or who has immediate German citizenship." This regulation was widely seen in public as a kind of final act in the founding of the Reich. In the Reichstag debate from 28 May 1913, the National Liberal Party saw it as an express sign of "German unity."[16] Still, the various citizenships of the German federal states continued to exist. In the Weimar Republic, for example, one was still a citizen of Prussia or Bavaria. This did not change until 1934 when in Nazi Germany a single, unitary citizenship was introduced for all citizens of the Reich.

The Reich Citizenship Law of 1913

On the matter of transnational migration, the Reich Citizenship Law of 1913 was first and foremost geared toward allowing German emigrants to retain their citizenship. Prior to this law, they would have lost it after ten years of emigration unless they had expressly applied for its renewal. On the immigration and naturalization of foreigners in Germany, the law was very defensive. The principle of ethnic heritage, finally codified in the 1913 citizenship law, placed the principles of nationhood and the national community above those of civil rights, in opposition to the principle of territoriality associated with the French republican ideal. The German understanding of citizenship, as expressed in the law of 1913, bound civil rights to the principle of ethnic descent. The law of 1913 aimed to prolong citizenship for German emigrants and at the same time sought to limit the acquisition of German citizenship by foreigners to exceptional cases.[17] At first ethno-national intentions gradually subsided, but since the late nineteenth century have increasingly influenced public understanding of the jus sanguinis principle. The law of 1913 originated in the Wilhelmine era of high imperialism before World War I. It was also an expression of the ethno-national idea of "protecting Germanness abroad [*Schutz des Deutschtums im Auslande*]" and of a fortress mentality against the suspected "flood from the East."

Two concurrent east-to-west movements across the Eastern German borders formed the background of this experience. The first was the transit migration of millions of East Europeans, mainly Jews and Poles from Russia, passing through German harbors on their ways to the United States. As Trude Maurer and Jack Wertheimer have shown, between 1880 and 1914, in spite of severe transit controls, about 78,000 "Eastern Jews" remained for some time in Germany. On the eve of World War I they made up about 12 percent (in 1925 about 19 percent) of the Jewish population of Germany. Xenophobic attitudes toward these East European migrants were strengthened by their high mobility. The idea of a general Jewish east-to-west migration was intensified by the experience of the internal Jewish migration from the Prussian East to the West, especially to larger cities. What contemporary anti-Semitic agitators mostly failed to realize was the fact that the small East European Jewish group did not regard Germany as their final destination but as a bridge between East and West and, first of all, as a country of transit or an intermediate stop on their ways to the New World.[18]

The second great east-to-west movement was the seasonal migration of hundreds of thousands of predominantly Polish "foreign labor migrants" crossing the Eastern borders of Prussia every year. Since the late nineteenth century, Prussian agriculture became increasingly dependent on the "willing and cheap [*willig und billig*]" foreign labor from the East. In Prussia, the largest group came from central Poland, at that time part of the Russian Empire. The Prussian government, however, was afraid of political destabilization in the Polish-populated border regions of the East, where the national-revolutionary dream of a revived Polish state could not be suppressed. Ethno-nationalistic propaganda of right-wing groups attacked the influx from the east as a severe cultural danger that threatened "Polonization" instead of "Germanization" of the Prussian East. The conflict between economic, political, and ethnonational interests was only resolved to some extent by the implementation of a compulsory rotation system that limited labor immigration to seasonal employment.[19]

Against this general background, anti-Semitic and anti-Polish resentment fueled nightmare visions of streams of unwanted immigrants moving across the eastern borders. As early as 1895, such resentment had prompted conservative members of the Reichstag to introduce a motion subsequently defeated by a substantial majority that banned new immigration of Jews into Germany. In the 1912/13 Reichstag debate on the new citizenship law, however, animosity focused on the "mass naturalization of Galician peddlers"—meaning East European Jews—and "poor farm workers"—meaning Polish migrant workers. Failure to exclude such people would mean "naturalization of elements of doubtful moral and economic standing."[20] This was the position of the Catholic Center Party (Deutsche Zentrumspartei), even though in the debate from 29 May 1913 it stressed that its position was "far from any anti-semitism" and only expressed its fear that a rightful claim to naturalization would create an unwanted incentive to immigrate. The right to naturalization after two years of residence had been demanded by the Social Democrats (Sozialdemokratische Partei Deutschlands or SPD) with the argument that it would lead "to the unhealthiest of situations" if hundreds of thousands of residents were "treated like pariahs" with "only half the citizenship rights" to which one was normally entitled. In their view, all foreigners should explicitly have the right to claim naturalization in order to prevent them from being turned away simply because of their religion or ethnic and national heritage. After all, among the 8,262 persons naturalized in 1910, only 91 were Jews.[21]

The Social Democrats' proposal was rejected. Over their opposition, a regulation was passed that sought to safeguard the Federal States' interests in the Reich Citizenship Law of 1913. This regulation stipulated that "Naturalization in a Federal State may take place only if and when the Reich Chancellor declared that none of the other Federal States had raised any objection against it; should any objection occur, the Federal Council [Bundesrat] decides." What sounded like a federal consensus model was in fact colored by anti-Polish and anti-Jewish resentment. In filing an application for naturalization, a claimant had to give both religion and nationality of the parents. These targets were apparent from a confidential remark by the Reich Ministry of the Interior, which suggested that this would see to it that "un-German elements from the East [*stammfremde Elemente aus dem Osten*] like Poles or Czechs, or, Jews below our cultural level, can be excluded from naturalization." However, this had to be treated in the strictest confidence to avoid "highly unwelcome" consequences in public discussions on the one hand and diplomatic repercussions with the allied Austro-Hungarian monarchy on the other. This strategy, which confirmed Social Democratic fears but escaped attention, was expressly denied by the representative of the Reich Ministry of the Interior in the Reichstag debate on 29 May 1913 but became the basis of practice following passage of the law. The basis of this practice were naturalization guidelines (*Einbürgerungsrichtlinien*) used in all German federal states and were modeled on those that were currently in effect in Prussia.[22] From this point of view, the Reich Citizenship Law of 1913 was also an ethno-nationalistic anti-immigration law, principally directed against the immigration of Jews and Poles from the East.

From *fremdstämmige* to *fremdrassige* Foreigners

The ambiguous position of Germany as a country of transatlantic emigration as well as of continental labor immigration led to a unique ambivalence which became readily apparent in the Weimar period: As a country of emigration, Germany opposed the increasing international protective restrictions against immigration, especially those of the United States, the main destination for German emigrants. As what I. Ferenczi called a "labor-importing country," however, Germany had to defend its own restrictive control system for continental immigration.[23]

With respect to immigration from the East, the Weimar Republic experienced fundamental changes because of its new balance of power.

Adversaries of a discriminative naturalization policy were now part of the government on both the Reich and state level. The question of naturalization guidelines became an eternal conflict with reversed fronts. On one side stood Prussia, which until 1932 was led by coalition governments consisting of the Social Democrats, the Center, and the liberal parties. On the other side was Bavaria, governed by the conservative Bavarian Peoples' Party (Bayerische Volkspartei), which had split from the Center Party in 1918/19. Bavaria's opposition to a Prussian-dominated naturalization policy was certainly influenced by its hostility toward the centralist tendencies of the Weimar Constitution. Whereas in imperial Germany Prussia had been the main opponent against the naturalization of "alien Easterners [*fremdstämmige Ostausländer*]," this position was now assumed by Bavaria, which constantly pointed out that the new Prussian naturalization policies would threaten this restrictive naturalization regime.[24] With Prussia suspending its former naturalization policy and opting for an examination of each individual case, Bavaria supported the continued imposition of general restraints on naturalization of "alien Easterners" by stipulating that, if at all, naturalization should be allowed for the second generation only. The new naturalization guidelines issued by the Reich Ministry of the Interior on 1 June 1921 included a ten-year residency requirement for "not culturally alien foreigners [*nicht kulturfremde Ausländer*]." The naturalization of "culturally alien foreigners," for which Bavaria demanded a residency requirement of at least twenty years, could not be resolved. The conflict thus dragged on, flaming up repeatedly. The naturalization guidelines of 1921[25] stipulated that it would no longer suffice that the claimant be of good reputation and willing to follow his civic duties. Naturalization should be possible only for persons who "in civic, cultural, and economic regard" would be "a valuable contribution to the German population." This was geared especially toward applications for naturalization by ethnic Germans who had kept their "Germanness" while abroad and who had performed their military service in Germany—a proviso that was abandoned with the end of compulsory military service.[26]

As in imperial Germany, this was meant for the descendants of German emigrants living in the Reich, and for Germans living in the former eastern territories of the Reich. Still, this did not mean a right to naturalization for descendants of German emigrants living in eastern Europe.[27] In hindering emigration as well as immigration of Russian Germans, Soviet and German interests even coincided. From 1918 to 1921 some 120,000 Russian Germans had managed to escape the turmoil of the Russian Revolution and Civil War; at the same time, the economic, social, and political crisis of the early Weimar Republic dampened its attractiveness. Around half of the Russian Germans moved on to the United States, Canada or South America. After the end of the Russian Civil War and the imposition of Soviet rule, emigration from the Russian German areas decreased, for the Soviet government sought to obstruct their emigration by administrative impediments. Its very restrictive emigration policy was linked to its large industrialization scheme which would only be realized by binding and directing all available labor forces. Hence during the 1920s, only a few thousand Russian Germans could leave the Soviet Union. Only the Mennonites' emigration reached any sizeable dimension. From 1923 to 1928, some 18,300 Mennonites—or a seventh of all Mennonites in the Soviet Union—managed to leave. Relatively few, however, migrated to Germany; the major destinations were Canada, Mexico, and the United States. The Soviet aim of obstructing emigration coincided with efforts by the Weimar governments to limit immigration because of the tight labor market.[28]

Leaving ethnic Germans from the East aside, the exclusionist tendencies in German naturalization policy, which Prussia no longer followed, focused once again on eastern European immigrants in general and Jews in particular. Xenophobic fantasies perceived enemies at both the bottom and the top of the social ladder. At the bottom was the "culturally lowest of the lowly," namely the Polish migrant worker, and the Jewish "sponger" from eastern Europe. At the top was the Jewish physician. The latter image reflected a growing interest in protecting certain branches of labor from competition from abroad, beneath the ethno-nationalist and increasingly racist character of the arguments.[29]

In 1929 Bavaria criticized the increase in naturalization applications from "typical Eastern foreigners, especially those of Eastern Jewish origin [*typischer Ostausländer, insbesondere solcher ostjüdischer Herkunft*]" in Prussia. Referring to the "membership in certain races [*Zugehörigkeit zu bestimmten Volksrassen*]," Bavaria now included not only ethno-nationalist, but overtly racist criteria. On 13 July 1929, the Reich Minister of the Interior Carl Severing, who formerly held the equivalent Prussian post, called a conference of all state ministers of the interior. He managed to reach a compromise according to which all applications for citizenship should be treated on an individual basis. On the basis of this compromise, no discrimination was to be made between "Eastern foreigners of alien descent [*fremdstämmigen Ostausländern*]" and other "foreigners of alien descent [*fremdstämmigen Ausländern*]." Other questions of naturalization were to be handled in the various federal states, which were not empowered to raise objections about other federal states' naturalization practices. However, the expected relief of the Federal Council (Reichsrat) from arbitrating differences between federal states in naturalization affairs was dashed as a consequence of the global economic crisis, mass unemployment and Nazi officials taking up posts in governments.[30] In 1930 the new Nazi minister of the interior in Thuringia Wilhelm Frick objected to Prussian applications for naturalization for persons of "alien races." In 1933 Frick became Hitler's Reich minister of the interior and prohibited any naturalization of "Eastern Jewish Foreigners." An ethno-national, ethno-nationalist, and latent racist interpretation of the naturalization guidelines turned into an openly racist interpretation, transforming immigrants of "alien stock [*Fremdstämmige*]" into immigrants of "alien races [*Fremdrassige*]."[31]

In the history of transnational migration, citizenship rights and related policies, the Nazi period introduced a new dimension, different in quality yet still representing an important line of continuity with the past. On the notion of "Germanness," there was after 1933 a concerted effort to indoctrinate Germans abroad with the ideas of National Socialism and to encourage them to re-migrate "home" to National Socialist Germany.[32] On the other hand, there many Germans were persecuted for political, religious, and racist motives, forcing them into an exile that often led to permanent emigration. On the matter of citizenship, the consequences of National Socialist "Germanness" policies were humiliation, deprivation of rights, and finally the stripping away of all civil rights, especially for Jews classified as "ethnic aliens," or *Fremdvölkische*. As long as the borders remained open, there was a chance to escape by emigration.[33] After closing the borders, the road finally led to the organized mass murder of the Holocaust.[34] In the area of continental immigration, the road led from the employment of foreign migrant labor to the unlimited exploitation of slave labor brought into the Reich especially through compulsory deportation from the conquered territories of eastern Europe.[35]

Immigration and Citizenship Rights in the German Federal Republic

Ambivalent attitudes toward emigration and immigration issues hardly changed in postwar Germany, while the shift in emphasis from emigration to immigration issues accelerated dramatically since World War II. The protection of emigrants represented an element of legislative continuity from the prewar to the postwar period and can be traced from 1950, when the Federal Emigration Agency (Bundesstelle für das Auswanderungswesen) was founded, until 1975, when the Law of Protection for the Emigrants (*Gesetz zum Schutz der Auswanderer*) was passed. In 1959–60, the Federal Emigration Agency was integrated into the Federal Administration Office (Bundesverwaltungsamt). The new office had to deal with questions and problems related to immigration as well as emigration.[36] After World War II, however, not emigration but immigration was most important.

Since the end of World War II, five phases in the immigration and integration process in Germany can be identified. The first and largest phase involved the integration of German refugees and expellees in occupied West and East Germany. The second phase took place until the construction of the Berlin Wall in 1961 and was related to the influx of Germans from East into West Germany offset by a smaller stream of West Germans heading to the East. The third phase was associated with the recruitment of "foreign labor" from the mid-1950s on and the transformation of the "guest worker" issue to a true immigration problem in West Germany. In united Germany the largest minority group is still composed of three generations of "domestic foreigners" or "foreign inlanders" originating from the former guest worker population with the first generation already entering retirement. The fourth phase included refugees and asylum seekers from the so-called Third World up to the mid-1980s and mostly from Eastern Europe today. Their numbers have increased sharply in the late 1980s and early 1990s. The new restrictive Asylum Law of 1993 resulted in a reduction in the number of applications for asylum, but has probably increased the weight of illegal immigrants. The arrival of immigrant minorities from Eastern Europe constitutes the fifth phase in the immigration and integration process. In this context, two groups are of special interest, the larger of which are the ethnic Germans from the East, or so-called *Aussiedler*, who since the early 1990s—but particularly since 1993—have come almost exclusively from the CIS countries. The smaller group comprises Jews, also emigrating from the CIS.[37]

Ethnic Germans from the East are not considered immigrants but Germans according to German laws, namely Article 116 of the Federal Constitution of 1949, the Federal Expellee and Refugees Act (*Bundesvertriebenen- und Flüchtlingsgesetz*) of 1953 and 1957, and finally the War Consequences Act (*Kriegsfolgenbereinigungsgesetz*) of 1993. German legislation states that minorities of German descent in Eastern Europe—and in other regions further in the East, where many descendants of Germans were settled after their deportation from the former Volga Republic in 1941—are still suffering from postwar "expulsion pressure," or *Vertreibungsdruck*. The preconditions for being accepted as an *Aussiedler* are German descent, the "confession of Germanness [*Bekenntnis zum Deutschtum*]," and a family fate of suffering from "expulsion pressure." This threefold combination enables ethnic Germans from the East to immigrate as Germans today and stands in sharp contrast to the Weimar period, when the wishes of Soviet citizens of German descent to "re-migrate" were fulfilled only in exceptional cases.[38] At that time, the German interest in surviving German minorities in Eastern Europe as well as the tight labor market in Germany were frequently cited as reasons for preventing the "re-migration" of ethnic Germans from the East.

The government of the newly unified Germany in the 1990s also reacted with restrictive measures when the immigration of ethnic Germans from the East turned to a mass movement. The War Consequences Act of 1993 restricted the ethnic Germans' right to immigrate to Germany to those born before 1993. For dependent children born after 1993, the last possible year of entry is 2010. At the same time, the act limited the number of entry permissions, or *Aufnahmebescheide*, to an annual maximum of

220,000. Together with other measures, the act of 1993 provoked a long-term decrease in the number of ethnic German immigrants down to the level of about 100,000 (103,080 in 1998)—for the first time in 10 years.[39] According to estimations, however, 1 to 2 million people in the CIS could still fulfil the conditions for being accepted as ethnic Germans.

All in all, the legal right of the descendants of Germans who had emigrated from Germany generations or even centuries before to "return" to the homeland of their ancestors as "Germans," belongs to the jus sanguinis tradition and to an ethno-cultural and ethno-national understanding of German identity. The policy toward ethnic Germans from the East, or *Aussiedlerpolitik*, works almost like an informal immigration policy based on ethnic criteria and, according to some, represents a peaceful German contribution to "ethnic cleansing" in the East European regions of origin.[40]

A similar continuity that we cannot follow in detail here can be seen in the defensive attitudes against regular immigration legislation and policies, which since the 1980s at the latest needed to shift from the pure jus sanguinis principle to one of jus sanguinis conditioned by elements of jus soli.[41]

From the beginning, there were generous integration programs for ethnic Germans from the East—in contrast to the "guest worker" population—supporting their permanent stay in Germany. As a consequence of these programs, although considerably cut back in the 1990s, the ethnic Germans from the East still are by far the most privileged immigrant group in Germany. The integration of large numbers of ethnic Germans from the East since the end of the 1980s made it clear that despite the federal government's demonstrative protestations to the contrary, this was a true immigration process, not in the sense of the law, but all the more with respect to social, cultural, and mental problems.[42] In addition to this, multicultural life in Germany was, to a certain extent, made more complicated by special group tensions caused by the Aussiedler immigration. On the one hand, many ethnic Germans from the East not only included in their "mental maps" openly ethno-nationalistic views in which they felt even confirmed by the German Aussiedler policy. On the other hand, many of them shared anti-Islamic as well as anti-Zionist and anti-Semitic attitudes. This is why some German transit camps took steps to separate Jews and ethnic Germans from the CIS.

The immigration of Jews from the CIS started during the agony of the German Democratic Republic (GDR) between the demise of the SED regime in November 1989 and unification with West Germany in October 1990. This postrevolutionary interval saw not only the introduction of the local franchise for foreigners which became invalid after unification. In 1990 the parliamentary delegations disagreeing with the former anti-Zionist SED doctrine published a declaration in which they affirmed their willingness to grant asylum to persecuted Jews. This was confirmed by the GDR's Ministerial Council (Ministerrat) in July 1990. Consequently, until mid-April 1991 almost 5,000 Jews applied for acceptance into the territory of the former GDR. From the fall of the Iron Curtain to the end of 1998, a total of 122,593 Jews were given permission to enter Germany. Between 1991 and 1998 almost 93,000 of these arrived, 17,781 in 1998 alone.[43] In the light of everyday anti-Semitism in the CIS, they were accepted as quota refugees, or *Kontingentflüchtlinge,* in Germany and enjoyed a collective status similar in many respects to that of recognized asylum seekers. This, in turn, explains why the treatment of applicants differs so strongly. In 1998, for example, only 0.48 percent of the Jewish applicants from the CIS were denied, while the denial rate was 96 percent among regular asylum seekers. The preferential treatment of CIS Jews in united Germany is an answer to the darkest chapter of German history, the Holocaust. Many Jews from the CIS, however, face problems of identity in Germany: They emigrated as Jews, were accepted and supported as such by Jewish communities, but only in their country of immigration did many of them rediscover a religious identity they did not, or could not, have at home.[44]

The feeling of guilt because of Nazi mass murder, however, did not extend to all minorities who suffered these crimes. This is amply demonstrated by the fate of the Roma who also immigrated during the early 1990s. The memory of Nazi crimes, from which "gypsies" suffered second only to Jews, did not build any bridges into Germany. The immigration of large numbers of Roma from East Europe became possible only as a result of the Rumanian revolution in December 1989, followed by chain migrations and intensified by the Yugoslav wars. Official estimates put the number of Roma refugees from January 1990 through 1 July 1993, when the new asylum law came into force, at 250,000. The largest group of Roma, some 60 percent, come from Rumania; another 30 percent come from Yugoslavia; and a further 5 percent from Bulgaria. Yet these "gypsy asylum seekers," or *Zigeuner-Asylanten,* were soon seen as evidence of how the right to asylum can be abused. Local and municipal authorities came under increasingly heavy pressure in 1992 and 1993 as the populace began to cite all sorts of harassment and disturbances in everyday life in a protest that was in some cases directed against the Roma's very existence in the community. Threats of physical violence against the immigrants from the East became a matter of increasing concern. Officially sanctioned "repatriations," "voluntary re-migrations," threats of deportation, deportations, and migration on to other countries caused the numbers of immigrants to fall. By mid-1993, a total of 125,000 Roma remained in Germany, although Roma organizations put the figure at only 75,000.[45] The figure has continued to fall against the background of measures that were the exact opposite of the favorable way in which Ethnic Germans and Jews from the CIS had been treated. *Their* migration was officially sanctioned and was accompanied by a commitment to effect their social integration and inclusion into the welfare state. For the unwanted "gypsies," on the other hand, exclusion and "repatriation" from Germany were the order of the day. This was tantamount to deportation to such countries as Romania, where they are disliked at least as much as Jews are in the CIS.[46]

Both the treatment of the Roma migrants as harbingers of a chain migration from the East and the eager acceptance of "nightmare migration prognoses" with the specter of "floods" of people from Eastern Europe showed that fears of a new movement of peoples (*Völkerwanderung*) from the East had not abated.[47] The same holds true for the treatment and strict insulation against those migrants from Eastern Europe who represented the bulk of the asylum seekers in the 1990s.[48]

Aside from this, the German government's position vis-à-vis the immigrant minority stemming from the former guest worker population shows that questions of immigration until the late 1990s were hardly viewed any more favorably. Since the late 1970s the so-called guest worker population had been turning more and more obviously into a true immigrant population. This economic, social, and mental process (which cannot be dealt with in detail here), was early recognized and brought to a broader public by experts of social services, trade unions, churches, and consultants for the integration of foreigners—known as *Ausländerbeauftragte*—as well as by migration researchers.[49] The government of the Federal Republic of Germany (FRG), however, consistently denied that Germany was increasingly becoming a country of immigration. It suppressed political action regarding immigration, thereby blocking any political discussion and administrative handling of true immigration issues as such. In the German Ministry of the Interior the word "immigration" remained a taboo term even in internal discussions.

Only in 1994 did the Christian Democratic Union (Christlich-Demokratische Union or CDU)—and only after crucial conflicts with her ethnonationally more conservative sister party, the Christian Social Union (Christlich-Soziale Union or CSU)—eliminate the taboo formula that "The FRG is not a country of immigration [*Die Bundesrepublik ist kein Einwanderungsland*]" from its platform for the election campaign. For the first time, the agreement between the CDU/CSU and the Free Democratic Party (Freie Demokratische Partei or FDP) in 1994 cabinet negotiations envisaged the reform of the citizenship law as a main, but ultimately unfulfilled, goal. Ethno-national thinking and the jus sanguinis tradition had severely retarded the general course of development, leading to a quite belated acceptance of social reality on the levels of programmatic and legal declarations.

In this respect, movement occurred only after the change of government in September 1998, when a red-green coalition of the SPD with the Alliance 90 (Bündnis 90) and the Greens (Die Grünen) replaced the CDU/CSU-FDP government. The new government declared the reform of the 1913 citizenship law—which in fact had been reformed several times before—in the sense of implanting jus soli elements and introducing dual citizenship to be one of its political aims. This meant a belated acceptance of social realities in Germany and the adoption of current practices in most European states despite the joint treaty against multiple nationality of 1963. According to the new citizenship law that was passed in May 1999 and that took force on 1 January 2000, children born in Germany to parents who are legally resident foreigners, i.e., with one parent who has stayed at least eight years in Germany and who has a secure resident status, have a right to dual and even multiple citizenship until the age of twenty-three. At this point they will have to choose between the German or any other citizenship, except under special circumstances. This was a compromise that came about because of an election victory of the opposition CDU in the state of Hesse and the consequent loss of an overall SPD majority in the Federal Council. The new law thus did not bring a full and clear acceptance of the jus soli principle. Still, it broke significantly with a long, ethno-national tradition that made the tackling of many problems of transnational migration unnecessarily difficult.

This was especially true for the exceptionally different treatment of ethnic Germans from the East, on the one hand, and the immigrant minority stemming from the former guest worker population, on the other hand, of whom the Turks, as citizens of a country that did not belong to the European Union, were hardest hit. Both were de facto immigrant groups, but neither was legally or politically accepted as such in Germany—not the "foreigners," because Germany was not willing to concede to becoming a country of immigration, nor the ethnic Germans from the East, because they were supposedly not immigrants but Germans. The social reality showed the opposite: As mentioned above, the guest worker population had developed early into a real immigrant population of "domestic foreigners," "foreign inlanders," or "Germans with foreign passport," while ethnic Germans from the East as "foreign Germans," however, are real immigrants with German citizenship. The resulting problems became all the more serious the less they were recognized and understood as such by the host society. The contradictory treatment of both immigrant groups has additionally led to considerable tensions, especially among young people on both sides who call each other "Turks" and "Russians." Tensions were sharpened by the withholding of dual citizenship for foreigners, but accepting it for ethnic Germans. This discrimination was another point where the consequences of ethno-national thinking and the one-sided jus sanguinis tradition played an important role.[50]

The naturalization of German Turks progressed quite slowly. This did not change before the late 1990s because of more frequent exceptional permits on the German side and often with the help of certain trickery on the Turkish side. According to the Turkish Ministry of Foreign Affairs, of the more than 2.1 million Turks living in Germany by the end of 1998,

196,000 held dual citizenship.[51] In reality, the number is even much higher: Turkey is interested in retaining Turkish citizenship and therefore, if it is applied for, tacitly annuls applications for deprivation of Turkish nationality in favor of the German one. There are different reasons for the hesitation of Turkish immigrants in Germany to make up their mind for German citizenship, even in the second generation: Explanations stress uncertainties among the Turkish immigrant population, enforced by the violent xenophobia of the early 1990s, influences of Turkish politics in Germany, and historically grown double bonds of loyalty arising from an immigration situation artificially kept unclear and open by the paradoxical German "non-immigration" migration policies. Another explanation includes the development of transcultural as well as transnational identities.[52] Ultimately such double bonds of loyalty or transnational identities can only be bridged by the grant of dual citizenship.

In 1999 this bridge has been built by the reform of the 1913 citizenship law over the strong resistance of CDU and CSU, which mobilized five million people in a mass signature campaign against dual citizenship.[53] This campaign evoked xenophobic reactions in many sectors of the population, clearly demonstrated by repeatedly occurring questions such as "Where can I sign against foreigners." The new minister of the interior, O. Schily from the Social Democrats, was quite right when he noted that in Germany the introduction of dual citizenship would "change our whole understanding of the state if we will no longer connect the belonging to the legal community with ethnic descent, but rather with the acceptance of our constitution and laws."[54] Moreover, the reform of the 1913 citizenship law with the adoption of elements of the jus soli definition of citizenship and the introduction of dual citizenship symbolized an acknowledgement of the republican idea, discussed in Germany under the key word "constitutional patriotism [*Verfassungspatriotismus*]," and challenged the contraposition of ethno-national identity. In this sense it was only consistent with the conservatives' views that they tried to prove the new 1999 citizenship law unconstitutional on the basis of ethno-national values in the German Constitution.[55] Long-established collective mentalities die hard and cannot be immediately altered by legal reform.[56]

Looking back from the close of the twentieth century to the courses of development of immigration, integration, immigrant minorities and of political acceptance, and legal and administrative management of the respective challenges in the Federal Republic of Germany, there seems to be a two-faced "German model" in the triangle of citizenship law, ethnonational thinking, and immigration policies. On the one hand, there was consistent political denial and a belated acceptance of social realities in immigration and a corresponding lack of clear and comprehensive legal conceptions, as well as of long-term perspectives needed for immigration management in the context of what, in German, came to be called *Gesellschaftspolitik*. On the other hand, there was a legal and administrative day-to-day immigration and integration management—not declared as such and not implanted in large political concepts, but meeting practical needs and challenges of the immigration situation—and by this "muddling through" gradually, at least partially, acceptance of an immigration situation that had been constantly denied in public. This shaped a regulative system of immigration and integration policies not declared as such, which all who wanted to accomplish objectives as migrants or for migrants had to accept.[57] The system worked at the price of accumulating many serious problems and resulting social difficulties, including collective emotional trauma among the immigrant population. Against this background, a one-sided reinterpretation of a "German model" of immigration and integration as having been just a pragmatic success path *per aspera ad astra*, however, would present a sanitized version of the two-faced history of German migration policies.

Notes

1. K. J. Bade, ed., *Population, Labour and Migration in 19th and 20th Century Germany* (Oxford, 1987); idem, ed., *Deutsche im Ausland – Fremde in Deutschland: Migration in Geschichte und Gegenwart* (Munich, 1992); idem, *Homo Migrans: Wanderungen aus und nach Deutschland – Erfahrungen und Fragen* (Essen, 1994); idem, ed., *Das Manifest der 60: Deutschland und die Einwanderung* (Munich, 1994).
2. K. J. Bade, *Vom Auswanderungsland zum Einwanderungsland? Deutschland 1880 bis 1980* (Berlin, 1983).
3. K. J. Bade, "Transnationale Migration, ethno-nationale Diskussion und staatliche Migrationspolitik im Deutschland des 19. und 20. Jahrhunderts," in *Migration – Ethnizität – Konflikt: Systemfragen und Fallstudien*, ed. K. J. Bade, Schriften des Instituts für Migrationsforschung und Interkulturelle Studien, 1 (Osnabrück, 1996), 431–50; idem, "From Emigration to Immigration: The German Experience in the 19th and 20th Century," in *Migration Past, Migration Future: Germany and the United States*, ed. K. J. Bade and M. Weiner (Providence, R.I., 1997), 1–37.
4. W. von Hippel, *Auswanderung aus Südwestdeutschland. Studien zur württembergischen Auswanderung und Auswanderungspolitik im 18. und 19. Jahrhundert* (Stuttgart, 1984); K. J. Bade, "Die deutsche Überseeische Massenauswanderung im 19. und frühen 20. Jahrhundert: Bestimmungsfaktoren und Entwicklungsbedingungen," in *Auswanderer – Wanderarbeiter – Gastarbeiter. Bevölkerung, Arbeitsmarkt und Wanderung in Deutschland seit der Mitte des 19. Jahrhunderts*, ed. K. J. Bade (Ostfildern, 1986), 1:259–99; W. Helbich, W. D. Kamphoefner, and U. Sommer, eds., *Briefe aus Amerika. Deutsche Auswanderer schreiben aus der Neuen Welt 1830–1930* (Munich, 1988).
5. H. Fenske, "Die deutsche Auswanderung in der Mitte des 19. Jahrhunderts. Öffentliche Meinung und amtliche Politik," *Geschichte in Wissenschaft und Unterricht* 24 (1973): 221–36.
6. M. Kuckhoff, "Die Auswanderungsdiskussion während der Revolution von 1848/49," in *Deutsche Amerikaauswanderung im 19. Jahrhundert. Sozialgeschichtliche Beiträge*, ed. G. Moltmann (Stuttgart, 1976), 102–45.
7. C. Hansen, "Die deutsche Auswanderung im 19. Jahrhundert – ein Mittel zur Lösung sozialer und sozialpolitischer Probleme?" in *Deutsche Amerikaauswanderung*, ed.

Moltmann, 8–61; G. Moltmann, "Auswanderung als Revolutionsersatz?" in *Die Deutschen und die Revolution*, ed. M. Salewski (Göttingen, 1984), 272–97.

8. F. Fabri, *Bedarf Deutschland der Colonien? Eine politisch-ökonomische Betrachtung* (Gotha, 1879); K. J. Bade, *Friedrich Fabri und der Imperialismus in der Bismarckzeit. Revolution – Depression – Expansion* (Freiburg, 1975), 80–99, 354–60.
9. F. C. Luebke, *Germans in Brazil: A Comparative History of Cultural Conflict During World War I* (Baton Rouge, La., 1987), 1–82.
10. K. J. Bade, "Das Kaiserreich als Kolonialmacht. Ideologische Projektionen und historische Erfahrung," in *Die deutsche Frage im 19. und 20. Jahrhundert*, ed. J. Becker and A. Hillgruber (Munich, 1983), 91–108; idem, "Die 'zweite Reichsgründung' in Übersee: Imperiale Visionen, Kolonialbewegung und Kolonialpolitik in der Bismarckzeit," in *Die Herausforderung des europäischen Staatensystems. Nationale Ideologie und staatliches Interesse zwischen Restauration und Imperialismus*, ed. A. M. Birke and G. Heydemann (Göttingen, 1989), 183–215.
11. K. J. Bade, "German Emigration to the United States and Continental Immigration to Germany, 1879–1979," *Central European History* 13 (1980): 348–77; idem, "Massenwanderung und Arbeitsmarkt im deutschen Nordosten von 1880 bis zum Ersten Weltkrieg: Überseeische Auswanderung, interne Abwanderung und kontinentale Zuwanderung," *Archiv für Sozialgeschichte* 20 (1980): 265–323.
12. R. Langbein and W. Henning, "Staat und Auswanderung im 19. Jahrhundert," *Zeitschrift für Kulturaustausch* 39 (1989): 292–301.
13. K. J. Bade, "Politik und Ökonomie der Ausländerbeschäftigung im preußischen Osten. Die Internationalisierung des Arbeitsmarktes im 'Rahmen der preußischen Abwehrpolitik,'" in *Preußen im Rückblick*, ed. H.-J. Puhle and H.-U. Wehler (Göttingen, 1980), 273–99.
14. R. Brubaker, *Citizenship and Nationhood in France and Germany* (Cambridge, Mass., 1992).
15. A. Fahrmeir, "Nineteenth-Century German Citizenship: A Reconsideration," *Historical Journal* 40 (1997): 721–52.
16. R. Just, "Gescheitertes Miteinander. Einbürgerungspolitik und Einbürgerungspraxis in Deutschland 1871–1933," *AWR (Association for the Study of the World Refugee Problem) Bulletin* 36, no. 2 (1998), 81–106, here 85.
17. Brubaker, *Citizenship and Nationhood*, 114–37.
18. J. Wertheimer, *Unwelcome Strangers: East European Jews in Imperial Germany* (New York, 1987); T. Maurer, *Ostjuden in Deutschland 1918–1933* (Hamburg, 1986); M. Just, *Ost- und südosteuropäische Amerikaauswanderung 1881–1914. Transitprobleme in Deutschland und Aufnahme in den Vereinigten Staaten* (Stuttgart, 1988); I. Blank, "'... nirgends eine Heimat, aber Gräber auf jedem Friedhof.' Ostjuden in Kaiserreich und Weimarer Republik," in *Deutsche im Ausland – Fremde in Deutschland*, ed. Bade, 324–32.
19. K. J. Bade, "'Preußengänger' und 'Abwehrpolitik': Ausländerbeschäftigung, Ausländerpolitik und Ausländerkontrolle auf dem Arbeitsmarkt in Preußen vor dem Ersten Weltkrieg," *Archiv für Sozialgeschichte* 24 (1984): 91–162; idem, "Arbeiterstatistik zur Ausländerkontrolle: Die 'Nachweisungen' der preußischen Landräte über den 'Zugang, Abgang und Bestand der ausländischen Arbeiter im preußischen Staate' 1906–1914," ibid., 163–283.
20. Bade, "Transnationale Migration, ethno-nationale Diskussion und staatliche Migrationspolitik," 416.
21. Just, "Einbürgerungspolitik und Einbürgerungspraxis," 85f.
22. Ibid., 88f.
23. I. Ferenczi, *Kontinentale Wanderungen und die Annäherung der Völker. Ein geschichtlicher Überblick* (Jena, 1930), 21; H. Bickelmann, *Deutsche Überseeauswanderung in der Weimarer Zeit* (Wiesbaden, 1980); K. J. Bade, "Arbeitsmarkt, Bevölkerung und Wanderung in der Weimarer Republik," in *Die Weimarer Republik – Belagerte Civitas*, ed. M. Stürmer (Königstein i.Ts., 1980), 160–87; idem, "Das 'Amt der verlorenen Worte': Das Reichswanderungsamt 1918–1924," *Zeitschrift für Kulturaustausch* 39 (1989): 312–25.

24. Just, "Einbürgerungspolitik und Einbürgerungspraxis," 89f.
25. Ibid., 100–102.
26. Ibid., 98f.
27. For the following, see K. J. Bade and J. Oltmer, "Einführung: Aussiedlerzuwanderung und Aussiedlerintegration. Historische Entwicklung und aktuelle Probleme," in *Aussiedler: deutsche Einwanderer aus Osteuropa*, ed. K. J. Bade and J. Oltmer, Schriften des Instituts für Migrationsforschung und Interkulturelle Studien, 8 (Osnabrück, 1999), 9–51, here 15–17.
28. For a more detailed analysis of the Weimar period, see the contribution of J. Oltmer in this volume.
29. Wertheimer, *Unwelcome Strangers*, 24–27; R. Koch, "Die 'Fremdvölkischen' im Blick der Einheimischen: Polnische Wanderarbeiter in Deutschland während der Weimarer Republik," *Deutsche Studien* 30 (1993): 39–56, here 46; Just, "Einbürgerungspolitik und Einbürgerungspraxis," 87f., 102.
30. Just, "Einbürgerungspolitik und Einbürgerungspraxis," 94f.
31. Ibid., 96.
32. R. R. Doerries, "German Transatlantic Migration from the Early 19th Century to the Outbreak of World War II," in *Population, Labour and Migration in 19th and 20th Century Germany*, ed. Bade, 115–34, here 130f.
33. W. Röder, "Die Emigration aus dem nationalsozialistischen Deutschland," in *Deutsche im Ausland – Fremde in Deutschland*, ed. Bade, 345–53; K. J. Bade and H. A. Strauss, eds., *Internationales Biographisches Handbuch der deutschsprachigen Emigration nach 1933/International Biographical Dictionary of Central European Emigrés 1933–1945*, 3 vols. (Munich, 1980–1983); E. Lacina, *Emigration 1933–1945. Sozialhistorische Darstellung der deutschsprachigen Emigration und einiger ihrer Asylländer aufgrund ausgewählter zeitgenössischer Selbstzeugnisse* (Stuttgart, 1982); W. Benz, ed., *Das Exil der kleinen Leute: Alltagserfahrungen deutscher Juden in der Emigration* (Munich, 1991).
34. R. Hilberg, *The Destruction of the European Jews* (New York, 1985); W. Benz, *Der Holocaust*, 3rd ed. (Munich, 1997); U. Herbert, ed., *Nationalsozialistische Vernichtungspolitik 1939–1945. Neue Forschungen und Kontroversen* (Frankfurt a.M., 1998); C. R. Browning, *Ordinary Men: Reserve Police Battalion 101 and the Final Solution in Poland* (New York, 1993); D. J. Goldhagen, *Hitler's Willing Executioners: Ordinary Germans and the Holocaust* (New York, 1996).
35. U. Herbert, *Fremdarbeiter: Politik und Praxis des "Ausländer-Einsatzes" in der Kriegswirtschaft des Dritten Reiches* (Berlin, 1985); idem, ed., *Europa und der "Reichseinsatz": Ausländische Zivilarbeiter, Kriegsgefangene und KZ-Häftlinge in Deutschland 1938–1945* (Essen, 1991).
36. Bade, *Homo Migrans*, 95f.
37. W. Benz, ed., *Die Vertreibung der Deutschen aus dem Osten. Ursachen, Ereignisse, Folgen* (Frankfurt a.M., 1995); idem, "Fremde in der Heimat: Flucht – Vertreibung – Integration," in *Deutsche im Ausland – Fremde in Deutschland*, ed. Bade, 374–86; R. Schulze, D. von der Brelie-Lewien, and H. Grebing, eds., *Flüchtlinge und Vertriebene in der westdeutschen Nachkriegsgeschichte. Bilanzierung der Forschung und Perspektiven für die künftige Forschungsarbeit* (Hildesheim, 1987); S. Bethlehem, *Heimatvertreibung, DDR-Flucht, Gastarbeiterzuwanderung. Wanderungsströme und Wanderungspolitik in der Bundesrepublik Deutschland* (Stuttgart, 1982); H. Heidemeier, *Flucht und Zuwanderung aus der SBZ/DDR 1945/1949–1961. Die Flüchtlingspolitik der Bundesrepublik Deutschland bis zum Bau der Berliner Mauer* (Düsseldorf, 1994); U. Herbert, *Geschichte der Ausländerbeschäftigung in Deutschland 1880–1980. Saisonarbeiter – Zwangsarbeiter – Gastarbeiter* (Berlin, 1986), 179–236; Bade, *Vom Auswanderungsland zum Einwanderungsland?* 59–124; idem, *Ausländer – Aussiedler – Asyl: Eine Bestandsaufnahme* (Munich, 1994); idem, "Tabu Migration: Belastungen und Herausforderungen in Deutschland," in *Das Manifest der 60*, ed. Bade, 66–85; R. Münz, W. Seifert and R. Ulrich, *Zuwanderung nach Deutschland. Strukturen, Wirkungen, Perspektiven* (Frankfurt a.M., 1997). On ethnic Germans from the East in the

GDR, see M. Krüger-Potratz, ed., *Anderssein gab es nicht: Ausländer und Minderheiten in der DDR* (Münster, 1991).

38. See the contribution of J. Oltmer in this volume.
39. *Süddeutsche Zeitung*, 2–3 Jan. 1999, 9.
40. R. Olt, "Zwischen Selbstpreisgabe und Hoffnung. Die Lage nationaler Minderheiten in Osteuropa," *Frankfurter Allgemeine Zeitung*, 28 Feb. 1994; Bade, *Ausländer – Aussiedler – Asyl*, 25–28, 147–74.
41. Bade, "Tabu Migration" (see n. 37), and idem, "Transnationale Migration" (see n. 3).
42. B. Dietz and P. Hilkes, *Integriert oder isoliert? Zur Situation rußlanddeutscher Aussiedler in der Bundesrepublik Deutschland* (Munich, 1994); K. J. Bade, ed., *Neue Heimat im Westen. Vertriebene – Flüchtlinge – Aussiedler* (Münster, 1990); idem, ed., *Fremde im Land. Zuwanderung und Eingliederung im Raum Niedersachsen seit dem Zweiten Weltkrieg*, Schriften des Instituts für Migrationsforschung und Interkulturelle Studien, 3 (Osnabrück, 1997).
43. P. A. Harris, "Russische Juden und Aussiedler: Integrationspolitik und lokale Verantwortung," in *Aussiedler*, ed. Bade and Oltmer, 247–63; J. Doomernik, *Going West: Soviet Jewish Immigrants in Berlin since 1990* (Aldershot, 1997), 2–5, 53–71; L. Mertens, *Alija. Die Emigration der Juden aus der UdSSR/GUS* (Bochum, 1993), 132–38, 185–89; S. I. Troen and K. J. Bade, eds., *Returning Home: Immigration and Absorption into their Homelands of Germans and Jews from the Former Soviet Union*, Hubert H. Humphrey Institute for Social Ecology, Ben-Gurion University of the Negev (Beer-Sheva, Israel, 1994).
44. J. H. Schoeps et al., eds., *Russische Juden in Deutschland. Integration und Selbstbehauptung in einem fremden Land* (Weinheim, 1996), 152f.
45. F. Blahusch, "Roma-Flüchtlinge in Deutschland. Zur aktuellen politischen und sozialen Situation," in *Sinti, Roma und wir anderen. Beiträge zu problembesetzten Beziehungen*, ed. R. Schopf (Münster, 1994), 73–96, here 82.
46. G. Mutz, "Die Gesellschaftliche Produktion von sozialer und kultureller Fremdheit in der Medienöffentlichkeit," in *Sinti und Roma in Deutschland*, ed. J. S. Hohmann (Frankfurt a.M., 1995), 116–175; M. Frost et al., "'Der bettelnde Zigeuner': Produktion eines Stereotyps und sein Nutzen für die Diskriminierung von Sinti und Roma," ibid., 216–30; M. Frost et al., "Roma-Feindlichkeit in fremdenfeindlichen Milieus. Thesen über einen spezifischen Rassismus," ibid., 231–51.
47. D. Vogeley, *Massenansturm aus dem Osten? Ursachen und Auswirkungen der Ost-West-Migration*, Deutsche Gesellschaft für die Vereinten Nationen, no. 139 (Bonn, 1991), 3.
48. Bade, *Ausländer – Aussiedler – Asyl*, 91–206.
49. F. Heckmann, *Die Bundesrepublik: ein Einwanderungsland? Zur Soziologie der Gastarbeiterbevölkerung als Einwandererminorität* (Stuttgart, 1981); Bade, *Vom Auswanderungsland zum Einwanderungsland.*
50. L. Hoffmann, *Die unvollendete Republik. Zwischen Einwanderungsland und deutschem Nationalstaat* (Cologne, 1990); idem, *Das deutsche Volk und seine Feinde. Die völkische Droge – Aktualität und Entstehungsgeschichte* (Cologne, 1994); D. Oberndörfer, *Der Wahn des Nationalen. Die Alternative der offenen Republik* (Freiburg i.Br., 1993); K. J. Bade, "Immigration and Social Peace in United Germany," *Daedalus* (Winter 1994), 85–106; idem, "Einwanderung und Gesellschaftspolitik in Deutschland – Quo vadis Bundesrepublik?" in *Die multikulturelle Herausforderung: Menschen über Grenzen – Grenzen über Menschen*, ed. idem (Munich, 1996), 204–23; idem, "Transnationale Migration, ethnonationale Diskussion und staatliche Migrationspolitik," 423–30; idem, "Was man tabuisiert, kann man nicht gestalten: Die große Ratlosigkeit: Einwanderungsprobleme ohne Einwanderungspolitik," *Frankfurter Rundschau*, 21 Nov. 1994, 12; H.-Å. Persson, "Foreigners, Historical Ethnic Immigration, and the Successful Western German Model," in *Encounter with Strangers: The European Experience*, ed. H.-Å. Persson (Lund, 1997), 9–84; R. Eckert, ed., *Wiederkehr des "Volksgeistes"? Ethnizität, Konflikt und politische Bewältigung* (Opladen, 1998); N. Piper, *Racism, Nationalism and Citizenship: Ethnic Minorities in Britain and Germany* (Aldershot, 1998), 136–44.
51. *Süddeutsche Zeitung*, 7 Jan. 1999, 6.

52. L. Pries, ed., *Migration and Transnational Social Spaces* (Aldershot, 1999); T. Faist, "Developing Transnational Social Spaces: The Turkish-German Example," ibid., 36–72.
53. *Süddeutsche Zeitung*, 21 May 1999, 7.
54. Ibid., 7 Jan. 1999, 1.
55. R. Scholz and A. Uhle, "Staatsangehörigkeit und Grundgesetz" *Neue Juristische Wochenschrift* 52 (1999): 5110–17.
56. A. Nassehi and M. Schroer, "Politische und rechtliche Inklusion oder gesellschaftliche Integration? Zur Überschätzung und Unterschätzung von Staatsbürgerschaft" (Paper given at the Conference on "Political Integration" at the Centre for Interdisciplinary Research, University of Bielefeld, 21–22 Jan. 1999).
57. M. Bommes, "Von Gastarbeitern zu Einwanderern: Arbeitsmigration in Niedersachsen," in *Fremde im Land*, ed. Bade, 249–322.

Chapter 2

Migration and Public Policy in Germany, 1918–1939

Jochen Oltmer

Looking back at the development of European migration in a structural-historical overview of the 130 years from the end of the Napoleonic wars until the end of World War II, two epochs can be distinguished: a "long" nineteenth century which lasted until the outbreak of World War I, characterized by free movement across borders that was scarcely regulated by the state, and a short "New Thirty Years' War" from 1914 to 1945 characterized by state intervention and millions of refugees. From this point of view, World War I is the boundary between these epochs because it was the first "total" war of modern times that massively influenced European migration patterns and caused new mass phenomena: forced migration, forced labor, mass refugee movement and expulsion. This was even more true of World War II, the final chapter of the New Thirty Years' War. By the end of World War II, though less than half of the twentieth century was over, it was already known as the "century of refugees," and can also legitimately be called a "century of expulsions" or a "century of forced migration."

The short "peaceful" period between both world wars was characterized by two main developments. First, there were large movements of refugees, expellees, and emigrants during the two decades from 1918 to 1939, primarily following World War I and on the eve of World War II. Second, the first Europe-wide trend to protectionist migration policies arose: the relationship of public policy and migration changed; state control, administration, and regulation became important features of migration and labor market policies focused on national protection and exclusion.

Research on the history of European migration during the New Thirty Years' War from 1914 to 1945 is still fragmentary. Forced migrations and refugee movements have been analyzed very intensively. Above all, this is true for emigration from Nazi Germany, for the absorption of these refugees, and for the immense Nazi forced labor system that covered the entire European continent. Much less research has been done on migration conditions during World War I and on resulting refugee movements, but also on the systems of forced migration and forced labor that played an important role in the supply of urgently needed workers to the expanding war economies. The relatively peaceful period between these extremes has received even less attention. When looking at overview descriptions of this topic, this paucity of research becomes obvious: the period from 1914 to 1945 is usually given very little attention or, alternatively, is totally ignored.[1]

In what follows, some of the fundamental traits of migration conditions between the wars shall be traced. The situation in Germany shall be placed in comparative perspective with the broader European context. In fact, Germany is an excellent starting point when considering the development of European migration conditions between the wars, as Germany was not only both country of emigration and immigration at the same time, but also one of the most important European destinations and, after 1933, countries of origin for refugees, expellees, and emigrants. The first question to be addressed will be how transnational migration manifested itself, the second identifying the political and administrative solutions used to control and regulate migration, and the third establishing the driving forces behind these protectionist migration policies.

Regulating Emigration

The "long" nineteenth century of European mass emigration ended with World War I. During the war, the number of emigrants had sharply decreased, however in the 1920s, 6.9 million emigrants left Europe. This was an annual average of nearly 700,000 people—approximately half the annual rates of the prewar decade.[2]

After World War I Germany was an exception to the pattern of European transatlantic emigration because the numbers of emigrants clearly increased when compared with prewar times. Between 1921 and 1930 Germany advanced to take the fifth position among the most important European countries of emigration, with 564,000 emigrants, twice as many as there had been between 1901 and 1910. The British Isles (2.2 million) and Italy (1.4 million) remained the leading emigration countries of Europe. With 560,000 emigrants, Spain had now dropped to the sixth position. Portugal took third position with nearly one million emigrants, followed by Poland (634,000) and Germany.

Several reasons can be found for the obvious increase in the number of German emigrants between World War I and the Great Depression.[3]

Basically, emigration was a phenomenon of the immediate postwar period. In view of the economic, social, and political postwar crisis, the number of emigrants could have been expected to reach millions. Yet this did not happen, even though statistics showed an increase in the course of the postwar crisis until 1923. In 1913 there were 22,100 emigrants, and the number had declined to less than half (10,700) in 1914. From 1915 to 1918, there were only 800 altogether. In spite of enormous difficulties in emigrating because of restrictions in the receiving countries and lack of available transport, the number of emigrants rose to 3,120 in 1919; to 8,458 in 1920, approaching the 1914 rate, and reached prewar levels with 24,173 in 1921. This level was surmounted in 1922 with 36,623 emigrants. In 1923, with its hyperinflation, numbers increased sharply to 115,431—an annual rate that had only been reached during the emigration wave of the 1880s and early 1890s.

Many people who had long before made up their minds to emigrate had to postpone this decision because of the emigration restrictions during and immediately after World War I, and could not realize their plans until the early 1920s. Together with these factors, the currency devaluation during the high postwar inflation in Germany and the hope of a better existence precipitated or contributed to the emigration of many who were already planning to leave. Many of these emigrants came from the ceded territories of the Reich, from the colonies, or from the German settlements in east, central east, and southeast Europe. Those who would not accept the political and social change during the transition from the Kaiserreich to the Weimar Republic, namely to having lost the war, were also among these "uprooted" people.

Following the general development in Europe, emigration from Germany strikingly decreased when in November 1923, the German currency stabilized, and in 1924, the U.S. imposed immigration restrictions. In the following years, emigration rates mirrored those of the last prewar years, and declined during the Great Depression of the early 1930s to an annual rate of 10,000 to 15,000. Even if the rise of German emigration numbers in the postwar crisis had no parallels in other European countries, the same substantial structural conditions and political courses were also true for other countries.

Not only destination countries like the U.S.[4] but also many countries of origin restricted or channeled migration by means of various and increasingly protectionist migration policies. The Soviet Union was an example of this development: in prewar times, Russia had been one of the most important European countries of origin for transatlantic emigration, but after World War I, the numbers of emigrants decreased to a very low level. Actually, there was no official prohibition of emigration, but emigration was made practically impossible by high bureaucratic hindrances: special documents, which were difficult to obtain, had to be presented and the fees were prohibitively high. These extremely restrictive emigration policies were directly connected to the massive Soviet industrialization program that only seemed to be practical with the binding and regulating of the entire labor force.[5]

Although Italy, for instance, remained one of the main emigration countries between the wars, controlling and restrictive migration policies developed in this country as well. For the fascist rulers in power since 1922, permanent or temporary emigration meant national disgrace that would reveal the economic backwardness of the country and aggravate this situation by the loss of important labor. The explicit intention of the Italian colonial policy that finally failed, had been to build up settlement colonies in order not only to transfer but also to limit streams of permanent or short-term emigration. Nevertheless, only 50,000 to 60,000 Italians had been settled in the new colonial areas in Libya and East Africa by 1930. After that, numbers increased, so that an estimated 400,000 emigrants in the colonies seem to be a realistic figure. In spite of this, re-migration was considerable: in the late 1930s, only 85,000 Italians were living in Libya and even less (60,000) in the East African colonies. In view of the 2 million Italian emigrants of the 1920s alone, plans to direct migration into colonial settlements must be considered a failure. Since 1927, Italian migration policies became more and more constrained, fighting above all against permanent emigration and trying to support re-migration at the same time. The recruitment of Italian migrant workers by foreign states or enterprises was submitted to strengthened controls.[6]

In the Weimar Republic, state influence on the extent and direction of emigration remained less open and less direct than in the USSR and in Italy. The growing governmental interest led to the foundation of the Reich Migration Agency (Reichsstelle für deutsche Rückwanderung und Auswanderung) in May 1918. One year later, this agency had become more important and was renamed Reich Migration Office (Reichsamt für deutsche Einwanderung, Rückwanderung und Auswanderung). In early 1924, however, it was reduced to a secondary Reich Emigration Agency (Reichsstelle für das Auswanderungswesen) with less expertise and resources. Apart from the beginning of this office at the end of World War I and its aftermath when the main task was to organize immigration of Germans and of people of German descent, the principal purpose, in spite of all institutional changes, was to control and administer emigration from the Reich.[7]

On the one hand, both the Reich Migration Agency and the Reich Migration Office were designed to protect emigrants by providing them with information on the situation as well as on the economic opportunities and dangers in different destination countries and by combating organizations and agents who might cheat emigrants. On the other hand, emigration was definitely to be controlled: a fully developed advisory network served as an advice center for emigrants. This was the most important device of state-controlled regulation of emigration, which was realized only indirectly because the Weimar Constitution assured everyone the right to emigrate. The agency's main intention was to prevent qualified workers from emigrating. When the emigration of a worker was not seen to be disadvantageous to the German labor market, the emigrant was whenever possible directed to such areas that allowed settlements of Germans, primarily in South America. Closed and permanent German settlements appeared possible there and were considered to be likely to preserve the emigrants' "Germanness." At the same time, German settlers as customers of German goods would help the economic development in the Reich as export would increase.

All in all, efforts to control and channel emigration from Germany remained primarily unsuccessful. In the end, the advisory practice did not prevent emigration, particularly as the strained German labor market could scarcely provide enough sources of income. Actually in the 1920s, Latin America had become a much more important emigration destination for Germans than in the nineteenth century. However, this had less to do with regulative policies of the Reich than, above all, with restrictions on emigration to the U.S. This lead to the choice of other destinations. In addition, the planned German settlements in South America were not able to be realized.

During the Great Depression of the late 1920s and 1930s, emigration from Europe sharply declined. Between 1931 and 1940, only 1.2 million emigrants were registered Europe-wide, a fifth of the rate of the 1920s. This meant an average annual number of 120,000 European emigrants, the lowest rate for over a hundred years. For example, the actual number of immigrants in the U.S. was even smaller than the already low U.S. quota allowed: in the 1930s, the U.S.-American quota for Great Britain and Ireland was 835,740, but only 110,094 immigrants arrived. Additionally, the Great Depression considerably contributed to restrict chances to immigrate and to support re-migration tendencies: Great Britain, one of the classical European emigration countries, had had the highest European annual number of emigrants for over one hundred years, apart from a few exceptional years. Because of rapidly decreasing emigration numbers and a stronger re-migration movement, 1930 was the first year that Great Britain registered an immigration surplus that, on the eve of World War II, had reached 500,000 people.

From 1930 to 1935, other countries that had long recorded more transatlantic or continental emigrants than immigrants, e.g., Belgium, Austria, Hungary, Yugoslavia, and Romania, reached a comparable immigration surplus. Between the Great Depression and the outbreak of World War II, emigration was no longer a decisive factor for the population development in Europe.[8] Germany was again an exception, although this was not a problem of voluntary emigration but of the politically and racial-ideologically motivated National Socialist expulsion.

Labor Market Control and Restrictive Immigration Policies

In 1930 the Hungarian economist Imre Ferenczi, an attentive observer of migration and migration policies in Europe between the two world wars on behalf of the International Labor Office in Geneva, identified two quite different stages: unregulated "proletarian mass migrations" before World War I, and those migrations after 1918 that were "regulated by social policy and internationally organized."[9] In the same year, the German economist Karl C. Thalheim described this development as follows: "today, the world migration economy is shifting from liberalism to state-planned national economies."[10] Unlike the epoch before 1914, the regulating, controlling, and administrating intervention of the protectionist welfare state became the essential feature of immigration policies between the wars.

In Germany, until 1914 the world's largest labor-importing country after the U.S., the protectionist transition between the wars became obvious as immigration policy was committed to labor market developments. Already before World War I, Prussia-Germany had developed a complex system to control foreign workers with the intention of strictly observing and regulating Polish immigration. However, this anti-Polish "defense policy" was not intended to cut down or block immigration as such and was not dependent on labor market development. For national political reasons, the main purpose was rather to prevent the extensive temporary immigration from Poland—urgently needed in view of labor shortages resulting from the economic boom—from expanding into permanent immigration.[11]

In the Weimar Republic, labor market policy was the basic element of migration policies rather than the anti-Polish "defense policy." As a consequence of serious economic and structural unemployment, the catchword "Protection Of The National Labor Market" as a determining factor and prevailing issue had now taken the place of the former slogan "Lack of People [*Leutenot*]" in industry and agriculture. "Protection of the National Labor Market" did not only stand for "rejection" and "repulsion" of foreign workers, but also for the above-mentioned prevention of permanent or temporary emigration of the skilled workers lacking in important economic areas. For this reason, immigration control as a crucial political issue was attached to labor market policy. As shown above, emigration was to be regulated in favor of labor market interests, since the Weimar Republic was both a country of emigration and a country of immigration.[12] Therefore, the purpose and strength of emigration or immigration policies cannot be examined separately.

In view of the high structural unemployment in Germany, the policy direction concerning foreigners was a clear "preference of domestic workers" in the labor market, while foreign workers simply had a substitutionary or additional function. This was in line with claims of the

German labor movement in prewar times, and it could be pushed through at the beginning of the Weimar Republic with the growing political power of labor movements: apart from the evident "preference of domestic workers," it was claimed that foreign workers should exclusively be employed under the conditions of wage agreements for Germans workers in order to prevent wage cuts. Furthermore, the admission of foreign workers should be regulated by committees equally representative of employers and workers. After a transitional stage specified by economic and personal demobilization, from 1920 the employment of foreign workers was regulated by a more and more differentiated system.

The intention to make the employment of foreign workers more flexible and to suit the economic situation was emphasized by the Labor Exchange Act (*Arbeitsnachweisgesetz*) of 1922. Existing single regulations were then standardized, all questions of foreign labor employment were directed to the Reich Employment Agency (Reichsamt für Arbeitsvermittlung), while the German Foreign Workers' Agency (Deutsche Arbeiterzentrale) managed labor recruitment abroad. In order to keep the employment of foreign workers flexible and to adapt it to the current economic situation, work and residence permits were principally granted for only one year—even shorter in agriculture—except for those foreigners who had been living in Germany for many years and been granted unlimited work and residence permits in the form of permanent visas, or *Befreiungsscheine*. The German-Polish Treaty on Polish Agricultural Migrant Workers of November 1927 was a means for German immigration control to intensify recruitment since this treaty guaranteed the recruitment and repulsion of Polish workers under German conditions. By centralizing decisive competencies at the Reich Labor Administration, the recruitment and management of foreign labor became merely government domains.

The requirement of residence and work permits facilitated far-reaching control and regulation. Consequently, the employment of foreign workers could be reduced compared to prewar times. At the end of World War I the number of foreign workers decreased to one-third (260,000), stabilized around 300,000 in the postwar period, and went down by one-fifth (227,000) in the Hyperinflation of 1923. In 1924, a stabilizing year but still characterized by depression, the number of foreign workers decreased again by one-fifth (177,000); in 1925, this rose to 263,000—50 percent more than in the previous year—followed by another decline between 1926 and 1930 when numbers fluctuated slightly from 220,000 to 240,000. During the Great Depression, the number of foreign workers employed in Germany decreased dramatically and plummeted to 109,000 in 1932. Anyway, the substitutionary or additional function of foreign workers was evident: during the Great Depression, their employment had become irrelevant, and, additionally, most of the remaining foreigners were regarded as being of German descent (*deutschstämmig*) and possessed permanent visas because of long-term employment in Germany. This was not changed by the National Socialists, who adopted, with the addition of some recruitment contracts, the entire control and regulation system of the Weimar Republic. However, the employment of foreign workers was tolerated to a greater extent during the militarization on the eve of World War II—in 1938/39 there were 370,000 foreign workers in Germany.

Compared with other countries, the French example indicates that increasing government influence on immigration cannot simply be attributed to economic crises.[13] Outside of Germany, the highest number of foreigners living in a European country is to be found in France before World War I. After the victory of 1918 the prospering French economy needed more and more workers who were not sufficiently available on the "national" French labor market as a result of decades of low birth rates and heavy war losses. Immigration as a solution to this dilemma was politically realized. After World War I, France became the center of intra-European, economic migration. In France, however, immigration policies were no longer implemented as liberally as in prewar times as this country, too, followed the tendency toward higher state intervention in migration. Regulation mechanisms were perfected, intergovernmental agreements with the countries of origin supported management and control of immigration.

In the 1920s France opened its borders widely to foreign workers. In 1931 there were 2.7 million foreigners, the most significant groups among them being, approximately, 800,000 Italians, 500,000 Poles, 350,000 Spaniards, and 250,000 Belgians. With two million immigrants in one decade, France became the second most important destination country for European permanent or temporary emigrants, apart from the U.S. In the second half of the 1920s, immigration into the U.S. clearly diminished because of the quota legislation, and France even turned out to be the most significant immigration country for Europeans.[14] Immigration in the 1920s made up no less than three quarters of the total increase in French population in this period. Soon after the end of the war in 1918, there was in France a broad consensus in favor of immigration with the economy presumably profiting from military success and France becoming the leading economic power on the continent rather than Germany. In view of prewar and war experiences, it was felt that immigration should be submitted to strict control and regulation, as in the Weimar Republic. Practically, this meant that foreign workers were directly recruited for those industries that did not have sufficient domestic workers. Foreign workers were not admitted unless they had an employment contract.

From the beginning, the recruitment policy excluded groups that were deemed unsuitable. These groups primarily consisted of workers from the French colonies in Africa and Southeast Asia and from China, who had been recruited during World War I but expelled immediately after. Their performance was said to be too low, their presence in France allegedly a cause of conflict. In order to safeguard the recruitment of foreign workers, France signed bilateral agreements with Poland, Italy, and Czechoslovakia between September 1919 and March 1920: these three states were allowed to control the number, regional origin, and qualification of the recruited workers, but not their working or living conditions nor their wages. Thus France granted these countries of origin some decision-making rights that Germany had not granted to Poland in the above-mentioned Treaty of 1927. Germany had not provided the Polish authorities any say in the regional origins or type of migrant workers recruited.

The French government, however, not only supported enterprises with recruitment treaties, but also directly intervened in employee-employer relations: breach of contract by foreign workers was punished by the state, as was the breaking of contracts by enterprises, as in Germany. Several measures were intended to prevent workers from changing jobs as well as from seeking work in certain industries and regions. Although France was far less affected by the Great Depression in the early 1930s than Germany or the U.S., the French government reduced permanent and short-term immigration, too. While in 1930, 120,000 immigrants were registered, in 1931 only 25,000 persons were admitted to the country. In 1932, the government completely closed the borders, and then restricted immigration of foreign workers to exceptional cases, applying restricted quotas.

In both Germany and France, the Great Depression clearly exhibited again the above-mentioned developments: state control and regulation became important features of migration policies that were focused on the labor market; temporary and permanent immigration were increasingly influenced by welfare state interventions and international agreements.

Refugee Movements and Expulsion as Mass Phenomena

The "century of refugees" began with World War I and intensified in the immediate postwar period. In 1914 Europe, an estimated five million people were living in states in which they were not born. World War I had basically changed the relationship between native and immigrant populations as well as between the belligerent state and so-called enemy aliens (*feindliche Ausländer*). By the outbreak of the War, high nationalistic spirits destroyed many forms of cross-border communication. World War I was a highly nationalized conflict: people originating from an enemy state were sweepingly declared "enemy aliens" in their own country and considered a danger to internal security. On all sides, these nationalist resentments resulted in the exclusion of individuals and was often followed by internment, repatriation, or expulsion. There were refugee movements in both the western and eastern theaters of war. Considering the figures alone, central east and southeast Europe were more heavily affected, because fronts were moving much longer than in the west.[15]

The Armistice of November 1918 and the peace treaties that followed did not put an end to such refugee movements. Indeed, each of the many border changes led to increasing numbers of refugees, expellees, and resettlers. In all cases, certain characteristics of emigration can be established: government officials, policemen, teachers, and other persons connected with the former ruling state were the first to leave the country. They were followed by employers and businessmen who felt threatened by the new customs boundaries, currencies, or laws. If the new governments pursued restrictive minority policies, emigration was liable to become a mass movement. Immediately after World War I, the defeated countries, the entire middle powers of World War I, were forced to take in at least two million people from their lost territories. It can be assumed that because of the political changes emerging from the peace treaties about five million people crossed European borders.[16] Immigration of former citizens reached high levels, for example, in the reduced Austrian territory. In the late 1920s more than 10 percent of the total Austrian population was born beyond the new borders. Around 1930, there were 764,000 people in Austria born outside the national territory, among them 440,000 from Bohemia and Moravia alone, the new heartland of the Czechoslovakian state created in 1918. Hungary was a parallel: after the war, it gave shelter to 200,000 people from Czechoslovakia, another 200,000 from Romania, and 100,000 from Yugoslavia.[17]

Such nationally and politically motivated ethnic cleansing was also practiced in other south European regions: at the end of the Greco-Turkish war from 1920 to 1922 and with the Peace Treaty of Lausanne, the prewar resettlement regulations were revived in the Balkans. All Greeks, for example, had to leave the Turkish territory, with the exception of Istanbul; at the same time, all Muslims had to move out of the Greek territory. As a final result, about 1.35 million Greeks and about 430,000 Turks were forced to resettle. As a consequence for the Greek population, this meant that after the resettlement, one-sixth of them had been born outside Greece. In the following years, the often forced "re-migration" of Muslims to Turkey continued.

The German Reich, diminished in size by the Treaty of Versailles, also experienced large-scale refugee and resettlement movements. The 1925 census recorded more than one million Germans from beyond the 1914 borders who were then living within the new borders of the Reich. According to the Reich Migration Office, 120,000 people from Alsace-Lorraine entered the reduced Reich, another 16,000 emigrants came from the former German colonies. Much more extensive, however, than these groups was the influx from the Reich's eastern areas ceded to Poland after the Treaty of Versailles. Until mid-1925, the Reich Statistical Agency (Statistisches Reichsamt) counted 850,000 German emigrants from those regions.[18] Many of them were initially brought to one of the many refugee camps, or *Heimkehrlager*, established along the eastern border and surveyed by the Reich Commissioner for Civil Prisoners and Refugees (Reichkommissar für Zivilgefangene und Flüchtlinge). Between 1920 and 1925 the Reich built twenty-six refugee camps. In 1923 they were occupied by about 40,000 people, the highest number in this period.[19]

The immigrants from the ceded territories were very unwelcome not only for reasons of preservation and "consolidation" of German minorities in the recently lost territories, but also because of the strained labor and housing market. This was also true for those immigrants officially called "foreigners of German descent and language" mainly from Russia in the immediate postwar period. In the confusion of the Russian civil war between 1918 and 1921, roughly 120,000 ethnic Germans left their settlements and headed to Germany. With the end of the Russian Civil War and the consolidation of Soviet rule, however, the number of emigrants from Russian-German settlements considerably declined. As the Soviet government sought to stop emigration with bureaucratic hindrances, as described above, only a few thousand ethnic Germans succeeded in leaving the Soviet Union in the 1920s.[20]

Soviet emigration restrictions were in the interests of German immigration policy. As in their fight against the crisis, the Weimar Republic governments not only pursued restrictive immigration policy toward migrant workers from abroad and toward Germans from the lost territories, as mentioned above, but their policies also affected "re-migrants of German descent." Their situation was actually deplored, but their immigration to the Reich was not appreciated at all. This was illustrated for the last time in 1929/30 when, as a result of the Soviet compulsory collectivization, 14,000 farmers of German descent went to Moscow in the hope of obtaining assistance from the German embassy to enable them to emigrate to Germany: it took many weeks of faltering negotiations until, finally, the German government allowed them to come. Nearly 6,000 of them were eventually able to leave the Soviet Union.[21]

One method to prevent immigration and long-term settlement in the Reich was the increasingly restrictive application of the citizenship law of 1913, a sharp contrast to the recent practice of granting German citizenship more or less automatically to ethnic Germans from the East, or *Aussiedler*, in the Federal Republic of Germany today. The Weimar Republic refused to grant equal legal status to "ethnic Germans with foreign citizenship" and citizens of the Reich, and thus rejected the speedy naturalization of "ethnic Germans." Two reasons were repeatedly given for this and for the refusal to support immigration of Germans from the ceded territories. First, equal rights for "ethnic Germans with foreign citizenship" and German citizens would alienate "ethnic Germans" from their home country and, therefore, weaken the German minority abroad, as equal rights would improve the attraction of the Reich and would only intensify the dissolution of minority groups.

Second, the generous admission of German citizenship would threaten the Reich's economic and labor market interests. In the Weimar Republic, the control of immigration of foreign workers was tightly connected to labor market policy, and the "protection of the national labor market" meant "refusal" and "repulsion" of foreign workers. To the same extent, immigration and settlement of "ethnic Germans with foreign citizenship" was restrictively integrated into the control system. This system, however, gave preference to "ethnic Germans" compared to other groups of foreigners in so far as they were more easily granted unrestricted work and residence permits in the form of permanent visas. Nevertheless, "the right to immigrate to the Reich was repealed for most ethnic Germans, too" in order not to endanger "the Reich's important political interests concerning economy and labor market."[22]

In 1930 the jurist R. von Broecker summarized the Weimar Republic's arguments pointing to the "all-German responsibility" of naturalization: "It cannot be in the interest of the Reich as a nation-state that the German cultural nation diminishes as a result of too many admitted naturalizations. The Reich as a closed national economy has equally little interest in expanding its national population with naturalizations exceeding its natural growth. Rather, there is a positive interest in the non-naturalization of ethnic Germans with foreign citizenship."[23] Consequently—and in strict opposition to the later National Socialist policy of "Home to the Reich [*Heim ins Reich*]"—the maxim of Weimar policy as regards "remigrants of German descent" was to preserve centers of settlement in east, central east and southeast Europe. This was done for reasons of domestic, foreign, and economic policy, against humanitarian interest if necessary, always in order to prevent immigration into the Reich. Again, the lines of argumentation were interweaving, even though there were different background interests: immigration was to remain limited and constantly under control, concerning "ethnic Germans with foreign citizenship," Germans from the ceded territories, as well as foreign workers.

Immediately after World War I Germany became the most important receiving country for refugees from revolutionary and civil war Russia. According to estimations of the "Russian Delegation for Prisoners of War and Re-migration in Germany," 100,000 refugees were supposed to have stayed in the Reich in 1919. In 1920, the U.S. Red Cross reported 560,000 Russians in Germany. This influx reached its peak in 1922 and 1923 when, according to the League of Nations and the German Foreign Office, 600,000 Russian refugees were living in the Reich. In Berlin alone, 360,000 people had been granted asylum in 1923. Then numbers decreased: for 1925, the High Commissioner for Refugees of the League of Nations reported 150,000 refugees, for 1933 another 100,000 Russian refugees in Germany.[24]

In the first years, "Russian Berlin" with its important cultural and political functions had been the center of European exile. When in the mid-1920s many refugees left Germany, the "Russian Paris" took over this role and maintained it until the invasion of German troops in 1940. It was primarily because in the 1920s, the French government encouraged immigration and the French economy lacked workers, that France, and more precisely Paris and the surrounding districts, became the most important destination for Russian refugees. However, this concentration of Russian refugees then shifted across the Atlantic. More and more frequently, North America was the final destination point in a gradual detachment from the Russian homeland. By World War II, the center of Russian exile had finally moved to the U.S. with a political and cultural emphasis on New York.

Similar processes of migration in stages and shifting centers can be identified in refugee movements from Nazi Germany after 1933.[25] Political opponents of the regime were concerned, but also all those who were made to feel alien in Germany by the racist ideology of National Socialism. First and foremost this was true for Jewish people. Refugee movements from Nazi Germany proceeded in phases. The first wave was precipitated by the takeover by Hitler in 1933 and the first measures against domestic political opponents and the first anti-Semitic laws. The racist "Nuremberg laws" provoked the next wave. The last great movement started with the open violence against Jews in the 1938 *Reichspogromnacht* and ended with the outbreak of World War II that largely cut down options for emigration. The emigration prohibition of 1941 marked the beginning of the genocide of German and European Jews.

The number of refugees from Germany is unknown. Jews make up by far the largest group; 280,000 to 300,000 are estimated to have left Germany. If one adds Jewish emigration from Austria after the "annexation" to the Reich in 1938 (150,000) and from Czechoslovakia after the Treaty of Munich (33,000), Jewish emigration alone from German-dominated central Europe amounted to between 450,000 and 600,000 people. More than eighty states world-wide received refugees from Germany. Most of them first fled to neighboring states, hoping for a swift collapse of the regime. Half of the Jewish refugees, however, continued their flight, and the U.S. exile increased in importance. In 1941 the number of refugees in the U.S. was estimated to be 100,000, followed by Argentina with 55,000 and Great Britain with 40,000. Particularly at the beginning but throughout World War II, the U.S. became increasingly important for Jewish refugees, as it was for Russian refugees—half of all found asylum there.

Compared with the large number of Jewish refugees from central Europe, those who went into exile for political reasons from Germany, Austria, and the German-speaking areas of Czechoslovakia after 1938 were a much smaller group, mainly consisting of Social Democrats and Communists—25,000 to 30,000 up to 1939. In this connection, a comparison with fascist Italy is very instructive. Given that the Mussolini regime did not implement any anti-Semitic measures before World War II, despite German pressure, refugee movements were nearly exclusively restricted to political refugees. Between Mussolini's takeover in October 1922 and 1937, an estimated 60,000 left the country for political reasons, 10,000 of them were living in France alone.[26] Emigration from Germany and Italy had one thing in common: in order to maintain political activities from abroad, most of the political opponents who fled stayed in Europe. France, Spain, Great Britain, and the Soviet Union were the most important European destinations. Germany had experienced a transition from the most significant European destination for refugees, expellees, and resettlers in the early 1920s to the largest point of departure for refugees in the 1930s.

The Search for Causes: Migration and Protectionism

In summary, one can say that in contrast to the period before 1914 transnational migration movements in Europe between the wars were not principally socio-economic phenomena but also (1) politically caused and (2) politically regulated.

First, forced migrations for political reasons (refugee movements, resettlement, expulsion) that were directly connected to World War I and to the revolutionary nation-building processes that took place in the immediate aftermath of the war assumed greater significance between the wars. A large part of migration movements can be attributed to this fact. The peace treaties formally bringing World War I to an end led to far-reaching shifts in the European political order. The three European empires broke up, and the formation of fourteen new states meant an additional 7,000 miles of state borders. Majorities became minorities, minorities became majorities, refugee movements and forced resettlements reached a scale that had not even been known during World War I. The entire European migration processes were undergoing change: in the large central and east European states that had become politically and territorially fragmented after the Paris Peace Settlement, many formerly internal migrations became migrations across borders. Some established migration traditions ceased completely as they were rendered impossible by the large number of closed borders and political conflicts between the new states. Conversely, some of the migrations crossing borders became internal migrations, for example in the reestablished Polish state. In the prewar period, a quarter of the Polish population had been dependent on migration.[27]

Second, migration was more and more subject to control, regulation, and protectionist limitation policies. Isolating the German example could lead to the assumption that such a turn to protectionism with all its far-reaching consequences for migration conditions must have been a response to the crisis-prone economic and labor market development. In the Weimar Republic, migration policy was facing quite different problems to that of the Kaiserreich, because the economic, political, and geographical basis and development conditions had largely changed. In the labor market, the "lack of workers" in industry and agriculture was no longer a determining factor or leading topic of discussion, rather the "protection of the national labor market" was. Immigration of foreign workers was therefore regulated by labor market policy that also tried to manage emigration. The question of immigration of Germans from the ceded territories, for example, or the return of Russians of German descent were not only affairs of foreign policies or of empowering minorities, but were directly related to questions of employment of foreign workers and to population policy. Although humanitarian interests were a feature of refugee policy, they always resulted in political conflicts concerning social security and the labor market.

In other parts of Europe also, the crisis-prone economic and labor market development was exacerbated by the consequences of war. Besides the problems of demobilizing armies of millions, problems of transition from war to peace economies arose. There was a currency devaluation in nearly all states involved in the war. The end of World War I was, at the same time, the end of European world-wide economic predominance that had lasted for centuries. Export opportunities were decreasing while competition in internal markets was growing, resulted in overproduction and a high level of structural unemployment in large sectors of European industry as well as, for example, in some segments of the agricultural sector. In the postwar economy, unemployment reached chronic proportions in some national economies and peaked during the Great Depression of the early 1930s. Estimations put the number of unemployed people in Europe at the end of 1932 at fifteen million. Given a background of deep economic crisis, unemployment became a serious problem in many countries. Consequently, labor market regulation became a crucial issue of policies. The basic call of the prewar labor movements for "protection of the national labor market" resulted in sharper immigration control leading to the protectionist blockade of labor competition from abroad.

This statement, however, cannot be generalized and does not account for all decisive factors in the German case: By no means had all European economies been suffering from serious crises after World War I. The French economy, for instance, was prospering even though a transition to protectionist migration policy was evident there, too. Because of low birth rates and heavy war losses, France became the most important European immigration country during the 1920s with a total of two million immigrants. Unlike prewar times, regulation mechanisms were perfected, and immigration was adapted to labor market development. In France, too, bilateral agreements considerably improved immigration regulation and control. Outside Europe, the most important immigration country for Europeans, the U.S., the economic winner of World War I, enjoyed a unique economic boom in the 1920s, notwithstanding accompanying protectionist immigration policies.

In recent literature, the question of decisive courses of development and determining factors of European migrations between the wars has been addressed in terms, and its many facets, continuities and discontinuities. Considering World War I and the time between the wars, Saskia Sassen mainly focuses on the enormous refugee flows. Her interpretation understands them to be a result of the numerous nation-building processes in central east and southeast Europe since the late nineteenth century, that reached their peak on the eve of World War I and with the succeeding peace treaties.[28] However, she does not take into account the protectionist migration policies between the wars. Leslie Page Moch, on the other hand, especially taking refugee movements and forced migration into consideration, describes the essential characteristics of the development of cross-border labor migration as well as the increasingly protectionist tendencies of migration policies in the era of the New Thirty Years' War. Yet she does not explicitly discuss the causes of these tendencies.[29]

Considering World War I and the period between the wars, Aristide R. Zolberg takes the perspective of the most important countries for European immigration of the late nineteenth and early twentieth century, the United States, Australia, and Canada. Unlike the European states, those countries did not experience World War I as a "total" war. From this point of view, Zolberg considers World War I merely as a minor break in a continuous development since the 1880s characterized by increasingly effective controls to enter the world's immigration countries. According to Zolberg, this was a nativist reaction to the global expansion of migration movements.[30] Neither Zolberg nor Leo Lucassen concentrate on the substantial refugee movements between the wars. As regards the question of reasons and background to the protectionist migration policies, Lucassen, too, refers to continuities in the development from 1880 to 1920. His emphasis is on the comparative analysis of the role of labor movements, increasingly integrated into the state since the late nineteenth century. They are said to have decisively influenced the introduction of immigration controls to protect "national" labor markets by the interventionist state in its striving for progress.[31]

Lucassen's interpretation seems to be an important starting point for research on crucial determining factors of migration between the wars, since the change toward modern national and social interventionist states decisively contributed to the fact that state control and regulation largely influenced European migration in this period. At that time, economic as well as labor market and migration policies were increasingly characterized by protectionism, partly aimed at self-sufficiency during the Great Depression. A general interpretation that takes into account the immense refugee movements, however, has to lay emphasis on the role that World War I played in Europe.

From this perspective, World War I with its massive state interventions in large sections of economy and society was not only an important break but also a crucial catalyst. First of all, the labor market had become the preferred object of state control and intervention. Recruitment of foreign workers had played a fundamental role in this, particularly in France and Germany.[32] Mainly due to these experiences, labor market policy was directly involved with foreign labor employment policy and hence they became essential political issues in postwar Europe.[33] The accelerated development of welfare-state structures during World War I, concentrating on war victims' benefits and regulation of labor market relations, strengthened the interventionist power of the state and demanded the definition and limitation of those groups entitled to benefits that separated citizens from foreigners.

Last but not least, the extremely nationalized conflict of World War I, almost a "clash of civilizations," led to the exclusion and expulsion of minorities, carried out or at least supported by the state. Another consequence was widespread xenophobia. Apart from the nationalist ethnic cleansing mainly in central east and southeast Europe that resulted in refugee movements and resettlement of millions of people, this was another postwar trend that contributed to more restrictive immigration and minority policies. Additionally, the chief significance of the European dictatorships that emerged from World War I should not be excluded from a consideration of the time between the wars: hundreds of thousands of political-ideological opponents—as well as victims of the racist persecutions in Nazi Germany of the 1930s—were expelled.

Notes

1. For example, see L. Page Moch, *Moving Europeans: Migration in Western Europe since 1650* (Bloomington, Ind., 1992), who very briefly deals with the complete period 1914–1945. See 161–70. D. Hoerder, *People on the Move: Migration, Acculturation and Ethnic Interaction in Europe and North America* (Providence, R.I., and Oxford, 1993), does not treat it at all. S. Sassen, *Migranten, Siedler, Flüchtlinge. Von der Massenauswanderung zur Festung Europa* (Frankfurt a.M., 1996), 99–114, concentrates mainly on flight movements. The same impression arises regarding overall descriptions on emigration. Unless they finish with 1914, the succeeding period is scarcely considered. For example, see D. Baines, *Emigration from Europe, 1815–1930* (Cambridge, 1995), 97–99. For an overview, see the emphatic plea for an inclusion of forced migration as a form of historically significant migration: J. Lucassen and L. Lucassen, "Migration, Migration History, History: Old Paradigms and New Perspectives," in *Migration, Migration History, History: Old Paradigms and New Perspectives*, ed. J. Lucassen and L. Lucassen (Bern, 1997), 9–38, here 11.
2. For an overall perspective on the development of emigration between the wars, see I. Ferenczi, *Kontinentale Wanderungen und die Annäherung der Völker. Ein geschichtlicher Überblick* (Jena, 1930), 28–40; idem and W. F. Willcox, *International Migrations* (New

York, 1929), 1:168–75, 192–95, 210–21, 230–33; W. Woodruff, *Impact of Western Man: A Study of Europe's Role in the World Economy, 1750–1960* (Washington, D.C., 1966), 60–100, as well as Tables, 103–11; D. Kirk, *Europe's Population in the Interwar Years* (Princeton, 1946), 72–96; W. S. Woytinsky and E. S. Woytinsky, *World Population and Production: Trends and Outlook* (New York, 1953), 66–110; W. Fischer, "Wirtschaft, Gesellschaft und Staat in Europa 1914–1980," in *Handbuch der europäischen Wirtschafts- und Sozialgeschichte*, ed. W. Fischer (Stuttgart, 1987), 6:36–44.

3. Primarily on German emigration between World War I and the Great Depression, see K. J. Bade, "Arbeitsmarkt, Bevölkerung und Wanderung in der Weimarer Republik," in *Die Weimarer Republik. Belagerte Civitas*, ed. M. Stürmer (Königstein i.Ts., 1980), 160–87, here 165–67; H. Bickelmann, *Deutsche Überseeauswanderung in der Weimarer Zeit* (Wiesbaden, 1980), 7–18; K. C. Thalheim, *Das deutsche Auswanderungsproblem der Nachkriegszeit* (Jena, 1926), 28–52.
4. For an overview, see E. R. Barkan, *And Still They Come: Immigrants and American Society, 1920 to the 1990s* (Wheeling, Ill., 1996), 8–53.
5. Yuri Felshtinsky, "The Legal Foundations of the Immigration and Emigration Policy of the USSR, 1917–27," *Soviet Studies* 34 (1982): 327–48, here 336–43.
6. L. de Rosa, "Italian Emigration in the Post-Unification Period, 1861–1971," in *European Expansion and Migration: Essays on the Intercontinental Migration from Africa, Asia, and Europe*, ed. P. C. Emmer and M. Mörner (New York and Oxford, 1992), 157–78; S. Bologna, "Kontinuität und Zäsur in der Geschichte der italienischen Migrationsarbeit," and C. Bermani, "Odyssee in Deutschland. Die alltägliche Erfahrung der italienischen 'Fremdarbeiter' im 'Dritten Reich,'" in *Proletarier der "Achse." Sozialgeschichte der italienischen Fremdarbeit in NS-Deutschland 1937 bis 1943*, ed. S. Bologna, C. Bermani, and B. Mantelli (Berlin, 1997), 17–252. On the repercussion of Italian policies on France as the most important European country of immigration, see G. S. Cross, *Immigrant Workers in Industrial France: The Making of a New Laboring Class* (Philadelphia, Pa., 1983), 112–19.
7. K. J. Bade, "'Amt der verlorenen Worte.' Das Reichswanderungsamt 1918–1924," in *Zeitschrift für Kulturaustausch* 39 (1989): 312–21; idem, "Arbeitsmarkt, Bevölkerung und Wanderung in der Weimarer Republik," 165–67; Bickelmann, *Deutsche Überseeauswanderung*, 52–107; Thalheim, *Das deutsche Auswanderungsproblem der Nachkriegszeit*, 111–39.
8. Woytinsky and Woytinsky, *World Population and Production*, 82; Fischer, "Wirtschaft, Gesellschaft und Staat in Europa 1914–1980," 37, 298.
9. Ferenczi, *Kontinentale Wanderungen*, 6.
10. K. C. Thalheim, "Gegenwärtige und zukünftige Strukturwandlungen in der Wanderungswirtschaft der Welt," *Archiv für Wanderungswesen* 3 (1930): 41–47, here 47.
11. K. J. Bade, "German Emigration to the United States and Continental Immigration to Germany in the Late Nineteenth and Early Twentieth Centuries," *Central European History* 13 (1980): 348–77.
12. For an overview, see Bade, "Arbeitsmarkt, Bevölkerung und Wanderung in der Weimarer Republik," 165–68; H. Kahrs, "Die Verstaatlichung der polnischen Arbeitsmigration nach Deutschland," in *Arbeitsmigration und Flucht. Vertreibung und Arbeitskräfteregulierung im Zwischenkriegseuropa*, ed. E. Jungfer et al. (Berlin and Göttingen, 1993), 130–94.
13. J. Singer-Kérel, "Foreign Workers in France, 1891–1936," *Ethnic and Racial Studies* 14 (1991): 279–93; Cross, *Immigrant Workers in Industrial France*; idem, "Towards Social Peace and Prosperity: The Politics of Immigration in France during the Era of World War I," *French Historical Studies* 11 (1980): 610–32; G. P. Freeman, "Immigrant Labour and Racial Conflict: The Role of the State," in *Migrants in Modern France: Population Mobility in the Later Nineteenth and Twentieth Centuries*, ed. P. E. Ogden and P. E. White (London, 1989), 160–76, here 162; P. Sicsic, "Foreign Immigration and the French Labor Force, 1886–1926," in *Migration and the International Labor Market, 1850–1939*, ed. T. J. Hatton and J. G. Williamson (London and New York, 1994), 119–38.
14. Kirk, *Europe's Population*, 105.

15. L. Kühnhardt, *Die Flüchtlingsfrage als Weltordnungsproblem. Massenzwangswanderungen in Geschichte und Gegenwart* (Vienna, 1984), 42, 47f.; M. R. Marrus, *The Unwanted: European Refugees in the Twentieth Century* (New York and Oxford, 1985), 53f.; D. Stola, "Forced Migrations in Central European History," *International Migration Review* 26 (1992): 324–41, here 341; M. Levene, "Frontiers of Genocide: Jews in the Eastern War Zones, 1914–1920 and 1941," in *Minorities in Wartime: National and Racial Groupings in Europe, North America and Australia during the Two World Wars*, ed. P. Panayi (Providence, R.I., and Oxford, 1993), 83–117, here 95–98.
16. Kirk, *Europe's Population*, 104.
17. Ibid., 102f.
18. *Vorläufige Ergebnisse der Volkszählung im Deutschen Reich vom 16. Juni 1925 mit einem Anhang: Die abgetretenen Gebiete und das Abstimmungsgebiet an der Saar nach den Ergebnissen der Volkszählung vom 1. XII. 1910* (Berlin, 1925), 8; "Denkschrift über Ein- und Auswanderung nach bzw. aus Deutschland in den Jahren 1910 bis 1920," in *Stenographische Berichte des Reichstags, 1. Wahlperiode 1920. Anlagen*, vol. 372, 4382–404, here 4382–88. For an overview, see E. M. Kulischer, *Europe on the Move: War and Population Changes, 1917–1947* (New York, 1948), 168f., 173–77; R. Just, "Ersatz der Bevölkerungsverluste oder zusätzliche Last – Die Haltung der deutschen Behörden zur Aufnahme von Deutschen aus Polen am Ende des Ersten Weltkriegs" (manuscript of a lecture at the German-Polish conference of the Forschungsgesellschaft für das Weltflüchtlingsproblem, AWR, "'Bleiben oder gehen?' Die deutsche Minderheit in Polen," 8.-11.6.1993 in Poznan), 1–19, here 8–11; R. Blanke, *Orphans of Versailles: The Germans in Western Poland, 1918–1939* (Lexington, Ky., 1993), 32–35.
19. Reichskommissar für Zivilgefangene und Flüchtlinge in Berlin an Reichsministerium des Innern in Berlin, 7.9.1923, Bundesarchiv (BA) Berlin-Lichterfelde, RMI 18401, Bd. 1; Reichskommissar für Zivilgefangene und Flüchtlinge – Abwicklungsstelle – in Berlin an Reichsministerium des Innern in Berlin, Febr. 1925, Bundesarchiv Berlin-Lichterfelde, RMI 18408, Bd. 6. On the media discourse, see U. Gerhard, "Flucht und Wanderung in Mediendiskurs und Literatur der Weimarer Republik," in *Die Sprache des Migrationsdiskurses. Das Reden über "Ausländer" in Medien, Politik und Alltag*, ed. M. Jung, M. Wengeler, and K. Böke (Opladen, 1997), 45–57; idem, *Nomadische Bewegungen und die Symbolik der Krise. Flucht und Wanderung in der Weimarer Republik* (Opladen, 1990).
20. I. Fleischhauer and B. Pinkus, *Die Deutschen in der Sowjetunion. Geschichte einer nationalen Minderheit im 20. Jahrhundert* (Baden-Baden, 1987), 166–69; K. J. Bade and J. Oltmer, "Einführung: Aussiedlerzuwanderung und Aussiedlerintegration. Historische Entwicklung und aktuelle Probleme," in *Aussiedler. Deutsche Einwanderer aus Osteuropa*, ed. K.J. Bade and J. Oltmer (Osnabrück, 1999), 9–51.
21. A. Eisfeld, *Die Rußland-Deutschen* (Munich, 1992), 103–8; S. Kraft, *Die rußland-deutschen Flüchtlinge des Jahres 1929/30 und ihre Aufnahme im Deutschen Reich. Eine Untersuchung über die Gründe der Massenflucht der deutschen Bauern und ein Beitrag zur Kenntnis der Behandlung volksdeutscher Fragen im Weimarer Zwischenreich* (Halle, 1939).
22 R. von Broecker, *Der Volksdeutsche fremder Staatsangehörigkeit im Reiche. Eine Darstellung seiner Rechtslage* (Berlin, 1930), 21.
23. Ibid., 39.
24. H.-E. Volkmann, *Die russische Emigration in Deutschland 1919–1929* (Würzburg, 1966); K. Schlögel, "Berlin: 'Stiefmutter unter den russischen Städten,'" in *Der große Exodus. Die russische Emigration und ihre Zentren 1917–1941*, ed. K. Schlögel (Munich, 1994), 234–59; idem, ed., *Russische Emigration in Deutschland 1918 bis 1941. Leben im europäischen Bürgerkrieg* (Berlin, 1995); B. Dodenhoeft, *"Laßt mich nach Rußland heim." Russische Emigranten in Deutschland von 1918 bis 1945* (Frankfurt a.M., 1993). On the refugee problem and policies in Europe on the whole with minor reference to Germany, see C. M. Skran, *Refugees in Inter-War Europe: The Emergence of a Regime* (Oxford, 1995); Marrus, *The Unwanted*; F. Caestecker and B. Moore, "Refugee Policies in Western European States in the 1930s: A Comparative Analysis," *IMIS-Beiträge* 7 (1998), 55–103.

25. For an overview, see *Handbuch der deutschsprachigen Emigration 1933–1945*, ed. C.-D. Krohn et al. (Darmstadt, 1998).
26. Kühnhardt, *Flüchtlingsfrage*, 48f.
27. Ferenczi, *Kontinentale Wanderungen*, 28–40. On Poland, see E. Morawska, "Labor Migrations of Poles in the Atlantic World Economy 1800–1914," *Comparative Studies in Society and History* 31 (1989): 237–72.
28. Sassen, *Migranten, Siedler, Flüchtlinge*, 93–114.
29. Page Moch, *Moving Europeans*, 161–74.
30. A. R. Zolberg, "Global Movements, Global Walls: Responses to Migration, 1885–1925," in *Global History and Migrations*, ed. W. Gungwu (Boulder, Colo., and Oxford, 1997), 279–307; idem, "The Great Wall Against China: Responses to the First Immigration Crisis, 1885–1925," in *Migration, Migration History, History*, ed. Lucassen and Lucassen, 291–315.
31. L. Lucassen, "The Great War and the Origins of Migration Control in Western Europe and the United States (1880–1920)," in *Regulation of Migration: International Experiences*, ed. A. Böker et al. (Amsterdam, 1998), 45–72.
32. J. Oltmer, "Zwangsmigration und Zwangsarbeit – ausländische Arbeitskräfte und bäuerliche Ökonomie im Ersten Weltkrieg," *Tel Aviver Jahrbuch für deutsche Geschichte* 27 (1998): 135–68.
33. G. A. Ritter, *Der Sozialstaat. Entstehung und Entwicklung im internationalen Vergleich*, 2nd ed. (Munich, 1991), 109. For further information, especially for Great Britain, see J. Paulmann, *Staat und Arbeitsmarkt in Großbritannien. Krise, Weltkrieg, Wiederaufbau* (Göttingen and Zurich, 1991).

Chapter 3

Racism as Public Policy in America's Cities in the Twentieth Century

Ronald H. Bayor

Today African Americans remain the most residentially segregated group in the United States, more so than Asians and Hispanics, and to a greater degree than the European ethnics or even the blacks of early twentieth-century America. Some of the story of how this situation developed is well-known. Federal mortgage insurance policies through the Federal Housing Administration and Veterans Administration that discriminated against all-black or racially mixed neighborhoods prevented a substantial African-American migration to the suburbs and confined this group to inner cities. Federal public policy was accompanied by private decisions of banks, realtors, and neighborhood whites using restrictive covenants to prevent black migration into white areas. Less known is the fact that throughout the twentieth century city governments accepted racism as a basis for policy decisions and used their powers to maintain segregated societies. This essay discusses the role and impact of city policies in residential segregation. Using ordinances, zoning, physical barriers, separate land grants and public housing site and tenant selection, cities as diverse as Chicago, New York, Atlanta, Miami, Detroit and others added an important third force to the federal and private initiatives for segregation.

Segregation ordinances were used in cities as early as 1910 supposedly "to preserve peace, prevent conflict and ill-feeling between the races, and to promote the general welfare of the city." They included a variety of odd stipulations as various city councils passed them into law. New Orleans stated that "members of either race were prohibited from establishing a residence in an area predominantly of a different race, without first securing permission of a majority of the residents." In St. Louis, the 1916 ordinance did not allow "invasion" of a block if the residents were 75 percent of another race. Atlanta had an ordinance in 1931 making it illegal for a member of one race to move into a house previously occupied by a member of the other race, if the dwelling was "within fifteen blocks from a public school." An earlier ordinance forbade a person moving into a house "where the majority of the residences on the street are occupied by those with whom said person is forbidden to intermarry."[1] Although there were still mixed race streets that were legal in some southern cities, these ordinances were often fortified with restrictive covenants and Klan and other terrorist violence.

Although in *Buchanan v. Warley* (1917) the U.S. Supreme Court declared these racial ordinances unconstitutional since they limited an individual's right to control his own private property, the ordinances still were being passed into the 1930s and effective for years afterward. Some cities such as Norfolk, Virginia just ignored the Supreme Court ruling; others such as Atlanta tried various tactics, e.g., denying moving permits to maintain the spirit of the ordinance.[2] Furthermore, racial zoning came into use in the 1920s. Atlanta, for example, passed such a plan in 1922 that divided the city into white and black residential areas and racially undetermined commercial and industrial districts. This was racial control on a grand scale signifying race as a land use classification similar to single-family residential or apartment house districts.[3]

Racial zoning also had a grander design, for it was supposed to regulate black migration in the city and create buffers and barriers between white and black areas. The same process was evident in St. Louis and Chicago. The City Plan Commission in St. Louis set zoning lines with race in mind and in an attempt to control black residential patterns. Often working with realtors and property owners, St. Louis and Chicago city officials applied the zoning regulations to strengthen neighborhood racial covenants. Chicago often pushed its African-American population into areas set aside for industrial or commercial development. City council members did express concern that the industrial fumes and pollution would hurt trees, grass and park space in these areas but saw these same areas as suitable for black housing.[4]

As in St. Louis and Chicago, Atlanta's zoning well into the 1960s was successful in segregating the black community and preventing residential movement into areas that were racially off limits. This practice resulted in vast areas of the city being politically unsuitable for black housing. An Atlanta Housing Resources Committee report in 1967 noted that the amount of land zoned industrial was excessive, especially in relation to finding land for low-income housing. Mayor Ivan Allen and other 1960s city officials acknowledged that an artificial shortage of land for blacks had occurred because the city used zoning to develop racial buffers between black and white areas. "The result was," Allen explained, that "Atlanta city maps were dotted with scores of these unused plots of land" at a time when land for housing was needed. A 1961 housing report concluded that there was an "artificial scarcity of land available for black housing in a community in which there are no natural barriers to geographic expansion and in which the white community has effective possession of considerable residential acreage which is vacant or thinly occupied."

As the Atlanta Bureau of Planning stated in 1965, "it should be remembered that there would be more than enough land for construction of Negro housing … if it were not for the restrictions inherent in our community customs." Zoning in Atlanta, as one expert concluded, "is utilized to preserve the status quo and to segregate the white and nonwhite populations."[5] While none of these ordinances and zoning laws in any city remained legal, they did effectively separate the races, set the city's racial residential divisions into the future, and as historian Christopher Silver writes of Richmond "legalized and codified the city's strong inclinations toward apartheid."[6]

Throughout the twentieth century, the attempt to fortify segregated black areas or ghettos continued. Unlike the walls of European ghettos, the American style was to use less obvious barriers to maintain separation, although in three cases, in the Detroit area in 1941, Miami in 1946 and Atlanta in 1962, walls were built to separate whites and blacks and to prevent black movement into a white area. The Detroit wall, "eight feet high and a half-mile long," was built at the urging of the Federal Housing Administration (FHA). The developer agreed since the FHA refused to provide mortgage insurance unless the races were separated. In Miami, in the Coconut Grove section, the planning board allowed the housing authority to build low-rent dwellings for blacks but only with the construction of a wall and buffer area to separate the races. Sections of the wall are still visible.[7]

The Atlanta wall was an interesting case of official white intransigence and overreaction. This case developed in 1962 when a black doctor tried to buy a house in the upscale white Peyton Forest subdivision on the city's west side. The white residents protested to the board of aldermen who responded with the closing and barricading of parts of Peyton and Harlan Roads. These roads led into the white subdivision south of the barriers. Mayor Allen approved the concrete and steel barriers as racial roadblocks. Although Atlanta had a long history of maintaining residential segregation, this was the first time a wall had been built to do so. The mayor justified his action by stating that the wall benefited both whites and blacks—by calming the whites and allowing the eventual rezoning of some land north of the barricades for black use. This land, which had been zoned commercial to prevent the building of black housing and to serve as a racial buffer, could possibly be reclassified once whites in the Peyton Forest neighborhood felt racially secure due to the wall.

Black opposition to the wall was intense. As the Student Nonviolent Coordinating Committee (SNCC) stated in 1962: "In past years, city officials have attempted to block Negro expansion by using parks, cemeteries and expressways as artificial buffer zones between whites and Negroes. The metal barricades represent the first instance of blocking roads to stop

Negro housing advances." Black leaders threatened political retaliation if the mayor and other city officials did not reconsider. This opposition had important implications for a mayor elected with strong black support. Finally, court rulings and the national embarrassment to the city which was always claiming that it was "too busy to hate" led to the wall's dismantling.[8] In another case, in North Memphis in the 1950s, the city commission required "developers to erect a steel fence to separate" black and white neighborhoods.[9]

However, American cities were more likely to zone and plan their cities with segregation in mind. As such, highways were often planned and constructed to deal not only with traffic flows and commerce but also with race. In Gary, Indiana, the post–World War II interstates served as barriers between the blacks in the northern part of the city and whites in the south. In Memphis, the highways "served as boundaries to the black community." Richmond's downtown expressway was planned to "form a barrier" between neighborhoods becoming black and "established middle-class white neighborhoods." Kansas City, Missouri's three radial parts of its highway system "entering the city from the east, north, and west followed curiously winding routes, each of which eliminated a black neighborhood enclave" and pushed blacks into the main ghetto. Miami saw the 1950s building of I-95 through the black Overtown area thereby destroying much of that community and pushing black residents out and into other black areas—a move that white commercial and political leaders had desired since the 1930s.[10]

Atlanta's highway system, including access roads, was specifically designed to protect white neighborhoods. To secure the white neighborhoods of Center Hill and Grove Park on the west side, an access road was planned as a racial dividing line. This road, which the city proposed, was designed to convince whites to stay in the area, an assurance that their property would not be subject to racial transition. In 1960, the Atlanta Bureau of Planning, in another case, stated that "approximately two to three years ago, there was an 'understanding' that the proposed route of the west Expressway would be the boundary line between the White and Negro communities" in the Adamsville neighborhood. The city marked out the road's route in the area: south of the road for whites and north for blacks. The city also blocked an effort by black developers to build south of the road. As the planning bureau noted, the city had "obligations to the Adamsville citizens to adhere to the expressway route boundary." Other cities that engaged in the use of highways as racial barriers were Charleston, West Virginia; Flint, Michigan; and Indianapolis, Indiana.[11]

Other barriers used were cemeteries, industry, commercial strips, and parks. Also decisions regarding road paving became part of city racial policy. In Atlanta's west side Mozley Park neighborhood in the late 1940s and early 1950s, the city, acquiescing to white demands, set the north side of Westview Drive as the southern boundary for black expansion. Black developers were only allowed to build up to 100 yards of Westview Drive. Streets that went from the black housing to Westview Drive over the 100 yards were left unpaved. In another case, to prevent black movement into a white area, the city decided to dead-end a through-street so that it would be impossible to travel from the black area into the white neighborhood. Part of this road (Willis Mill Road) was left abandoned and remains so today. In similar fashion, some roads were paved so as to give black residents access to their neighborhoods without going through white areas. To cross any of these boundaries meant trouble—either in the form of violence, or as in Miami in 1945 when two black couples bought houses across the unofficial racial boundary line, they "were harassed by county health, zoning and police officials and were eventually jailed for zoning violations."[12]

African Americans, confined to their overcrowded ghettos, had great difficulty securing residential property. Property was sometimes secured by using sympathetic whites to buy land and then reselling it to blacks. But this would not stop white harassment. One way to avoid problems was to secure city government approval for property acquisitions. In Atlanta, in the late 1940s, the city privately approved six expansion areas for the black community. Working with the Atlanta Urban League, the Atlanta Housing Council, set up by black leaders, selected the land as suitable for peaceful black development. All the areas were near sections of black housing and most were already owned by black landowners. The city and Metropolitan Planning Commission eventually publicly endorsed the concept of the expansion areas in 1952. These lands were considered "safe" for black migration and occupancy. Since the migration to this territory did not threaten any white neighborhoods, it was considered suitable. However, in one situation "white objectors as far as two miles away had to be placated."[13]

The attempt to control black migration was evident in other cities as well, such as Miami. As historian Ray Mohl reports about Miami, "any shifts in black residential patterns were usually dictated by public policy decisions." One 1930s Miami plan that was discussed for years although not implemented involved the Dade County Planning Board. The board laid out a "Negro resettlement plan" that, with Miami city officials' aid, was to force the movement of the whole central black ghetto out of downtown Miami to three resettlement areas or black towns on the outskirts of the city. Part of this plan, the development of a public housing project for blacks outside the city, built with federal funds and designed to relocate people out of the central ghetto, was accomplished in 1937.[14]

There are a number of issues involved in these Atlanta and Miami plans. Part of the black support for the 6 sites in Atlanta came from a desire to avoid white violence and to secure needed space. The white support was somewhat based on the desire to prevent violence also, but city and county officials were clearly trying to control black residential migration to suit the long-term segregation plans of the city. In essence, what was being created were reservations for African Americans—an official attempt to separate the races in an apartheid policy reminiscent of South African black townships.

Racism as an entrenched city policy did not end with ordinances, barriers, highways and separate land. The urban renewal period of the 1950s and 1960s provided an enormous opportunity to direct and control racial migrations and to reinforce the black ghetto. This goal was accomplished either through public housing tenant selection based on race or by destroying black neighborhoods through renewal and rebuilding and sometimes relocating the ghetto into huge public housing projects. Segregated public housing was evident as early as the 1930s. New York's La Guardia administration in the 1930s and 1940s had the opportunity to break up the ghetto and create a dispersed public housing plan for the city. Instead, the choice was to keep the projects in the ghetto area, especially in Harlem, and to enlarge that area, as one historian has noted, into "a racial preserve." Separate public housing application offices for whites and blacks and the New York City Housing Authority's relocation of most blacks into all-black housing during the 1930s set the city's racial patterns.[15]

Chicago was cited in federal court in the late 1960s for "fostering segregation by systematically constructing public housing in black neighborhoods." Ghetto placement and control were part of the massive renewal and public housing project plans of that city. Black residential mobility was manipulated to maintain and expand the ghetto. Arnold Hirsch, the historian of Chicago's renewal experience, writes that "government powers under the guise of 'urban planning' [were used] in order to reshape the local environment and control the process of [racial] succession." Efforts to protect white neighborhoods such as Hyde Park from racial transition led to the systematic removal and relocation of black residents not only in this city but in others. In Hyde Park, for example many whites uprooted from the neighborhood due to urban renewal were relocated back in this section. Few blacks were so allowed.[16]

Philadelphia saw similar city actions. In that city, spot clearance in an area of southeast Philadelphia "removed every house occupied by a black household," although there were also some efforts in this city to support integrated public housing in the 1950s. In "Baltimore County, Maryland, some suburban black enclaves were zoned for nonresidential use even though adjacent white areas were zoned residential." This tactic would remove blacks from that section. In Miami's Overtown area, the city used home inspections and long-forgotten code violations to push black residents out, beginning in the late 1940s. Detroit was faced with blighted white as well as black areas but chose to demolish the black section in their renewal. Furthermore few plans were made for rehousing the displacees. When city officials wanted to manipulate population movements, for whatever reason, it was easy to do so.[17]

Atlanta also saw removal of black residents according to a plan to maintain segregation. The renewal decades of the 1950s and 1960s fit in with a long-standing use of public power to shift and confine the black population to certain parts of the city. The most extensive plan was suggested in the all-white Metropolitan Planning Commission's *Up Ahead* plan of 1952 which laid out a widespread removal of the central city black population, including the elimination of the main black business area along Auburn Avenue and the shifting of the black business center to the western part of the city. This avenue had been for decades the center of African-American life in Atlanta. It was not a low-income section and contained well-built cottages and established businesses. The decision, which the black community strongly opposed, would have kept this group out of any expansion or improvement of the downtown business section, and thereby out of the economic boon coming to the city.

While the city's plans to demolish the Auburn Avenue block were never fulfilled, the surrounding area was deeply affected by renewal and a north-south highway cut through the avenue which respectively diminished the area's customer pool and divided the business center. Auburn Avenue never rebounded from this destructive planning. By 1968, 95 percent of those removed by renewal were black. Essentially African Americans were displaced out of the central business district to public housing projects in other parts of the black community. The ghetto was not demolished by renewal but simply moved, reshaped and fortified. The National Committee for the Advancement of Colored People (NAACP) commented in 1967 in regard to Atlanta that "the pattern was established and continues through the past twenty-five years or more where all available housing for Negroes, publicly aided or not, has been done either in the ghetto or adjacent to it." Using public housing site selection, separate application offices for blacks and whites, and segregated white or black housing projects, city officials maintained a segregated city. Other cities saw urban renewal destroy black businesses. In Detroit, as one study stated, renewal devastated many small black-owned businesses. "Very often the city's lack of sufficient reimbursement to businesses for their property and for relocation left these merchants without a livelihood and the community without needed commercial enterprises.[18]

There was also an effort in Atlanta to disperse public housing and break up the ghetto. Black leaders supported a dispersal of this housing with special attention to fringe neighborhoods, where the housing would attract black and white tenants. The reasoning for this was simple. The west side, where most of the projects were built, was becoming overcrowded. Schools and city services were strained by the excess of population. Mayor Ivan Allen, faced with an angry black constituency and a federal government insisting that no more public housing be built in majority black areas, worked with the Housing Resources Committee to study low-income housing needs. The committee recommended the dispersal of low-income projects to all parts of Atlanta. Faced with opposition from the white business community if he supported dispersal and anger from the black leadership if he did not, the mayor rejected a general dispersal plan and said he would consider individual sites one at a time. The only low-income housing developed from that point on was either in outlying areas or in sections earlier determined as areas for black expansion. Attempts to place public housing in white areas failed.

In one case, in 1972, a white north side site that a federal court-appointed housing committee recommended for public housing was quickly rezoned by the Atlanta Board of Aldermen for commercial development, even though the board had turned down two earlier requests for this rezoning. The neighborhood civic association that had earlier opposed commercial zoning for this property now supported this action. Furthermore, housing torn down was not always replaced with new housing. Atlanta built both a stadium and a civic center on land that had once served low-income blacks. Black displacement was extensive on both sites. On the stadium site, the initial intention was to build housing but for the middle class. Failing to interest developers, city officials planned a housing project for whites. At a time when there was a housing shortage for black Atlantans, the city saw the land as a good buffer against black encroachment on downtown rather than a place to provide housing for those displaced by renewal. The final decision to locate a baseball stadium on that site served the purpose of still constructing a buffer while providing the city with a good commercial enterprise. The only ones to suffer for this decision were the former residents of this renewal area. The civic center plan, also to be a racial buffer on the city's eastside, was scaled down after the federal government insisted that more pubic housing be built.[19]

In Chicago, efforts to prevent the construction of more public housing in the mid-1960s in majority black areas led to a court decision to build the projects elsewhere in the city. The federal court found that 99 percent of the Chicago Housing Authority's family housing was filled by blacks and that "99.5 percent of its units were in black or racially changing areas." The court ordered "that the next 700 units built by the housing authority had to be placed in white areas." The city's response was to stop the further development of such housing over the next ten years even though there was a housing shortage in the city, particularly among minorities.[20] For public housing in Chicago that did contain both black and white tenants, segregation still was often the norm. In the Jane Addams Homes, the Chicago Housing Authority limited the black tenants to the number that had resided on that property before the project was built. Within the project, black tenants were relocated to a certain part of the project. In contrast, in Atlanta there was little pretense regarding integrated housing. During the 1950s, for example, white-only projects were built in order to serve as racial buffers or barriers in black-white fringe neighborhoods.[21]

Other cities saw the same scenario. In Norfolk, Virginia, twenty-one out of the twenty-two housing projects in the city were placed in black neighborhoods and had only black tenants. In Yonkers, New York, a federal judge charged the city with 40 years of intentional segregation in its public housing site selection and ordered the building of low-income public housing in various white neighborhoods. Yonkers had placed 90 percent of its projects in one part of the city. This case was decided in 1986 after five years of litigation, but it was 1991 before construction began. In the interim, the mayor and city council refused to comply even when faced with large fines. After $12 million in legal fees and $450,000 in fines, the housing was built. However, the new housing did not affect the segregation patterns of the city since the judge had ordered the construction of only 200 housing units. They were built on eight sites in white areas. The intransigence of this northern city even extended to its earlier refusal to accept a $2.8 million federal aid package for the city because it also meant accepting the public housing.[22]

One final scenario reveals the role of city racism in developing private housing that had a public component. A good example comes from New York City and relates to the construction of Stuyvesant Town, a middle-income housing development built in the mid-1940s. Supported by the La Guardia administration and its master builder Robert Moses, Stuyvesant Town was a public-private enterprise built by the Metropolitan Life Insurance Company. The goal was a worthy one: to clear a slum area and replace it with needed housing. The city provided tax breaks, city-owned land and its eminent domain powers to the company but also one other factor. The city agreed that Metropolitan would be allowed to bar black tenants. The company, claiming the need to protect property values and their investment, insisted on control of tenant selection, which included its racist policy. La Guardia acquiesced to this policy because the city needed housing and needed private companies that would be interested in rebuilding New York. Whatever the rationale—and there were always many—the city had furthered the development of segregated housing and established it as a policy. To make amends to the black community, La Guardia in 1944 convinced Metropolitan to build the Riverton housing project in Harlem. But the effect of this gesture was simply to maintain and expand the Harlem ghetto. Also, La Guardia secured the passage of a bill in 1944 which prevented racist tenant selection in future public-private housing. However, this bill did not deal with Stuyvesant Town. Although Stuyvesant Town was eventually integrated in the 1950s due to city actions, its tenant selection policies reveal that even in a city run by progressive mayors, racism could become an aspect of official policy.[23]

Many American cities have used racism as a public policy and either directly created or helped to create the segregated cities that stand today. In that way, cities became what they had been planned to become. The process of maintaining segregation and using zoning, renewal and other tactics to ensure it, was a purposeful policy. Had the cities enacted policies that encouraged integration, the racial dynamics would be different today. These policies could have involved placing public housing on the borders of white and black neighborhoods thereby encouraging integration in the projects, developing highways strictly on traffic flow and topographical information, rather than racial considerations, and allowing zoning to correctly designate areas as industrial or residential rather than forcing these designations for racial purposes. While city officials might claim that housing would have sorted out in a racial way regardless of city action due to income levels, various studies indicate that income explains only a part of the segregation pattern. For example, in Atlanta in 1967, the U.S. Civil Rights Commission's research division noted in hearings that "segregated housing patterns ... have increased since 1940, although the economic justification for them has diminished." By 1960, more then two-thirds of the residential segregation could not be explained by differences in economic status between the races.[24]

Since racism through private, federal and city action has played such a major role in residential segregation, how can the cities remake their neighborhoods into more open housing areas now? The federal government, beginning in 1962 with President Kennedy's Executive Order 11063, first took a clear stand against housing discrimination in regard to "federally supported housing."[25] But like the court decisions, the president's order meant little unless failure to comply led to some form of punishment. Although there was some punishment outlined in the order for violators, it was not enforced. As Douglas Massey and Nancy Denton write in *American Apartheid*: "At nearly every level, the federal bureaucracy resisted a broad application of Kennedy's order." Efforts to deal with housing discrimination through congressional action also met great resistance. Opening up housing and permitting ghetto dwellers to secure the housing of their choice was not something many whites in Congress supported, even during the 1960s when other civil rights legislation was passed. Nonetheless, various events including the 1968 Kerner Commission report detailing the racial problems the country faced and the role of housing discrimination within it and the assassination of Dr. Martin Luther King, Jr., spurred Congress to pass a housing measure. The 1968 Fair Housing Act further put the government in support of open housing, but it too was not always carried out effectively. The enforcement provisions of the act were very weak. For the individual facing residential-housing discrimination, there was still no way to punish those who discriminated and thereby no way to discourage this practice. As Massey and Denton state: "Investigations carried out during the 1970s revealed that only 20% to 30% of complaints filed with the Secretary [of Housing and Urban Development] ever reached formal mediation, and nearly half of the complaints that did so remained in noncompliance after conciliation efforts had terminated. Moreover, HUD made virtually no effort to follow up or to monitor compliance in the conciliation agreements it reached." However, amendments passed in 1988 provided stricter enforcement and higher penalties and gave the legislation a chance of succeeding.[26]

Given the long history of institutional racism, the process of dismantling the ghetto will be arduous. Bank mortgage policies, attitudes of landlords and real estate agents, the process of public housing site selection and the slow bureaucratic response to discrimination must all change before open housing is a reality. The city government's role in maintaining segregation has diminished particularly as black mayors have been elected. But the decades of city policies based on racism have left these mayors with divided cities as a legacy.

Notes

1. G. T. Stephenson, "The Segregation of the White and Negro Races in Cities," *South Atlantic Quarterly* 13 (1914): 3; Michael J. O'Connor, "The Measurement and Significance of Racial Residential Barriers in Atlanta, 1890–1970" (Ph.D. diss., University of Georgia, 1977), 20; Barbara J. Flint, "Zoning and Residential Segregation: A Social and Physical History, 1910–1940" (Ph.D. diss., University of Chicago, 1977), 306–7. See also the Atlanta General Council Minutes, 16 March 1931, 518, and 20 May 1929, 525. For references to Atlanta throughout this essay, see R. H. Bayor, *Race and the Shaping of Twentieth-Century Atlanta* (Chapel Hill, N.C., 1996).
2. E. Lewis, *In Their Own Interest: Race, Class and Power in Twentieth-Century Norfolk, Virginia* (Berkeley, Cal., 1991), 77. See also *Report*, Box 44, 1–G, Branch files, NAACP papers, Library of Congress.
3. Bayor, *Race*, 54–55.
4. Flint, "Zoning and Residential Segregation," 344, 349, 352–56.
5. Housing Resources Committee memo, "Report on Vacant Land in Atlanta," 9 August 1967, Southern Regional Council papers, Atlanta University Center Library (hereafter cited as AUC); Atlanta Branch, NAACP, "Citywide Housing Conference," 11 February 1967, Samuel Williams Collection, AUC; Atlanta Chamber of Commerce, Board of Directors, 13 September 1967, Grace T. Hamilton papers, AUC, Ivan Allen, Jr., with Paul Hemphill, *Mayor: Notes on the States* (New York, 1971), 71; Hamilton Douglas, Jr., "Housing the Million," report on Atlanta Housing (prepared by a group of Atlanta business leaders), 10 January 1961, Cecil Alexander papers (privately held); Atlanta Bureau of Planning, "The Story of Negro Housing in Atlanta," 1965, Atlanta Bureau of Planning papers, Atlanta History Center; N. O. Ordway, "A Study of Select Political and Social-Economic Factors Influencing Zoning Decisions in the City of Atlanta during the period December 22, 1954, to December 22, 1975," (Ph.D. diss., Georgia State University, 1978), 34, 37, 329, 354–55, 360–61. See Bayor, *Race*, 81–82.
6. C. Silver, *Twentieth-Century Richmond: Planning, Politics and Race* (Knoxville, Tenn., 1984), 111.
7. J. T. Darden et al., *Detroit: Race and Uneven Development* (Philadelphia, 1987), 113; K. T. Jackson, *Crabgrass Frontier: The Suburbanization of the United States* (New York, 1985), 209; M. Dunn, *Black Miami in the Twentieth Century* (Gainesville, Fl., 1997), 207.
8. Allen, *Mayor*, 71–72; *Atlanta Journal*, 17, 19, and 20 December 1962; *Atlanta Daily World*, 14 December 1962, O'Connor, "Measurement," 112; L. Blumberg, "Segregated Housing,

Marginal Location, and the Crisis of Confidence," *Phylon* 25 (1964): 323–24. See also Bayor, *Race*, 66–67.

9. C. Silver and J. Moeser, *The Separate City: Black Communities in the Urban South, 1940–1968* (Lexington, Ky., 1995), 133.
10. Y. Rabin, "The Roots of Segregation in the Eighties: The Role of Local Government Actions, "in *Divided Neighborhoods: Changing Patterns of Racial Segregation*, ed. G. Tobin (Newberry Park, Cal., 1987), 215–16; R. Flowerdew, "Spatial Patterns of Residential Segregation in a Southern City," *Journal of American Studies* 13 (1979): 106; Silver, *Twentieth-Century Richmond*, 287; R. Mohl, "The Settlement of Blacks in South Florida," 1990, unpublished paper, 23.
11. "Report on the Adamsville Transition Area, 26 August 1960," Atlanta Bureau of Planning papers, Atlantic History Center. See Bayor, *Race*, 61,63, and Rabin, "Roots," 219.
12. R. Thompson, H. Lewis and D. McEntire, "Atlanta and Birmingham: A Comparative Study in Negro Housing, in *Studies in Housing and Minority Groups*, ed. N. Glazer and D. McEntire (Berkeley, CA, 1960), 21, 27–32; S. Adams, "Blueprint for Segregation: A Survey of Atlanta Housing," *New South* 22 (1967): 76; Douglas, "Housing the Million"; author's interview with Robert Thompson (housing secretary for the Atlanta Urban League beginning in 1940s), 15 August 1986. See also Bayor, *Race*, 65–66; R. Mohl, "Making the Second Ghetto in Metropolitan Miami, 1940–1960," in *The New African American Urban History*, ed. K. Goings and R. Mohl (Thousand Oaks, Cal., 1996), 277.
13. "Proposed Areas for Expansion of Negro Housing in Atlanta, Georgia" Atlanta Housing Council, May 1947; *Atlanta Constitution and Journal*, 30 July 1950. See Bayor, *Race*, 59–60, 71–72.
14. Mohl, "Settlement of Blacks," 19–20.
15. J. Schwartz, *The New York Approach* (Columbus, Oh., 1993), 56, 58, 89.
16. A. R. Hirsch, *Making the Second Ghetto: Race and Housing in Chicago, 1940–1960* (Cambridge, 1983), 9–10, 36, 133, 136, 153, 168–69, 225, 254, 274; G. Squires et al., *Chicago: Race, Class, and the Response to Urban Decline* (Philadelphia, 1987), 114.
17. Rabin, "Roots," 216–17; J. F. Bauman, *Public Housing, Race and Renewal: Urban Planning in Philadelphia, 1920–1974* (Philadelphia, 1987), 128–29; J. M. Thomas, *Redevelopment and Race: Planning a Finer City in Postwar Detroit* (Baltimore, Md., 1997), 58, 60; Dunn, *Black Miami*, 158.
18. Atlanta Branch, NAACP, presentation before the Advisory Committee of the U.S. Civil Rights Commission, 8 April 1967, Southern Regional Annual papers. See also Thomas, *Redevelopment and Race*, 61–62, and Bayor, *Race*, 70–72, 74, 76–77.
19. Bayor, *Race*, 74–76, 78–79.
20. Hirsch, *Making the Second Ghetto*, 265–66.
21. Ibid., 218. In Atlanta this refers to the Joel Chandler Harris Homes. See Bayor, *Race*, 80–81.
22. Rabin, "Roots," 220; *New York Times*, 25 November 1985, 9 September 1986, and 14 April 1991; D. Massey and N. Denton, *American Apartheid: Segregation and the Making of the Underclass* (Cambridge, Mass., 1993), 228.
23. R. H. Bayor, *Fiorello La Guardia: Ethnicity and Reform* (Arlington Heights, Ill., 1993), 167–70.
24. "Toward Equal Opportunity in Housing in Atlanta, Georgia—A Report to the Georgia State Advisory Committee to the U.S. Commission on Civil Rights," 13 October 1967, 26, Southern Regional Council papers. See Bayor, *Race*, 77.
25. Massy and Denton, *American Apartheid*, 189–97.
26. Ibid., 196–97, 210–11.

PART TWO

NEW PERSPECTIVES ON THE EXPERIENCES OF JEWISH REFUGEES FROM GERMANY

Chapter 4

GROWING UP JEWISH IN THE NAZI ERA

School, Emigration, and War

Werner T. Angress

Two years ago, while facing the fact that I was approaching the age of eighty, I set out to write the recollections of my youth. My main purpose in doing so was my desire to let my children and grandchildren know a little about my life, something about which they had often asked me questions. But I was especially interested in telling them how I became an American—not only in the technical sense but in every respect—and this included the story of my growing up in Nazi Germany, then immigrating to the United States, and ultimately joining the American army during World War II. The following account is an abstract of what I have written so far in the draft of my recollections.

Going to School in Berlin

When Hitler came to power, I was twelve and a half years old, lived in Berlin-Lichterfelde, a conservative district populated by retired officers and bureaucrats, and attended a *Realgymnasium*, or high school, where I was the only Jew in my class, ultimately in the entire school. My fellow pupils were sons of retired officers and bureaucrats, and in January 1933 many of them were still enrolled in nationalist, but not National Socialist youth groups, or Bünde. Only a few of them were members of the Hitler Youth. This was to change rapidly, however, and a few months after the "Seizure of Power" most of my classmates were *Pimpfe* in the Jungvolk, the junior branch of the Hitler Youth.

We had moved to Lichterfelde in 1932, several months prior to Hitler's appointment as chancellor on 30 January 1933. But even then I had been an outsider. When after a lengthy illness I entered the classroom for the first time in the fall of 1932, a somewhat older boy than the rest of us, Arndt G., already a member of the Hitler Youth who wore his swastika pin hidden under the lapel of his jacket, confronted me at once by asking whether I was Angress, and if I was a Jew. When I answered yes to both questions he replied: "Then stand with your back to the wall and don't move, or else you'll get lynched." This was my reception. Nobody else intervened, and I stayed with my back to the wall until the form teacher entered and assigned me a seat. How did Arndte, as we called him, know I was "the Jew"? Of course, it could be found in the class register in which the attendance, grades, behavior, and personal data of every student in the class were entered.

In contrast to a good many of my Jewish friends elsewhere in Berlin, I was exceedingly fortunate, despite this odd beginning, in that I spent until March 1936 in that school without ever being physically attacked. On the other hand, it was from the outset a time of frequent humiliation. Only a handful of kids were and remained on friendly terms with me. Among them was Wolfgang Sauer who decades later became my successor in the Department of History at the University of California, Berkeley. The majority of my classmates simply ignored me, did not talk to me, and treated me as if I did not exist. A few of them openly flaunted their anti-Semitism by making offensive remarks in my presence, notably the aforementioned Arndt and a kid named Schmidt, called "Schmidtchen." The latter was a weakling, who tried to compensate for his sickly appearance by emphasizing at every opportunity that he was "Aryan" and I was not, though without thereby winning the respect of his peers.

Equally differentiated was the attitude my teachers adopted in dealing with "the Jew." Between 1932 and 1936 I had consecutively two *Klassenlehrer*, or form teachers—Dr. Walter Muchall and his successor, Dr. Martin Lampel. Neither made anti-Semitic remarks to my face, but both treated me—a child after all, even though a Jewish one—with a mixture of sarcasm and contempt. Whenever Muchall, or subsequently Lampel, called upon me to recite, answer a question, in short do anything pupils do, it was the sneer on their faces that was so painful to watch, especially as it was an invitation to the class to do likewise. Then there was the history teacher who had lost a leg in the war and who tried to liven up his otherwise boring lessons with anti-Semitic comments. There he sat, leaning back in his chair, addressing the ceiling and never even looking at me, the near-sighted Jewish boy in the front row, while he made his Nazi comments. Finally, the Falstaffian music teacher who had us regularly sing Nazi songs. When I walked up to him after the first or second class session I attended and told him politely that I was a Jew and would not sing anti-Semitic songs, he looked at me contemptuously and said: "You don't need to sing with us at all." We never exchanged another word.

In all fairness, however, the majority of my teachers treated me no differently than they treated the rest of the class. In fact, some of them went out of their way to spare me embarrassment. One example was *Oberstudienrat* Max Naumann, an elderly gentleman who told us proudly that before the war he had been repeatedly among those who accompanied the Kaiser during his annual North Sea cruises. Naumann had the unpleasant task of having to instruct us on Saturdays in "National Politics" (*national-politischer Unterricht*), while the majority of the class was out drilling with the Hitler Youth. One day his assigned lesson was the National Socialist Party program. When he reached the sections dealing with the party's attitude toward the Jews, he glanced at me nervously and said, "Well, these points are obvious; let's skip them" and moved on to the subsequent sections. Another example was our gym teacher. When I first saw him, my heart sank as he wore the brown uniform of a low-ranking storm trooper, a fact my perpetual antagonist Arndte lost no time rubbing in.

For the first few weeks nothing unusual happened, but one day I was told to come to his office. My knees shook as I knocked at his door while Arndt sneered. To my utter surprise, the man said that we had a gymnastics contest with another school coming up, and he was herewith appointing me team leader to whip the boys on the team into shape for the contest, notably on the horizontal and parallel bars. He had watched me and felt sure I would do a good job. Well, I walked out, found Arndt waiting for me, and told him. He rushed to the office, but returned a minute later without looking at me, his face crimson red. We won the contest and I expected to be relieved of my new position, but I was not. A few months later, about to leave school to attend an agricultural training farm for Jewish boys and girls in Silesia for subsequent emigration and settlement overseas, I went to say goodbye to the gym teacher. He asked what my future plans were and advised me to leave Germany as soon as possible as I had no future there. Then he shook hands with me and we parted.

Finally, also during my last year at school, there was the teacher of German literature, a Herr Heyse. He was young, imaginative, full of vitality, and very much liked by the class. I soon noticed with surprise that he never made any references to National Socialism, something that I would have expected at the time for a man of his generation. One day—we had just been reading Theodor Storm's "Der Schimmelreiter"—he told us that we were going to hold a "trial" in class of the story's main character, Hauke Haien, who would be indicted for negligence. Then Heyse started to appoint requisite roles for the court trial and to my amazement picked me for the position of examining magistrate, or *Untersuchungsrichter*. The looks on the faces of my classmates clearly revealed surprise that I had been assigned such a position, but nobody said a word. Sometime later during the year—it was 1935—as my fellow pupils were going down to the schoolyard during recess, Heyse signaled to me to stay and wait for him as he wanted to talk to me. When we were alone in the classroom, he questioned me about my relations with my fellow pupils. When I told him that, given the circumstances, their behavior was reasonably tolerable, he nodded and remarked that I was fortunate in that most of them seemed to be decent fellows. Then he asked me about my plans for the future and whether I would like to go to Palestine. When I replied that I was no Zionist, he surprised me by telling me about a recent meeting he had with a Zionist revisionist group, Brit Trumpeldor, and then added that he had been really shocked because "they are fascists." Decades later I learned that Heyse had been a communist, something he obviously had kept well hidden from the authorities, and that after World War II he had been superintendent of a school district in East Berlin where he was constantly at odds with the party hierarchy. The latter did not surprise me.

How representative were my school experiences compared to those of other Jewish children at the time? Although I found a few memoirs in which the authors' experiences resembled my own, the overwhelming majority of Jewish children in the first half of the 1930s was much worse off than I, despite the humiliations, slights, and nasty comments I encountered. To be sure, luck had a lot to do with this. I happened to attend a school where most of my fellow pupils came from a conservative, middle-class background; and although many of them disliked Jews, theirs was the traditional anti-Semitism of German conservatives. Thus, when I left the school early in 1936, their anti-Jewish stance had not yet attained the vicious and violent stage it was to reach a couple of years later. Furthermore, there was the principal, also called Schmidt, son of a China missionary. He was a tall man who was a conservative nationalist, but no anti-Semite. When my mother—behind my back, by the way—went to see him early in 1933 and suggested that she would like me to transfer to a Jewish school, Schmidt replied that he saw no need for that. As long as he was principal, nothing would happen to me. He was forced to retire prematurely not very long after I had left the school. If one adds that I did not look the way many Germans imagined Jews to look, that I was a mediocre student and particularly poor in mathematics, a subject in which Jews supposedly excelled, but that I had "A" grades in two subjects rated particularly high at the time—German and physical education—the combination of these facts may well have protected me from real abuse.

Furthermore, despite the nastiness I encountered on the part of several teachers and peers, and despite my considerable, though not complete, isolation within the class, I was not excluded from any school activities common to all. On the contrary, whenever an important speech by Hitler was broadcast, I was expected to join the other pupils in the auditorium, the *Aula*, and listen to the Führer's voice. On each 1 May from 1933 through 1935 those of us not enrolled in the Jungvolk or Hitler Youth went with the form teacher to the Lustgarten, where Goebbels and Hitler would address us. I remember that in 1933 I even climbed a tree to see better. In the early spring of 1934, my class, including me, lined both sides of a narrow street behind our school to cheer Hitler and Ernst Röhm—the chief of staff of the storm troopers (Sturm-Abteilungen or SA) who was subsequently murdered on orders from his Führer a few months later—on their way to inspect the SS Leibstandarte Adolf Hitler (Hitler's personal body guard) stationed in the former Prussian Cadet Academy (Kadettenanstalt). And I was also taken along to watch the movie *Hitlerjunge Quex* during school time with my classmates. Finally, while all of my Jewish friends in other Berlin schools were forbidden to render the so-called German salute, I had to stand every morning alongside my peers with my outstretched arm and yell "Heil Hitler" when the teacher entered the classroom.

Why did I not transfer to a Jewish school in 1933 as my younger brother did and as my mother had wanted me to do? The idea was at the time repugnant to me. I considered myself, above all, a German, though one who happened to be Jewish. I was nationalistic to the core and did not want to go to a "ghetto." Therefore, I put up with a lot of daily unpleasantness, although I never told my parents of the humiliations I encountered in school. Moreover, from the fall of 1933 on, I compensated by joining a German-Jewish youth movement whose members generally held the same views that I did. Its general outlook was somewhat to the right of the predominantly liberal German-Jewish community.

I never finished high school, but left with what is now called *Mittlere Reife* in March 1936. A couple of months later, I enrolled in the recently founded agricultural emigration training farm Groß Breesen in Silesia to learn farming alongside other Jewish boys and girls my age. The ultimate objective was to settle together somewhere overseas, though not in Palestine. At Breesen, I spent eighteen happy intensive months, established friendships that have lasted until today—though our ranks are thinning every year—and also began to look at the world in a more realistic and mature way than I had while still going to school in Berlin.

Emigration and Exile

Turning to the theme of emigration and exile, ours was more of a flight than an ordinary emigration. My father, then the owner of a very small private bank, had already decided after passage of the Nuremberg laws in 1935 that his three sons should leave Germany as soon as possible because he saw no future for us there. For this reason I, the oldest, was sent to Gross Breesen to prepare myself for emigration. My parents meanwhile resolved to stay on, at least for a while yet, waiting to see how the situation would develop. By the fall of 1937, however, my father realized that he was barely holding his own in business and decided, rather suddenly, to leave the country with the entire family, taking his money along. This, of course, constituted a violation of the prevailing currency laws. In mid-October 1937 I was summoned to Berlin, where my mother informed me—my father was in Amsterdam to arrange for the illegal monetary transfer—that all of us would be leaving Germany within two weeks. Until then I could return to Groß Breesen. I was shocked beyond belief at the prospect of having to part with my friends, notably my first girl friend, and leave with my family with whom I—a difficult teenager—was then not on good terms. Thus, while my mother was visiting somewhere I sneaked out of our apartment, went to the station and returned to Breesen, leaving a note in which I told my parents that I would not join them while wishing them the best of luck wherever they were going.

Needless to say the director of Breesen, Curt Bondy, who met my father in Berlin a few days later, told me that I would have to leave with my family. By staying behind I would risk becoming a hostage to the Nazis as they would compel my father to return from abroad. I had to yield and met with my father on 30 October 1937 in Berlin, from where he and I intended to fly to Amsterdam a few hours later with London as our final destination. As it turned out, the plane was grounded by fog, and we left Germany that evening by separate routes. My mother and brothers had left the night before as "ordinary tourists" by railway and boat for London. My father, having secretly dispatched his money the same day, ultimately did not join me on the night train to Amsterdam but traveled to Prague instead, a destination he did not tell me as we parted when I went to catch my train. After visiting customers—all refugees—in Prague, Vienna, Switzerland, and France on a route referred to at the time as the *jüdischer Südring*, my father arrived in Amsterdam a week later. From there he and I went together to London to join my mother and brothers.

Exile began for me when the train reached Oldenzaal in Holland early Sunday morning on 31 October 1937. Shortly before, at Bentheim-Grenze, lying in bed in a sleeping car, I was woken up and asked some questions by two men in bowler hats and black leather coats—the "uniform" of the low-ranking Gestapo. They asked me to spell my last name and wanted to know where my parents were. "In Berlin," I lied, and at the end they handed me my passport and let me go. This was a mistake on their part because, as we found out a few weeks later when my father's secretary visited us in London, hours earlier all major German border crossings had received a telegram: "Stop the five-member Angress family! [*Fünfköpfige Familie Angress aufhalten*]" I still remember my mixed feelings as the kind Dutch conductor checked my ticket and passport and wished me a good journey. Nazi Germany lay behind me, but within it were still all my friends who I might never see again and before me lay a very uncertain future.

The next two years taught me the experience common to most refugees, that of not belonging. To be sure, in Nazi Germany I had not "belonged" either, but that had been due to the arbitrary political policies enforced by those who governed the country since 1933. And as far as I was concerned at the time, they could not tell me who I was and what I felt myself to be. But it was different living abroad. We spent four months in London, knowing only other refugees, trying to find a country overseas that would let us in. I still remember walking with my father from one South American consulate to the next, getting nowhere. Many South American countries at the time had good political and above all trade relations with Nazi Germany and, therefore, were unwilling to admit German Jews. A few of the latter managed to get in, anyway, mostly by bribing one or two consular officials—something which my father, very much of a Prussian, rejected out of hand. Nor did we feel comfortable in England. None of us spoke English beyond a few basic phrases. My contact with Englishmen was largely restricted to bus conductors and the police at Bow Street, where we had to register as aliens and keep reporting in. Early in 1938, my father decided to take us to Amsterdam where he had made contact with another refugee from Berlin who wanted to open a lingerie store, but lacked the necessary funds to do so. My father, who had the funds, now became a silent partner in that store that prospered very fast, though he was not to benefit from this new venture for very long as Holland was invaded by Germany in May 1940.

In Amsterdam we encountered once again another culture and another foreign language. With my family settled now, I spent a lot of time during the next year and a half trying to join one of the Breesen emigration projects. But being already abroad, thus "safe," I was given low priority by the U.S. consulate in Rotterdam even after I had been placed on a list of Breeseners who were to settle on a farm in Virginia. The immigration number assigned to me then, making me eligible for a visa provided I fulfilled all other immigration requirements, was due to come up in 1943! For many months I worked on and off (and unpaid) in the store of which my father was now part owner. When, after the November pogrom of 1938, a group of Breesen boys just released from Buchenwald were accepted into a Jewish refugee transit camp in the north of Holland, I eventually joined them. Once again I did farm work while waiting and hoping to get to the United States. In 1939 the farm project in Virginia finally materialized and my frustrating contacts with the U.S. consulate finally bore fruit. The farm had been bought by a wealthy southern department store owner, William B. Thalhimer, to enable roughly thirty young Jews trained in agriculture to come to the United States, settle on a farm called Hyde Farmlands as shareholders, and thereby qualify for preference visa. Thanks to the efforts of the American Joint Jewish Distribution Committee, an organization founded in 1914 to help people just like us, a well-known American banker and Eisenhower's subsequent chairman of the Atomic Energy Commission, Lewis L. Strauss, provided me with an affidavit that made it possible for me to secure an agricultural preference visa from the U.S. consulate in Rotterdam.

At the beginning of November 1939, over two months after World War II had begun and with several German divisions massed at the Dutch border, I boarded the Dutch ship SS *Veendam* in Antwerp. The boat was crowded with fellow refugees and at night was illuminated with the Dutch colors to keep German submarines from torpedoing us. And thus I was finally on my way to the United States. My parents and brothers stayed behind in Amsterdam. On 10 November 1939, one year after "Crystal Night," I arrived in Hoboken, New Jersey, and a week later took a Greyhound bus to Richmond, Virginia. After a brief meeting with Thalhimer, I was taken by truck to Hyde Farmlands.

What followed was a year and a half of failure to integrate into the country to which I had come as a refugee, where I had at once taken out First Papers, as it was called, to indicate my intent to become a citizen, and where for half a century I was ultimately to live, work, and raise a family. But initially, at Hyde Farmlands, we remained isolated. Beyond the farm manager, one or two neighbors and a few occasional visitors, we had virtually no contact with Americans. Except for a few older Gross Breesen boys and one girl who had come to Hyde Farmlands earlier than we had and who did speak some English, we mostly spoke German among ourselves—except on Friday. That was the day of the week we were supposed to speak only English and which was, therefore, always a rather quiet day whenever we sat around the supper table.

Nottoway County, where Hyde Farmlands was situated sixty miles southwest of Richmond, Virginia, was then still a largely rural, wooded area where one encountered wild turkeys, copperheads and other "exotic" animals. We worked under the supervision of an American farm manager, Urban Koenig Franken from Missouri whom Thalhimer had hired for this purpose. Franken, who lived on the farm with wife and children, not only supervised our work, but also tried to familiarize us with the "American way of life." Whenever he did not like something we were doing, he would admonish us by saying "We don't do that in this country." We worked hard, I as a specialist in raising "small fruit," and enjoyed it. Starting everything from scratch, we built chicken houses from logs we had cut in the woods, raised chickens and sold eggs, planted grapes, strawberries, vegetables, planted fruit trees, but also potatoes and corn, hoping that after a few years the farm would start paying for itself and even make some profit. We were glad to have come to the United States and did not worry overly much about our subsequent future. We were grateful being where we were, received $4.00 pocket money a month for which one could buy considerable more at the time than one can today, and all of our expenses, including health coverage, were taken care of by Thalhimer.

Some of us who had been unable to translate our adolescent dreams of adventure into action while growing up in Nazi Germany now seized the opportunity to make some of these dreams come alive. From the little money my father had been able to give me when I left for the United States, I bought myself a .22 caliber rifle and went hunting rabbits. Occasionally, against all good sense and, of course, all regulations, a friend and I clandestinely each took a work horse out of the barn at night and rode bareback through the nocturnal woods, seeing ourselves as American Indians on the war path.

The War Years

The farm project came very suddenly and unexpectedly to an end in the spring of 1941. After Thalhimer suffered a heart attack and was in the hospital, his brother Morton, a real estate agent, decided to sell the farm. His main reason was that during the two years we had operated it, the farm had never paid for itself. Under these circumstances, I saw only two acceptable choices: either become a farm hand at $21.00 a month on the apple farm of Virginia Senator Harry F. Byrd to whom Morton Thalhimer wanted to "sell" me, or volunteer for the draft and enter the Army of the United States, which then also paid $21.00 a month to its rookies. Together with a couple of other friends I chose the latter. For one, we knew that thereby we would finally learn English and, as the length of service was then still only one year, hoped that thereafter we might even go to a college. Ignorant of American life as we were we did not realize how difficult it might be to enter a college without a German high school degree which most of us lacked. So we went ahead and volunteered for a year's service under the draft. We were sworn in on 7 May 1941 in Richmond and inducted into the newly created Army of the United States. In contrast to the traditional U.S. Army composed of regular enlisted soldiers serving for many years, this was an army of civilian draftees.

I was sent to Fort George G. Meade in Maryland and, after a few days of taking tests and drawing my uniform and equipment, was assigned to Company B, 116th Infantry Regiment of the 29th, the Virginia National Guard Division. Here, during basic training, I made rapid progress learning English as well as soldiering. As to the former, I received help from two fellow soldiers shortly after I was inducted. One morning during the first week I had been assigned to the 29th Division, these two men walked up to me, and the older of the two, a tall and ugly looking man, asked me where I was from. When I told him in halting English where I came from and why I had left, he asked whether Hitler did not have good reasons to get rid of the Jews. I got terribly upset, stuttered, and tried to explain what the Nazis were like. Ignoring my comments, he then suggested that I buy the *New York Times* every day, read the political section, and report to him and the other fellow, a Washington journalist who was soon transferred elsewhere, what I had read. They would then correct my errors, and in this way I should learn fairly soon to speak English properly. Strange as it may sound, this was the beginning of a friendship with the tall and ugly fellow, John G. Barnes, a civil engineer from Newport News, Virginia, who continued to look out for me as long as I remained in Company B. He was killed on D-Day, coming in with the second wave of the regiment to land at Omaha Beach.

Instead of just one year, as I had expected, I stayed in the army for four and a half years. In the summer of 1941 President Roosevelt extended the draft to two years, and on 7 December the Japanese extended it "for the duration" by bombing Pearl Harbor. Until the summer of 1942 I served as an infantryman in the 29th Division, rising to the rank of corporal. Most of the time we were on maneuvers in the South, battling the heat, poison oak, chiggers, and intermittently also incapable National Guard officers who got us lost in the woods as they were unable to read a map properly. But my Americanization continued steadily and I came to know people from parts other than just Nottoway County. My being a foreigner—I was only naturalized in October 1943—never bothered anybody in the 29th Division, nor did my accent. Barnes and others corrected my diction and pronunciation when necessary, while otherwise largely illiterate kids furthered my education by giving me lessons in the history of the American Civil War and cursing the "damn Yankees."

I would have liked to stay with the 29th Division, where on account of my knowledge of German I had been transferred early in 1942 to the intelligence section of headquarters company. But a few months after the division had been sent to Camp Blanding, Florida, in the late spring of 1942, it was shipped to Northern Ireland to await the anticipated invasion of the continent. To my dismay, I was not allowed to go along because I had not yet received my American citizenship papers. I was transferred to the 79th Infantry Division where I spent a little more than a year, most of which was rather miserable.

In November 1942 I was removed from the company and placed for the next nine months in a so-called alien detachment. This was composed of German-Jewish refugees like myself, non-Jewish Germans from predominantly Chicago and a few other lost souls. All of us were soldiers from throughout the division who had not yet become U.S. citizens, and we were segregated from the other soldiers and assigned to an area situated at the edge of the regular army camp. All we were allowed to do was menial labor, and as long as we stayed in Camp Blanding it was my task to supervise the cleaning of the officer's club, notably the toilets. All efforts to obtain assistance from some higher authority failed, though we tried hard. Why did all this happen? As we found out later, the culprits who deprived us of nine months of training and, incidentally, of leaves and furloughs as well, were the colonel in charge of the division's intelligence section, a nearly senile old bird, and the ranking master sergeant of his section, a Jew from Brooklyn. The latter had manipulated the old colonel to issue the segregation order that created the "alien detachment" with the argument that all of us who were coming from Germany and Nazi-occupied Europe were Nazis, although some kept posing as Jews.

In late June 1943 we were suddenly and without any explanation transferred back to our old infantry companies, and within a few weeks of local maneuvers my company commander had me promoted to the rank of sergeant. But my dislike for the division as such remained strong, and when I was given the chance to transfer to a military intelligence training camp—we subsequently referred to the abbreviation "MITC" as "Military Institute of Total Confusion"—in order to become an interrogator of German prisoners of war, I volunteered at once. In August 1943 I bade farewell to Captain Roundtree and my buddies and was shipped to Camp Ritchie, Maryland (today a retreat of the American president, Camp David). There we were instructed on the organization of the German Wehrmacht, including the Waffen-SS, but in particular on how to interrogate prisoners of war.

The makeup of our, the eleventh class, was fascinating. There were German-Jewish refugees and non-Jewish Germans from all over the United States, but the unit also included GIs originating from South America, France, and other European countries. A babel of languages was spoken in every barrack. Many of my fellow trainees became subsequently academicians, journalists, or authors. For instance, the man who slept in the double-decker bunk next to mine and with whom I usually went to eat in the mess hall was Corporal Fred Hechinger, subsequently education editor of the *New York Times*. And one Private Stefan Heym—later on a prominent and controversial author in the German Democratic Republic—gave me a lot of trouble during the few days that I was barrack sergeant after I had ordered him to sweep under his bunk.

After approximately three months of intensive training, we had to undergo a final examination and, if we passed, were to be promoted to a higher rank. The man who tested my capabilities as an interrogator was Second Lieutenant Bartholomew from Utah, a Mormon who had suffered battle fatigue while participating in General Eisenhower's North African campaign and had been assigned as an instructor to Camp Ritchie. All of us took turns posing as prisoners of war, and when it was my turn to be tested I faced a buddy of mine who could barely refrain from grinning while the mock interrogation proceeded. Quite consciously I interrogated in a manner friends had warned me to refrain from: I treated the "prisoner" kindly, made him sit down, offered him a cigarette (which I had borrowed as I only smoked pipe), and then asked my questions. As a result I flunked this particular interrogation examination.

The lieutenant stared at me icily, but did not say anything until the prisoner had "collapsed" and told all. But then Bartholomew let me have it. When he had interrogated men of Rommel's Afrika Korps, he shouted at me, he had never allowed any one of them to sit down, had not offered cigarettes, but had yelled at them as "this was the only language Germans understand." So he flunked me because I did not yell at the kid who posed as a German prisoner but did all sorts of things which my examiner considered unforgivable. Despite the fact that my overall average in the course was over 90 percent, I was only promoted to the next highest rank, that of staff sergeant. A couple months later when it came to the real thing, I followed exactly the same approach I had taken during the test. How was I, young looking and small, to impress tough German prisoners by yelling at them? Instead, I tricked them, chatted, asked what seemed to be harmless questions, never took notes in their presence, and usually got results. Those who refused to talk, pleading the Geneva Convention, I dismissed at once and got another prisoner instead.

In January 1944 I shipped out of Brooklyn Harbor on the HMS *Rangitata*, British command boat of a convoy to Liverpool. Once in England, I spent the spring awaiting combat assignment at military intelligence headquarters in Broadway, the Cotswolds, and in May was assigned to an interrogation team attached to the 508th Parachute Infantry Regiment, 82nd Airborne Division—as a nonjumper. Upon arrival at division head quarters the coordinator of the interrogation teams, First Lieutenant Bushman, a Jewish officer whose highest ambition was to become an opera singer (and who subsequently, during his occasional interrogations in the field, would question the prisoners in Yiddish) asked me whether I wanted to become a paratrooper. I assented and was promised the appropriate training. This I never received—bad weather, no plane available, trainer sick—the excuses were staggering. Then, on 4 June 1944, the regiment was alerted to be moved to a hidden airfield for the upcoming invasion. My team's second in command, Lieutenant Hauff, instructed me to stay behind with him and a few other nonjumpers and follow the regiment a few days later by boat. I ignored Hauff, ran to divisional headquarters, requested to see the commanding general, Matthew Ridgway, and was told that he was busy. But I could see the deputy division commander, General James M. Gavin. When I reported to Gavin and stated my request to jump with the regiment he replied, "Well, why not? My chauffeur never jumped before, and he's coming along." I ran back to grab my stuff and, again ignoring a now fuming Hauff, was off to join my buddies just being loaded into trucks on the way to the airfield.

This marked the beginning of ten months of combat duty. Around 2 A.M. of 6 June 1944, I did the first jump of my life. As I had noticed when boarding the plane, a C-47, it bore a picture of Donald Duck in bathing trunks, and underneath the caption, "Son of the Beach." Standing near the exit door of the plane I watched with amazement what went on outside it. I was at the head of the "stick," the term for a squad of paratroopers ready to leave the plane, hooked to the static line which held the release of my chute. Being "number one" was no coincidence, as I then found out. Because I was not yet a qualified paratrooper, I had the privilege to refuse the jump, even at the last minute, without risking a court-martial. All it would have taken was merely to step aside and make room for the rest of the troopers to go out. Suddenly the "rigger sergeant" came to the door. (The night before he had given me ten minutes worth of instructions on how to jump, using a table for that purpose. It was the job of the riggers to collect the chutes after the jump so that they could be used again). He told me that I was to leave the plane before he tossed out the two equipment bags. Once I and the baggage were out, the "stick" would follow. Staff Sergeant Angress was, therefore, simply another piece of baggage.

We drew the first fire approaching the Channel Islands Guernsey and Jersey, flying very low to frustrate the German anti-aircraft gunners. Shortly after we hit the Normandy coast and the C-47 plane had climbed to the level from which we were to jump—roughly a thousand feet—we were hit. Tracer bullets flew all around us, and one of them had knocked out the plane's electrical system by means of which the pilot was to give us the signal when to jump. The rigger sergeant cursed, muttered that we were now on verbal orders from the pilot, and trudged off to the cockpit to wait for the pilot's command. Meanwhile, I talked to the kid standing behind me, being careful not to move my left hand from the leather strap that connected my chute to the static line lest it tear off my arm when I left the plane. Commenting on the mess we were obviously in—the plane next to us was downed in front of our eyes—the kid only muttered, "What else is new? Snafu," meaning "situation normal, all fucked up." And then the rigger sergeant came pushing his way by the troopers behind me, yelling, "Jump, chicken!" And "chicken," his nickname for me, stepped out of the door.

It was all very different from what I had expected. Outside the plane it was quiet. I noticed that I was oscillating and, following the rigger sergeant's instructions, pulled on the risers—the straps that connected my harness with the shroud lines—to steady the chute and succeeded to do so. I did not have the feeling of falling but saw the ground come rushing up to meet me. I landed softly in an apple orchard, my chute getting hung on top of a apple tree while a white horse, scared beyond its wits, kept running along the orchard's fence and neighed wildly. After getting out of my harness and detecting that I could not follow instructions and fold up the chute for the riggers because it was firmly embedded on top of the tree, my first reaction was to urinate as I had been told I would. Then I checked my equipment, got out a flashlight and compass and, still assuming that I had been dropped near Ste. Mère-Église, proceeded to move east in search of a blue light that was to mark the assembly point for the troopers of the several regiments.

What I did not know was that the pilot of our plane had taken "evasive action," had dodged the anti-aircraft fire around Ste. Mère-Église, had taken us to Quettehou, a little southeast of Cherbourg and approximately thirty miles north of the proper dropping point, and there had given us the order to jump. Thus, instead of taking us back to England and letting us return in another plane, he dropped us far behind the German lines. In fact, the last two men of the stick landed in the sea, though fortunately in shallow water close to the beach. The pilot was subsequently court-martialed for his action.

Somewhat to my surprise I found myself alone and set off to find the blue light. After falling off a hedgerow—which fence off the many orchards in Normandy—and losing my flashlight I needed to read the map, I walked east. Suddenly a German voice came from a dugout in front of me. The moon was light enough to reveal three German soldiers in the dugout behind a machine gun that was pointed at an open field. I stopped, pulled the trigger from one of the two hand grenades I carried and stepped forward, shouting: "Non-commissioned officer on patrol [*Unteroffizier auf Patrouille*]." This, although spoken in clear German, was wrong. Non-commissioned officers rarely went on patrol by themselves, and the proper term—as I should have remembered from my time in Camp Ritchie—was "Streife," not "Patrouille." When the voice ordered me to step closer, I tossed my grenade and then ran as quickly as I could along the path. I heard excited voices behind me and then felt something hit my helmet. One of the Germans had fired his pistol and the bullet hit my helmet, tearing the camouflage net and making a small dent. This, at a distance of about thirty meters and at night was pretty good shooting, I'd say! I jumped at once into the bushes next to the path and proceeded to bury my "Order of Battle" book that Hauff had ordered me to take along—strictly against regulations as the book contained all the information that U.S. Army intelligence had collected about the German armed forces. For this reason it was not to fall into German hands. Alongside the book I also buried my gas mask which I felt I would not need and then, for good measure, threw my entrenching tool into the bushes as well, as I wanted to travel light.

After sneaking off into what seemed an enormous forest, I crawled into a blackberry patch and slept until well after dawn, then spent a day walking through the woods trying unsuccessfully to find my unit. It was only in the evening of that day when I discovered that I was in the forêt de Vidcauville, far away from where I should have been. The next days I found more stragglers like myself, mostly artillery people from the 101st Airborne Division. Being the only one who could speak some French, I became the chief contact with the local population on which we depended for information and food. We moved at night behind the German lines from hideout to hideout, trying to rejoin our units south of us. In the evening of 15 June we were suddenly attacked by a German antiaircraft unit—some Frenchmen with whom I had negotiated for food had given us away—and, after a short skirmish in which I was lightly wounded in the leg, we were taken prisoner and ultimately moved to Cherbourg. Liberated on 27 June, my twenty-fourth birthday, when the Germans holding Cherbourg surrendered I rejoined my regiment.

There I was welcomed like a long-lost child. My fellow interrogators saw to it that I got clean clothing—my duffel bag with all my clothing had "disappeared" after I had been listed as "MIA," missing in action—and that I finally could take a bath and get shaved. The regimental intelligence officer (S-2), Captain John A. Breen, saw to it that the division's chief medical officer who examined the little wound in my upper thigh did not order me sent back to England for "proper treatment and recovery." Interrogators were too few and far between and couldn't be spared. As my team commander, First Lieutenant Alfred Diamant—he survived and for many years taught political science at Indiana University—had been gravely wounded and captured, my old friend Hauff had taken over as deputy team commander when he got to Normandy by boat a few days after the initial invasion.

He and I did not get along any better than we had before. One day Captain Breen asked me discreetly why the interrogation reports Hauff submitted dealt mainly with the military situation in Russia. I told him that Hauff, a descendant of a German family, or Volga Germans, that had settled in Russia during the reign of Catherine the Great, was trying from personal interest to obtain such information from German prisoners who had fought on the Russian front. As a result, Captain Breen had me transferred from my team directly to regimental intelligence (S-2) so that I could reinterrogate all prisoners after Hauff was through with them. Then I was to write my own report about what was of immediate concern to us—who was facing us, unit strength, casualties suffered, and other matters of tactical interest. Fortunately, Lieutenant Hauff never found out what Captain Breen and I had cooked up between ourselves.

For the balance of the war, I did what I had been trained to do in Camp Ritchie: interrogate German prisoners of war. After Normandy I participated in the Dutch campaign which lasted from 17 September until 14 November 1944. It was my second and last combat jump, and it was a satisfying experience not to land all by myself, as in Normandy, but together with hundreds of fellow troopers in a beet field at the edge of the city of Nijmegen. Initially, nobody was even shooting at us. Although a German anti-aircraft battery stood right in the middle of the field where we landed, the German gunners surrendered without firing a shot, approaching us with raised hands while we were still struggling out of our jump harnesses. But shortly thereafter, as my division advanced into the city of Nijmegen proper and eventually succeeded in capturing the bridge that spanned the river Rhine, the fighting became fierce and remained so until we were finally relieved and sent to Camp de Sissonne near Reims that was to become our base camp in France. Compared to our Canadian fellow troopers who jumped into Arnhem and virtually on top of two Waffen-SS divisions just moving through, we could count ourselves lucky.

At Sissonne we were looking forward to Christmas leave in Paris. This pleasant prospect did not materialize in that Hitler decided to send an army under the command of General von Rundstedt into Belgium to try and capture Antwerp and chase the Allied forces into the sea. In mid-December we were alerted, loaded into open trucks and, in the midst of ice and snow, were transported to the Ardennes forest where we fought until the end of February 1945 in the so-called Battle of the Bulge. It was by far the most grueling and toughest campaign, partly because of the cold weather and the snow in which we often had to sleep, but also because of the fanatical way in which the Waffen-SS attacked. As word circulated that German soldiers in American uniforms were trying to infiltrate our lines, I was warned not to speak to anybody outside my own unit where I was known because my German accent might put me in danger. And sure enough, one day as I gave hell to a trooper from a neighboring regiment when he dunked a dead chicken, prior to plucking it, into a barrel of rainwater used for drinking, I was immediately arrested and threatened to be shot. My captors marched me at the point of a rifle to their battalion headquarters, where I was able to persuade one of the officers to call my regiment to identify me over the field phone. Then I was released.

On 15 March, back at Sissonne, I made my third and last parachute jump, a practice jump that for a number of my buddies turned out to be fatal. With a nearly hysterical Marlene Dietrich, who was visiting our division, watching from the ground—she had been told, falsely, that the jump took place in her honor—a number of troopers were killed when a malfunctioning plane swooped down out of control, hitting and killing jumpers from other planes as they were drifting to the earth, including my team commander, First Lieutenant Nick C. Emanuel.

On 4 April 1945 the division then pushed eastward until we reached Cologne. A few days earlier my regiment, the 508th P.I.R., had been detached from the division and sent to Frankfurt am Main to guard Eisenhower's headquarters. For the first time I found myself once again in a German city where we encountered widely differing reactions to our presence, ranging from open defiance to cringing servility and self-pity. While in Cologne I served temporarily as General Gavin's interpreter whenever he moved around the city and its outskirts by jeep, talking to people and trying to assess their attitude. At the end of April, after the Germans in the Ruhr pocket had surrendered, we moved rather fast toward the Elbe, crossed that river early in May and proceeded toward Ludwigslust, Mecklenburg, where we not only experienced the end of the war, but also met up with the Russians. A few days before, after hearing of Hitler's suicide, we had toasted the news with captured brandy and the fervent imprecation: "Long may he rot!"

As soon as I heard that the war was over, I asked that a battlefield commission for which I had been recommended and which had been in progress for several weeks, be stopped because I no longer wanted it. All I desired was to get back to the States and, if possible, enter a college. Yet, there was still a good deal of work to be done before we could think of returning home. Two occurrences deserve mention. When the division settled in Ludwigslust where the palace of the grand duke (who had wisely fled to Denmark in order to put himself under the protection of his brother-in-law, the Danish king) became division headquarters, we liberated a small forced labor camp, Wöbbelin, an *Aussenlager* of the Neuengamme Concentration Camp, a few miles outside of Ludwigslust. After taking the guards prisoner, we had them move two hundred victims from all over occupied Europe, who had been starved to death in the camp, to the palace garden in Ludwigslust; had them dig the graves; and then had a formal burying ceremony. The entire population of Ludwigslust was compelled to attend the burial, including a group of captured German officers who, for this occasion only, were placed into my charge.

I was also assigned the task of screening roughly two thousand imprisoned members of the Waffen-SS who were held behind barbed wire in a nearby patch of woods. Together with three fellow interrogators, none of whom was an officer, we spent about a week separating the "sheep from the goats." Those who had been drafted into the Waffen-SS, notably during the closing months of the war, were eventually moved into a prisoner of war camp for soldiers of the regular army. The rest, about one-half of the contingent, was then handed over for trial to the British who had requested the screening process in the first place. To carry out the project, we distributed questionnaires and briefly interrogated everyone except for the SS officers who were "automatic arrest," checked through their identification booklet (*Soldbuch*), where on pages 4 and 17 all the relevant information of their past assignments and duties had been duly entered, without letting them know what we were up to. They finally found out when we moved half of them to one of the numerous improvised for the regular German army, leaving the other half, the "goats," where they were, ready for the British to pick them up.

We left Ludwigslust in mid-June, moved first back to Sissonne, then onto Épinal near Vichy to wait for a transport home. In September, I actually sailed from Marseilles to Boston from where I was sent to Fort George G. Meade, Maryland, to be discharged. In the meantime, I had found my mother and brothers in Amsterdam. They had survived underground while my father had been murdered in Auschwitz.

In Retrospect

What was it like, in retrospect, to have served for four and a half years as an American soldier, and specifically during the eleven months of combat as an interrogator? For me as a German-Jewish refugee, it had been a strange experience to talk nearly daily with German prisoners of war, trying to extract information from them on what was happening on the enemy side of the front lines. We needed tactical information, and we usually got it. Did I hate these German POWs? The answer is "no." Many of them were my age group, most were relieved that for them the war was over, and I often could empathize with them. I believe that one reason for my detachment—I only learned of the "Final Solution" and my father's death in Auschwitz after the war was over—was the awareness that I was now an American, a paratrooper, and an interrogator in the "All American Airborne Division." I had a job to do that had to be carried out efficiently and in a civilized manner—no threats, no physical abuse—because, after all, I was not a Nazi.

Let me add that my fellow interrogators on the team, most of them likewise Jewish refugees, behaved the same way I did. We, and others beside us, all had made the transition, each in his own way, from children who on account of their non-Aryan background had been humiliated (if not worse) in school by Nazi teachers and fellow students, to immigrants eager to be integrated into the society of their new homeland. This most of us did during World War II. In the last analysis, it was the Army of the United States, an army of civilians in uniform, that was instrumental in making me an American.

Selected Bibliography

School

Angress, W. T. *Between Fear and Hope: Jewish Youth in the Third Reich*. Trans. W. T. Angress and C. Granger. New York, 1988.

Dwork, D. *Children with a Star: Jewish Youth in Nazi Europe*. New Haven, Conn., and London, 1991.

Friedlander, S. *Nazi Germany and the Jews*. New York, 1997.

Kaplan, M. *Between Dignity and Despair: Jewish Life in Nazi Germany*. New York and Boston, 1998.

Walk, J. "Jüdische Schüler an deutschen Schulen in Nazideutschland." *Bullletin des Leo Baeck Instituts* 19 (1980): 101–9.

Emigration

Benz, W., ed. *Das Exil der kleinen Leute. Alltagserfahrung deutscher Juden in der Emigration*. Munich, 1991.

Benz, W., and M. Weiss, eds. *Die Erfahrung des Exils. Exemplarische Reflexionen*. Berlin, 1997.

Feidel-Mertz, H., ed. *Schulen im Exil. Die verdrängte Pädagogik nach 1933*. Hamburg, 1983.

Kwiet, K., and J. A. Moses, eds. "On Being a German-Jewish Refugee in Australia." *The Australian Journal of Politics and History: Experiences and Studies*, special issue, vol. 31, no. 1 (1985).

Loewald, K. G. "A Dunera Internee at Hay 1940–41." *Historical Studies of the University of Melbourne* 17 (1977): 512–21.

Mosse, W. E., ed. *Second Chance: Two Centuries of German-Speaking Jews in the United Kingdom*. Tübingen, 1991.

War

Bentwich, N. *Understanding the Risks: How Those Who fled to England from Hitlerite Oppression Fought against Nazism*. With a foreword by the Marquess of Reading. London, 1950.

Dawson, W. F., ed. *Saga of the "All American."* Chicago, 1946.

Gavin, J. M., *On to Berlin: Battles of an Airborne Commander 1943–1946*. New York, 1978.

Lord, W. G., II, ed., *History of the 508th Parachute Infantry*. Washington, D.C., 1948.

Ryan, C. *June 6, 1944: The Longest Day*. New York, 1959.

Chapter 5

WILLIAM STERN (1871–1938)

A Word-View at Risk

Supriya Mukherjee

When William Stern arrived in the United States in 1934 as a refugee scholar, he already had significant accomplishments to his credit. He had served as a lecturer, or *Privatdozent*, and later as associate, or *außerordentlicher*, professor at the University of Breslau where he taught psychology, philosophy and pedagogy between 1897 and 1916. Thereafter he became a full, or *ordentlicher*, professor in philosophy, psychology, and pedagogy at the Colonial Institute in Hamburg and played an instrumental role in its transformation into a full-fledged university after World War I. Between 1916 and 1933 he made the University of Hamburg into a world-renowned center for pedagogical psychology, specializing in the diagnosis of gifted and talented school children. His scholarly achievements throughout his career were exceptional both qualitatively and quantitatively. He had done path-breaking work in child, pedagogical, forensic, and industrial psychology. His formulation of the Intelligence Quotient (IQ) won him an international reputation. In recognition of his work, he was elected President of the German Psychological Society in 1931. Two years later, with the Nazi seizure of power, he was dismissed from his university position for being a Jew.

The story of Stern's subsequent emigration to the United States, where he joined William McDougall's Department of Psychology at Duke University, forms a chapter in the narrative of that great "intellectual migration" about which much has been written.[1] The literary and cultural personalities, academics and research scientists who left Germany and German-occupied Europe en masse between 1933 and 1940 is a modern exodus tale of escape and new beginnings, flight and rebirth. It is also a tale of losses and gains for individuals and nations, although here the symmetry of outcomes is by no means unequivocal. Alvin Johnson was right to say, "Hitler shakes the tree and I gather the apples." On the other hand, there is no gainsaying that for many of the refugees, there was little, if anything, providential about their fate.

In recent years the morality play version of the "exodus of the mind" (*Auszug des Geistes*) has undergone scrutiny and modification. The prominent and eminent continue to receive their attention, but scholars have rightly questioned the literature's neglect of lesser-known personalities. They also draw our attention to the uncritical presumption that it was the circumstance of forced migration alone that led to the subsequent innovations and accomplishments of the well-known personalities. A more nuanced, if less dramatic, picture of émigré history has emerged in recent years. As scholars pay attention to entire disciplines and the processes of acculturation in all their aspects, they show us that the discourse of "loss" and "gain" is not incorrect, but simplistic in its assumptions and focus. Intellectual "contributions" are the outcome of a number of negotiations that include factors of personality, sociocultural background, national variations in styles of thought and research, the demands as well as support structures of academic departments, universities and grant organizations, and finally, audience receptivity both within and without academe.[2]

The Nazi civil service law of 7 April 1933, the Nuremberg laws of 1935, the pogroms of November 1938, and the invasions of Austria and Czechoslovakia saw to the expatriation of approximately 2,000 German-speaking academics and scientists. For some disciplines, such as physics, mathematics, and psychology, the qualitative dimensions of the loss were as significant as the quantitative. Although only 14.6 percent of the 308 members of the German Psychological Society emigrated, they included in their number the directors of four of the five best-known psychological institutes and a number of senior researchers and associate professors. The full professors who were dismissed on account of the 1933 discriminatory laws included William Stern (Hamburg), Max Wertheimer (Frankfurt/Main), David Katz (Rostock), and Wilhelm Peters (Jena). Other scholars were dismissed later or left voluntarily, such as Wolfgang Köhler, who left the directorship of the Psychological Institute at Berlin in 1935 for Swarthmore College.[3]

The civil service law of 1933 affected some universities more than others, reflecting the concentration of Jewish academics in these institutions. The number of Jewish professors at the University of Hamburg did not exceed the national average and was considerably less compared to Berlin and Frankfurt.[4] Still, it was a fairly extensive purge that the university experienced over the course of the year.[5] Aside from Stern, other prominent faculty members included Ernst Cassirer in philosophy, the economists Eduard Heimann and Theodor Plaut, Richard Salomon in East European history, Walther Küchler in Romance languages (who was also dean of the faculty of philosophy), and the well-known art historian Erwin Panofsky. At the Psychological Institute, regarded as a hotbed of "Jewishness"[6] by the new regime, the gruesome process of racial "purification" was accomplished through the dismissal of professors and research assistants who were either Jews or "Jew-sympathizers" (*Judengenossen*). Most noteworthy of those dismissed were Heinz Werner, who possessed an international reputation in his discipline, and Martha Muchow, a well-known child psychologist, assistant to Stern, as well as a close friend of the family. Stern himself was officially relieved of his duties without pay on 31 October. However, he had been prohibited from teaching since the passage of the law in April. His friends, students, and colleagues were warned against him, his books removed from the libraries. He was even denied entry into the Institute. "The exile had begun even before he went into exile."[7]

Doubtless Stern's experiences were similar to many of those of his background and position. This fact does nothing to lessen their poignancy, however. Not only was he deprived of his livelihood and status, his family members were torn away from him as well. His writer and philosopher son Günther Anders left for France in April 1933, to be followed by his wife, the prominent émigré personality Hannah Arendt. They divorced later. The youngest daughter, Eva, whose Zionistic enthusiasm had disturbed her father before, now worked with the Berlin Jugend Aliyah, the movement to send Jewish youth to Palestine, with her father's blessing. Stern's eldest daughter Hilde was a communist sympathizer and was given a prison sentence of two years. Her two children were entrusted to her parents, who took them along to Holland in the winter of 1933. Luckily for Stern, his international reputation opened the way for several lecture tours in Holland, while he continued in his search for a more permanent position.

Unfortunately, this bit of good fortune was tarnished by the loss of two of his closest friends and associates. The first to pass away was Martha Muchow, who committed suicide in September and whose tragic death "remained a secret that will never be explained." There is no question that she was a casualty of recent political developments. The next to pass away was Otto Lipmann, Stern's co-editor for nearly thirty years of *Die Zeitschrift für angewandte Psychologie*. Lipmann died of a heart attack that was brought on, Stern speculated, by recent events and in particular, the termination of the *Zeitschrift*, "the single tie that connected him with the scientific world."[8] Both of these deaths affected Stern deeply. His daughter Eva recalls her father was able to survive these disappointments only because of the strength and support of her mother, Clara Stern.[9]

In Holland Stern received a piece of good news. Eva Stern recalls her father being extremely pleased when the Dutch publishing house of Nijhoff gave him a book contract for his *Allgemeine Psychologie*. It was not the contract itself, but the fact that the book was to be published in German, that gave him comfort.[10] "It seemed to him a personal victory of international collaboration over Hitler," wrote Günther Anders.[11] While in Holland Stern received an offer from Duke University, thus ending the uncertainty of his professional situation. The chair of the psychology department was the well-known English psychologist William McDougall, who strongly supported a position for Stern. This was no surprise, as McDougall was one of the very few representatives in the United States of the "hormic" (holistic) school of psychology, which bucked the dominant trend of behaviorism and was closer to German (and Stern's) research practices and orientations. However, the initial impetus for Stern's appointment came from the Emergency Committee in Aid of Displaced German Scholars. In a confidential letter to President William P. Few of Duke, the Emergency Committee prefaced their recommendation in the following words:

> He is about 62 years of age, alert, almost boyish in his manner and enthusiasm. His wife is charming and gracious, a woman who has in her own right a first class reputation as a psychologist. They understand English and speak it well enough for conversational purposes, but Stern is quite certain that he will lack freedom of intellectual formulation in the English language and must therefore be allowed to lecture in German.[12]

It was the Emergency Committee, along with the Rockefeller Foundation, that also funded Stern's $6,000 salary for the one-year renewal appointment. It is important to recognize that without such outside funding, Duke would not have been able to employ a foreign-born scholar. These were also the Depression years and universities were hard-pressed to keep on existing personnel. In the end, Duke employed six émigré scholars during the 1930s. Four of these were brought in with the assistance of the Emergency Committee.[13]

Adjustment to America and American customs was not easy for Stern. Though he had visited the country twice before (once for the celebrated Clark conference in 1909, where he was given the first of his American honorary doctorates, and a second time for the Ninth International Congress at New Haven in 1929), he spoke little English. Lack of facility in the language troubled him deeply, used as he was to being appreciated as a fluent and lively speaker in Germany. The human geographical aspects of American life were puzzling and alien. It astonished him that people without cars could become so completely isolated, that the streets had no proper sidewalks so that it was virtually impossible to take a leisurely walk. "The Americans need their legs only to play football," he quipped.[14] Intellectually, the atmosphere at the university was less of a problem. McDougall had put the stamp of his scholarship on the department. Additionally, two of his assistants, Karl Zener and Don Adams, had studied in Berlin and were "therefore somewhat familiar with Germanic thinking [*deutsche Denkweise*]." Stern acknowledged that he had found a unique supportive niche:

> The psychology practiced here represents an exception in this country. McDougall is a strong opponent of the dominant American tendencies and

> both he and his colleagues are very much interested in the relationship between psychology and philosophy, something that is singular for this country. Furthermore, his "Purposive Psychology" has much in common with my own way of thinking, so that the differences are not so great, as they are for the other European psychologists who have come to this country. Still, the discrepancies are big enough, as I have discovered in my various attempts to translate certain concepts and expressions into English.[15]

Obviously, it was not a perfect match.

It should be noted that there existed a significant set of differences between German and American academic psychology in terms of research practices and theoretical orientations. The dominant orientation in American psychology during the 1930s was a particular form of behaviorism that was committed to the idea of psychology as a practically useful science of human performance. Psychology as a discipline had instrumental value. In Germany psychology was a subdiscipline of philosophy. Its institutional basis until 1941[16] (with some exceptions) was philosophical chairs, and practicing psychologists were also trained philosophers. Almost from the very beginning, therefore, German psychology had to answer to a long tradition of philosophical inquiry that had formed the discursive core of German scholarship since the foundation of the University of Berlin in 1810. This resulted in two related orientations. First, there was a heightened awareness of the theoretical and philosophical ramifications of their research among German psychologists. In fact, the doyen of German psychology, Wilhelm Wundt, held that psychology was essentially a propaedeutic to philosophical questions. Second, the idealistic and metaphysical bases of German philosophy could not be easily discarded.

At the level of discourse, these positions translated into a rejection of "elementarism," "associationism," and "aggregate" psychology, all of which were said to typify American research practice. From Wundt to Dilthey to the Gestalt psychologists, German psychology endeavored to see the human mind as something more than the mechanical adding up of individual sensations. There was an a priori aspect to the human mind that needed to be taken into account. Experimental techniques and quantification were to be utilized within this discursive context. It is no small wonder then that the American psychological establishment viewed with great suspicion the European refugees and their commitment to such an "unscientific" and "mentalistic" approach to human conduct. Unlike the psychoanalysts, who had no established tradition to contend with, refugee academic psychologists were only minimally successful in the United States. Even the technically sophisticated experiments of the Gestalt psychologists were received with much ambivalence by the American psychological establishment, mainly because at a practical level, their results seemed irrelevant.[17]

This difference in basic orientations did not mean, however, that the social relevance of psychology or the need for quantification were ignored by German-speaking psychologists. In fact, it has been seen that an important factor in the genesis of the various subdisciplines of the field was the recognition that psychology can and ought to be applied to the solution of practical problems.[18] And although there was a deep-seated anti-utilitarian bias in the academic culture of Germany in the early twentieth century that was both ideologically and philosophically conditioned, many psychologists found themselves addressing issues of public concern, in education, industry, social work, and crime. This development was partly the result of the keen interest shown by the pedagogues, teachers, criminologists, social workers, and industrialists in the applied potential of laboratory work. The outcome was interdisciplinary collaboration that had immediate practical consequences.

Thus it was that early in his career Stern worked with the famous criminologist Friedrich von Lißt of the University of Berlin to test the reliability of eyewitness testimony. And it was this involvement in *Aussagepsychologie*, or the psychology of testimony, that led him to the editorship, along with Otto Lipmann, of the *Zeitschrift für angewandte Psychologie und psychologische Sammelforschung* in 1907. This publication was the journalistic organ of the Institute for Applied Psychology that had been founded a year earlier in Berlin.

Applied psychology in its various forms was a thriving business within the German psychological profession. Stern himself was one of its foremost practitioners, having played a pioneering role in the development of the special sciences of forensic, pedagogical, aptitude, and vocational psychology. His reputation as the formulator of the IQ was well-known.[19] Moreover, his appointment to the University of Hamburg came about because of the practical needs of that great commercial city. Hamburg also had an extremely active school reform movement.[20] It was with the help of the highly progressive teachers' association of the city that Stern was able to develop the so-called Hamburg Method of selection for schools, which won international recognition for its thoroughness and high rate of success, particularly in the diagnosis of gifted and talented children.

The work of Stern and others like him points to a significant fact: in a modernizing society a status-based characterization of individuals no longer suffices; hence the need for a scientific psychology that is relevant for social and social engineering purposes. In the United States the practical requirements of the state and educational system from early on played a critical role in the instrumental character of American psychology. While "pure science" and cognition psychology had its defenders, particularly among those grouped around Edward Titchener, the technocratic orientation was far more widespread and less controversial among American psychologists. Even those involved in traditional psychophysics or in the field of development (child and adolescent psychology) were keenly aware of the social implications of their work. In Germany, this was also true. However, as Mitchell Ash has pointed out, there were important underlying distinctions between the American and German discourses. "The differences appeared in the purposes, the referents, and the preferred styles of quantification."[21] Thus in America there was an increasing preference for "group data," studies that focused less on the individual than on the variations or differences among groups or across individuals. In terms of methodology, this meant a comprehensive substitution of descriptive and qualitative data by statistical data, which could be effectively employed, for example, by education administrators.

In Germany, however, the normative importance of the individual was not eclipsed by group standards. Thus individual differences and requirements in the classroom continued to play a big role in German "experimental pedagogy" (the psychology of learning and teaching), and the practical requirements of the administration were balanced by idealistic and humanist concerns regarding the unfolding of individual personality, as expressed in the traditional concept of *Bildung*, or personal self-cultivation. As a consequence, German psychology was also more concerned with the individual as a "subject" than as an "object."

As Stern vehemently argued throughout his career, psychology as a discipline had become far too influenced by the methods of the natural sciences and the experiments and measurements that were reified at the expense of the individual. It discounted individual attitude; human beings responded or reacted in a measurable way to measurable stimuli (behaviorism). He, on the other hand, felt that it was extremely vital to recognize human experience and its meaning connotations. Psychology for him was the science of the person having experience or capable of having experience. It looked at human beings as subjects, not objects. And he noted, "In the contemporary research a distinction is drawn between a 'subjectless psychology' (which would turn the fertile working concept of analysis into a principle of being) and a 'subject psychology' that enlists my sympathies."[22] This is not to say that he rejected the rational, analytical, experimental and quantitative point of view. He fully accepted the findings and methods of "exact" psychology. However, he felt that these should be given their "due weight and application" in a fundamentally subject-oriented system, one that he called "personalistic psychology."

However, there is no doubt that it was as a practical psychologist that Stern built his international reputation. The book that received widest notice in the English-speaking world was his child psychology,[23] which had important implications for educational and vocational psychology as well as intelligence testing. But he himself regarded such work as secondary to his main pursuit, which was the development of a *Weltanschauung* that would at a metaphysical level transcend the familiar dualisms of philosophy: mind and body, whole and aggregate, teleology and mechanics, nature and nurture. All the special sciences of human beings, which would include not just psychology, but biology, physiology and the cultural-historical sciences would receive, within this system, their theoretical coherence. Psychology was simply the application within a special area of a general ontology that he called Critical Personalism. The basic ideas of Critical Personalism were outlined in a three-volume work, *Person and Thing*, the first volume of which appeared in 1906 and the last in 1924.

A critical evaluation of this philosophy cannot be addressed at present. In the final analysis, its purpose was to reorient philosophical discourse from a concern with epistemological issues to ethical and existential ones. The central philosophical question was not that of Mind and Matter, but Person and Thing, Teleology and Mechanics. It is not whether consciousness exists, but whether there are purposive units in this world that have intrinsic value, i.e., Persons, as opposed to Things, non-purposive units which derive their direction and value from outside.

Stern defined a Person as an entity that, despite its manifold parts and partial functions, forms a real, unique and intrinsically valuable unity that is also purposive and self-initiated in its activity. In contrast, a Thing is merely a "pseudo-entity," resoluble into constituent parts, an aggregate that is subject to the extrinsic force of mechanical laws and is not self-determined. As a *weltanschauliche* philosophy in search of a unified world-view, Critical Personalism aimed at transcending this existential dichotomy by incorporating Things within Persons. The existence of mechanical processes in the world is beyond dispute. However, a Person, as a unity in multiplicity (*unitas multiplex*) manifests its unitary nature and efficiency in its parts by bringing them into definite relations with one another, so that what, from the point of view of the whole, is personal, from the point of view of the parts, is impersonal and mechanical. In other words, mechanical laws functioned within the context of immanent purposes ("teleomechanics").

The most significant consequence of Critical Personalism for psychological thought was its reconciliation of a subject psychology that emphasized the centrality of the experiencing subject with the special findings of the "mechanistic" and "elementaristic" scientific approach. It was intended to be a "critical" Personalism as opposed to the "naive" Personalism of conventional theological thinking that cannot successfully stand up to scientific objections. Its aim was to maintain the personalistic standpoint sans a naive Personalism by subordinating into its system the irrefutable evidence of (impersonalistic) scientific analysis.

Stern, therefore, developed a psychology that was fundamentally antimechanistic and teleological but which made room for mechanical explanations in context. The methods and findings of natural science had their place, and Stern carried out many experiment-based investigations throughout his career with a thoroughness and attention to detail that was commendable by any standard. He was acknowledged for his mastery of the technical aspects of the field: quantification, measurements, instruments, tables, and questionnaires; all had a role to play for this philosopher psychologist. He was the inventor of the *Tonvariator*, an acoustic apparatus to measure changes in auditory perception that came to be widely used in psychological laboratories prior to the introduction of electronic equipment. Günther Anders gives us a very insightful comment about his father's scientific work:

> The most astonishing fact was that although not a natural scientist by disposition, he [Stern] was able to satisfy all the requirements of experimental work and even pioneer special areas of investigation for the science. He was, if one might use the expression, a "Multi-Specialist." What was even more astonishing was that his Hegelian passion for the "Whole" and his skepticism regarding the results of experiments never inclined him to carry out his experiments superficially. He was scrupulous to the extreme. However, although he was rigorous in his experimental work, he was also insistent on limiting its value [*Werteinklammern*], observing that experiments can only discover relations; *no experiment in the world can ever prove that "reaction" is the essence of man*. (italics mine)[24]

The last statement was a clear and obvious indictment of behaviorism. Behaviorism focused on psychological variables and their quantification and eliminated from its investigations any reference to "self" or "I," which smacked of metaphysics. This was completely unacceptable to Stern:

> We define psychology "as a science of the person having experience or capable of having experience." The immediate subject-matter of psychology, experience, is therefore to be interpreted in terms of its matrix, the unitary, goal-directed person.[25]

It is not surprising that Stern made few converts to his personalistic system in America, where behaviorism was all the rage. Even those appreciative of Stern's ideas felt their theoretical underpinnings to be far too metaphysical and Germanic. R. B. MacLeod, a colleague of the Gestalt psychologist Wolfgang Köhler at Swarthmore who was no doubt familiar with German psychology, made the following observation:

> To recognize goal-directedness as psychologically contained within the behavior of persons is one thing; to interpret this directedness in terms of transcendent goals which are logically implied by the behavior is an altogether different matter. The one is psychology, the other is metaphysics.[26]

In other words, it was not as a philosopher that Stern found his niche at Duke. But he fitted in with the department well, and there was some understanding for his intellectual point of view. His expertise in child, vocational, forensic and aptitude psychology was put to good use, and he gave numerous public lectures in these fields. His colleagues also appreciated his modesty and the obvious sincerity of his convictions, familiar or alien. His students held him in high regard. Among them he was known for the liveliness and carefully devised simplicity of his lectures, as well as for his *sympathische* and friendly personality. For example, he deliberately eschewed the role of the "superior" German professor. His courses were taught in German, and the classes averaged less than ten graduate students. Perhaps with such a captive audience his personalistic psychology (which he taught during his second semester at Duke) got the hearing it deserved.

The years at Duke were not unhappy, although the eldest daughter Hilde had to be placed in a sanitarium for a period, a source of constant sorrow and concern for the family. Friendships accumulated, and the language problem became less taxing. His *General Psychology* found an English translator and was published by Macmillan in 1938. He began fresh work on aspects of child psychology, and spent the summer of 1936 lecturing at Harvard, about which he commented, "This old university has its own atmosphere, which reminds one of the best of the European traditions."[27] The scholarly life of research and teaching had picked up again on alien soil. His premature death on 27 March 1938 was felt acutely by all. President Few reported, "We had all come to be attached to him and Mrs. Stern. Our whole community is deeply distressed by his sudden death."[28] The funeral rites were conducted by Rabbi Bernard Zigler of Chapel Hill and Professor Alban Widgery of the Duke philosophy department. Services were held at the university chapel.

To look at Stern's life from the perspective of his last years, from his dismissal in 1933 till his death, is to get a limited picture of the man. But these were not insignificant events in his life. His eviction and forced migration was a traumatic experience. He was, after all, 63 years old in 1933, and at the height of his career and reputation. As with many other refugee intellectuals and academics, his emigration assured safety and survival, but also a decline in status and income. His American audience did not accord him that special place of honor that he was accustomed to in Hamburg, as a member of the German academic community. The English language was a handicap he never successfully overcame, and he felt this hardship acutely; one can never underestimate the loss of language to one who lives by the lectern and the pen. Most of all, American psychology represented the kind of "wrong thinking" he had been struggling against throughout his career. He worried that the IQ tests he had conceived had been mechanized in America, whereas for him the IQ gave only a very partial and limited understanding of intelligence or the individual. While in the United States, he earnestly wished to undo the harm he believed done by his own earlier invention of the IQ.

The discordant note struck by the last years of his career, however, stood in contrast to a by-and-large harmonious and successful life. The Germany that eventually ousted him had also given him opportunities. Günther Anders remarked that before the catastrophe of 1933 his father had been a lucky man, lucky in the sense that he had achieved almost all he had set himself out to do as a writer, thinker and scholar. Anders further noted that there was also a fortuitous element in his career, because he was able to achieve professional success without having to undergo the "formality" of conversion. His father's modesty prevented him from recognizing the exceptionality of his situation. Not only that, it proved to him that dishonorable and evil motives had no place in the world. "Because he was modest, he overestimated the world; because he was generous, he underestimated its evil."[29] This "innocence" was reflected in his philosophy, in which there was no consideration of evil, power, death, and violence. As Fichte put it, ultimately the kind of philosophy one adopts depends on the kind of man one is.

Stern was an optimist. "Father's goodness and optimism made it very difficult for him to deal with things that could not be accommodated into his positive world-view," wrote Eva Stern.[30] This was partly a matter of temperament, but it also reflected his nineteenth-century heritage. He was no positivist, to be sure, but he held a belief in progress that was a part of nineteenth-century bourgeois thought and which rested on the achievements of the natural sciences. He firmly believed that all problems and conflicts were capable of resolution, if one took the proper philosophical position. Günther Anders, who changed his last name as a symbolic rejection of his father's philosophy,[31] thought his father deluded himself. As a philosophy, Personalism was a defense of individual autonomy and value in a society that tried to treat human beings as objects and things. Yet because it was so abstract, it was not a compelling humanitarianism. It certainly did very little for Germany's Jews.

Anders felt that politically, his father was uncritical and naive. His initiatives in the area of school reform, vocational psychology and the like bespoke of a real faith in the bourgeois political and social order, which to him was the basis for individual and social good. His politics was bourgeois liberal. He supported the Kaiserreich while it lasted, and after the war, the German Democratic Party (Deutsche Demokratische Partei or DDP). He was no jingoist, but he shared the exaggerated patriotism of most Germans at the outbreak of World War I. During that time he even dropped his middle name, which was Louis, because he said that he did not want to be known by two foreign names. He insisted that his family live on the rations allotted to it when most other families tried to find other sources of food, and changed his mind only after a colleague of his died from malnutrition. Eva Stern, who became a Zionist and eventually migrated to Israel, was critical of her father's faith: "Somehow the great psychologist and philosopher could not bring himself to face in time the serious threat which would cut off his roots later on in a sudden and brutal way."[32]

His roots were Jewish, but it was a highly assimilated Jewish family that he came from. His grandfather on his mother's side was Sigismund Stern (1812–1867), who was a leader of the Berlin Reform movement and an important if controversial personality among German Jewry. Stern recalled that although the family was Jewish, it felt itself to be completely German (*vollständig zum Deutschtum gehörig*). Within the family religious customs were no longer followed, although prayer and confirmation classes were important and these had a very strong impact on Stern. However, he acknowledged that his interest for religion was mostly intellectual. The emotional side of the religious experience was alien to him.[33]

Stern considered himself a German who happened to be of the Jewish faith. All the same, he remained unwilling to convert, even though his career would have profited from such an act. The bias against Jews in the upper ranks of academia in imperial Germany is well documented. Fewer than 3 percent of full professors were Jews. It took him ten years, despite a very impressive academic record, to be promoted to associate professor in Breslau. Hamburg was a rare exception in its willingness to give him a full professorship. The same position in Breslau, for example, had been made conditional on his conversion. Despite these obstacles, for the greater part of his life he remained convinced, like many assimilated German Jews, that anti-Semitism was an anachronism that would disappear in a progressive Germany. In holding this view he was not being particularly naive or singular. His birth coincided with the time when Jews achieved full legal emancipation, and although the Kaiserreich witnessed bursts of popular anti-Semitism, the latter was not a significant political force. German anti-Semitism seemed surmountable and weak compared to Dreyfus France and pogrom infested Russia. Stern's attitude was typical of many German Jews of the upper and middle classes. The process of embourgeoisment that, for many German Jews, determined the road to respectability and a stake and place in society had a widespread impact.

Anders recalls that his father was so assimilated that he felt affronted by the presence of the less-assimilated Eastern European Jews. As a teenager Anders's closest friend was a highly gifted and well-read Ukrainian Jew. This friendship disturbed his father greatly:

> My father was concerned that he might find himself in association with East European Jews. Not only was he unhappy about my friendship with this young man (without whose influence I never would have become a writer), he was downright indignant about it. The situation led to scenes between us, and even a long period of estrangement.[34]

Religion was never a significant force in Stern's life, except when it was made an issue by society. His refusal to convert was the threshold of his tolerance for a discriminatory society. It was the point beyond which he would not go. "He held on to a minimum, but it was only a minimum," was Anders's assessment.[35] Mostly he remained diffident in the face of open confrontations, even ambivalent toward Jews less passive than he. In Hamburg, where a large section of the student body became rightist after the war and then very quickly Nazified, and where racist and hate-mongering professors were allowed to slander with impunity,[36] Stern seems to have practiced a policy of conscious detachment and self-effacement. In response to certain acts of anti-Semitism at German universities, Stern wrote his philosopher friend and lifelong correspondent Jonas Cohn, "We Jewish academics must out of necessity hold back from any initiative, especially when our kind is prone to agitation [*nostra res agitur*]."[37]

Eight months passed before Stern would write to Cohn again. By this time, he was ready to leave for Holland. The letters to Cohn that follow are revealing in their silence about the recent turn of events. The decision to leave Germany had already been made, even though a close friend suggested that he "wait out" the Nazi regime. To this friend he replied, in a rare admission of his inner turmoil, "My *Weltanschauung* has collapsed."[38] Looking back on those years, Anders concluded that his father had positively repressed (*positiv verdrängt*) the coming of National Socialism. "He couldn't risk his view of the world, which fell apart in 1933."[39] While this was understandable, it seems astonishing that he never truly came to terms with the political events of his time. As a philosopher and humanitarian, he must have been aware of the need and responsibility to do so. As a psychologist, he ought to have tried to clarify the psychopathology of Nazism. As a member of the intelligentsia, it behooved him to rethink his world-view in the light of recent events.

Such a reappraisal never came. Through all the years of his exile, which in fact had begun in Germany, he doggedly persisted on completing his earlier projects and plans. In this he showed a discipline of purpose that was both admirable and blinkered. The American psychologist Gordon Allport, who had studied with Stern, wrote, "Already at the age of nineteen he had planned the intellectual road that he would travel, and, never doubting, he pursued it to the day of his death."[40] In America, he strove earnestly to introduce and popularize his personalistic psychology, and was deeply gratified by the appearance in February 1938 of the English translation of his *Allgemeine Psychologie*. To the end, therefore, he clung to the intellectual optimism that he had learned to live by, although inwardly he must have been troubled. And while he was grateful to America, it was for him a temporary refuge. There is no doubt that he hoped to go back to Germany as soon as political conditions permitted. It was ironical that he was spared a real test of his faith by virtue of his premature death. Whether his unflagging optimism would have survived the destruction of European Jewry remains an open question.

Notes

1. For a sample of the works available in English, see D. Fleming and B. Bailyn, eds., *The Intellectual Migration: Germany and America, 1930–1960* (Cambridge, Mass., 1969); L. C. Coser, *Refugee Scholars in America: Their Impact and Their Experiences* (New Haven, Conn., 1984); A. Heilbut, *Exiled in Paradise: German Refugee Artists and Intellectuals in America from the 1930s to the Present* (New York, 1983); and J. C. Jackman and C. M. Borden, eds., *The Muses Flee Hitler: Cultural Transfer and Adaptation, 1930–1945* (Washington, D.C., 1983).
2. For example, see M. Ash and A. Söllner eds., *Forced Migration and Scientific Change: Emigré German Speaking Scholars and Scientists after 1933* (Cambridge, Mass., 1996); and U. Teichler and H. Waser, eds., *German and American Universities: Mutual Influences, Past and Present*, Werkstattberichte, no. 36 (Kassel, 1992).
3. M. Ash and A. Söllner, Introduction, in Ash and Söllner, eds., *Forced Migration and Scientific Change*, 1–9.
4. In terms of the number of Jewish academics, Hamburg was at par with Göttingen and Cologne. See B. Vogel, "Anpassung und Widerstand: Das Verhältnis Hamburger Hochschullehrer zum Staat, 1919 bis 1945," *Zeitgeschichte* 16 (1988): 12.
5. For a full account of the dismissals at the University of Hamburg, see E. Krause, L. Huber, and H. Fischer, eds., *Hochschulalltag im Dritten Reich. Die Hamburger Universität 1933–45* (Hamburg, 1991), passim.
6. Helmut Moser, "Zur Entwicklung der akademischen Psychologie in Hamburg bis 1945," in Krause, Huber, and Fischer, eds. *Hochschulalltag im Dritten Reich*, 496.
7. Günther Anders, "Bild Meines Vaters," in W. Stern, *Allgemeine Psychologie auf personalisticher Grundlage* (The Hague, 1950), xxiv.
8. Letter from Stern to Jonas Cohn, 19 Dec. 1933, MSS Division, Hebrew University at Jerusalem, William Stern Collection, MS Varia 431.
9. E. Michaelis-Stern, "Erinnerungen an meine Eltern," in W. Deutsch, ed., *Über die verborgene Aktualität von William Stern* (Braunschweig, 1989), 116.
10. Ibid.
11. Anders, "Bild Meines Vaters," xxiii.
12. Quoted in W. E. King, "Duke University Opens Its Doors," in H. A. Landsberger and C. E. Schweitzer, eds., *They Fled Hitler's Germany and Found Refuge in North Carolina* (Chapel Hill, N.C., 1996), 29–30.
13. Ibid., 25–29, 30.
14. Letter from Stern to Jonas Cohn, 5 Sept. 1934, MSS Division, Hebrew University at Jerusalem, William Stern Collection, MS Varia 431.
15. Ibid.
16. During the Third Reich, the military's demand for trained psychologists required a revision of the state and doctoral examination systems that until 1941 allowed for professional degrees in psychology only in a few universities of the Reich. Elsewhere one had to sit for philosophy or pedagogy where the psychological training was more philosophical and theoretical in its orientation than diagnostic, a key requirement of the military. See U. Geuter, "German Psychology during the Nazi Period," in M. Ash and W. Woodward, eds., *Psychology in Twentieth-Century Thought and Society* (Cambridge, 1987), 178.
17. K. Danziger, "Social Context and Investigative Practice in Early Twentieth Century Psychology," in Ash and Woodward, eds., *Psychology in Twentieth-Century Thought and Society*, 13–35.
18. S. Jaeger, "Zur Herausbildung von Praxisfeldern der Psychologie bis 1933," in M. Ash and U. Geuter, eds., *Geschichte der deutschen Psychologie im 20. Jahrhundert* (Opladen, 1985), 83–84 and passim.

19. Alfred Binet had constructed a series of tests to measure, applied particularly to young people. In 1911 he developed the concept of the mental age, the age at which a child is functioning intellectually regardless of his or her chronological age. In 1912 Stern pointed out that by dividing the mental age by the chronological age, the IQ could be determined to indicate a child's relative standing in comparison with other children, at any particular chronological age.
20. For a history of the Hamburg school reform movement and its historical-organizational roots, the reader is referred to H. Weimer, *Geschichte der Pädagogik* (Berlin, 1976).
21. M. Ash, "Emigré Psychologists after 1933: The Cultural Coding of Scientific and Professional Practices," in Ash and Söllner, eds., *Forced Migration and Scientific Change after 1933*, 119.
22. W. Stern, "William Stern," in C. Murchison, ed., *History of Psychology in Autobiography* (Worcester, Mass., 1930), 346–47.
23. The first edition of this book appeared in 1914. The third edition was translated into English and appeared under the title *Psychology of Early Childhood up to the Sixth Year of Age* (London, 1924).
24. Anders, "Bild Meines Vaters," xxvi.
25. W. Stern, *General Psychology from the Personalistic Standpoint* (New York, 1938), viii.
26. R. B. MacLeod, "William Stern," *The Psychological Review* 45 (1938): 349.
27. Letter from Stern to Jonas Cohn, summer 1936, MSS Division, Hebrew University at Jerusalem, William Stern Collection, MS Varia 431.
28. Quoted in W. King, *If Gargoyles Could Talk: Sketches of Duke University* (Durham, N.C., 1997), 136.
29. Anders, "Bild Meines Vaters," xxv.
30. Michaelis-Stern, "Erinnerungen an meine Eltern," 114.
31. "Anders" in German translates as "other." Although he loved his father deeply, the son felt that they came from two different worlds. He was the "other" Stern.
32. E. Michaelis-Stern, "William Stern, 1871–1938: The Man and His Achievements," *Leo Baeck Institute Yearbook* 17 (1972): 145.
33. W. Stern, *Anfänge der Reifezeit. Ein Knabetagebuch in psychologischer Bearbeitung* (Leipzig, 1925), 111–12.
34. Quoted in M. Greffrath, *Die Zerstörung einer Zukunft. Gespräche mit emigrierten Sozialwissenschaftlern* (Hamburg, 1979), 20.
35. Ibid., 21.
36. The geography professor Siegfried Passarge's "anti-Semitism of the lectern" is a case in point. For more details on the Passarge incident, see G. Giles, *Students and National Socialism in Germany* (Princeton, N.J., 1985). Giles has argued that although the University of Hamburg was set up in the liberal atmosphere of the newly born Weimar Republic, the attitudes of the professoriate were generally antidemocratic and inclined to a tacit support of right-wing groups.
37. Letter from Stern to Jonas Cohn, 6 Jan. 1933, MSS Division, Hebrew University at Jerusalem, William Stern Collection, MS Varia 431.
38. Michaelis-Stern, "Stern," 147.
39. Greffrath, *Zerstörung einer Zukunft*, 21.
40. G. Allport, "The Personalistic Psychology of William Stern," in B. B. Wolman, ed., *Historical Roots of Contemporary Psychology* (New York, 1968), 27.

Chapter 6

EXCLUSIONS AND INCLUSIONS OF A COSMOPOLITAN PHILOSOPHER

The Case of Ernst Cassirer

Michael Hänel

Speaking at the ceremonies commemorating the fourth anniversary of the graduate faculty of the former "University in Exile" and the New School for Social Research, Alvin Johnson expressed the view that "scholarship never has been bound to a particular environment."[1] With these words Johnson sought to stress that the essence of scholarship was cosmopolitan and universalist and that it therefore transcended the boundaries of nationality and culture. Johnson concluded that "a university, that is, a collective attempt to make the universality of culture productive and useful, can hardly be in exile."[2]

This was not, however, a view with which the philosopher Ernst Cassirer would have readily concurred. Born in Breslau in 1874 and one of the first German-Jewish intellectuals to leave Germany in 1933, Cassirer most likely would have regarded such a view as an oversimplification and would have added that being rooted in a certain culture or nation does not contradict universality as an aim or "ideal task." For while Cassirer was deeply rooted in German culture, he remained profoundly humanist and cosmopolitan in his general outlook and saw no contradiction whatsoever between the highest values of German culture as embodied in the lives of Lessing, Mendelssohn, Kant, and Goethe and those of the European humanist tradition with its origins in the culture of classical antiquity. From Cassirer's perspective, Hitler represented not the logical culmination but rather an aberration of German history culture. As he explained to Henry Pachter, his erstwhile neighbor in New York City: "You know Mr. Pachter, this Hitler is an error [*Irrtum*] of History; he does not belong in German history at all. And therefore he will perish." To which Pachter laconically added: "This is what all decent people felt at the time."[3]

To understand Cassirer's attitude toward the profound changes that were taking place in his own life as well as his confidence in the future, it is necessary to take a closer look at Cassirer's path through imperial Germany and the Weimar Republic. It is also necessary to reflect upon the reception of Cassirer and his works by his contemporaries after the end of World War II, because this will shed light on the conditions of publicity for "philosophical" perspectives or even "world-views." What this will reveal is that Cassirer was decidedly democratic from the beginning of his academic career and that, as the importance and influence of democrats in the Weimar Republic diminished, he became more and more an "outsider." But in a way this was nothing new, for he had already been an outsider because he was a Jew. His books were to be banned from the shelves of the libraries and university seminars throughout Germany in the twelve years of the Third Reich.[4]

The intellectual climate of the defeated Germany was not particularly hospitable to a philosophy that could not be easily fit into the broader spectrum of "political" or "abstract" points of view. Broadly speaking, the Cold War confrontation prolonged the need for a decision between "left" and "right." Those not willing to sacrifice their interests to political "world-views" sought to escape into the field of what they thought to be the neutral positions of "historicist" or "scientific" philosophy. "Liberal" positions were clearly a minority in postwar German philosophy, despite many declarations about the need for a "new humanism."[5] Cassirer, who remained true to a tradition of neo-Kantian idealism, had little in common with the more popular and mainstream positivistic, Marxist, or existentialist modes of thought. Cassirer's "historical" works were too "humanist" in their perspectives.

While these works remained a source of interest for historians of philosophy on account of their remarkable erudition, his systematic philosophy attracted little attention outside a small circle of specialists until the 1980s.[6] What Cassirer wrote about culture in general in his *Essay on Man* thus holds true for the fate of his own work: "In order to possess the world of culture we must incessantly reconquer it by historical recollection."[7] From such a perspective, the act of writing history is a struggle to preserve ideas and ideals that are in danger of being forgotten. This conception sheds light on Cassirer's early "nonpolitical" writings in imperial Germany as well as on his works during the Weimar Republic. It is the aim of this essay to show that Cassirer was not only a defender of the liberal and humanist ideals that would eventually lose out in Germany but also that this made his integration in the countries of his exile easier. This essay will examine how Cassirer himself experienced the changes that were forced upon him and how this experience was then reflected in his work.

* * *

Like many other German-Jewish intellectuals in imperial Germany, Ernst Cassirer was an advocate of cosmopolitan ideals and a supporter of the liberal movement. In his case, these ideals were grounded in his understanding of Kant as well as in his interest in Renaissance individualism. At the same time, however, he saw himself as a German patriot in the classical sense of the word, something that is clearly distinct from the nationalist abuse of the term. The same Enlightenment position also helped shape his attitude toward religion. His wife Toni Cassirer reported in her memoir that he counted among his friends "as many Jews as non-Jews and it would never have come to his mind to research for someone's descent."[8] In his 1978 study of Cassirer's political attitudes, David Lipton claimed that for Cassirer "being a German was of primary importance and his religion merely modified the type of German he was."[9] Yet this never led Cassirer to deny his Jewish origins.

Cassirer's first step into the public political arena was taken in 1912, when he became a member of the League for International Understanding (Verband für internationale Verständigung), a moderate pacifist association founded in 1911 with connections to French and American peace-associations. In 1913 the organization had 350 members, including renowned politicians and scholars like Friedrich Naumann, Hugo Preuß, Rudolf Breitscheid, Ernst Troeltsch, and Max Weber.[10] Cassirer's commitment to international peace was demonstrated in 1914 when he was awarded the Kuno-Fischer Gold medal by the Heidelberg Academy and requested that he be given the bronze medal instead so that the difference in monetary value—3,000 Reichsmark—could be sent to the Red Cross.[11]

At the time Cassirer was still a lecturer at the University of Berlin. He remained at this relatively undistinguished academic rank until 1918 despite the international recognition he had received from the publication of the first two volumes of his *The Problem of Knowledge* in 1906/1907 and his book on *Substance and Function* in 1910. A barometer of his growing reputation was a two-term invitation to Harvard University in 1913, which Cassirer declined out of consideration for his family. Only much later did the long-term consequences of this decision become clear. When he was searching for new career options in the United States from his Swedish exile in 1940, his friends were told that no offers from Harvard would be forthcoming because of his earlier refusal to come there.[12]

Cassirer never seemed to have participated in the surge of nationalist feeling that swept through Germany after the outbreak of World War I. In surprising contrast to his academic teachers Hermann Cohen and Paul Natorp,[13] Cassirer remained skeptical of the legitimacy, sense, and aims of the war. According to his daughter Anne Appelbaum, her family never "flew the flag" after German victories. Upon asking her mother why they had no flag, she was reminded that victories also mean blood and death and that the soldiers of the Allies had parents too. "I don't fly the flag when someone dies. I am not for war" her mother concluded, "and your father is not for war either."[14] But it was not merely because of his pacifism that Cassirer felt obliged to defend his views during the war.

In 1916 a fellow "neo-Kantian" Bruno Bauch launched an attack against the core of Cohen's and Cassirer's self-esteem as Germans as well as against their philosophical integrity. While already involved in several disputes about the appropriate interpretation of Jewish religion and the place of Jews in Germany, Cohen was defamed by Bauch in an article in the prestigious *Kant-Studien* as a "foreigner" incapable of fully understanding the philosophy of a "German" thinker like Kant. Accompanied by other anti-Semitic attacks from extreme nationalists, Bauch's article triggered a bitter fight that eventually led to his resignation from the editorial board of the *Kant-Studien*. To be sure, the leaders of the Kant Society (Kant-Gesellschaft), Hans Vaihinger and Arthur Liebert, tried to mediate between the two parties, but in the end they did more harm than good. Cassirer's answer to Bauch, entitled "Zum Begriff der Nation: Eine Erwiderung auf den Aufsatz von Bruno Bauch," was never published, and Bauch's supporters were able to embellish their picture of a Jewish conspiracy by claiming that his resignation from the *Kant-Studien* was necessary because he was not willing to accept a "board of Jewish censors."[15]

Concerned about what might happen if the forces of German nationalism continued to abuse the best traditions in Germany for shortsighted political purposes, Cassirer began to write a collection of essays on great German personalities that was published in 1916 under the title *Freiheit und Form*. Here he not only analyzed the concept of freedom as articulated by Leibniz, Kant, Goethe, and others, but he also stressed the universal and cosmopolitan character of this concept when combined with concepts of responsibility and equality. Several passages from his introduction, written in June 1916, may very well have anticipated the fight with Bauch that was to erupt only weeks later. For as Cassirer argued, the German traditions of freedom can only truly be understood in terms of the liberation of man and not from a narrowly "chauvinist" point of view.[16]

It is not known how Cassirer became aware of the social and political realities in Germany or if he was member of a political party. Still it is clear that he was debating problems of great political, social, and cultural consequence with other prominent intellectuals of his times. In Berlin he took part—along with the likes of Ernst Troeltsch, Walter Rathenau, the historian Gustav Mayer, and the sociologist Alfred Vierkandt—in Friedrich Meinecke's "Sunday walks."[17] In May 1919 he signed a petition in support of the Munich "revolutionary" Eugen Leviné, appealing to the court for a delay in the proceedings against him until after the political situation calmed down. The telegram also carried the signatures of Albert Einstein, Hugo Haase, and Maximilian Harden, among others.[18] Despite their appeal, Leviné was sentenced to death on 3 June for his involvement in the revolutionary government and executed three days later.[19]

At first sight Cassirer's commitment to a clearly "anti-bourgeois" revolutionary writer seems somewhat surprising. The scant sources available, however, indicate that even before the war he had become friends with Kurt Eisner, later one of the leading persons in the short-lived Bavarian "republic" of 1918/19. Eisner had studied in Berlin and had then worked for several news agencies and newspapers. After 1892 Eisner's work occasionally led him to Marburg, where he made friends with Hermann Cohen and was apparently influenced by Cohen's philosophy. The strong influence that neo-Kantian ethics exercised upon many socialist and Social Democratic theorists of the early twentieth century stands in sharp contrast to the image of neo-Kantianism as merely an abstract collection of "professorial systems," estranged from and not interested in the realities of everyday life. Eisner, an experienced journalist, was not the only person who believed that "ethical socialism" was well suited as a guide for practical political activity.[20]

In Berlin Cassirer and his family were also part of the larger circle of the extended Cassirer family, which included the publisher Bruno Cassirer and the renowned sponsor and promoter of modern arts, Paul Cassirer. Ernst's cousin Paul, later a member of the Independent Social Democratic Party (Unabhängige Sozialdemokratische Partei), was the center of a circle that constantly discussed not just art but politics as well. Among his friends were Walter Rathenau and Harry Graf Kessler. No doubt this provided Cassirer, who also refereed manuscripts for his cousin's publishing house, with another first-hand source of information about German politics.[21] His involvement in circles like these might very well have encouraged Cassirer to believe that acceptance and discussion were still possible across the artificial boundaries of "schools," parties, and academic disciplines, and—what was even more important—without prejudice. For even if the anti-Semitic propaganda of World War I had done a great deal to renew and confirm certain stereotypes about the Jew, this did not erode Cassirer's belief in the ultimate goodness of humanity.

From 1916 until the end of the war Cassirer served in the war office, where he worked for the French section of the press office. According to his wife, he immensely disliked this activity and the systematic deception of the German people. At the same time, he had access to confidential information that led him to believe that Germany was losing the war long before this dawned on the vast majority of his contemporaries.[22] Still, he performed his duties well, and the experience in general helped increase his sensitivity to the tactics of deception and may very well have provided him with his first insight into the modern techniques of myth-creation.

* * *

Cassirer had almost come to terms with his situation as an "eternal *Privatdozent*" when he was appointed as a full professor at the new University of Hamburg in 1919.[23] The years in Hamburg not only marked the height of his career but were also a period of relative security. At Hamburg Cassirer was able to develop his philosophy in new directions. Here he published the three volumes of his *Philosophy of Symbolic Forms* as well as numerous articles and essays on such diverse subjects as religion, language, psychology, physics, and history.[24] He also made the acquaintance of Aby Warburg and the project known as the "Kulturwissenschaftliche Bibliothek."[25] From the beginning Cassirer was excited about the project and what it meant for his own intellectual development. Fritz Saxl, assistant director of the Warburg Library after Aby Warburg's death, remembered that

> on a day memorable in the annals of the Warburg Institute, Cassirer came to see the library collected by professor Warburg over a period of about thirty years. Warburg's nerves had broken down in 1920 under the strain of postwar events, and he had been sent to Switzerland for recovery. Being in charge of the library, I showed Cassirer around.... Cassirer understood at once. Yet, when he was ready to leave, he said, in the kind and clear manner so typical of him: "This library is dangerous. I shall either have to avoid it altogether or imprison myself here for years. The philosophical problems involved are close to my own, but the concrete historical material which Warburg has collected is overwhelming." Thus he left me bewildered. In one hour this man had understood more of the essential ideas embodied in that library than anybody I had met before.[26]

Warburg's project profoundly influenced Cassirer's philosophy, and Cassirer's philosophy in turn stimulated the studies of the "Warburg circle."[27] At the same time, a deep bond of friendship developed between Cassirer and Warburg. Ties between the two men became stronger after Cassirer visited Warburg in 1924, where Warburg's illness was being treated by Ludwig Binswanger, a famous psychiatrist of the time.[28] Not only did the two men immediately understand each other's way of thinking, but the fact that they were both Jews no doubt strengthened their friendship and their resolve to fight against racism and blind nationalism.[29]

In Hamburg Cassirer also made friends with the psychologist and philosopher William Stern. As in his relationship with Warburg, Cassirer and Stern constantly exchanged scholarly views and occasionally worked together, as in the organization of the Twelfth Congress of the German Society for Psychology in 1931 that Cassirer used as a forum to present his important essay on language and the construction of the world of objects.[30] Stern, famous for his own work on the psychology of children, was later forced to emigrate, as was Cassirer. Before Cassirer ever came to Hamburg, Stern had warned him of the anti-Semitic tendencies at the university, but fortunately the clamor of right-wing students temporarily abated in the early and mid-1920s. In 1921, however, Cassirer had clashed with the geographer Siegfried Passarge, a follower of the extreme nationalist German Racist Protective and Resistance League (Deutschvölkischer Schutz- und Trutzbund). Passarge propagated racist and especially anti-Semitic myths in his lectures and was convinced of the direct determination of the individual through race. When personally confronting Cassirer, however, Passarge tried to exempt his colleague from the allegedly base features of the Jewish race by allowing for exceptions in the case of the "bedouin" tribe of Jews. Cassirer responded that for him the whole theory was "complete nonsense."[31]

From Cassirer's writings on political philosophy, freedom, and the importance of the individual, one can easily conclude that Cassirer found his political home in the left-liberal German Democratic Party (Deutsche Demokratische Partei).[32] That he identified with the basic values of German democracy is beyond dispute. In his book on Kant, for instance, Cassirer wrote about the great Königsberg sage's attitude toward the French Revolution, arguing that in the ideals of 1789 Kant had seen "the promise of the realization of the pure laws of reason."[33] And, as Cassirer emphasized, Kant had come to the conclusion, that only "through the medium of society could the ideal task of moral self-consciousness find its factual fulfillment."[34] Although the individual is dependent on society, this was also a program of individualism insofar as the capability of autonomous reflection was the focus of moral and social reasoning. But it also followed that the individual was responsible to do its utmost in constructing and supporting a society of the greatest possible freedom without diminishing the rights of other legal subjects. This Kantian perspective not only contradicted the older view of the role of the state that prevailed in imperial Germany, but it also opposed the nationalist and *völkisch*, or racist, assertion that participation in the life of the community as a whole constituted the decisive factor in politics and political reasoning.[35]

To be sure, every attempt to employ Kant's moral philosophy in the spheres of politics and law was open to the reproach of being "formalistic" and that it was not applicable to the necessities of "real life." The only values that counted were those taken from "life." While such a claim had a long history and could be traced back at least to Schiller's criticism of Kantian ethics, it still played an important role in contemporary debates about political philosophy and ethics. In the Weimar Republic the charge of "empty formalism" was frequently used against democratic theorists such as Hans Kelsen and Hugo Preuß.[36]

Cassirer's defense of democracy, however, went far beyond the academic defense of democratic ideas and values. In 1926 Cassirer became a member of the Association of Liberal Academics (Vereinigung freiheitlicher Akademiker), also known as "Der Bund." This association was part of the small group of German professors who openly declared their support of the Weimar Constitution. Their activities, however, were rather ineffectual and had little influence on the general course of German political development during the Weimar Republic. Still, the very existence of the Association could be taken as a sign that supporters of the democratic state did in fact exist.[37] Another association that Cassirer joined was more closely related to his professional life, namely, the "Philosophical Academy" that had been founded shortly after World War I with Ernst Troeltsch as its first president. The "Academy," whose general aim was reconciliation and mutual understanding in international philosophy, was founded on the premise that neither national boundaries nor social and economical obstacles should hamper cooperative work between disciplines and schools. The first volume of the Academy's journal *Symposion* reflected this ideal with contributions by Moritz Schlick, Rudolf Carnap, and Hans Reichenbach on scientific rationalism and logical positivism alongside articles on the psychology of religion, Eduard Spranger's conception of pedagogy, and Vedanta philosophy. The membership roles for 1925 includes scholars from many countries, including Norway, India, and Japan, but interestingly none from France. Among the German scholars who belonged to the organization were Cassirer and Spranger, as well as Martin Heidegger and Hans Freyer.[38]

Cassirer also served on the editorial board of the *Kant-Studien* for many years and was one of the founders of the local chapter of the Kant Society in Hamburg. This afforded him with an outlet for scholarly exchange that was far removed from the everyday pressures of anti-Semitism and the demise of Germany's liberal culture. Almost until the end of the Weimar Republic there were possibilities for Cassirer to speak and act as if the ideal of the "Republic of Scholars" was actually within reach. By the same token, Cassirer was also among the organizers of the International University Courses of Davos in Switzerland, where in 1929 he had his famous debate with Heidegger.

The dispute between Cassirer and Heidegger has not yet been fully analyzed, although a reevaluation is currently under way.[39] The commonly accepted version of the dispute is more or less as follows. The issue at debate was Kant's philosophy, but there was far more at stake than the proper understanding of what Kant had intended. Eye-witness accounts of the event suggest instead that to the audience Cassirer and Heidegger represented two "irreconcilable" world-views, two generations, two temperaments. For while Cassirer supposedly stood for the neo-Kantian orientation toward the natural sciences as well as for the moral cosmos of the German *Bildungsbürgertum*, Heidegger represented a new and radical style of calling into question the philosophical and moral foundations of the European intellectual tradition in light of the experiences of the younger generation. Like expressionist literature, Heidegger's terminology reflected the dangers in modern life to which people saw themselves exposed. Although Heidegger always insisted that his philosophy was not to be read as simple cultural criticism or even pessimism, he nevertheless projected this aura, a fact that at least partially explains the enormous success he enjoyed in the broader public. To those at Davos, it seemed that Heidegger had triumphed over the "world of Kant and Goethe." In contrast to the allegedly abstract, professorial "school philosophy" of yesterday, the new "radical" philosophy had seemingly demonstrated its contact with life.[40]

There are, however, some elements of this story that are misleading. Aside from the fact that focusing on the contrast between their personal styles and political attitudes of the two thinkers obscures the differences between the substance of their respective philosophical arguments, there are other sources of confusion in the commonly accepted version of the dispute. In the first place, almost all later accounts of the events at Davos have more or less uncritically accepted the one-sided picture of neo-Kantianism that Heidegger's disciples painted of it.[41] This, in turn, undercut the historical outlook of the Kantian movement and, in doing so, greatly oversimplified the issues at stake.[42] It is not even certain that Cassirer could still be called a "neo-Kantian" at that point in his life or, indeed, if Cassirer was defending his own position or that of Hermann Cohen.[43]

Only weeks before the meeting at Davos Cohen and Cassirer had both been attacked by the extreme nationalist Othmar Spann, a sociology professor at the University of Vienna. In a speech delivered in Hitler's presence in Munich in February 1929, Spann defamed Cohen and Cassirer as "foreigners" and asserted that it was a pity for Germandom that they should be allowed to take the lead in interpreting Kant.[44] Reports of Spann's speech appeared in many of the larger German newspapers, so that a broad public would have almost certainly have known of it. It is not inconceivable that Cassirer—attacked in Davos as a "neo-Kantian"—defended Cohen's interpretation of Kant because otherwise it would have looked as if he were not loyal to his teacher in times of distress.

David Lipton is certainly right in suggesting that "Cassirer's fate, like the fate of the German Jews, was bound up with the survival of the Weimar Republic."[45] But this did not lead Cassirer to embrace Jewish "nationalism" or Zionism. Nor was he ready to accept the denial of his Germanness by others. And as rector of the University of Hamburg, Cassirer explicitly chose to defend the endangered republic, but in a way that was appropriate for a philosopher rather than for a party politician.[46] In public speeches and articles aimed at a wider public, he defended the Weimar Constitution as a ground for political competition. Cassirer also followed Kant and Max Weber in claiming that the universities should abstain from partisan political activity.[47] Again he tried to demonstrate that the political ideas of the European traditions were interwoven and that the concept of democracy cannot be reasonably seen as "foreign" to the German mind.[48]

The first of these speeches, delivered as an academic address in honor of the Weimar Constitution at the University of Hamburg at the request of the city senate, deserves special attention. As Hans Liebeschütz observed:

> At this time such a function was already a sign of political courage: probably not many of the professor's colleagues would have been ready to take over such a commission. Read in retrospect this confession of Hermann Cohen's favorite pupil appears also as a piece of Jewish self-defence.... Cassirer's capacity as lecturer was recognized among the students. But on this occasion he scarcely convinced anybody in the middle-sized auditory who had not already been on his side. The theme defined him as the speaker of a group with which only a small minority of students wished to be linked.[49]

Cassirer was the voice of reason and political rationality. But appealing to reason in Germany in 1932 meant fighting a losing battle.

* * *

If politics were at the heart of the dispute at Davos, then they would not have favored Cassirer's position. Nor was time on his side. Within four years of his debate with Heidegger at Davos, Cassirer had to leave Germany while his protagonist became rector of the University of Freiburg. From the beginning Cassirer's emigration was marked by bitter ironies. As Werner von Melle, honorary rector and former inaugurator of the University of Hamburg, wrote in November 1933: "You have been the pride of our university for many years. I don't need to affirm that to you. But perhaps I am allowed to let you know that again today."[50] Such sentiments, as noble as they might have been, inadequately reflected the highly charged political situation in which they were written. For by then Cassirer, convinced that nothing more could be done under the conditions of the Third Reich, had already left Germany for exile in Great Britain.

Shortly after the Nazi assumption of power and just before Cassirer's decision to flee, the Nazi party had organized the first national boycott against German Jews. "As Kurt Tucholsky had predicted," as the historian Anthony Heilbut observed, "the Right had mastered the orchestration of imagery and symbolism. Those early actions, such as the book burning and the dismissal of academics, had succeeded in making independent thought appear criminal."[51] Cassirer's daughter remembered having once asked her father if he was surprised that something like this could have happened in a country like Germany. His answer, she recalled, was: "No, civilization is only a thin layer on a volcano."[52] This remark was perfectly consistent with a report by Dimitry Gawronsky, a close friend of the Cassirer family who related that "already years before Cassirer had recognized the great danger of this [Nazi] movement.... [He] seemed to know with uncanny foresight what Nazism was about to do to Germany and the rest of the world."[53] Hitler as an "error of German history" is perhaps best understood as the negative expression of Cassirer's fragile vision of a "better Germany."

Years later in an article commemorating the hundredth birthday of his teacher Hermann Cohen, Cassirer noted that "in Germany the greatest efforts have been made to forget the name of Hermann Cohen, and to efface or suppress his philosophical work." Yet despite Nazi attempts to erase or redefine major parts of Germany's traditional intellectual landscape, Cassirer remained optimistic that "future historians of German philosophy in the second half of the nineteenth century will regard Cohen as one of the greatest representatives of that period."[54] What Cassirer wrote about Cohen was pregnant with meaning for himself. For like Cohen and countless hundreds of German intellectuals, philosophers, and academics who suffered a similar fate, Cassirer was one of those whose works were no longer studied or recognized in the twelve years of the Third Reich.

Cassirer's colleagues and friends were astonished, if not embittered, by his sudden decision to resign his position and leave Germany. Cassirer resigned his post as an individual act, but not without protesting Nazi policies: "I think too highly of the meaning and dignity of an academic office to remain in it at a time when my involvement in German culture is being denied to me as a Jew."[55] His protest went unpublished. In her memoirs Cassirer's wife Toni reveals that because of her objections Cassirer decided not to write a pamphlet against the Nazis. "I took the position in principle that no German Jew should take up the fight at this moment," she later wrote.[56] Toni Cassirer feared the negative consequences for their family and relatives. The ominous "Law for the Restoration of the Civil Service" from 7 April 1933 had helped create a climate of fear and a "wait-and-see" mentality that kept opponents of the regime like Cassirer from pursuing a more spirited course of action.

This is something that must be kept in mind when answering the reproach in much of the literature on Cassirer that he failed to do everything that was "possible" to oppose the regime. As one critic, Joseph Mali, wrote: "One might have expected indeed that as the first rector of a German university … he would raise his voice more often and more forcefully for the Jewish cause, which was generally identified with his own liberal ideas."[57] Such a reproach, however, conveniently ignores the fact that Cassirer had relatives all over Germany who were unable at that point in time to follow him into exile.

Shortly after his resignation and formal dismissal in July 1933, Cassirer discovered another way to become actively involved in the struggle against the new regime by joining rescue efforts for persecuted German intellectuals. Cassirer joined forces with anatomist Philipp Schwarz in Zurich, economist Moritz Julius Bonn in London, physicist Max Born at Cambridge, and the former director of the Political Academy in Berlin

Fritz Demuth in the Emergency Committee of German Scholars Abroad (Notgemeinschaft deutscher Wissenschaftler im Ausland) to place an estimated two thousand émigré German scholars in academic positions throughout the non-Nazi world in the fourteen years of the organization's existence.[58] Cassirer also acted as an advisor for the Academic Assistance Council, the most important British association for émigré scholars that had been founded in 1933 on the initiative of Sir William Beveridge of the London School of Economics for the support of refugee scientists in Great Britain.[59]

Despite their best efforts, these two organizations were not always able to fulfill their mission because of inadequate financial resources, the lack of suitable jobs, or the failure of German officials to cooperate. In 1939, for example, Cassirer appealed to the Academic Assistance Council—by then it had renamed itself the Society for the Protection of Science and Learning—from Sweden on behalf of Max Herrmann, former professor of literature at the University of Berlin and one of Cassirer's early teachers. In a letter to Dame Edna Purdie Cassirer wrote: "Their [Max Herrmann and his wife] situation is getting more and more dangerous and almost unbearable.... If it would be possible to bring him to England, that would mean a real rescue for him." Although the Council responded quickly, it was no longer possible to get Herrmann and his wife out of Germany, and Max Herrmann died in Theresienstadt in 1942.[60] Cassirer was also apparently involved in efforts to support activities for the Austrian-born writer Robert Musil, author of *The Man without Qualities* who had escaped in 1933 from Berlin to Vienna and had later taken refuge in Switzerland, where he was forced to live under difficult circumstances. In 1934 Cassirer offered to join the Association of Supporters of Robert Musil, but Musil declined his help as apparently too embarrassing or dangerous for him.[61]

After 1933 Cassirer lectured for two years at Oxford before accepting an invitation to come to Sweden. Despite whatever difficulties he may have had because of his lack of command of the English language,[62] Cassirer was able to integrate himself into British academic life more easily and more extensively than many of his fellow refugees.[63] Not only had Cassirer taken English lessons before delivering a lecture at the King's College in London in 1927, but he had relied upon English-language sources for his recently published study of the seventeenth-century Cambridge Platonists[64] and had written several articles for Alvin Johnson's *Encyclopaedia of the Social Sciences* as well as for the *Encyclopaedia Britannica*.[65] But, as Raymond Klibansky recalled, it was not always easy for Cassirer to spark student interest in the history of philosophy or in concepts different from those in vogue because of the widespread popularity of "analytic philosophy" and its claim that the history of philosophy was merely the history of errors and that all problems of philosophy would soon be solved by the "logical analysis of language."[66] Still, Cassirer was flexible and managed to adjust, in part because his concerns in the classroom were always overshadowed by those that he and his wife felt regarding the fate of friends and relatives still under the control of or within reach of the Nazis.

Because of an uncertain future in England and better employment prospects in Sweden, the Cassirers moved to Göteborg in 1935.[67] In Sweden Cassirer again had to overcome the problem of expressing himself in a foreign language. Amazingly he managed it a second time and had, in the words of one biographer, "so thoroughly imbued himself with Swedish art, philosophy, literature, and history that he was able to make a very important contribution to the development of Swedish philosophy with his book on Hägerström."[68] But Cassirer's publications were still in German. It was only in the last country of his exile, the United States, that he began to publish in English rather than his native German. Cassirer's interest in learning about the culture of Sweden was due in no small part to his sense of indebtedness to the country that had given him another chance and had offered him good working conditions.[69]

In his inaugural lecture at Göteborg Cassirer reflected at some length for the first time in public about the situation of European culture in the face of National Socialism. Speaking on the topic of "The Concept of Philosophy as a Philosophical Problem," Cassirer expounded on his own responsibility and the failure of philosophy to achieve its ethical task. Quoting from Albert Schweitzer that "in the hour of peril the watchman slept, who should have kept watch over us" and admitting that if the philosopher, in general, can be seen as a kind of "watchman," Cassirer conceded that he could not exclude himself from such a reproach:

> I do not exclude myself and I do not absolve myself. While endeavoring on behalf of the scholastic conception of philosophy ... we have all too frequently lost sight of the true connection of philosophy with the world. But today we can no longer keep our eyes closed to the menacing danger. Today the urgency of the time warns us more strongly and more imperatively than ever that there is once again a question for philosophy which involves its ultimate and highest decisions. Is there really something like an objective theoretical truth, and is there something like that which earlier generations have understood as the ideal of morality, of humanity?[70]

In 1936 Cassirer was presented a Festschrift, edited by his friend and former student Raymond Klibansky and the English philosopher Herbert James Paton, that contained contributions that had been written two years earlier for the occasion of his sixtieth birthday. Of a total of twenty-one contributions, only three were by former German colleagues: Theodor Litt in Leipzig, his old-time friend Ernst Hoffmann in Heidelberg, and Friedrich Gundolf, who had died in 1931. In a gesture that suggested a cordial relationship between the famous erstwhile member of the "George Circle" and the liberal "neo-Kantian," Gundolf's widow provided the editors with papers from his literary estate.[71] Of the living German philosophers, only Litt and Hoffmann dared to have their names appear in a Festschrift for a liberal Jew in exile who had been persona non grata in Germany since 1933. The official Nazi view of Cassirer, expressed by Max Wundt in his review of Cassirer's book on the philosophy of the Enlightenment, was that this book represented "an exemplary case of a false view … on the philosophy of the Enlightenment, one in which Germany is treated as an appendage of western Europe. It is an example also of how our own history has been taken away from us by the Jews."[72]

During his time in Sweden Cassirer was as productive as he had been during his best years in Hamburg. Besides teaching he was invited to deliver public lectures throughout the country and managed to rework his philosophy. What he had identified as central problems for contemporary philosophy in his Göteborg address now became the focus of his work as he began to explore the causes of the crisis of his age and ask whether or not it was possible to employ a concept of ethics as a cure to this crisis.[73]

In 1939 the Cassirers became Swedish citizens, but Cassirer was forced to retire the following year on account of his age. Following an invitation from Yale University, Cassirer and his wife left Sweden in May 1941 "on the last ship permitted to go out."[74] Charles Hendel, with whom Cassirer had become friendly soon after his arrival in the United States, said that in the final station of their exile the Cassirers "made themselves at home in America." He believed "that we can say that Ernst Cassirer was happy here, both in New Haven where he first came to live, and then in New York."[75] Cassirer's last move was made easier by the fact that he had the chance to renew contacts with former friends and colleagues who also lived in exile. The United States had been the country of refuge for Albert Einstein, whom Cassirer had known since 1921 when Einstein proofread his manuscript of his study on the philosophical relevance of the theory of relativity. Cassirer was also acquainted with art historians Erwin Panofsky and Edgar Wind, with the Gestalt psychologist Max Wertheimer, and with Walter Solmitz, the favorite disciple of Cassirer and Aby Warburg in Hamburg who had suffered in Dachau before his escape.[76] Cassirer, however, did not reestablish contact with another former disciple who became quite famous after the war, Leo Strauss. Although he had received his doctorate in 1921 under Cassirer's direction, Strauss severely criticized the absence of natural rights theory in the work of his former teacher.[77]

Although it was difficult for a Swedish citizen and man of his age to secure long-term appointments in the United States, the climate of tolerance, compared to what he had experienced particularly in Germany, and the politics of President Franklin Delano Roosevelt seem to have attracted him. His appointment to the editorial board of the newly founded *Journal of the History of Ideas*, where he published some of his last articles, can only be seen as a sign of Cassirer's quick integration into American academic life. On the other hand, he refused to take part in the "Council for a Democratic Germany" centered around the famed theologian Paul Tillich.[78]

When Cassirer left Yale University for New York's Columbia University, he delivered a farewell address to his colleagues that afforded him an opportunity to reflect upon his life and academic career.

> Looking back on my long academic life I must regard it as a long Odyssey. It was a sort of pilgrimage that led me from one university to the other, from one country to the other, and, at the end, from one hemisphere to the other ... at any new place I was lucky enough to find new friends. I found colleagues who were ready to help me in my work, and I found students who were interested in my philosophical views.[79]

Cassirer enjoyed the American way of teaching with its emphasis upon close contact with students and was fond of the so-called joint seminars with other teachers. But in another part of his address he seemed to reminisce about the "generational" theories that had become so popular in Weimar Germany.

> We are told that there is a deep and insurmountable gap between the generations; that every generation must feel in its own way, think its own thoughts and speak its own language. I regard this as a misleading and dangerous dogma—and as a dogma that throughout my life I found constantly contradicted by my own personal experience. The older I grow, so much the more I become interested in the work and thoughts of the younger men. And I always found that they readily answered to my interest.[80]

Cassirer's main goal in his last years was to understand the fatal turn of "civilized" mankind toward mythical and quasi-religious thought. This he saw as part of a more general change in the concept of man since the Renaissance, a phenomenon that he discussed at length in his *Essay on Man* from 1944 in a way appropriate to a philosopher and historian of ideas rather than as a prophet or philosopher of history. Reflecting in his last book, *The Myth of the State*, upon what this meant for philosophy and its place in the world, Cassirer observed that "it is beyond the power of philosophy to destroy the political myths. A myth is in a sense invulnerable. It is impervious to rational arguments.... But philosophy can do us another important service. It can make us understand the adversary. In order to fight an enemy you must know him."[81]

The fight against intolerance and Nazism was not only fought in the streets or the parliaments. It also was a "war of ideas" and involved the mystifying and "Germanizing" of thinkers like Luther, Leibniz, Kant, Fichte, Hegel, and even Plato. On that special "frontline" Cassirer not only did the best he could but perhaps more than any other of the

German academic philosophers of his times to defend the history of philosophy against this political misuse. The importance of the interpretation of the past and the philosophical tradition for political ends must not be underestimated. Cassirer in his last work concentrated on the power of mythical thinking—which in a more general respect he already had treated before—in the field of politics. This power can be and was used as an instrument in the technique of exclusion and inclusion. While it builds "identity" and stability of world-views for one, it excludes the other as a factor of irritation and therefore "evil." And the power of myth, though often disguised as "common sense," political theory, sociology or philosophy, is surely still at work today and perhaps always will be.

Notes

I wish to express my gratitude to Aron Fogleman of the University of South Alabama for proofreading an early version of this text and to Larry Eugene Jones of Canisius College for helpful suggestions.

1. A. Johnson, "The Intellectual in a Time of Crisis," *Social Research* 4 (1937): 282–85, here 285.
2. Quoted from the foreword to *Social Research* 4 (1937): 263.
3. H. Pachter, "On Being an Exile: An Old-Timer's Personal and Political Memoir," *Salmagundi*, nos. 10–11 (Fall 1969–Winter 1970), 16.
4. For a general introduction into the life and thought of Cassirer, see H. Paetzold, *Ernst Cassirer – Von Marburg nach New York. Eine philosophische Biographie* (Darmstadt, 1995), and A. Graeser, *Ernst Cassirer* (Munich, 1994). On the German-Jewish existence in Weimar Germany, see *Juden in der Weimarer Republik*, ed. W. Grab and J. H. Schoeps, Studien zur Geistesgeschichte, 6 (Stuttgart and Bonn, 1986. On the neo-Kantian movement in Germany, see T. E. Willey, *Back to Kant: The Revival of Kantianism in German Social and Historical Thought, 1860–1914* (Detroit, Mich., 1978), and K.-C. Köhnke, *Entstehung und Aufstieg des Neukantianismus. Die deutsche Universitätsphilosophie zwischen Idealismus und Positivismus* (Frankfurt a.M., 1986).
5. For example, see K. Jaspers, *Über Bedingungen und Möglichkeiten eines neuen Humanismus. Drei Vorträge*, ed. K. Rossmann (Stuttgart, 1982). On the postwar reception of Cassirer's work in Germany, see L. Hajen and T. Janssen, "Die doppelte Heimkehr. Ernst Cassirer und die Bibliothek Warburg," in *Dialektik – Enzyklopädische Zeitschrift für Philosophie und Wissenschaften* 1 (1995): 31–36.
6. For example, Marburg Neo-Kantianism and Cassirer were not discussed in the classic study by H. Schnädelbach, *Philosophie in Deutschland 1831–1933* (Frankfurt a.M., 1983). For a subsequent reassessment of Cassirer and his place in German philosophy, see H. Schnädelbach, "Unser neuer Neukantianismus," in *Philosophisches Denken – Politisches Wirken. Hermann-Cohen-Kolloquium Marburg 1992*, ed. R. Brandt and F. Orlik (Hildesheim, Zurich, and New York, 1993), 204–21. In this respect, the inspiring study by J. M. Krois, *Cassirer, Symbolic Forms and History* (New Haven, Conn., and London, 1987), as well as the efforts of the Heidelberg-based International Ernst Cassirer Society to make Cassirer's thought accessible to a broader public warrant special mention. See also the special issue on Cassirer in the *Internationale Zeitschrift für Philosophie* 2 (1992), as well

as the insightful essay by H.-J. Sandkühler, "Republikanismus im Exil – oder: Bürgerrecht für den Philosophen Ernst Cassirer in Deutschland. Zum 50. Todestag Ernst Cassirers," in *Einheit des Geistes. Probleme ihrer Grundlegung in der Philosophie Ernst Cassirers*, ed. M. Plümacher and V. Schürmann, Philosophie und Geschichte der Wissenschaften, Studien und Quellen, 33 (Frankfurt a.M., 1996), 13–36.

7. E. Cassirer, *Essay on Man: An Introduction to a Philosophy of Human Culture* (New Haven, Conn., and London, 1944), 185.
8. T. Cassirer, *Mein Leben mit Ernst Cassirer* (Hildesheim, 1981), 40.
9. D. R. Lipton, *Ernst Cassirer: The Dilemma of a Liberal Intellectual in Germany, 1914–33* (Toronto, 1978), 54. For a somewhat different perspective, see G. J. Giles, "The Academic Ethos in the Face of National Socialism," *Minerva Review of Science, Learning and Policy* 18 (1980): 171–79, and J. M. Krois's review of Lipton's book in *Journal of the History of Philosophy* 20 (1982): 209–13.
10. For further information on the League, see K. Holl, *Pazifismus in Deutschland* (Frankfurt a.M., 1988), 95ff., and R. Chickering, "A Voice of Moderation in Imperial Germany: The 'Verband für internationale Verständigung' 1911–1914," *Journal of Contemporary History* 8 (1973): 147–64, as well as the more general study by W. Eisenbeiß, *Die bürgerliche Friedensbewegung in Deutschland während des Ersten Weltkrieges. Organisation, Selbstverständnis und politische Praxis 1913/14–1919* (Frankfurt a.M., 1980).
11. D. Gawronsky, "Cassirer: His Life and Work," in *The Philosophy of Ernst Cassirer*, ed. P. A. Schilpp (Evanston, Ill., 1949), 3–37, here 22.
12. J. M. Krois, "Ernst Cassirer 1874–1945," in *Die Wissenschaftler: Ernst Cassirer, Bruno Snell, Siegfried Landshut*, ed. Verein für Hamburgische Geschichte, Hamburgische Lebensbilder, 8 (Hamburg, 1994), 16, as well as T. Cassirer, *Mein Leben*, 108–9.
13. On Natorp, see the balanced study by N. Jegelka, *Paul Natorp – Philosophie, Pädagogik, Politik* (Würzburg, 1992). On Natorp's wartime writings, see H. Lübbe, *Politische Philosophie in Deutschland. Studien zu ihrer Geschichte* (Basel and Stuttgart, 1963), 188–96.
14. The interview with Anne Appelbaum was recorded in 1994 by Patrick Conley for a feature on Cassirer, which was broadcast in 1996 by Sender Freies Berlin and has been published, along with Conley's interviews with Raymond Klibansky, Paul Oskar Kristeller, and Hans-Georg Gadamer, in W. Vögele, ed., "Die Gegensätze schließen einander nicht aus, sondern verweisen aufeinander," in *Ernst Cassirers Symboltheorie und die Frage nach Pluralismus und Differenz* (Loccum, 1999), 184–92. A longer and different version of Conley's radio feature was broadcast by the Hessischer Rundfunk in April 1995. I would like to thank Conley for having provided me with a copy of this interview.
15. U. Sieg, "Deutsche Kulturgeschichte und jüdischer Geist. Ernst Cassirers Auseinandersetzung mit der völkischen Philosophie Bruno Bauchs. Ein unbekanntes Manuskript," *Bulletin des Leo Baeck Instituts* 88 (1991), 59–91. Cassirer's reply to Bauch was edited by Sieg and is printed as appendix to his essay on pages 73–91. For general background, see U. Sieg, "Bekenntnis zu nationalen und universalen Werten. Jüdische Philosophen im Deutschen Kaiserreich," *Historische Zeitschrift* 263 (1996): 609–39.
16. E. Cassirer, *Freiheit und Form. Studien zur deutschen Geistesgeschichte*, 5th reprint (Darmstadt, 1991), xi, xvi. See also Lipton, *Cassirer*, 54–69.
17. F. Meinecke, *Autobiographische Schriften* (Stuttgart, 1969), 232–37. A letter from Ernst Troeltsch to Heinrich Rickert confirms Meinecke's account. See Troeltsch to Rickert, 22 Jan. 1917, in "Ernst Troeltschs Briefe an Heinrich Rickert," ed. F. W. Graf, *Mitteilungen der Ernst-Troeltsch-Gesellschaft* 6 (1991): 108–28, here 120.
18. W. T. Angress, "Juden im politischen Leben der Revolutionszeit," in *Deutsches Judentum in Krieg und Revolution 1916–1923*, ed. W. E. Mosse (Tübingen, 1971), 137–315, here 297, n. 676.
19. U. Sieg, *Aufstieg und Niedergang des Marburger Neukantianismus*, Studien und Materialien zum Neukantianismus, 4 (Würzburg, 1994), 225–27, and 329, n. 130.
20. For the theoretical background of Eisner's "ethical socialism," see *Ethischer Sozialismus. Zur politischen Philosophie des Neukantianismus*, ed. H. Holzhey (Frankfurt a.M., 1994).

21. On the Cassirer circle, see G. Brühl, *Die Cassirers. Streiter für den Impressionismus* (Leipzig, 1992), and W. J. Mommsen, *Bürgerliche Kultur und künstlerische Avantgarde 1870–1918. Kultur und Politik im deutschen Kaiserreich* (Berlin, 1994), esp. 51–54, 140–49, as well as the memoirs of Paul Cassirer's wife Tilla Durieux, *Eine Tür steht offen. Erinnerungen* (Berlin, 1971). Durieux, however, does not mention Ernst Cassirer in her account of Paul Cassirer's political activities (see 223–38), but then neither does Toni Cassirer mention Paul Cassirer or his wife in her memoirs. That Ernst was consulted by Paul on philosophy manuscripts is reported by Krois, *Cassirer*, 16.
22. T. Cassirer, *Mein Leben*, 117–20.
23. Paetzold, *Cassirer*, 46–85, here 46, and T. Cassirer, *Mein Leben*, 121–23. On Cassirer's Hamburg years, see also B. Vogel, "Philosoph und liberaler Demokrat. Ernst Cassirer und die Hamburger Universität von 1919 bis 1933," in *Ernst Cassirers Werk und Wirkung*, ed. D. Frede and R. Schmücker (Darmstadt, 1997), 185–214.
24. See the titles in W. Eggers and S. Mayer, *Ernst Cassirer: An Annotated Bibliography* (New York and London, 1988). A fourth volume of Cassirer's *Philosophy of Symbolic Forms* has been discovered in Cassirer's literary estate. See E. Cassirer, *Nachgelassene Manuskripte und Texte*, vol. 1: *Zur Metaphysik der symbolischen Formen*, ed. J. M. Krois et al. (Hamburg, 1995).
25. On Warburg's life and work, see H. Liebeschütz, "Aby Warburg (1866–1929) as Interpreter of Civilisation," *Leo Baeck Institute Yearbook* 16 (1971): 225–36, as well as the standard biography by E. Gombrich, *Aby Warburg: An Intellectual Biography* (London, 1970). On the "Kulturwissenschaftliche Bibliothek," see the various contributions to *Porträt aus Büchern. Bibliothek Warburg und Warburg Institute, Hamburg – 1933 – London*, Kleine Schriften des Warburg-Archivs im Kunstgeschichtlichen Seminar der Universität Hamburg, 1 (Hamburg 1993).
26. F. Saxl, "Ernst Cassirer," in *The Philosophy of Ernst Cassirer*, ed. Schilpp, 47–51, here 47–48.
27. For further information, see R. Klibansky and P. Conley, "Ein Gespräch über Ernst Cassirer und die Bibliothek Warburg," *Merkur. Deutsche Zeitschrift für europäisches Denken*, 564/3 (March 1996): 274–77. On the influence that this had upon Cassirer's thought and intellectual development, see M. Jesinghausen-Lauster, *Die Suche nach der symbolischen Form. Der Kreis um die Kulturwissenschaftliche Bibliothek Warburg* (Baden-Baden, 1985), and U. Raulff, "Von der Privatbibliothek des Gelehrten zum Forschungsinstitut. Aby Warburg, Ernst Cassirer und die neue Kulturwissenschaft," *Geschichte und Gesellschaft* 23 (1997): 28–43, as well as the perceptive essay by J. Habermas, "Die befreiende Kraft der symbolischen Formgebung. Ernst Cassirers humanistisches Erbe und die Bibliothek Warburg," in *Ernst Cassirers Werk und Wirkung*, ed. Frede und Schmücker, 79–104.
28. Saxl, "Cassirer," 50.
29. In this respect, see C. Schoell-Glass: *Aby Warburg und der Antisemitismus. Kulturwissenschaft als Geistespolitik* (Frankfurt a.M., 1998).
30. For the text of Cassirer's talk, see E. Cassirer, "Die Sprache und der Aufbau der Gegenstandswelt," reprinted in E. Cassirer, *Symbol, Technik, Sprache. Aufsätze aus den Jahren 1927–1933*, ed. E. W. Orth and J. M. Krois (Hamburg, 1985), 121–51. On Cassirer's relationship with Stern, see E. Cassirer "William Stern. Zur Wiederkehr seines Todestages," in W. Stern, *Allgemeine Psychologie auf personalistischer Grundlage*, 2nd ed. (The Hague, 1950), xxiii–xxxii. On Stern, see S. Mukherjee, "William Stern (1871–1938): An Intellectual Biography of a German Psychologist and Philosopher" (Ph.D. diss., Buffalo, N.Y., 1996).
31. T. Cassirer, *Mein Leben*, 133–34; Lipton, *Cassirer*, 84. For further information on Passarge and his attacks upon Jewish faculty at the University of Hamburg, see B. Vogel, "Anpassung und Widerstand. Das Verhältnis Hamburger Hochschullehrer zum Staat 1919 bis 1945," in *Hochschulalltag im "Dritten Reich." Die Hamburger Universität*

1933–1945, ed. E. Krause, L. Huber, and H. Fischer (Berlin and Hamburg, 1991), 3–83, here 11–12.

32. Cassirer apparently voted for the DDP. See Lipton, *Cassirer*, 85, n. 9.
33. E. Cassirer, *Kants Leben und Lehre* (Darmstadt, 1994), 398.
34. Ibid., 238. See also Lipton, *Cassirer*, 42–82.
35. On the importance of community (*Gemeinschaft*) in Weimar political discourse, see O. G. Oexle, "Das Mittelalter und das Unbehagen an der Moderne. Mittelalterbeschwörungen in der Weimarer Republik und danach," in idem, *Geschichtswissenschaft im Zeichen des Historismus*, Kritische Studien zur Geschichtswissenschaft, 116 (Göttingen, 1996), 137–62.
36. In this respect, see *Hans Kelsen and Carl Schmitt: A Juxtaposition*, ed. D. Diner and M. Stolleis, Schriftenreihe des Instituts für deutsche Geschichte Tel Aviv, 20 (Gerlingen, 1999); C. Graf von Krockow, *Die Entscheidung. Eine Untersuchung über Ernst Jünger, Carl Schmitt, Martin Heidegger*, Göttinger Abhandlungen zur Soziologie, 3 (Stuttgart, 1958); and H. Hofmann, *Legitimität gegen Legalität. Der Weg der politischen Philosophie Carl Schmitts* (Neuwied, 1964).
37. For further details, see H. Döring, *Der Weimarer Kreis. Studien zum politischen Bewußtsein verfassungstreuer Hochschullehrer in der Weimarer Republik*, Mannheimer sozialwissenschaftliche Studien, 10 (Meisenheim am Glan, 1975).
38. No history of the Philosophical Academy has yet been written. For its objectives, range of interests, and membership, see "Mitteilungen der Philosophischen Akademie," published as an appendix to *Symposion – Philosophische Zeitschrift für Forschung und Aussprache* (Berlin 1927), 3.
39. The literature on the Cassirer-Heidegger debate is quite extensive. The most important contributions are K. Gründer, "Cassirer und Heidegger in Davos 1929," in *Über Ernst Cassirers Philosophie der symbolischen Formen*, ed. H.-J. Braun, H. Holzhey, and E. W. Orth (Frankfurt a.M., 1988), 290–302; D. A. Lynch, "Ernst Cassirer and Martin Heidegger: The Davos Debate," *Kant-Studien* 81 (1991): 360–70; W. Cristaudo, "Heidegger and Cassirer: Being, Knowing, and Politics," *Kant-Studien* 82 (1991): 469–83; F. Schalow, "Thinking at Cross-purposes with Kant: Reason, Finitude and Truth in the Cassirer-Heidegger-Debate," *Kant-Studien* 87 (1996): 198–217; and the first chapter in K. W. Zeidler, *Kritische Dialektik und Transzendentalontologie*, Studien zum System der Philosophie, Beiheft 1 (Bonn, 1995), esp. 31–44. See also Cassirer's unpublished Critique of Heidegger in *Philosophy and Rhetoric* 16 (1983): 147–63. For eyewitness accounts of the dispute by Ludwig Englert from Germany and Jean Cavaillès from French, see *Die II. Davoser Hochschulkurse/Les IImes Cours Universitaires de Davos 1929* (Davos, 1929). The protocol of the debate is printed as an appendix to M. Heidegger, *Kant und das Problem der Metaphysik*, 5th ed. (Frankfurt a.M., 1991), 274–96. As Heidegger himself points out in note 5 to his preface, the protocol is a reconstruction from notes and is not verbatim.
40. For a general overview of the ideological situation in the late Weimar Republic, see A. Schwan, "Zeitgenössische Philosophie und Theologie in ihrem Verhältnis zur Weimarer Republik," in *Weimar – Selbstpreisgabe einer Demokratie*, ed. K. D. Erdmann and H. Schulze (Düsseldorf, 1980), 259–85, and H. Kiesel, "Aufklärung und neuer Irrationalismus in der Weimarer Republik," in *Aufklärung und Gegenaufklärung in der europäischen Literatur, Philosophie und Politik von der Antike bis zur Gegenwart*, ed. J. Schmidt (Darmstadt, 1989), 497–521.
41. On Heidegger's use of "neo-Kantianism" as a polemical gambit, see W. Kluback, "Hermann Cohen und Martin Heidegger. Meinungsverschiedenheit oder Entstellung?" *Zeitschrift für Philosophische Forschung* 40 (1986): 283–87. See also the contemporary accounts of the Davos dispute by H. Herrigel, "Denken dieser Zeit, Fakultäten und Nationen treffen sich in Davos," *Abendblatt der Frankfurter Zeitung* (22 April 1929), no. 297, and a series of articles by Heidegger's disciple F. J. Brecht, "Die Situation der gegenwärtigen Philosophie," *Neue Jahrbücher für Wissenschaft und Jugendbildung* 6 (1930): 42–58, and "Grundfragen der gegenwärtigen Philosophie," ibid., 672–86.

42. This point is particularly relevant with respect to the "Marburg School." See S. Schwarzschild, "Judaism in the life and work of Ernst Cassirer," *Il cannocchiale, rivista di studi filosofici*, nos. 1/2 (1991), 327–44.
43. This has been argued by Krois in Cassirer's unpublished critique of Heidegger (see above, n. 40) and "Aufklärung und Metaphysik. Zur Philosophie Cassirers und der Davoser Debatte mit Heidegger," *Internationale Zeitschrift für Philosophie* 2 (1992): 273–89.
44. See J. Haag, "The Spann Circle and the Jewish Question," *Leo Baeck Institute Yearbook* 18 (1973): 93–126, esp. 103–5.
45. Lipton, *Cassirer*, 85.
46. See Vogel, "Philosoph und liberaler Demokrat" (see above, n. 24), 185–214, and C. Naber, "... die Fackel deutsch-jüdischer Geistigkeit weitertragen." Der Hamburger Kreis um Ernst Cassirer und Aby Warburg," in *Die Juden in Hamburg 1590–1990. Wissenschaftliche Beiträge der Universität Hamburg zur Ausstellung "Vierhundert Jahre Juden in Hamburg,"* ed. A. Herzig (Hamburg, 1991), 393–406.
47. E. Cassirer, "Die Idee der republikanischen Verfassung. Rede zur Verfassungsfeier am 11. August 1928," reprinted in *Dialektik. Enzyklopädische Zeitschrift für Philosophie und Wissenschaften* 1 (1995), 13–30; idem, "Wandlungen der Staatsgesinnung und der Staatstheorie in der deutschen Geschichte (Rede anläßlich des Weimarer Verfassungstages 1930)," in *Enge Zeit. Spuren Vertriebener und Verfolgter der Hamburger Universität*, ed. A. Bottin, ed., Hamburger Beiträge zur Wissenschaftsgeschichte, 11 (Hamburg and Berlin, 1992), 161–69; idem, "Vom Wesen und Werden des Naturrechts," *Zeitschrift für Rechtsphilosophie* 6 (1932): 1–27.
48. For example, see E. Cassirer, "Deutschland und Westeuropa im Spiegel der Geistesgeschichte," *InterNationes. Zeitschrift für die kulturellen Beziehungen Deutschlands zum Ausland* 1 (1931), nos. 3–4, reprinted in E. Cassirer, *Geist und Leben. Schriften zu den Lebensordnungen von Natur und Kunst, Geschichte und Sprache*, ed. E. W. Orth (Leipzig, 1993), 218–34, as well as E. Cassirer, *Die Philosophie der Aufklärung*, 5th ed. (Tübingen, 1973).
49. H. Liebeschütz, "The Relevance of the Middle Ages for the Understanding of Contemporary Jewish History," *Leo Baeck Institute Yearbook* 18 (1973): 3–25, the quoted passage 18.
50. Quoted in T. Cassirer, *Mein Leben*, 122–23. See also Vogel, "Philosoph und liberaler Demokrat" (see above, n. 23), 186. On the situation at the University of Hamburg during and after the Nazi assumption of power, see the articles by B. Vogel, "Anpassung und Widerstand" (see above, n. 31); P. Borowsky, "Die philosophische Fakultät 1933–1945"; and J. Meran, "Die Lehrer am Philosophischen Seminar der Hamburger Universität während der Zeit des Nationalsozialismus," all in *Hochschulalltag im "Dritten Reich,"* ed. Krause, Huber, and Fischer, 1:3–83, 3:441–82, as well as G. J. Giles, "Academic Ethos" (cited above, n. 9), and idem, *Students and National Socialism in Germany* (Princeton, N.J., 1985), esp. 44–72.
51. A. Heilbut, *Exiled in Paradise: German Refugee Artists and Intellectuals in America from the 1930s to the Present* (Berkeley, Calif., Los Angeles, and London, 1983), 25.
52. Interview with Conley (see above, n. 14), 190. For a similar expression, see Cassirer's last book, *The Myth of the State* (New Haven, Conn., and London, 1946).
53. Gawronsky, "Cassirer," 28.
54. E. Cassirer, "Hermann Cohen, 1842–1918," *Social Research* 10 (1943): 219–32.
55. Letter from 27 Apr. 1933, quoted in T. Cassirer, *Mein Leben*, 202. For the circumstances under which the letter was conceived, see 196–205.
56. T. Cassirer, *Mein Leben*, 197.
57. J. Mali, "Ernst Cassirer's interpretation of Judaism and its Function in modern political Culture," *Juden in der deutschen Wissenschaft*, Jahrbuch des Instituts für Deutsche Geschichte, Beiheft 10 (Tel Aviv, 1985), 187–215, quotation from 206.
58. N. Bentwich, *The Rescue and Achievement of Refugee Scholars: The Story of Displaced Scholars and Scientists, 1933–1952* (The Hague, 1953), 17–18.

59. For further details, see G. Hirschfeld, "The Defence of Learning and Science ..." Der Academic Assistance Council in Großbritannien und die wissenschaftliche Emigration aus Nazi-Deutschland," *Exilforschung. Ein internationales Jahrbuch* 6 (1988): 28–43.
60. For further information, see J. L. Flood, "Émigré Germanists and the University of London," in *Keine Klage über England? Deutsche und österreichische Exilerfahrungen in Großbritannien 1933–1945*, ed. C. Brinson et al. (Munich, 1998), 224–40, for the letter 232–33. On the situation of German refugee scholars in Great Britain, see G. Hirschfeld, "Durchgangsland Großbritannien? Die britische "Academic community" und die wissenschaftliche Emigration aus Deutschland," *In England? Aber wo liegt es? Deutsche und österreichische Emigranten in Großbritannien 1933–1945*, ed. C. Brinson et al. (Munich, 1996), 59–70.
61. In this respect, see Musil's letters to Toni Cassirer, 1 Jan. 1934, and to Ernst Cassirer, 15 Jan. 1934, in R. Musil, *Briefe 1901–1942*, ed. Adolf Frisé (Reinbek bei Hamburg, 1981).
62. Gawronsky, "Cassirer," 29. See also T. Cassirer, *Mein Leben*, 155.
63. On the language barrier for German refugee scholars, see H. Maimann, "Sprachlosigkeit: Ein zentrales Phänomen der Exilerfahrung," in *Leben im Exil. Probleme der Integration deutscher Flüchtlinge im Ausland 1933–1945*, ed. W. Frühwald and W. Schieder, Historische Perspektiven, 18 (Hamburg, 1981), 31–38.
64. E. Cassirer, *Die platonische Renaissance in England und die Schule von Cambridge* (Berlin 1932).
65. In this respect, see the entries by Cassirer on "Kant" and "Leibniz" in *Encyclopaedia of the Social Sciences* (New York, 1932–33), 8:538–42; 9:400–402, and on "Neo-Kantianism," "Rationalism," "Substance," "Transcendentalism," and "Truth" in *The Encyclopaedia Britannica*, 14th ed. (London and New York, 1929).
66. Klibansky and Conley, "Gespräch über Cassirer" (see above, n. 27), 277. On the problems the Cassirers faced in England, see T. Cassirer, *Mein Leben*, 211–16.
67. On the circumstances that prompted the move from Oxford to Göteborg, see Paetzold, *Cassirer*, 153, 157–61, and T. Cassirer, *Mein Leben*, 222–32, 245–48.
68. Gawronsky, "Cassirer," 31. The book to which Gawronsky is referring is E. Cassirer, *Axel Hägerström. Eine Studie zur schwedischen Philosophie der Gegenwart* (Göteborg, 1939).
69. On Cassirer's exile in Sweden, see G. Korlén, "Politik und Wissenschaft im schwedischen Exil," *Berichte zur Wissenschaftsgeschichte* 7 (1984): 11–21. On exile in Sweden in general, see H. Müssener, *Exil in Schweden. Politische und kulturelle Emigration nach 1933* (Munich, 1974).
70. E. Cassirer, "The Concept of Philosophy as a Philosophical Problem," in E. Cassirer, *Symbol, Myth, and Culture: Essays and Lectures of Ernst Cassirer, 1935–1945*, ed. D. P. Verene (New Haven, Conn., and London, 1979), 49–63, the quoted passage on 60–61.
71. R. Klibansky and H. J. Paton, eds., *Philosophy and History: The Ernst Cassirer Festschrift* (Oxford 1936).
72. M. Wundt, "Christian Wolff und die Deutsche Aufklärung," in *Das Deutsche in der deutschen Philosophie*, ed. T. Haering (Stuttgart and Berlin, 1941), 229–46, quotation from 230.
73. Cassirer's most important works from this period are his book on "Determinism and Indeterminism in Modern Physics" (1936), his argument with the positivist Swedish philosopher Axel Hägerström, the fourth volume of his "Problem of Knowledge," and the collection of essays published in 1942 under the title "The Logic of the Cultural Sciences." His book on Descartes and the Swedish queen Christine seems to have been almost a commercial success. For a full list of Cassirer's publications during his stay in Sweden, see Eggers and Mayer, *Cassirer: An Annotated Bibliography* (cited above, n. 24).
74. C. W. Hendel, "Ernst Cassirer," in *The Philosophy of Ernst Cassirer*, ed. Schilpp (Evanston, Ill., 1949), 55–59, quotation from 55.
75. Ibid.
76. On Solmitz's strange fate, see J. Grolle, *Bericht von einem schwierigen Leben: Walter Solmitz 1905 bis 1962. Schüler von Aby Warburg und Ernst Cassirer*, Hamburger Beiträge zur Wissenschaftsgeschichte, 13 (Berlin and Hamburg, 1994).

77. L. Strauss, review of Cassirer's *The Myth of the State*, in *Social Research* 14 (1947): 125–28.
78. T. Cassirer, *Mein Leben*, 323–24. On the Council for a Democratic Germany, see U. Langkau-Alex and T. M. Ruprecht, eds., *Was soll aus Deutschland werden? Der "Council for a Democratic Germany" in New York 1944–1945. Aufsätze und Dokumente*, Quellen und Studien zur Sozialgeschichte, 15 (Frankfurt a.M. and New York, 1995), and E. Bahr, "Paul Tillich und das Problem einer deutschen Exilregierung in den Vereinigten Staaten," *Exilforschung. Ein internationales Jahrbuch* 3 (1985): 31–42.
79. Quoted in Hendel, "Cassirer," 56.
80. Ibid., 57.
81. Cassirer, *Myth of the State*, 296.

PART THREE

THE STRUGGLE FOR EQUAL RIGHTS IN GERMANY AND THE UNITED STATES

Chapter 7

SELECTING THE "BETTER ELEMENTS"

Jewish Students and the Admission of Women to German Universities, 1890–1914

Patricia Mazón

In imperial Germany, tremendous anxiety existed about the "wrong" people getting into the university. Just how seriously officials took the whole idea of credentials is illustrated in an incident from 1904. When a Swedish woman lost her *Mädchengymnasium*—or girls' high school—certificate, the machinery of state was set in motion on her behalf. The Swedish embassy alerted the German foreign office, which in turn contacted the Prussian education ministry. Another foreign female student, a Jewish woman, probably from Russia, was suspected of stealing the paper with the intention of using it to apply to German universities. To combat this potential swindle, the education ministry passed the word on to individual universities.[1]

In this chapter I would like to explain why this episode may have exemplified certain anxieties associated with the admission of women to German universities, known in Germany as the *Frauenstudium*. The debate over admitting women began around 1865 and continued even after their matriculation in the various German states between 1900 and 1909. Yet the entrance of women to German higher education was no smooth, even transition but a course of trial and error that took over a decade to complete, lasting from the time when a significant number of women were allowed to audit courses in the 1890s to women's formal matriculation after 1900. During this process, the question changed from whether to admit women at all, to which women to admit—and thus from the admission of women as individuals, to the admission of "qualified" groups of women. Here I will argue that the admission of women in general ultimately hinged on the exclusion of many foreign women, mostly Russian Jews, who were held to a higher standard than their male countrymen. In this case, as we shall see, the traditional hospitality and openness of the German academy toward foreigners did not apply.[2] Moreover, the question of female students was decided amidst the crisis of the late nineteenth-century German university. At the height of the development of the modern research university, widely copied elsewhere, German academics worried about booming enrollments and the erosion of academic standards.[3] In such a climate, it was only natural that women's qualification to study would come under intense scrutiny.

The loopholes and irregular policies that had allowed a handful of women to audit courses at several German universities in the late 1860s and early 1870s were formally closed almost everywhere by 1880. By the 1890s, most universities began to allow auditing by women again, at first on an experimental basis, then in a more systematic way. For example, the University of Berlin admitted a lone American woman, Ruth Gentry, to audit lectures in 1892 and thereafter began slowly to allow female auditors on a regular basis.[4] Despite officials' and professors' fears to the contrary, auditing could not be undertaken frivolously, as the process of obtaining permission was far too complex: obtaining permission from the state education ministry, the university, and the instructor was standard procedure.[5] After the first batch of test cases at each university, the numbers of auditing women increased rapidly.

State and university officials were caught between extending the same principles for admission to women and creating new standards for them. Following long-established custom, the formal requirements to study at a German university were relatively generous and fairly straightforward. In order to audit a lecture course, a person had only to demonstrate sufficient knowledge of the subject under discussion. In order to be matriculated as a regular student, a German needed to pass the *Abitur*, the final exam of the *Gymnasium*, the college preparatory high school. Foreign students generally required whatever entitled them to study in their home country.[6]

For academic policymakers, it was not just a matter of deciding to let women present the necessary credentials because in many cases women were not able to obtain the credentials in the first place. For example, women were not allowed to take the Abitur, as girls' schools did not prepare students for it. During the 1890s, women were admitted solely as auditors, not as formally matriculated students, regardless of their qualifications. Throughout the decade, university officials searched for a way to control the flow of women. Ironically, restricting women to auditing left officials with little to guide them in their admissions decisions precisely because the traditional auditing guidelines were so lax. As the ranks of female auditors swelled, it became obvious to state education ministries that formally admitting women would actually limit their numbers by holding women to a much higher standard than that required merely to sit in on courses. After 1900, appreciable numbers of German women gained permission to take the Abitur and thus possessed a credential equivalent to the men's. But by setting the Abitur as the standard for women's admission, German officials were also deliberately moving to exclude foreign women, as it would be difficult or impossible for them to obtain this credential.

Many modifications in auditing policy occurred before the decision was reached to enroll women on an equal basis with men. The most significant change occurred between 1900 and 1902, when the requirements for female auditors were made stricter at several universities. The revised guidelines did not set a higher educational standard but instead were directed against the foreign women who were coming to German universities in increasing numbers, in particular the so-called *Russinnen*, or "Russian women." Ironically the Russians under discussion here appear to have been ethnically largely non-Russian and mostly Jewish. While Russian Jewish men were kept out of Russian universities by quotas, educational prospects for Russian Jewish women in their homeland were starker still. Advanced courses for women founded in Russia in the 1870s were closed in the next decade. University courses were entirely closed to women throughout this period, except for a brief spell between 1906 and 1908, when women could audit. In 1897 an independent medical school for women was established in St. Petersburg, with another established in 1906 and two more by 1910.[7] Finally, the few institutions open to women did not always admit Jews, as appears to have been the case at the St. Petersburg women's medical school.[8] Thus, Russian Jewish women went abroad, often to Germany. There they attracted attention for a variety of reasons, partly because of the memory of the radical Russian women in Switzerland in the 1870s, and partly because of a growing climate of anti-Semitism and prejudice against Russians and Slavs at German universities and in imperial German society at large.[9]

The issue that triggered the concern with foreign women was precisely that of qualifications and standards. A widespread perception arose that the Russinnen especially were unqualified to study and that their education was not equivalent to that of German girls' schools. The question, then, was to what degree Russian girls' schools resembled their German counterparts. Even today historians are divided on whether the Russinnen were indeed less qualified. At the time, the discussion was extremely one-sided and dominated by German officials. Few voices from the Russinnen were heard.[10]

More important, and ultimately more interesting, than whether these women received an education equal to that of their German counterparts is the fact that foreign women were treated far differently than foreign men. The *Ausländerfrage*, or foreigner question, was a burning issue at German universities from about 1901 on. The largest contingent among the male foreign students was composed of Russian men, again mostly

Jewish, whose numbers nearly quadrupled in the period from 1900 to 1914. Many of the prejudices surrounding the Russinnen clung to their male countrymen as well, most notably anti-Semitism and the suspicion of socialism and political radicalism. Although in the period before World War I many students and professors called for a crackdown on foreign students, particularly Russians, state education officials had a more internationalist outlook and shied away from limiting foreign enrollment.[11]

When it came to female foreign students, though, both ministries and faculties were of another opinion. The change in auditing guidelines for women between 1900 and 1902 that occurred in many German states was not so much a step toward the admission of women as toward the determination of what kind of woman would eventually be admitted. Two cases from Berlin and Leipzig illustrate two different and contradictory pressures that led to the policy change: in Leipzig male students, professors, and state bureaucrats pushed to restrict the numbers of foreign women, while in Berlin German women with an Abitur advanced similar arguments.

Around 1900 at the University of Leipzig, the credentials of foreign female auditors, especially Russians and Americans, were called into question. While the matter of the Americans was soon solved, opposition to the Russian women continued, especially in the medical faculty. As had recently occurred at Halle, male medical students again protested against female students. This time, though, their complaints were directed mainly at foreign women.[12] In a petition submitted to the medical faculty in January 1901, the men asked that women without a German Abitur not be allowed to study medicine. The male students saw the admission of such women as "an injustice and a danger to the reputation [*Ansehen*]" of their "estate." It quickly became apparent that their main demand was to ban foreign women without distinction. Citing the rising numbers of foreign women, the petitioners feared crowding in their courses as reportedly was the case in Zurich, "where 40 per cent of the medical students are women." The presence of women disadvantaged German men, who had worked for years in order to enroll in the medical faculty, the Leipzig medical students continued. They saw the foreign women as a threat to the standards and honor of the medical profession if the Russinnen were to remain in Germany as "quacks."

To bolster their position, the male medical students assembled a wide array of common arguments against the admission of women to medical studies at all. Women labored under the "greater liability of their nervous systems and their physiological weaknesses," the petitioners argued. More worrisome still was the prospect of competition in a field seen as already overcrowded. Medicine, they feared, was the only logical place for women to turn. "A flooding of our lecture halls by women will, moreover, occur for the simple reason that medicine, next to the [faculty of] philosophy is the only subject ... with which the women can earn a living." It was not fair, the men pointed out, that medicine was open to women while law and theology remained closed. "It could almost appear to be a degradation of our estate if it is intended to function, in a manner of speaking, as a means of support [*Versorgungsanstalt*] for emancipated women," the petitioners complained. Women driven into medicine by the need to support themselves could hardly be expected to share the same ideal view of the medical profession as men who had chosen it freely. If women were to be admitted at all, the petitioners concluded, they should have the same qualifications as the men.

As the male medical students had demanded, the medical faculty passed their concerns along to the Saxon education ministry in February 1901. The dean of the medical faculty reported to the ministry that at the beginning of the current winter semester 1900/1901, twenty-two women had arrived in Leipzig with the intent of studying medicine. Their petitions for auditor's certificates had been approved by the ministry, so they were allowed to take part in medical lectures and dissection courses. In the meantime, however, the medical faculty discovered that the preparation that the Russian women had received "lag[ged] substantially behind that required from German women studying medicine." Closer investigation revealed that the majority of the Russinnen had attended Russian Mädchengymnasien where no Latin was taught. In fact, the medical faculty had learned that the education that most of these women had would not even qualify them for courses at the medical women's academy in St. Petersburg, which required Latin. The dean argued that it would hurt the reputation of the university if many foreign female auditors came to study medicine who could not even do so in their own country. He added that it seemed unfair that German women had to meet a higher standard than foreign women in terms of their preparation. Almost all of the Russinnen were Jewish, the dean noted, and thus had not been admitted to the female medical academy in St. Petersburg. The women's appearance was also an issue. The dean complained that "the women in question, almost without exception Jews, showed themselves in such a disheveled toilet as to give offense … in the auditoriums." A large number of female students in clinics and "practical" lectures would lead to "serious abuses"—the appearance of the Russinnen had already led to the enclosed petition. The dean contended that the university was sure to be "flooded" by foreign women. Academic freedom, the dean noted, meant that every professor could simply turn the women away, but it would be easier not to admit them in the first place.

The medical faculty asked the minister not to let in any female foreigner without the equivalent of the male qualification for any subject, not just medicine. The minister rapidly agreed.[13] In November 1901 the Saxon education ministry announced that it would not accept certificates from Russian Mädchengymnasien any more. At the same time it decided to extend auditing certificates for five years (in the case of medicine, seven years) for women with the German Abitur.[14] The new standards resulted in only thirty of fifty-six requests to audit being granted by the ministry that semester.[15]

This change in policy provoked an immediate response from twenty-one of the Russinnen, who petitioned the minister in December 1901. The women explained that in October they had asked for permission to audit in the philosophical faculty, assuming that their Russian Mädchengymnasium certificate would suffice, as it had in the past. The demand that they show a German Abitur was a "terrible blow to us all."

> Trusting in the continuing validity of the prior policy, we made the long trip, some from Siberia, mostly under unspeakably difficult material sacrifice for ourselves and our families, rented apartments here ... only to find out now, when every opportunity to attend another German or foreign university is closed to us ... that the gates of the university of Leipzig are closed to us.

The women, of whom at least eight seem to have been Jewish and one Armenian, asked to be allowed to audit on the old terms, and two of them appeared to plead their case personally in the ministry.[16] Although the policy was not changed, the women were allowed to stay for the rest of the semester.[17] It is not clear whether they were able to continue their studies at other German universities.

In fact, it seems highly unlikely that they could, because the same changes that had been made at Leipzig with regard to Russian credentials occurred at other German universities around the same time. The way in which this change was instituted at Berlin shows that male students, professors, and bureaucrats were not the only ones worried about the influx of foreign women. Beginning in 1900, pressure began to come from the first sizable cohorts of German women who had passed the Abitur.

The particular concerns of German *Abiturientinnen* as an interest group first came to the attention of the Prussian education ministry in a petition submitted in February 1900. The document was signed by Anita Augspurg on behalf of her association for Frauenstudium in Berlin. In general the petition asked the ministry to raise its standards for the Frauenstudium. Admitting insufficiently prepared women would degrade the whole idea of women's university studies, Augspurg asserted. German women should be required to have an Abitur. Male and female foreigners alike should be admitted only on the basis of a separate entrance examination such as that administered in Switzerland. Furthermore, the prerequisites for auditing should be made the same for men and women. The *collegia publica*, general lectures free to students, were geared to a nonspecialist level, so men and women who studied part-time or on the side should be admitted on equal terms. Augspurg contrasted these dilettantes with "such women who take up a course of study in the sense of a serious life calling [*eines ernstes Lebensberufes*]." These women, who had achieved the right to take the Abitur in all German states, should be given the chance to fulfill the same requirements demanded of male students. Such a policy was in the best interests of the male students, the female students, and scholarship itself, Augspurg argued.[18]

Although the ministry ignored Augspurg's demand that women be matriculated, her mistrust of the qualifications of many foreign women was shared by state officials. Only recently Professor Schliemann of the University of Berlin had assured both the university and the ministry that German girls' schools provided more advanced instruction than Russian Mädchengymnasien in all subjects except pedagogy. He believed that the only Russian women qualified to audit were those who had attained the title of *Erzieherin*, or governess.[19] In the same month as Augspurg's petition, February 1900, the university of Berlin announced that it had changed the requirements for female auditors. Women still needed to get the rector's permission every semester. German women would now need one of four credentials: a certificate for at least the fifth-level class, or *Obersekunda*, of a German *Gymnasium*, *Realgymnasium*, or *Oberrealschule*; a teaching exam; the completion of the girls' school along with good grades from state art institutes; or certificates attesting to outstanding achievement as a writer or artist. Foreign women had to show that their preparation was the same as that demanded of German women. Certificates from Russian Mädchengymnasien would only suffice if they were at the level of "governess," given after the seventh-level class, or *Selecta*. But most Russian women had completed only the sixth class, since this entitled them to pursue higher education in Russia. Russian women already in Berlin were allowed to continue their studies, but newcomers would have to meet the new standard.[20]

The implications of this new policy were immediately clear. Already in June 1900 Berlin newspapers reported that the new admission guidelines for women were perceived by the Russinnen as discriminatory. No other German or Russian university was this picky, one article commented, explaining that few women earned the certificate of Erzieherin now required at Berlin. Those who did usually remained in Russia because they received preferential admission to special female "higher courses" and other benefits. Because Jews and Armenians were barred from this, they came to Berlin. If the policy persisted, the Russinnen would be as good as barred, the article concluded.[21] In fact the numbers of female auditors in the winter semester of 1900/1901 showed a slight increase over those of the previous winter, from 431 to 454. But by the summer of 1901, the effect of the policy became more apparent as the growth in the number of female auditors (temporarily) stopped. The number of women held virtually steady compared with the previous summer semester of 1900. Yet stricter standards for the Russian women notwithstanding, the number of female auditors at Berlin continued to rise, reaching 634 in the winter semester of 1901/1902.[22]

The change in auditing guidelines, which amounted to tougher standards only for foreign women, pleased neither Augspurg nor German women with an Abitur. In March 1900 an anonymous article almost certainly written by Augspurg appeared in *Parlamentarische Angelegenheiten und Gesetzgebung*, which she edited. Striking a pessimistic tone, the article repeated many of the arguments of the petition she had submitted the previous month. The adoption of the new policy had imposed "the official seal of inadequacy on the study by women at the university of Berlin." The new standards would cultivate only "dilettantism" and revealed "the intention of holding the academic study by women from the very start at the level of an academic proletariat, in order to attach to it the unmistakable label of its inferiority." Augspurg's association for Frauenstudium had tried to avoid this through its petition to the Berlin university senate and the education ministry, which demanded "equal rights on the basis of equally performed duties," but in vain. Stricter preparation for university work was needed if female students were to be taken seriously. As long as women were not enrolled, they could not be held to the male standard, so the only thing women could do in the meantime was to try to reach the higher standard themselves, the article concluded.[23]

German women who had done so by passing the Abitur continued to petition the education ministry to recognize their achievement and enroll them officially. One letter from the Association of Women Studying in Berlin in March 1901 appealed for the matriculation of women with the Abitur. The petition asked the ministry to distinguish between serious, qualified women and others. Although no overt mention of foreigners was made, the implication was clear that women with the Abitur would almost certainly be German.[24] Other letters were more direct. In July 1901 Elise Taube, a Berlin medical student, wrote to Count Adolf von Posadowsky, the state secretary in the Prussian ministry of the interior, requesting that she and other women at Berlin with an Abitur be allowed to complete their medical studies there. Currently they were barred from dissection courses and clinical exercises. The surgical clinic refused to take any women on the grounds that it would then have to take all of them. Taube pointed out that all women should not be lumped together. Most of the foreign women were badly prepared and spoke poor German. "The foreign women crush us with their superior numbers, and in addition to the foreign women come a number of German women as well who, also without the appropriate educational background," merely dabbled in medicine, she wrote. The official who received Taube's letter noted that in the Berlin medical faculty there were twenty-nine women, of whom six were German and seventeen Russian. Two of the Germans had the Abitur.[25]

A third petition from fifty-one women at Prussian universities reached Education Minister Studt in February 1902. The women argued that those with a German Abitur should be formally enrolled, since those with the credential were at a disadvantage compared to those without it. In Berlin, the petitioners claimed, only thirty-one out of 611 auditing women had an Abitur. The letter also pointed out that since Baden had matriculated women in 1900, admitting them to Prussian universities would keep them in the state.[26]

There is some evidence that this last petition prompted the education minister to survey Prussian universities on the matriculation of women with a Prussian Abitur the same month. Despite the policy changes with regard to foreign women, the University of Berlin's opinion on female students in general remained deeply ambivalent, as shown by its response in May 1902. The philosophical faculty was in favor, as was, surprisingly, the theological faculty. What might explain this positive stance was that even the arguments in favor of the Frauenstudium focused on the fact that a career as a theologian or lawyer was not an issue, so the question was really a matter of women in medical and philosophical faculties. Although some members opposed enrolling women in this faculty because no career was open to them, the same persons recognized that if women were matriculated, academic freedom would not allow their wholesale banning from the faculty. The legal faculty deemed matriculation "pointless" since no profession requiring university study was yet open to women. Strictly speaking, this was not true, as women had been admitted to state certification as physicians in 1899 on the basis of audited coursework. The medical faculty opposed the idea, as did the university curatorim (*Universitätskuratorium*).[27]

In July 1902 forty-three Russian women at Berlin wrote to the education ministry protesting the decision not to recognize the Russian Mädchengymnasium credential. They argued that their final exam was not inferior to the German female teachers' exam or even the Abitur. Comparing the Russian Mädchengymnasium with the German female teachers' exam, which was the minimum standard for German women, the Russians claimed that their curriculum was comparable and even offered more math. The only difference was, of course, less German. The petitioners also argued that the Russian courses were more academically oriented, while in Germany girls' schools were more practical and pedagogical.[28]

Despite the Russian women's appeal, the University of Berlin announced stricter standards for them in the fall of 1902. Russian Mädchengymnasium certificates, even at the level of "governess," would no longer suffice. Instead the Russinnen would need to have finished the academic women's courses in St. Petersburg or prove outstanding scholarly achievement.[29] Although the ministry stood by its decision, women who had already been allowed to audit on the basis of these papers were permitted to continue.[30] The effect of the new policy was quite dramatic in the short run and noted in the press. *Neue Bahnen*, an organ of the women's movement, reported in July 1903 that the number of women auditing at German universities had gone from 1,271 in the winter semester of 1902/1903 to only about 850 in the following summer semester of 1903. In Prussia the numbers had decreased even more in the same period, from about 900 to 529; in the case of Berlin, female auditors had gone from 560 to 293 and had fallen by about half at other Prussian universities, too.[31]

The *Neue Bahnen* had put its finger on a key point: the reforms of fall 1902 helped to slow sharply the rate of increase in female enrollment. The number of female auditors at Berlin had increased an average of 60 percent every winter semester from 1895/96 to 1899/1900. In the summer semester of 1900, just before the first restrictions aimed at the Russinnen, the number of all women at the university increased another 60 percent from the previous summer semester. Nominal increases in female enrollment followed until the winter semester of 1901/1902, which saw a 40 percent jump, and the summer semester of 1902, which saw a 22 percent increase. The effect of the stricter standards for Russian women announced in the fall of 1902 seems to have extended right up to the time of women's matriculation in 1908: between the winter semester of 1902/1903 and that of 1907/1908, the number of women at Berlin increased only an average of 4 percent each winter semester.[32]

Specific data on the nationality of the auditors at Berlin is not available for all semesters, so it is difficult to determine if the measures against the Russinnen were really triggered by a significant increase in their numbers or by their mere presence. It does appear that the proportion of Russians among the women rose from about 14 percent in the winter semester of 1898/99 to about 21 percent in the summer of 1901.[33] That the absolute numbers of Russian women then sank after the reform of fall 1902, which was harsher than that of the summer of 1900, seems probable. Anja Burchardt shows that the absolute number of female Russian auditors in the medical faculty alone dropped from thirty in the winter term of 1901/1902 to thirteen a year later and to ten in the winter term of 1903/1904.[34]

The figures from Leipzig tell a similar story. At Leipzig in the summer of 1900, there were twenty-nine female auditors, of whom twenty were German and seven Russian. In the medical faculty there were four German and two Russian women. The next semester the number of female auditors shot up to eighty-nine, including thirty-two Germans and forty-one Russians. Suddenly the medical faculty found itself with eight German and twenty-three Russian women. In the summer of 1901, there were seventy-one female auditors, twenty-six Germans and thirty-two Russians; the medical faculty had eight German and eighteen Russian female students. Although the university tightened its standards for Russian women in November 1901, the twenty-two Russian women currently auditing were allowed to complete the semester. That winter there were seventy-three female auditors, of whom twelve Germans and ten Russians studied medicine. In the following winter of 1902/1903, the Russians numbered only seven out of the eighty-one female auditors. By the winter semester of 1904/1905, the absolute number of Russian women began to increase, but they remained a small fraction of all female auditors; that winter Russian women numbered eleven out of 102 women total, the following year fifteen out of 123.[35]

Prussia and Saxony were not the only German states to crack down on foreign women. In the case of Baden, standards for Russian women were raised after the matriculation of women at Heidelberg and Freiburg in 1900. A few years following admission, the medical faculty at Freiburg complained that foreign female auditors, especially Russians, were not well-prepared enough and asked for stricter enforcement of the auditing rules. The education ministry complied in December 1903 with stunning results. From one semester to the next the number of auditors at Freiburg was nearly halved: in the winter semester 1903/1904 there had been ninety-nine female auditors but just fifty-four the next semester.[36]

In the wake of the auditing reforms, a consensus developed around the issue of the Russian women. A 1902 article in the *Vossische Zeitung* summarized the dilemma at hand neatly. Reporting on the stricter standards for Russinnen at Halle, the reporter observed that many problems with foreign students stemmed from the fact that German university rules said that the foreign student's credential for university study was valid in Germany as well. But standards in each country were different. An important part of solving the Ausländerfrage was to hold foreign students to the same standards as Germans.[37] Yet it was the female, not the male students, who were made to measure up to the German standard and found lacking. Complicating matters further was that the standard itself was still in dispute. In contesting who the *Studentin* would be and what qualifications she would have, male medical students at Leipzig and German Abiturientinnen at Berlin both converged on the *Russin*, who became the scapegoat for both groups. Only by sacrificing her could the admission of women proceed from the efforts of bureaucrats and faculty to control the Frauenstudium.

The formal matriculation of women was decided state by state between 1900 and 1909. Baden was the first state to admit women in 1900. Elsewhere women's formal enrollment took several years longer. Bavaria followed in 1903, Württemberg in 1904. Saxony admitted women in 1906, Prussia in 1908, and last, Mecklenburg in 1909. In most of these states, admitting women was, ironically, a course of last resort to control a problem that could not be solved by simply reforming auditing policies. In various contexts, it became clear that only by admitting women would their numbers be decreased. The case of the University of Berlin illustrated what was really at stake: the standard set for female admission was not a neutral measure of academic ability but a conscious political decision.

In March 1905 Friedrich Althoff, a senior official in charge of Prussian university policy, tipped his hand on the matter before the Prussian House of Deputies. He noted that foreign women amounted to 657 auditors in Berlin alone, raising the question of whether women should not be matriculated. Matriculation, he continued, "would not be … an expansion in the admission of women but rather a limitation." Althoff then explained how standards for auditors were lower than for enrolled students. He urged the deputies to see the admission of women as a "limitation, or more correctly a regulation, through which firm and specific guidelines will be introduced for the admission of women … in place of the lax test, with which the admission of the female auditors is usually associated." Such a policy, Althoff argued, would "benefit the better elements" and "keep away the less desirable ones, namely those from foreign countries."[38]

Ultimately, the solution to the problem of women at the university was more symbolic than absolute. Female enrollment continued to rise as more Mädchengymnasien were founded, producing more Abiturientinnen, although their numbers never approached the flood traditionalists had feared: in 1914, less than 7 percent of all students at German universities were female. The number of students of both sexes was increasing rapidly during this period. In 1900, students at all German universities had numbered 33,000. By 1914, this figure had grown to over 60,000 students, of whom 4,000, or 6.7 percent, were female.[39]

The decision about the credentials women should present was crucial in controlling not just how many women got in but what kind of women. Making a German Abitur, or its equivalent, the standard eliminated many of the foreign women. In the end, foreign women were held to a different and stricter standard than their male counterparts, who for the most part continued to enjoy the tradition of German academic hospitality: what qualified men to study at home was also recognized in Germany.[40]

The fact that female foreigners were restricted and not male foreigners proves that German women gained admission through a corporatist logic. As I have argued elsewhere, the latter were admitted not as individuals who happened to be women but as members of a group that had a part to play in the German nation, whereas foreign women did not. The compromise that emerged from the long debate over the Frauenstudium was that women would study only certain subjects and pursue socially useful careers, such as medicine.

The admission policies produced a group of matriculated women who had an even more elite and exceptional social profile in almost all respects than their male peers. The *Studentinnen* were more upper-middle class and urban, as well as disproportionately Protestant and Jewish; Catholic women were even more underrepresented in German higher education than Catholic men.[41] The price of women's formal admission was an admissions policy that was highly restrictive, not just against foreigners but against certain groups underrepresented in German higher education. In many respects officials were able to impose on women a far stricter standard than they imposed on German men, who at this time were diversifying in all of the social categories mentioned above. Amidst the crisis of the universities of the late Wilhelmine period, professors demanded from the female student what they could no longer require of the male.

Notes

1. Geheimes Staatsarchiv Preussischer Kulturbesitz, Berlin-Dahlem (hereafter cited as GStA Berlin-Dahlem) Rep. 76 Va Sekt. 1 Tit. VIII Nr. 8 vol. X, 343–46.
2. This chapter draws on my dissertation, "Academic Citizenship and the Admission of Women to German Universities, 1865–1914" (Stanford, 1995), and appears in revised form in my manuscript in progress, "'Intellectual She-Monsters': The Admission of Women to German Universities, 1865–1914."
3. K. H. Jarausch, *Students, Society, and Politics in Imperial Germany: The Rise of Academic Illiberalism* (Princeton, N.J., 1982).
4. R. Drucker, "Zur Vorgeschichte des Frauenstudiums an der Universität Leipzig," in *Vom Mittelalter zur Neuzeit*, ed. H. Kretzschmar (Berlin, 1956), 283. See also Leipziger Universitätsarchiv (hereafter cited as LUA), Rep. II Cap. IV Nr. 35, 37. For further information, consult J. C. Albisetti, *Schooling German Girls and Women: Secondary and Higher Education in the Nineteenth Century* (Princeton, N.J., 1988), 223–37; H. Krabusch, "Die Vorgeschichte des Frauenstudiums an der Universität Heidelberg," *Ruperto-Carola* 8, no. 19 (June 1956), 135–39; E. Boedeker, *25 Jahre Frauenstudium in Deutschland. Verzeichnis der Doktorarbeiten von Frauen 1908–1933*, 4 vols. (Hanover, 1935–39), 1:xxx.
5. E. T. Nauck, *Das Frauenstudium an der Universität Freiburg i.Br.* (Freiburg, 1953), 48–51.
6. B. vom Brocke and P. Kruger, eds., *Hochschulpolitik im Föderalismus. Die Protokolle der Hochschulkonferenzen der deutschen Bundesstaaten und Österreich 1898 bis 1918* (Berlin, 1994), 70.
7. C. Weizmann, *Trial and Error: The Autobiography of Chaim Weizmann* (New York, 1949), 34; L. H. Edmondson, *Feminism in Russia, 1900–17* (Stanford, Calif., 1984), 18–19, 91, 147; M. Bessmertny, "Die Geschichte der Frauenbewegung in Russland," in *Handbuch der Frauenbewegung*, ed. H. Lange and G. Bäumer, 5 vols. (Berlin, 1901–1906), 1:338–49.
8. LUA, Medizinische Fakultät B VII No. 8, Bl. 66–72; LUA, Rep. II, Cap. IV Nr. 35, 73–76; and *Berliner Börsen-Courier*, 1 June 1900 (evening edition, 1st supplement), in GStA Berlin-Dahlem, Rep. 76 Va Sekt. 1 Tit. VIII Nr. 8 vol. VIII, 285.
9. *Hochschul-Nachrichten* 11 (1900/1901), no. 2, 36; *Vossische Zeitung*, 8 Nov. 1898 (evening edition), in GStA Berlin-Dahlem, Rep. 76 Va Sekt. 1 Tit. VIII Nr. 8 vol. VII, 184. See also W. Lexis, *Die Ausländerfrage an den Universitäten und Technischen Hochschulen* (Leipzig and Berlin, 1906), 25. On anti-Semitism in German universities, see N. Kampe, *Studenten und "Judenfrage" im Deutschen Kaiserreich. Die Entstehung einer akademischen Trägerschicht des Antisemitismus* (Göttingen, 1988). On anti-Semitism in Germany, see the work of R. S. Levy, *The Downfall of the Anti-Semitic Political Parties in Imperial Germany* (New Haven, Conn., 1975), and P. G. Pulzer, *The Rise of Political Anti-Semitism in Germany and Austria* (London, 1964)
10. Albisetti, *Schooling*, 245; Bessmertny, "Frauenbewegung in Russland," 3:331–38.
11. Brocke and Kruger, *Hochschulpolitik*, 95–97, 433; Jarausch, *Students*, 64–68.
12. Drucker, "Vorgeschichte des Frauenstudiums," 286–87.
13. LUA, Medizinische Fakultät B VII No. 8, 66–72; LUA Rep. II, Cap. IV Nr. 35, 73–76. See also Drucker, "Vorgeschichte des Frauenstudiums," 286–87; L. Buchheim, "Als die ersten Medizinerinnen in Leipzig promoviert wurden," *Wissenschaftliche Zeitschrift der KMU*, Mathematics and Natural Science Series 6 (1956–57), 367.
14. LUA Rep. II, Cap. IV Nr. 60, vol. 2, 144–47.
15. *Hochschul-Nachrichten* 12 (1901/1902): 62.
16. LUA Rep. II, Cap. IV Nr. 60, vol. 2, 155–59.
17. Buchheim, "Medizinerinnen," 367.
18. GStA Berlin-Dahlem, Rep. 76 Va Sekt. 1 Tit. VIII Nr. 8 vol. VIII, 173–174. Petition published in *Parlamentarische Angelegenheiten und Gesetzgebung* [supplement to *Die Frauenbewegung*] 2 (15 Jan. 1900): 5.
19. The professor's name is unclear; it might be Schiemann. GStA Berlin-Dahlem, Rep. 76 Va Sekt. 1 Tit. VIII Nr. 8 vol. VIII, 139–43.

20. *Hochschul-Nachrichten* 10 (1899/1900), no. 5, 108; no. 6, 126–27.
21. *Berliner Börsen-Courier*, 1 June 1900 (evening edition, 1st supplement) in GStA Berlin-Dahlem, Rep. 76 Va Sekt. 1 Tit. VIII Nr. 8 vol. VIII, 285.
22. *Vossische Zeitung*, 25 July 1901 (morning edition) in GStA Berlin-Dahlem, Rep. 76 Va, Sekt. 1 Tit. VIII No. 8 Adh. II vol. I, 66; *Chronik der königlichen Friedrich-Wilhelms-Universität* 13 (1899/1900), 14 (1900/1901), 15 (1901/1902).
23. *Parlamentarische Angelegenheiten und Gesetzgebung* 5 (1 Mar. 1900): 18–19.
24. GStA Berlin-Dahlem, Rep. 76 Va Sekt. 1 Tit. VIII Nr. 8 vol. IX, 19–22.
25. GStA Berlin-Dahlem, Rep. 76 Va Sekt. 1 Tit. VIII Nr. 8 vol. IX, 97–98.
26. GStA Berlin-Dahlem, Rep. 76 Va Sekt. 1 Tit. VIII Nr. 8 vol. IX, 127–35, 346.
27. Albisetti, *Schooling*, 246. See also GStA Berlin-Dahlem, Rep. 76 Va Sekt. 1 Tit. VIII Nr. 8 vol. IX, 346–48; GStA Berlin-Dahlem, Rep. 76 Va Sekt. 1 Tit. VIII Nr. 8 vol. X, 92–97.
28. GStA Berlin-Dahlem, Rep. 76 Va Sekt. 1 Tit. VIII Nr. 8 vol. IX, 352–61, 390–96.
29. "Die Zulassungsbedingungen für die Frauen zu den Vorlesungen an der Berliner Universität," *Allgemeine Deutsche Universitäts-Zeitung* 16, no. 19 (15 Nov. 1902): 147.
30. *Neue Bahnen* 37, no. 3 (1 Dec. 1902): 288.
31. *Neue Bahnen* 38, no. 14 (15 July 1903): 178. The comparison in the case of Berlin is perhaps a bit misleading, since Berlin always experienced higher enrollments in the winter semester than in the summer because students preferred to spend the summer semester in sunnier, more pleasant cities like Munich and Heidelberg. The official figures for Berlin in the winter of 1901/1902 were 634 women, and in the following winter semester, there were 560 women. Consult *Chronik der königlichen Friedrich-Wilhelms-Universität* 15 (1901/1902).
32. Statistics figured from data in the *Chronik der königlichen Friedrich-Wilhelms-Universität* of each year.
33. *Vossische Zeitung*, 25 July 1901 (morning edition), in GStA Berlin-Dahlem, Rep. 76 Va, Sekt. 1 Tit. VIII Nr. 8 Adh. II vol. I, 66; ibid.; GStA Berlin-Dahlem, Rep. 76 Va Sekt. 1 Tit. VIII Nr. 8 vol. VIII, 23–27.
34. A. Burchart, *Blaustrumpf – Modestudentin – Anarchistin? Deutsche und russische Medizinstudentinnen in Berlin 1896–1918* (Stuttgart, 1997), 271. Another factor complicating any figures is that German women, admitted formally in other states after 1900, probably chose to study elsewhere, so this could also have left Berlin with a disproportionate share of Russian women. This possibility was discussed at the time. Burchardt writes that many German women avoided the Berlin medical school because of its hostile atmosphere. See Burchardt, *Blaustrumpf*, 110–12. Burchardt also observes that the reforms of the winter term 1901/1902, in which a Russian Mädchengymnasium certificate was found insufficient qualification to audit, did not affect the number of Russian women at the Berlin university medical faculty and that the faculty, despite outward protest, continued to accept the Russian Mädchengymnasium plus an additional Latin certificate in the cases of all 112 Russian women who wrote medical dissertations there between 1905 and 1918. Russian women, she argues, were less concerned about formal enrollment because they needed only the doctorate (which could actually be earned by an auditor) to qualify for the Russian medical state exam. On the other hand, German women were more under pressure to take and pass the Abitur. See Burchardt, *Blaustrumpf*, 47–78, 90–91. Nonetheless, Burchardt argues, not many German women earned a doctorate at the Berlin medical faculty before 1908 because it was an "unfriendly" place for women. In fact, the vast majority of the 191 dissertations between 1905 and 1918 were supervised by only 12 of the 200 professors of medicine. Ibid., 110–15.
35. LUA Rep. II Cap. IV Nr. 60 vol. 1, 133–149.; LUA, Rep. II Cap. IV Nr. 60, vol. 4, 59–59a; LUA, Rep. II Cap. IV Nr. 60, vol. 5, 63–65; and LUA, Rep. II Cap. IV Nr. 60, vol. 6, 53, 106–107.
36. Nauck, *Frauenstudium*, 48–52, 54, 56–57. It is difficult to trace the effects of these changes in auditing policy over the long term because policies changed frequently until matriculation, which came at different times to German states between 1900 and

1909. Moreover foreign women with outdated credentials were often allowed to stay on for an extra semester or two, thus distorting the number of auditors. Finally many universities experienced seasonal fluctuations in enrollment, with more students in one semester than the next.

37. *Vossische Zeitung,* 4 Jan. 1902 (morning edition, 1st supplement) in GStA Berlin-Dahlem, Rep. 76 Va Sekt. 1 Tit. VIII Nr. 8 vol. IX, 264.
38. GStA Berlin-Dahlem, Rep. 76 Va Sekt. 1 Tit. VIII Nr. 8 vol. XI, 195–97.
39. See the enrollment figures in vom Brocke and Kruger, *Hochschulpolitik,* 424.
40. LUA, Rep. II Kap. IV No. 61 vol. 1, 157–168.
41. On the social background of the *Studentinnen,* see C. Huerkamp, "Frauen, Universitäten und Bildungsbürgertum" in *Bürgerliche Berufe. Zur Sozialgeschichte der freien und akademischen Berufe im internationalen Vergleich. Acht Beiträge,* ed. H. Siegrist (Göttingen, 1988), 200–222; Jarausch, *Students,* 109; and L. Mertens, *Vernachläßigte Töchter der Alma Mater. Ein sozialhistorischer und bildungssoziologischer Beitrag zur struckturellen Entwicklung des Frauenstudiums in Deutschland seit der Jahrhundertwende* (Berlin, 1991).

Chapter 8

THE CENTRAL ASSOCIATION OF GERMAN CITIZENS OF THE JEWISH FAITH

Jews and the Struggle for Civil Rights in Imperial Germany

Trude Maurer

In 1905 the journal of the Central Association of German Citizens of the Jewish Faith (Centralverein deutscher Staatsbürger jüdischen Glaubens) assured its readers that "one cannot deprive one hundredth of a population of [its] liberty without other groups falling victim to the arbitrariness of privileged circles as well."[1] The same sentiment was echoed in "The Call" for the National Negro Conference in 1909: "Discrimination once permitted cannot be bridled; recent history in the South shows that in forging chains for the negroes, the white voters are forging chains for themselves.... Hence we call upon all the believers in democracy to join in a national conference for the discussion of present evils, the voicing of protests, and the renewal of the struggle for civil and political liberty."[2]

These statements, so similar in their underlying arguments, raise a number of questions that were central to both the civil rights movement in the United States and the fight against anti-Semitism in Germany. Who, in the final analysis, is affected by the discrimination against a minority? Whose problem is it, and who should fight it? What were the arguments employed for redressing the situation, and what were the underlying principles? What did equality mean for the organizations claiming it, or rather for precisely which rights were they struggling? And by what methods did they hope to achieve their aims?

The following discussion will address these questions by focusing on the Central Association of German Citizens of the Jewish Faith (subsequently referred to as the Central Association) with occasional references to and comparisons with the League for Defense against Anti-Semitism (Verein zur Abwehr des Antisemitismus). As both the position of the Jews and the nature of anti-Semitism changed after World War I, efforts to combat anti-Semitism changed as well. On the one hand, Jewish equality, though never perfect, became a reality in a fuller sense than ever before. On the other hand, anti-Semitism had gained additional momentum during the war, and the rise of National Socialism threatened both democracy and Jewish equality in an unprecedented way. Thus, the fight against Nazism and cooperation with democratic parties and other anti-Nazi organizations became the main activity of the Central Association in the last years of the Weimar Republic.[3] Inasmuch as the situation changed drastically as a result of the work, this presentation will confine itself to the period between the founding of the League for Defense against Anti-Semitism in 1890 and the outbreak of World War I.

The circumstances in which these organizations came into existence, the socio-political, religious and ethnic affiliation of their founders, and the composition of their membership were decisive for the definition of their respective aims. Approximately 13,000 people belonged to the League for Defense against Anti-Semitism in 1893, while the Central Association of German Citizens of the Jewish Faith had an estimated 34,000 members in 1912.[4] By 1926 the membership of the Central Association had grown to 60,000, or one-fifth of the 300,000 German Jews it claimed to represent by virtue of the societies or local Jewish communities that enjoyed corporate membership.

Like American civil rights movements such as the all-black Niagara movement in 1905 or the biracial National Association for the Advancement of Colored People (NAACP) in 1909, the German organizations were founded several decades *after* emancipation, that is, after legal equality had been granted. But unlike the situation in the United States, where African Americans had been disenfranchised in the American South, where segregation had been reintroduced and sanctioned by the Supreme Court, and where anti-black riots had occurred even in the North, Jewish equality in Germany had *not* been revoked. Nevertheless, since the late 1870s, anti-Semitism in Germany had organized itself into a number of parties, congresses, and conventions and was propagated in numerous journals and pamphlets. In January 1890, for example, five anti-Semites had been elected to the Reichstag on an explicitly anti-Semitic program, and a number of prominent anti-Semites had begun to intensify their attacks on Jews.

In response to these developments, a group of twelve concerned individuals met toward the end of the year to issue a public protest and to form the League for Combating Anti-Semitism (subsequently referred to as the League). Although all but one of those involved in this undertaking were Christian, the initiative had been taken by a Jew. Still, the League presented itself as a Christian organization. In its initial proclamation from January 1891, the League's founders called upon their "fellow-citizens" to join them in their efforts to end the hateful campaign against "our Jewish fellow-citizens," a campaign that sought nothing less than the revocation of their civil equality. Such a commitment was defended as a matter of honor for the German people and especially "for us Christians."[5]

Two years later, in January 1893, a pamphlet published anonymously by Raphael Löwenfeld and entitled *Schutzjuden oder Staatsbürger?* called upon German Jews to take action in their own self-defense.[6] The preface was signed on New Year's Day, and within eight days the third edition of Löwenfeld's pamphlet was published. Whereas in 1890 Jews had been reluctant to step forth publicly, this appeal for self-defense obviously met a need. In the meantime, anti-Semitism had gained further ground. In 1891 an allegation of ritual murder had done much to provoke widespread anti-Semitic agitation. Even more ominous was the fact that the authorities did not question the allegation, took a Jewish butcher into custody, and investigated the case. In 1892 the German Conservative Party (Deutsch-konservative Partei) revised its program to call for restraints on "Jewish influence" and demanded "Christian authority and Christian teachers for Christian pupils."[7] In Prussia anti-Semites, conservatives, and members of the National Liberal Party (Nationalliberale Partei) created electoral alliances with each other. The fact that the German Radical Party (Deutsche Freisinnige Partei) that had served as the political home of the Jews since 1884 had split in two and that its two successors had lost nearly half of their predecessor's popular vote encouraged the anti-Semites to boast of their gains at the ballot box.

In the meantime, conditions within German Jewry had also begun to change. Since the early 1880s Jewish students had responded to the rise of anti-Semitism and their exclusion from general student fraternities by forming societies and organizations of their own. Although the League for Combating Anti-Semitism had already begun to recruit more heavily among Germany's Jewish population,[8] the League also insisted that Jews commit themselves to their own cause. Moreover, the League's demands for complete assimilation did not meet with the approval of the majority of German Jewry.[9] But in organizing themselves for the fight against anti-Semitism, German Jews were responding not merely to the increasing virulence of anti-Semitic agitation or the emergence of a new leadership cadre but also to a more general change in German political culture. Public interest in politics had greatly increased, and the masses had broken the monopoly over political power that had been previously held by the notables.

With the increasing democratization of German public life, pressure groups began to confront authorities directly, used the press for their purposes, and tried to influence parliamentary deputies. They conceived of themselves as the representatives of particular groups and appealed to those groups for mass support. It was only natural for German Jews to respond to the challenge of anti-Semitism in ways consistent with Germany's general political development. As Eugen Fuchs, one of the leaders of the Central Association of German Citizens of the Jewish Faith, explained in 1896: "In an age of pressure groups [*Interessenverbände*] the Jews had discovered how important it is to create such an association [*Verband*] for themselves."[10]

This change is also borne out by an analysis of the motives that lay behind publication of the pamphlet *Schutzjuden oder Staatsbürger?* The executive board of the Berlin Jewish community had intended to send a delegation to the Kaiser in hopes that he might be induced to take a stand against anti-Semitism. This plan, however, was severely criticized by the anonymous author, who argued: "He who does not enjoy any rights or whose rights are being curtailed beseeches protection. But we are in the full possession of our civil rights, and the riotous crowd of anti-Semites has no power to curtail them."[11] Instead of petitioning the monarch, the pamphlet's author demanded a "manifestation [*Kundgebung*] of modern Jewry."[12] In clarifying this idea, he explained: "We do not want to be protected Jews, but citizens. This, however, entails two things. With all our might we must strive to make the equality to which we are entitled only on paper a reality of life. And we must earn this equality through the continuous work of self-education."[13] The author then concluded his pamphlet with the six tenets that were subsequently incorporated with minor changes into the political platform of the Central Association of German Citizens of the Jewish Faith.[14]

F. Simon, the author of another pamphlet from 1893, concurred with Löwenfeld in his appeal for Jewish self-defense of their rights to citizenship. But his argument was not confined to the first author's universal and humanitarian perspective. He strongly identified with the Jewish community and demanded a thorough knowledge of Jewish heritage: "We want to be Germans and remain Jews, faithful citizens of the new Reich and respectful confessors of the old God."[15] Simon went on to suggest that Jews learn from their adversaries and form an efficient organization of regional branches with a central office in the capital as a way of combating them more effectively.[16]

The idea of self-defense lay at the heart of the political credo of the Central Association of German Citizens of the Jewish Faith. It could be found in the Association's first public appeal of May 1893 and was subsequently reiterated time and time again.[17] The Central Association regarded it as a duty and a matter of honor for Jews "to stand up for one's civic rights when they are being threatened and to do it at one's personal risk in the hour of danger."[18] Self-defense of Jewish civil rights was seen as a necessary precondition for success in the struggle against anti-Semitism.[19] The Central Association, therefore, did not confine its work to the mere refutation of anti-Semitic allegations but consistently sought to articulate its defense of Jewish interests in terms of abstract constitutional rights, that is, by defending "that which has been guaranteed to us by law and the constitution."[20] Proclaiming its aims to be "the maintenance of the civic rights of Jews in Germany and the struggle for their full equality,"[21] the Central Association insisted that anti-Semites were striving to curtail the civic rights of the Jews[22] and that the full equality that Jews had supposedly received from 1869 to 1871 had yet to be translated into reality.[23]

In its campaign for civil equality the Central Association of German Citizens of the Jewish Faith repeatedly drew attention to the fact that administrative measures had consistently excluded Jews from positions in the civil service, including education, and had denied them access to the reserve officers corps. Nor did it ignore discrimination in the economy.[24] In 1906 the Central Association published a survey that detailed the extent to which social relations between Jews and Christians and the position of Jews in society as well as in the economy had deteriorated over the past several decades.[25] Jewish employees were consistently discriminated against by non-Jewish firms. Chemical engineers could hardly find a job, even big banking firms sometimes would not consider a Jewish applicant.[26]

In addition to its main activities—the close monitoring and refuting of anti-Semitism and the legal actions it took against such trespasses—the Central Association thus assumed the lead in the fight against economic and professional discrimination. When hospitals, for example, refused to accept Jews for the so-called year of practice that was required for all medical students after graduation, the Central Association induced medical associations and the self-governing disciplinary bodies, or *Ärztekammern*, to intercede on behalf of Jewish candidates.[27] By the same token, the Association drew attention to professional discrimination against Jews by publishing advertisements that came to its attention for positions for Christians only and urged Jewish customers to boycott firms that refused to employ Jews.[28] At the same time, it wrote letters of protest when a hospital demanded a certificate of baptism from doctors applying for a vacancy,[29] or when big firms discriminated against Jews.[30]

Inasmuch as "the efforts to deprive Jews of their civic rights went hand in hand with attacks on their economic equality," the Central Association complemented the political struggle for equality with measures aimed at achieving economic security.[31] In 1913, for example, when Jewish merchants came under heavy attack from local anti-Semites in the Prussian province of Posen, the Central Association responded by creating a center of economic affairs with an information office.[32] In the public sphere it lodged complaints with the responsible cabinet officer when a tax office advertised a post for a Christian assistant[33] or when school administrators allowed the employment of Jewish teachers only in exceptional cases and only for religious instruction.[34] It also took action to ensure the admission of Jews as notaries and judges[35] and pressured to have Jews appointed as jurors in localities where they had been systematically excluded from jury duty.[36]

An instructive example of the way in which the Central Association defended Jews against discrimination appeared in a short report of 1895. All Jewish inhabitants of the East Prussian district of Marggrabowa that bordered on the Russian part of Poland had been called upon by the local authorities to prove their citizenship by either birth or naturalization certificates. In addition, they had to provide information on the birthplaces of their fathers and grandfathers. The Central Association exhorted all Jews not to carry out this "imposition" because it was presumed that the data would be used to prepare the expulsion of foreign-born Jews. Thus, "the Jewish fellow-citizens are, in a way, to contribute" to expulsion by "denunciation." At the same time, it interpreted the demand for such data as a violation of the law of 1869 because it amounted to unequal treatment of citizens of different confessions. In this instance at least, the Central Association, often censured for not devoting sufficient attention to the plight of the East European Jews, in fact defended them.[37]

To be sure, the Central Association tried to pursue all the cases that were brought to its attention but was not always successful in securing a redress of grievances.[38] From 1904 on, part of these tasks was taken over by the newly created Federation of German Jews (Verband der deutschen Juden), which conceived of itself as the official representative of German Jewry and whose leadership overlapped with that of the Central Association.[39]

What the Central Association demanded in all these cases was equality for Jews, that is, that German Jews should enjoy the same rights and the same opportunities as any Christian citizen of the state. The Association did not seek political representation for Jews that was proportional to the Jewish share of the overall population. On the contrary, such ideas were unequivocally rejected whenever they were brought up. When this was suggested in the Bavarian state parliament, or *Landtag*, in a transparent effort to reduce the number of Jewish judges, a Jewish journalist denounced it as "paper emancipation diametrically opposed to reality." His comments also revealed the origins of what was meant by "parity" at that particular point in time.

During the *Kulturkampf*—the conflict between the Prussian state and the Catholic church in the 1870s and 1880s—the Catholics had demanded justice. But later when the government realized its own mistakes and tried to repair them, the Catholics demanded parity defined as proportional representation in every sphere. But that, the author claimed, was the equivalent of injustice, not justice. Equality in modern times meant that the state did not concern itself with the religious but also with the intellectual and moral qualifications of applicants. Strictly speaking, the author claimed, even asking for a person's religion was a violation of the constitution. If one applied the standard of proportionality to actual conditions, one would soon find out that in most German states the *Jews* were the "confession" that was most badly underrepresented. In high schools and universities, however, the application of this standard would be detrimental to Jews because here they were more strongly represented than they were in the population at large.[40] In this case, as a modern historian commented succinctly, "principles squared with political convenience: as a religious corporation the Jews would have been entitled only to an insignificant proportion of public positions."[41]

The advocates of such propositions pointed time and time again to the population's rejection of Jewish officials. In the Prussian Landtag even the minister of justice conceded that German sensibilities deserved greater attention than German law. Speaking before an audience of approximately seven hundred at a rally in Berlin in 1901, one of the Central Association's most prominent leaders asked when it had become Prussian tradition to interpret the Constitution and conduct the bureaucracy according to the will of the people.[42] And in its monthly journal the Central Association went on to suggest that those sectors of the population that were not ready to accept a Jewish judge should be reeducated so as to become more tolerant.[43]

In addition to demanding equality for Jews as individual citizens, the Central Association of German Citizens of the Jewish Faith also demanded equality for Judaism with the Christian churches. Christian religious instruction was compulsory in German schools. Thus, in the Central Association's first public meeting Löwenfeld, the author of *Schutzjuden oder Staatsbürger?*, demanded that Jewish children should also receive such instruction.[44] In the ensuing debate, the Central Association was frequently supported by people who in principle would have preferred to have no religious instruction in school at all.[45] As long as Catholics and Protestants received their respective confessional instruction in school and the state made some kind of officially acknowledged religious instruction obligatory even for children whose parents had seceded from church, it seemed indispensable for the sake of equality to "demand the same for us." In this case, the term "parity" was applied by Jews to themselves[46] and in accordance with its original meaning in German constitutional and ecclesiastical history.[47]

The question of Jewish equality in education was taken up in 1905 by the Federation of German Jews (subsequently referred to as the Federation), when a new school bill was introduced in the Prussian Landtag. Whereas the government wanted to organize the school system along confessional lines, the Federation lobbied to prevent the abolition of existing Jewish schools, to facilitate the establishment of new schools where the Jewish communities requested them, and to provide religious instruction paid for by the state in any public school where there were twelve or more Jewish students. On this point, even the Conservatives agreed that the Jewish communities should receive subsidies for providing religious instruction.[48]

State subsidies to the Catholic and Protestant churches of Prussia were also at issue. Inasmuch as these subsidies were paid out of the general tax revenue to which the Jews also contributed payments, Jews resented the fact that they had to pay taxes for the maintenance of their own religious communities without any subsidies from the state.[49] The Federation of German Jews took up the case in 1908 and, in the absence of a formal response from the government, took it to the Chamber of Deputies. The authorities proceeded to argue that a positive decision would set a precedent for other religious communities, namely, Protestant denominations outside the state church, or *Landeskirche*. In addition, they pointed to disagreement between Orthodox and Liberals within the Jewish community. But by 1914 both "the parties in parliament and ministry policy-makers conceded that 'reasons of fairness' spoke for the proposal."[50]

Thus, from its very beginning the Central Association for German Citizens of the Jewish Faith struggled both for the equality of individual Jews as citizens and for religious equality between Judaism and Christianity. It did not, however, demand compensation for previous discrimination, nor did it expect a policy of affirmative action aimed at redressing previous economic and professional inequities. Behind this attitude lay the conviction "that the Jewish question is not a question of party politics, but a question of law. Any citizen who fulfills his moral and material duties towards the state must enjoy the protection of the laws and be equally entitled to the benefits of the state.... Any attempt to undermine or infringe upon this foundation of legal equality is to betray the constitution of the German Empire."[51] When they had been insulted in the ghetto, Jews had had to remain silent. But after emancipation? "Never! Giving up such struggle as hopeless would mean to despair of the constitutional state [*Rechtsstaat*] and of mankind."[52] From this perspective, the Central Association consistently rejected any exceptional law regardless of whom it might affect.[53]

From the outset, the ideology of the Central Association was informed by constitutionalism, and its aim was to translate the aim of civic and legal equality into reality. In that respect, the Association's ideology might be compared to the famous "Call" of 1909 that in the United States had led to the founding of the National Association for the Advancement of Colored People. At the same time, the position of the Central Association clearly paralleled the attitude of the League for Combating Anti-Semitism, whose founders considered the attack of the anti-Semites on the principle of equality as a direct threat to the Rechtsstaat. But the motivation here appears to be different. The leaders of the League for Combating Anti-Semitism not only insisted that "their perspective was greater than the special concerns of a single creed" but also warned "that ultimately the assault against the Jews was ... a repudiation of liberalism" as well.[54] Thus, in defending equality as one of the underlying principles of the Rechtsstaat they were also defending their own political position, for without exception the leaders of the League for Combating Anti-Semitism were Liberals, mostly left Liberals. In accordance with their upholding of constitutional principles, however, they denied being a pressure group and defined their role as helping the political parties in the struggle against anti-Semitism.[55] In contrast, the primary concern of the Central Association was the rights of both individual Jewish citizens and the Jewish community at large. In this respect, its leaders frankly admitted that they considered their organization a pressure group and hoped that in the end it would embrace all German Jews.[56] Some even considered it to be a movement,[57] a claim that may not necessarily have reflected the views of the vast majority of the organization's membership.

Even though they agreed on their basic aims—that is, the struggle against anti-Semitism and the maintenance of equality of all citizens—there were a number of further differences between the League for Combating Anti-Semitism and the Central Association of German Citizens of the Jewish Faith. One was tactical. For whereas the Jewish organization fought anti-Semitism in the courts,[58] the nondenominational one rejected that strategy on the grounds that this would only provide anti-Semites with a sounding board for their ideas.[59] More important was their different view of Jews and Jewishness. For whereas the League for Combating Anti-Semitism refused to acknowledge any peculiar cultural distinctiveness or social separateness in the struggle for Jewish rights,[60] the fight against their adversaries led Jews to reflect on their own identity and reinforced their identification with Judaism.[61] To be sure, their identity was complex and included German as well as traditionally Jewish components. But it was also formed by regional influences and professional experience. As Eugen Fuchs, generally regarded as the Central Association's "chief ideologue," said in the general meeting of the Association in 1913:

> By virtue of my nationality I am a German; a Jew, by virtue of religion and heritage. My Silesian homeland, the business of my parents, and my academic-legal profession have left a certain imprint on my character, so has my Jewish home. The Jewish environment in which I was raised and continue to live left as strong a mark on my personality as my belonging to Prussia. But this Jewish heritage does not separate me in the national sense from German Christians, does not influence my belonging to the genus "Volk," and it estranges me from *Deutschtum* as little as the heritage of a Friesian farmer estranges him in the national sense from a proletarian on the Rhine or one in Berlin.[62]

In a similar vein, Fuchs would declare in the same year: "We want to take part in the renaissance of Judaism."[63]

In striving to protect the constitutional rights of Jewish citizens, translate them into reality, and attain equality for Judaism with the Christian churches, the Central Association of German Citizens of the Jewish Faith was more than an association for countering anti-Semitic agitation. If it was not a civil rights movement, it was certainly a civil rights organization.[64]

In conclusion, it would be useful to touch upon the similarities and differences between the organizations discussed above and the early phase of the civil rights movement in the United States. Both the League for Combating Anti-Semitism and the NAACP were founded by members of the majority committed to preventing discrimination against a minority, although in Germany this took place at the initiative of a member of the minority. In both organizations, however, members of the minority would soon prevail. Even then, their roles seem to have been different. For whereas in Germany the main function of the increasingly Jewish membership was to contribute to the League's budget, in the NAACP representatives of the minority in whose name the organization had been founded would come to provide more and more of its leadership. In Germany this situation reflected "the deep insecurity felt by most Jews."[65] But within a few years German Jews would create their own organization, the Central Association of German Citizens of the Jewish Faith, as a counterpart to the predominantly Christian-led League for Combating Anti-Semitism in what must have been seen as a tactical sharing of roles that afforded different avenues of influence.

The methods used by the Central Association of German Citizens of the Jewish Faith and the early civil rights movement in the United States were similar and included litigation, lobbying, protest, and publicity. The important role of legal activities might, of course, have been a general characteristic of late nineteenth-century minority movements or those that represented oppressed sectors of the population. But this leads us to another, more specific parallel. For both in Germany and the United States the struggle for equality was waged with reference to the constitution with the ultimate aim of integrating the minority into society at large. In both cases, however, the struggle for equality made the minority more conscious and prouder of itself. The struggle for equality thus enhanced awareness of a specific identity among both German Jews and African Americans. To be sure, in each case the struggle for equality and integration developed its own dialectic. It has even been suggested that the ultimate goal of the Central Association of German Citizens of the Jewish Faith was the creation of a pluralistic society,[66] *avant la lettre*, of course. Such a synthesis, however, did not develop in Germany for the balance of time that Jews were still allowed to live there.

Notes

1. *Im deutschen Reich. Zeitschrift des Central-Vereins deutscher Staatsbürger jüdischen Glaubens* (hereafter cited as *IdR*) 11 (1905): 525.
2. "The Call." A Lincoln Emancipation Conference, reprinted in C. F. Kellogg, *NAACP: A History of The National Association for the Advancement of Colored People*, vol. 1: 1909–1920 (Baltimore, Md., 1967), 1:297–99, here 298.
3. On this phase of the Centralverein's history, see the basic study by A. Paucker, *Der jüdische Abwehrkampf gegen Antisemitismus und Nationalsozialismus in den letzten Jahren der Weimarer Republik*, 2nd rev. ed. (Hamburg, 1969).
4. On the League for Defense against Anti-Semitism, see I. Schorsch, *Jewish Reactions to German Anti-Semitism, 1870–1914* (New York, London, and Philadelphia, 1972), 82. There is no independent confirmation of the number of 20,000 in 1904 as reported in *Allgemeine Zeitung des Judentums*. See B. Suchy, "The Verein zur Abwehr des Antisemitismus [I]. From its Beginnings to the First World War," *Leo Baeck Institute Yearbook* (hereafter cited as *LBIYB*) 28 (1983): 205–39, here 210. For the Centralverein, see *IdR* 19 (1913): 52. For an analysis of Centralverein's membership in 1893–1895, see J. Borut, "'Not a Small Number of Notables': The Geographical and Occupational Structure of the Central Verein Membership During Its First Years," *Jewish History* 9 (1995): 51–77.
5. Here I follow closely the major contribution on the League for Defense against Anti-Semitism by Suchy, "Verein zur Abwehr des Antisemitismus," 205–8, quotations from the appeal, 205. See also the chapter on the organization in Schorsch, *Jewish Reactions*, 79–101.
6. [R. Löwenfeld], *Schutzjuden oder Staatsbürger? Von einem jüdischen Staatsbürger*, 3rd ed. (Berlin 1893).
7. English quotations taken from J. Reinharz, *Fatherland or Promised Land: The Dilemma of the German Jew, 1893–1914* (Ann Arbor, Mich., 1975), 38.
8. Suchy, "Verein zur Abwehr des Antisemitismus," 210. On the systematic recruitment effort, ibid., 208, and Schorsch, *Jewish Reactions*, 93–95.
9. For a survey of conditions in 1893, see A. Paucker, "The Jewish Defense against Anti-Semitism in Germany, 1893–1933" in *Living with Anti-Semitism: Modern Jewish Responses*, ed. J. Reinharz (Hanover and London, 1987), 104–32. On the defense league's demand for assimilation, see below, n. 60. For its criticism of Jewish indifference in the face of anti-Semitic attacks, see Schorsch, *Jewish Reactions*, 93.
10. In this respect, see J. Borut, "Der Central-Verein und seine Vorgeschichte. Deutschlands Juden am Ende des 19. Jahrhunderts," in *Jüdischer Almanach 1996/5756 des Leo Baeck Instituts*, ed. J. Hessing, 4 (1996): 99–110, particularly 100–106. See also the quotation from *IdR* 2 (1896): 170. On the correlation between this change and "the higher education, higher than average social and economic standing, and apparently younger than average age of Central Verein members with respect to the overall Jewish population," see Borut, "Not a Small Number of Notables," 54ff., 65. For an earlier classification of the Jews as a pressure group after 1898, see M. Lamberti, *Jewish Activism in Imperial Germany: The Struggle for Civil Equality* (New Haven, Conn., 1978), x. This insight reconciles the apparent contradiction between the argument that the Jews looked upon the Catholic Center Party (Deutsche Zentrumspartei) as a model for their own political aspirations (see Reinharz, *Fatherland*, 37, 44) and the assertion that Jews rejected "confessional politics" because of their commitment to the separation of religion and politics and because they represented too small a minority to gain anything from proportional representation. In this respect, see E. Friesel, "The Political and Ideological Development of the Centralverein before 1914," *LBIYB* 31 (1986), 121–46, especially 131. For one Jewish journalist's idea how the Jews should model their own organization after the Center Party, see M. Lamberti, "The Attempt to Form a Jewish Bloc: Jewish Notables and Politics in Wilhelmian Germany," *Central European History* 3 (1970): 76. In addition, their participation in general political parties was symbolic of their belonging to *Reich* and *Volk*. See A. Paucker, "Zur Problematik einer jüdischen

Abwehrstrategie in der deutschen Gesellschaft," in *Juden im wilhelminischen Deutschland 1890–1914*, ed. W. E. Mosse and A. Paucker (Tübingen, 1976), 479–548, esp. 506.

11. [Löwenfeld], *Schutzjuden oder Staatsbürger?*, 8. For an English summary of Löwenfeld's pamphlet, see Reinharz, *Vaterland*, 39–42.
12. [Löwenfeld], *Schutzjuden oder Staatsbürger?*, 16.
13. Ibid., 12.
14. Political views were considered matters of individual choice. German Jews had no special ties with the Jews of other countries, their moral standards did not differ from those of other German citizens, and they condemned unethical behavior of any individual, but rejected any responsibility for the individual Jew. For our purposes, the first two tenets are central: "We are not German Jews, but German citizens of the Jewish faith." And: "As citizens we neither need nor demand any protection beyond our legal rights." See [Löwenfeld], *Schutzjuden oder Staatsbürger?*, 26f.
15. F. Simon, *Wehrt Euch! Ein Mahnruf an die Juden. Mit einem offenen Briefe der Frau Baronin Bertha von Suttner an den Verfasser* (Berlin, 1893), as quoted in [P.] Rieger, *Ein Vierteljahrhundert im Kampf um das Recht und die Zukunft der deutschen Juden. Ein Rückblick auf die Geschichte des Centralvereins deutscher Staatsbürger jüdischen Glaubens in den Jahren 1893–1918* (Berlin, 1918), 18.
16. Rieger, *Vierteljahrhundert im Kampf*, 17.
17. *An die deutschen Staatsbürger jüdischen Glaubens. Ein Aufruf* (Berlin, 1893), 5f. See also M. Mendelssohn, *Die Pflicht der Selbstverteidigung* (Berlin, 1894), 7, as well as *IdR* 1 (1895): 235, and ibid., 9 (1903): 4.
18. *IdR* 4 (1898): 5. For a further indication of the emphasis upon "duty" or "obligation," see the title of Mendelssohn's pamphlet (cited above in n. 17). On the question of honor, see *IdR* 19 (1913): 50.
19. *IdR* 1 (1895): 2.
20. *IdR* 1 (1895): 146.
21. *IdR* 4 (1898): 235. See also ibid., 1 (1895): 235, and ibid., 9 (1903): 198. Consult also the organization's statutes, which are reprinted in *An die deutschen Staatsbürger* (see above, n. 17), 11–16, esp. p. 11.
22. See also *An die deutschen Staatsbürger*, 3, and *IdR* 3 (1895): 147.
23. *IdR* 12 (1906): 298.
24. *IdR* 4 (1898): 236; ibid., 9 (1903): 201. See also Rieger, *Vierteljahrhundert im Kampf*, 9f., 24f.
25. *IdR* 12 (1906): 279–298.
26. Rieger, *Vierteljahrhundert im Kampf*, 43f. See also Schorsch, *Jewish Reactions*, 137.
27. Rieger, *Vierteljahrhundert im Kampf*, 44f. For an example of such a refusal, see *IdR* 16 (1910): 76f.
28. Rieger, *Vierteljahrhundert im Kampf*, 43.
29. *IdR* 1 (1895): 157; ibid., 4 (1898): 10.
30. *IdR* 11 (1905): 143.
31. Rieger, *Vierteljahrhundert im Kampf*, 43.
32. Ibid., 45. On the complex situation that existed in the province that Prussia had acquired through the partition of Poland, see W. W. Hagen, *Germans, Poles, and Jews: The Nationality Conflict in the Prussian East, 1772–1914* (Chicago, 1980), especially 232f., 262f., 305–9. See also R. Jaworski, *Handel und Gewerbe im Nationalitätenkampf. Studien zur Wirtschaftsgesinnung der Polen in der Provinz Posen (1871–1914)* (Göttingen, 1986), 132–36 and passim.
33. Centralverein deutscher Staatsbürger jüdischen Glaubens, *Arbeitsbericht für die Zeit vom 1. August 1914 bis zum 25. November 1914*, "Streng vertraulich! Nur zur perönlichen Information! Als Manuskript gedruckt!" (N.p. [Berlin], n.d. [1914]), 7.
34. *IdR* 2 (1896): 593–600. See also ibid., 3 (1897): 67–69, and for a temporary settlement ibid., 6 (1900): 126.
35. Rieger, *Vierteljahrhundert im Kampf*, 35.
36. Schorsch, *Jewish Reactions*, 132. For a successful example, see *IdR* 1 (1895): 157.

37. *IdR* 1 (1895): 173. For protests by the Federation of German Jews (Verband der deutschen Juden) against expulsions of foreign Jews, see Schorsch, *Jewish Reactions*, 163.
38. Rieger, *Vierteljahrhundert im Kampf*, 35.
39. On the Federation of German Jews, see Schorsch, *Jewish Reactions*, 149–77, and W. Breslauer, "Der Verband der Deutschen Juden (1904–1922)," *Bulletin des Leo Baeck Instituts* 7 (1964): 345–79. On the Federation's creation, see Lamberti, "Attempt," 77–87.
40. *IdR* 8 (1902): 1–7. For a summary of the debate in the Bavarian Landtag, see ibid., 7 (1901): 651–558 [recte: 658].
41. Friesel, "Political and Ideological Development of the Centralverein before 1914," 131.
42. Schorsch, *Jewish Reactions*, 151. For the text of the speech, see Fuchs, "Jüdische Notare und Konitzer Ritualmord," in E. Fuchs, *Um Deutschtum und Judentum. Gesammelte Reden und Aufsätze (1894–1919)*, ed. L. Hirschfeld (Frankfurt a. M., 1919), 197–214.
43. *IdR* 7 (1901), 558 [recte 658].
44. *Bericht über die erste Versammlung des Centralvereins deutscher Staatsbürger jüdischen Glaubens (…) 29. Juni 1893* (Berlin, n.d. [1893]), 3. For a fuller discussion of this question see the chapter "Lobbying and Government School Policies" in Lamberti, *Jewish Activism*, 123–75, esp. 123–39.
45. *IdR* 1 (1895): 291–93.
46. *IdR* 1 (1895): 231–238, quotations from 232, 233. For this use of "parity," see also *IdR* 1 (1895): 151.
47. H. Fenske, "Gleichgewicht, Balance," in *Geschichtliche Grundbegriffe. Historisches Lexikon zur politisch-sozialen Sprache in Deutschland*, ed. O. Brunner, W. Conze, and R. Koselleck, 8 vols. (Stuttgart, 1975–92, reprinted 1994) 2:959–96. For this reference, see 963. For the "principle of parity" defined as *aequalitas exacta mutuaque* in the Peace of Westphalia (1648), see G. Besier, "Toleranz," ibid., 6:445–523.
48. See Lamberti, *Jewish Activism*, 129–75.
49. For a fuller discussion of this problem, see *IdR* 19 (1913): 54–57.
50. See Marjorie Lamberti, "The Jewish Struggle for Legal Equality of Religions in Imperial Germany," *LBIYB* 23 (1978): 101–16, the quotation from 116.
51. *IdR* 1 (1895): 6.
52. Ibid., 160.
53. *IdR* 14 (1908): 23, quoted in Paucker, "Zur Problematik," 530.
54. Schorsch, *Jewish Reactions*, 89–90.
55. Suchy, "Verein zur Abwehr des Antisemitismus," 231.
56. This hope, which distinguished the Central Association from the committees that had previously existed, lay at the heart of the following statement: "All [Jews] shall cooperate, we want to be an association of all, not just a committee which by its very nature implies an exclusive small number of members." See *IdR* 1 (1895): 151. For further information, see Rieger, *Vierteljahrhundert im Kampf*, 23. On the various committees that had been founded in response to periodic eruptions of anti-Semitic agitation, see Schorch, *Jewish Reactions*, 53, 59–65, 113, 242 (n. 46).
57. *IdR* 1 (1895): 160, and ibid., 9 (1903): 205.
58. The relevant articles of the Criminal Code were Section 130 which forbade inciting one class to violence against the other, Section 166 which proscribed blasphemy as well as the defamation of the institutions and practices of any incorporated religious body, Sections 185–200, which dealt with libel, and Section 360, paragraph 11, which forbade disturbing the peace or committing a gross nuisance. See Schorsch, *Jewish Reactions*, 123. For the psychological importance of this strategy, see *IdR* 9 (1903): 6, as well as Paucker, "Zur Problematik," p. 509. For the results of this tactic, see *IdR* 1 (1895): 158 and 195; ibid., 4 (1898): 9; ibid., 6 (1900): 120; and ibid., 9 (1903): 7.
59. Schorsch, *Jewish Reactions*, 84.
60. Suchy, "Verein zur Abwehr des Antisemitismus," 222, 226–28. See also Schorsch, *Jewish Reactions*, 96–99, and Lamberti, "The Attempt," 91.

61. Borut, "Centralverein," 99; Paucker, "Zur Problematik," 489, 518; Schorsch, *Jewish Reactions*, 117.
62. *IdR* 19 (1913): 224f. For the English translation, see Reinharz, *Fatherland*, 77. This passage was slightly reworded and incorporated in an article of 1917. See E. Fuchs, "Glaube und Heimat," *Neue Jüdische Monatshefte* 1 (1916–1917): 629–41 (for this passage, see 633f.), reprinted in Fuchs, *Um Deutschtum und Judentum*, 247–62.
63. Fuchs, "Referat über die Stellung des Centralvereins zum Zionismus in der Delegierten-Versammlung vom 30. März 1913, in Fuchs, *Um Deutschum und Judentum*, 230–46, esp. 237.
64. For the relevant definitions, see M. Konwitz "Civil Rights" in *International Encyclopedia of Social Sciences*, ed. D. L. Sills, 17 vols. (New York, 1968), 3:312–18. See also J. Hampel, "Bürgerrechtsbewegungen" in *Staatslexikon. Recht – Wirtschaft – Gesellschaft*, ed. Görres-Gesellschaft zur Pflege der Wissenschaft im katholischen Deutschland, 7th ed., 7 vols. (Freiburg, 1985), 1:1058–63. For the classification of the Centralverein as a civil rights organization, see Friesel, "Political and Ideological Development of the Centralverein before 1914," 97.
65. Suchy, "Verein zur Abwehr des Antisemitismus," 207.
66. Lamberti, *Jewish Activism*, 178; Paucker, "Zur Problematik," 544.

Chapter 9

OBJECTIVITY AND INVOLVEMENT

Georg G. Iggers and Writing the History of the Little Rock School Crisis

Tony A. Freyer

"It is perhaps inescapable," wrote Georg Iggers, "that the historian approaches history from a standpoint that reflects the imprint of his personality and of the social and cultural framework within which he writes." True to this insight, Iggers explored the "time bound political and social conceptions and norms in the historical perspective" of many historians. A measure of his success was the masterpiece, *The German Conception of History*. David A. Gerber's biographical work and Georg's autobiographical fragments further establish a basis for evaluating how Georg reconciled values of objectivity and involvement. Undoubtedly, the most important influence shaping his own "standpoint" was that of a Jewish émigré whose flight from Germany as a boy in 1938 reflected the real and symbolic evil of Crystal Night. Additionally, Gerber and Georg himself indicate that Georg's and Wilma's commitment to the cause of racial justice—particularly their role in the origins of the Little Rock desegregation crisis from 1957 to 1959—was an extension of the Jewish immigrant experience.[1] This essay examines Georg's place in the Little Rock confrontation from the perspective of the complementarity existing between one historian's life in books and life in action.

Certain initial caveats are in order. Neither Gerber nor the brief statement Georg published in a teaching documents collection in 1960 gives a full account of the Iggerses' involvement in Little Rock's civil rights struggle. Thus as far as I know, the most thorough discussion is a letter he wrote me replying to a series of questions. Dated 17 September 1980, the letter became a leading source for my understanding of the origins of the 1957 crisis. In addition, over the years Georg has contributed to the University of Arkansas at Little Rock's archives a collection of primary records that amplify—and to some extent modify—what is stated in this letter. These sources very much influenced my own study of the crisis and its significance. I must emphasize also that this material reveals how much Georg and Wilma worked as a team; their civil rights activity in Little Rock was indeed a mutual endeavor. The personal nature of this source material helps to explain why, when at the end of my questions I asked Georg if, "as an experienced historian," he could give me any general advice as to how I might proceed in the project, his reply was characteristically modest and true to the highest standards of historical enquiry: "It would be ... presumptuous for me to do so. I have worked in very different kinds of history," he wrote.[2]

Although Georg's assessment was essentially descriptive, it suggested an irony characterizing scholarly study of the Little Rock crisis. An understanding of Georg's contribution reveals how central was the city's African-American community to the origins and outcome of this historic civil rights confrontation. Most recent civil rights historiography has focused on the growth of African-American group identity within local communities. This same historiography, however, has generally ignored the Little Rock crisis, probably because of the prominence there of the New York-based National Association for the Advancement of Colored People (NAACP), the federal courts, the white governor, and national military power. But approached in terms of the Iggerses' role, it is clear that Little Rock is more representative of the broader civil rights movement than its current treatment by historians seems to allow.

Below the surface of media (and textbook) attention, there was a long tradition of local black protest, centered in the local branch of the NAACP. As historians are discovering for other southern areas, the local branch was not wholly directed by the national office, but represented a genuine indigenous activism. The challenge to the local school board in the 1950s demanded greater mobilization of the local black population than had ever been attempted before, aggravating divisions within the black community and engendering opposition from white moderates and segregationists alike. The Eisenhower administration's dramatic deployment of troops was entirely a reaction to these local trends, neither continuing nor initiating any program of federal executive action. Finally, the very ambiguity of the outcome at Little Rock—a limited though important victory for local black activists, and Governor Orval E. Faubus's remarkable success as he moved from racial moderate to skillful exploiter of white supremacy—is more representative of the overall outcome of the movement than the clear-cut showdowns on which historians have focused elsewhere.[3]

Racial Moderation Contested

Studying the Iggerses' Little Rock story may help, then, to strengthen the historiographical record. From 1950 to 1956, Georg and Wilma taught at the black, Protestant-affiliated Philander Smith College in Little Rock. Gerber's essay and Georg's Stafford Lecture at the University of Richmond in 1994 describe the life experiences that Georg brought to the Arkansas capital. These biographical and autobiographical sources recount the significance of his German-Jewish refugee cultural heritage, the personality traits reflected in the tensions with his parents, his intellectual precocity and acuity, and his anti-racist activism and internationalism at Richmond College.[4] But I think that several additional points regarding Georg's experiential baggage are noteworthy. First, at the time Georg and Wilma arrived in Little Rock the anti-Semitic strain within the University of Chicago Department of History, which conferred the doctorate upon Georg in 1951, and the American historical profession generally was becoming weaker. In 1952 a Chicago historian wrote a colleague that leading publishers and foundations were "now in the hands of Jews" and "Enrollments have declined [and] the main cause … probably is the distaste for such an overwhelming number of Jewish refugees on the faculties." At about the same time, however, another Chicago historian, Louis Gottschalk—who was on Georg's dissertation committee—was, according to Peter Novick, chosen president of the American Historical Association, in part "because it would establish the precedent of honoring a Jew."[5]

The Iggerses' cultural "otherness" did not inhibit their being accepted within certain white and black community groups. In his letter to me Georg said: "Almost from the beginning of our stay in Little Rock … we lived in the black community, in houses owned by Philander Smith College.… Our three children were born while we were living on the … Campus. We were well integrated into the Black community—I was even pledged into the Phi Beta Sigma Fraternity." Despite the omnipresence of Jim Crow, moreover, "relatively quickly we also became acquainted with individuals and groups—Quakers, Unitarians and others, who represented the 'liberal' point of view in the white community." Georg contrasted this interracial and culturally pluralistic acceptance with the social class divisions and racism that characterized the wider white society. "In the 1950s in Arkansas," he wrote, "racism was still a powerful force, particularly, but not solely, among lower income people who felt insecure in their economic and even more so their social status. In a sense what Arkansas experienced after 1954 was an awakening of the white masses exploited by populists like Faubus against the political control of the state and of the cities by a comfortable middle class." The emergence of heightened, white class consciousness and the persistent strength of racism was, Georg suggests, due to the state's less-developed "industrialization and urbanization."[6]

Georg and Wilma also carried on their activism within a broader social and academic life. When they arrived in Little Rock to begin the 1950/51 academic year, both Iggerses were nearing completion of their dissertations, he in European intellectual history, she in German literature. During the mid-1950s, Philander Smith's average student enrollment was about 920; the faculty teaching load was fifteen to sixteen hours, the same as the students. Library resources were minimal. Faculty taught across disciplines, with few if any colleagues in main academic fields: Georg, for example, was associate professor of history and foreign languages.[7] Most of the faculty and students were from black middle-class backgrounds with strong family support and segregated community networks; thus many had, Georg observed, "a stake in the dual society." In this setting Georg remained professionally active. He completed his Ph.D. in 1951, published a journal article drawn from the dissertation two years later, began work on two other dissertation-based articles, which were subsequently published, and, by the time the family left Arkansas in the summer of 1957, a revised version of the dissertation had taken book form, to be published in 1958 as *The Cult of Authority*. During the period he also developed job contacts at the University of Arkansas in Fayetteville and at Dillard and Tulane universities in New Orleans.[8]

Each of these factors contributed to Georg's activist perception. If his German-Jewish immigrant background was the dominant influence, then, the conflicted but nonetheless improving racial views regarding his Ph.D. mentor presented a lesson to be hopeful about overcoming racism. The racially integrated living and teaching experience, moreover, gave Georg direct involvement with the complex interdependencies between race and class *among blacks themselves*, which Jim Crow fostered. It should be emphasized that relatively few whites, especially southerners, would have had such a complete connection with any part of the black community. Meanwhile, these concrete realities coexisted with intellectual and professional endeavors that remained relatively compartmentalized from activist pursuits. The input from academic study was, accordingly, indirect.

Not long after arriving in Little Rock, this experiential ambivalence encouraged Georg's initial activist act. Both Georg's personal accounts and Gerber note that his action resulted in the public library board ending "racial segregation" in the city's libraries by January 1951. Less known, however, are the tactics Georg used to achieve desegregation. In addition to personal meetings with the library board, he published an appeal to the editor of Little Rock's progressive newspaper, the *Arkansas Gazette*. It appeared between two stories involving the Korean conflict. Identifying its author as a "recent white newcomer to Little Rock," Georg's letter employed a moderate discourse that combined a description of the gross inequities in the book collections that significantly disadvantaged blacks with reference to the failure to comply with the "equal" part of the Supreme Court's separate but equal doctrine. He commented further that strict compliance with constitutional principle would require a level of duplication that was "impractical and wasteful. The only practical and democratic solution is that of opening the doors of the main library to all readers, irregardless of race." He emphasized that such a "step would not be radical." In his "former hometown" of Richmond, Virginia, "Negroes" had gained equal access to public libraries "without any friction." Admitting "our Negro fellow citizens" to Little Rock's public libraries "would be a meaningful expression" by the city's white citizens of "democracy and … American ideals at a time of intense international crisis when democratic belief is challenged in many areas of the world."[9]

Following the "victory," which Georg said "received a minimum of publicity," the local NAACP branch invited him to join. Initially, he observed, he was the "only white person to be active in the branch, also the sole 'intellectual.'" The board's trust in Georg grew after he negotiated an end to racially separate drinking fountains in the city's department stores. Early on, he assumed the chairmanship of the branch's education committee, which was charged with the "planning of strategy in regard to school integration." He was also elected chairman of the executive committee. "From the beginning" he said, "I was involved in organizing challenges to school segregation in the city and state by gathering evidence on the inequality of facilities."[10]

In 1952 he and Wilma prepared separate reports on three Arkansas school districts, including particularly, Little Rock. Georg visited the white and black schools, Wilma gathered the statistical data. Coincidentally, the design of the reports roughly followed the moderate logical argumentation of Georg's letter seeking equal admission to the public library. The appeal for school "integration" was based on a factual demonstration that facilities were grossly unequal by any reasonable standard, especially the Supreme Court's separate but equal doctrine. There was a clear showing too that achieving equal access was "ethically" and economically efficient, and required relatively limited institutional accommodation. Unlike the library argument, however, the reports concluded with a comprehensive assessment of the practical policy options and outcomes rather than a broad assertion of democratic and humanitarian values. "Segregation in public facilities is bound to pass," the Little Rock report concluded. "With the increasing social and political awakening of the Negroes in the South, increasing pressure is being brought upon this system and is finding increasing sympathy among enlightened white citizens."[11]

Underlying the argument was a cautious hope that moderate action might succeed. Indeed, the report observed, in Arkansas relative progress had come primarily through "mediation" rather than litigation. Even so, "[f]ull integration may come in two ways: either suddenly through court action or gradually through planned integration." The "likelihood" of court action "becomes greater as planned integration is pushed into a distant future or rejected." Litigation, moreover, engendered "social tension … resentment on the part of pupils and teachers … and unemployment for many Negro pupils and teachers." Accordingly, the preferred alternative was "planned integration" in order to introduce black teachers and students "into the common school system step by step as they become ready. Such a plan would also condition white public opinion to a situation that in the long run would result in greater social harmony and a better trained citizenry." An appeal to justice was couched in pragmatic terms of social inequality and its consequences. Employing the theory the Supreme Court had acknowledged in the recent University of Texas Law School decision, which recognized the value of intangibles in the educational process, the "crux of the matter" was, the report stated, that the "Negro children, members of a minority group ... generally excluded from the fullness of American life and its heritage, are not admitted to the cultural advantages of the privileged majority. The segregated school system perpetuates this semi-isolation of the Southern Negroes."[12]

The report's moderation engendered ambivalent outcomes. Indicative of interracial cooperation in Little Rock, the report was published by an ad hoc council on schools, which included members of the NAACP, the Urban League, and the Southern Regional Council. Georg wrote later that the objectives were limited to allowing black Dunbar High School students to "share facilities they lacked at underutilized Little Rock High School (e.g., print shops, etc.) and to be admitted to courses not offered at their school." This was, he said, "conceived as a first step toward a gradual integration of the schools." Initially, the gradualist strategy seemed effective because the white school board agreed to discuss confidentially the feasibility of its implementation. On the board, three members "appeared sympathetic," the superintendent, hostile.[13] A breach of confidentiality, however, ended these exchanges. The *Gazette* reported that NAACP branch president and black attorney Thaddeus D. Williams had publically announced an impending meeting with the school board. According to the paper, Williams had said that "to abolish complete segregation was not the Association's immediate plan, but they wanted more study opportunity in colored schools." The *Gazette* contrasted Williams's statements with those of an NAACP regional secretary in Dallas who asserted that "We are seeking the immediate and complete abolition of segregation!" The NAACP wanted a decision in a "local lawsuit ... outlawing segregation to set a precedent."[14]

The disruption of informal negotiations by the local branch's own president undercut the gradualist strategy. Georg commented later that he did not know why Williams publicized the meeting with the school board, but the action "produced consternation" within the local branch. Clearly, the attorney "sincerely" favored integration; he may have, however, "wanted recognition in the black community." In any case, the board voted down the report's limited desegregation objectives. After a few months quite informal contacts between sympathetic whites on or associated with the school board and the NAACP branch led to the board's formal reconsideration and rejection of restricted black access to the white high school. At this point in mid-1952 the branch's executive committee for the first time seriously considered bringing a desegregation suit to achieve their modest objectives. The move coincided with the NAACP Legal Defense Fund's litigation that two years later climaxed in the Supreme Court's decision of *Brown v. Board of Education* (1954). The NAACP's New York headquarters thus urged the Little Rock branch to delay bringing its suit pending the outcome of *Brown*. With this request the branch complied.[15]

Once the Court decided *Brown* on 17 May 1954, local proponents of desegregation and members of the School Board met. The board's new superintendent, Virgil Blossom, presented the plan he had developed to comply with the Court's historic decision. This initial Blossom plan was significant in part because it reflected what the city's white leadership thought would constitute minimal compliance with the Court's reversal of the separate but equal doctrine. At this point—nearly a year before the Court handed down the *Brown* II remedial decree permitting implementation "with all deliberate speed"—the Blossom plan was reasonably progressive. As Georg later described it: "Two new high schools under construction, Horace Mann on the east side and Hall on the west side, would be opened upon completion, projected in fall of 1956, without racial designation. With the opening of these schools, all the high schools in the city would be desegregated. There would be three attendance zones, including Little Rock Central." By 1957 the junior high schools were to be integrated, with the elementary schools following over a three-year period ending in 1960. Notwithstanding the "somewhat gerrymandered school zones," the result would have been genuine desegregation along the moderate lines suggested in the Iggers's 1952 report.[16]

The moderate character of the Blossom plan and its acceptance by the branch requires emphasis. Throughout the period between the initial *Brown* decision of 1954 and the remedial decree the Court announced on 31 May 1955, desegregation efforts in Little Rock and elsewhere in Arkansas reflected a course that Georg later described to be moderate. He recalled that there was "consensus in the branch that the plan was acceptable, good faith in the intentions of the board and a relative optimism that the Little Rock community would accept this stage-by-stage plan of integration."[17] Correspondence during 1954/55 between Georg and Mrs. Franz Adler, a spokesperson for a desegregation group in Fayetteville, suggested that the Blossom plan was consistent with moderate opinions shared by accommodationist whites and the local NAACP branch members. Mrs. Adler "agreed" with Georg that "informal negotiations should be the approach employed in changing the pattern of segregation as long as there is hope of success by that means." Then, on the eve of the Court's *Brown* decision of 1954, Georg wrote Mrs. Adler that the NAACP regional lawyer in Dallas contended that the "purpose" of the litigation was "not the forcible merger of white and colored schools but rather the establishment of the principle that schools serve a community rather than a racial group and that the individual student has the right to attend the school which is closer or offers a better curriculum. In practice this would mean that most school children would continue to attend the same schools."[18]

The Court's *Brown* II decision undercut the cautious optimism that such moderation could succeed. "By the summer of 1955," Georg recalled, "the atmosphere regarding integration had changed." The Supreme Court's "implementation decision seemed to leave the door open to slow, gradual compliance. The white citizens councils now became active. Political pressure now built on the school boards to move toward minimum compliance. It is in this setting that the school board modified its original plan."[19]

The political dynamics were nonetheless confused. Orval Faubus had campaigned for and won the governorship in 1954 as an economic liberal. This liberalism explained why blacks across Arkansas, including Little Rock, voted for him. During his first term, moreover, Faubus successfully avoided political entanglement with the white citizens council's efforts to enact states' rights interposition laws aimed at impeding the enforcement of *Brown* II.[20] As the legislature debated these measures early in 1955, Mrs. Adler wrote Georg expressing "shock" at the "segregation bill" the legislature was considering. Members of her group intended to "write the Governor asking his opposition and veto should it pass." A law faculty member had told her that if enacted into law it "would definitely be a violation of due process, and could be taken at once into federal courts on those grounds."[21] Meanwhile, Faubus did not resist limited desegregation successes in northern Arkansas; he also managed to stay out of a school confrontation in Hoxie where a federal court order finally prevailed over the white citizens council's threatened violence.[22]

It soon became apparent how tenuous was the moderation the school board and the branch shared. Georg summarized the retreat from the initial Blossom plan that was underway by the summer of 1955. The plan Superintendent Blossom had presented to the desegregation advocates the year before, "would have involved large scale integration of at least Horace Mann and Central high schools," he wrote later, "residential factors would have limited integration at Hall, although even on the West Side there were several Black enclaves." The revised Blossom plan that emerged during the second half of 1955, however, instituted "freedom of choice" and the "assignment of black teachers to Horace Mann and white teachers to the other two high schools would have established a racial identity for each of the schools and resulted in token integration at the best." Additionally, the board, seeking to mollify extreme segregationists, "no longer felt it necessary to consult black leadership which it could expect to be dissatisfied with these modifications." Still, at this time, the NAACP branch "did have contact with [the city's] white liberal sympathizers … as well as with established leaders in the community, in commerce, the professions and organized labor." Many of these liberal whites, in turn, influenced the Pulaski Heights business elites who, through their control of the suburban Fifth Ward, "until the crisis of 1957 decided school board elections while voting participation in the other four working class wards was slight."[23]

A New "Community Action" Strategy Emerges

The School Board's retreat also aggravated a split among the NAACP branch's membership. In his 1960 essay Georg described a "sharply divided sentiment" within the branch. From the beginning a "more militant" group resisted the Blossom plan "on the grounds that it was vague, indefinite, slow-moving, and indicative of an intent to stall further on public-school integration." The militants had urged filing suit "immediately," while the "moderates," including Georg, had wanted to give the board "adequate time to demonstrate their good faith." The victory in *Brown* I quieted the disagreement, but it revived once Blossom began altering his plan following the *Brown* II decree of 1955. Now, however, the "militants" and "moderates" switched places. According to Georg, the "conviction was growing among those of us who previously opposed a suit from the standpoint of community relations that without a court order the Board would never integrate a single school." But the former militants, identified with two local black attorneys who usually did the branch's legal work, did not support bringing a case because, they believed, the Blossom plan was sufficiently consistent with the "all deliberate speed" standard that federal judges in and outside Arkansas might readily uphold it. A bad precedent for the desegregation cause would be the inevitable result. Instead of challenging what Thaddeus Williams called the "phoney" Blossom plan, the lawyers advised filing suit against one of the many central-Arkansas school districts that had made no attempt whatever to comply with *Brown* II.[24]

The disagreement reflected deeper tensions within Little Rock's black community. As Georg later described it, the "NAACP represented the militant position" in the city; it was "committed to the abolition of segregation in the public school system ... [and] to the abolition of the dual society generally. At the same time the NAACP did not believe in direct confrontation. It did not even at this time engage in civil disobedience. It relied primarily on legal recourse." A militancy based on legal action was nonetheless central to an African-American protest tradition reaching back in Arkansas at least to Reconstruction. Most notably, from 1889 to 1944 Scipio A. Jones was prominent among a small number of African American lawyers whose practice included challenges to racially discriminatory jury selection, voting, and criminal justice administration. One of the lawyers the local NAACP relied on was J. R. Booker, an associate of Jones's from the 1920s. Prior to the Iggerses' arrival in 1950, the city's NAACP had won, in conjunction with the Legal Defense Fund (LDF), teacher salary equalization cases. Meanwhile, in urban areas like Little Rock and Pine Bluff, some of the more affluent African Americans carried on the acommodationist tradition of Booker T. Washington, who like many of Georg's colleagues at Philander Smith College, "had a stake in the dual society" and thus were "ambivalent about the NAACP." Even so, the number of members actively involved in the branch's activities was quite small; nearly all were on the executive committee that Georg chaired. Among this group, and the branch as a whole, Georg and Dr. Lee Lorch, who arrived to teach at Philander Smith in the fall of 1955, were fully accepted. Unlike Georg and Wilma, however, Lorch and his wife Grace quietly espoused radicalism. Still, the branch was, Georg emphasized, truly "color-blind."[25]

These tensions shaped the decision to sue the school board. In retrospect, Georg recalled, the branch's initial trust in the board's good faith moderation was "overly optimistic." He and other executive board members were "much too optimistic when we believed that economic motivations were an important factor in racial discrimination, and that racial antagonism would disappear as educational and economic opportunities became available to blacks." But along with an awakening to the problem posed by the racism of whites, Georg and his fellow activists had to maneuver among the divisions within the black community. Georg believed that the "NAACP had the sympathy of a very broad segment of the Black community, how broad is difficult to determine." He suggested that the "strength of the political divisions" among blacks was represented by the two black newspapers: the more "militant *State Press*," edited by NAACP branch members L. C. and Daisy Bates, and the "accommodationist *Southern Mediator*." Even so, the *Southern Mediator* editorialized in January 1956 about "some sort" of disagreement within the branch over the question of bringing a suit. In fact, some members of the NAACP, working through a sympathetic white attorney, attempted to avoid litigation by urging the school board to return to the integration plan it had discussed in the fall of 1954. But this effort got nowhere.[26]

In the late fall of 1955 the executive committee voted to challenge the Blossom plan in court. This shift occurred after it became clear that the new Horace Mann High School would open in February 1956 as a segregated institution. Of further concern was the likelihood that under the proposed transfer guidelines only a handful of black children would be able to attend Central High School. Most black children living near Central would have to walk past the school to reach Horace Mann, some two miles away. Finally, no date was announced for the integration of the rest of Little Rock's public schools.

Georg and a majority of his colleagues agreed that litigation was now essential. The executive committee sought advice from U. Simpson Tate, a Dallas-based attorney affiliated with the NAACP Legal Defense Fund.

Georg discussed with him the advisability of seeking an injunction against opening Horace Mann as a segregated school. Tate counseled against this, urging instead that the children living near Central petition for admission there. The motivation for bringing suit came solely from the local branch. The executive committee had solicited Tate's opinion at least partly because of the disagreement with Williams about challenging the "phoney" Blossom Plan. The local branch of the NAACP notified the New York office about its decision. The national headquarters supplied no direct input regarding the suit, but the Legal Defense Fund agreed to review legal briefs prepared by local counsel provided that the local branch pay for its attorney and bear all other costs. Frank Smith, New York's field representative, played virtually no role, although the branch informed him of its actions.[27]

By January 1956 the executive committee endorsed a litigation plan Georg had proposed. Before the NAACP could file a suit it was necessary for black parents to attempt to register their children at one or more of the city's schools and for school officials to refuse to register them. Then parents could apply for legal aid. In addition, however, the NAACP needed to raise $300 to hire an attorney. Williams and J. R. Booker, who usually did the Little Rock branch's legal work, were not enthusiastic about serving. Georg and Lee Lorch, with the full support of the executive committee, took the lead. Georg suggested, and the committee accepted, a plan for getting parents involved as plaintiffs. When Horace Mann High opened, parents would attempt to register children in their neighborhood schools. To locate interested parents, four, mostly interracial teams (including Georg and Wilma, Lorch, J. C. Crenchaw, and Mr. and Mrs. Bates) visited homes throughout black residential areas. The groups found parents supportive of the litigation idea and willing to become parties to it. The parents agreed to gather with their children on the stipulated date in January at several collection points and attempt to register them. This positive response indicated a change of attitude among the city's blacks, most of whom had not given the NAACP a great deal of support in the past.[28]

Georg and Wilma wrote to family members and friends in the United States and Canada for contributions to finance the Little Rock litigation. They wrote that "public opinion on the whole is moderate" in the city, and it was "likely that school integration can be accomplished with little social tension." But, the appeal emphasized, "School board officials, for political and other reasons, are generally unwilling to move unless directed by court order." Even though the school board had announced its willingness to comply with the *Brown* decision, it stated, the NAACP considered the board's plan "so vague as to appear more like circumvention than like compliance." A move to file suit was therefore under way because of the impending opening of Horace Mann, "originally announced to be interracial but now restricted to Negroes. As a result … several dozen Negro children will be passing the white high school, which at present has no space problem, on their way two miles farther to the new Negro high school." The purpose of the suit was to get the school board to integrate Central and, eventually, Little Rock's other public schools.[29]

The Little Rock NAACP was soon able to procure the services of Wiley Brandon, a lawyer in Pine Bluff, about forty-five miles from Little Rock. His work for the NAACP's Legal Redress Committee took him throughout Arkansas and Mississippi and he was well-known to the Little Rock executive committee. His family had lived in Pine Bluff for several generations, was well-established in business there, and was on good terms with the white community. He was among the first blacks to graduate from the University of Arkansas School of Law, which had been integrated in 1948. By the mid-1950s, Brandon, as one of the few black attorneys in the state, was involved in several NAACP-sponsored cases. The Little Rock suit seemed in no way exceptional.[30]

When Horace Mann High School opened, the NAACP, parents, and children were ready to implement the registration plan. The parents—many more than had been approached by the NAACP—gathered at collection points in their neighborhoods and walked to nearby schools. Only a few of the children were from professional or middle-class backgrounds. Most were from working-class families. Because these parents were vulnerable to recrimination (some were employed as service personnel by the school board), several were dissuaded from participating. After attempting to register their children and being turned away, the parents formally appealed to the local NAACP branch for legal aid. The unexpected numbers of parents seeking to participate indicated growing support in the black community for a more activist role by the NAACP.[31]

On 8 February 1956, through the NAACP as legal representative, thirty-three of the children who were not allowed to register filed suit in the United States District Court for the Eastern District of Arkansas. The plaintiff children ranged in age from six to twenty-one; their names appeared on the suit in alphabetical order, the first being John Aaron. The defendants were listed as the president and secretary of the Little Rock School District, the superintendent of schools, and the district itself. The president of the school board was William G. Cooper, a prominent Little Rock physician and civic leader. Upon the filing of *Aaron v. Cooper*, members of Little Rock's black community contributed about a thousand dollars in support of the litigation, another indication of a change of mood among the city's blacks.[32]

Shortly before the suit's filing, Philander Smith's president revealed equivocation among other members of the black community. President M. LaFayette Harris had come to "understand" that Georg and Lorch had "been visiting Horace Mann High School in the act of soliciting students to transfer. This would certainly seem to be improper." Harris acknowledged that faculty "must have academic freedom," but "freedom always entails responsibility." Thus he told Georg that "you will take the consequences of anything which follows as a result of your action." The school did not seek to interfere with Georg's "community activities. The College will tell you in rather definite terms if the consequences of your action affects the Institution adversely. Therefore, I am not arguing the merits of the case either way." Harris felt that the only permissible course was to visit the parents of the Horace Mann students. "After all," he concluded, "the parents must file the suit." In a hand-written reply, Georg agreed with the president that "academic freedom also entailed responsibility" and that "it would have been highly improper to have solicited students on any public school campus to transfer." He explained, accordingly, that "Mrs. Iggers, Dr. Lorch, and I visited Negro parents in their homes; each time we were accompanied by a prominent person in the Negro community." Georg closed asserting that "I fully understand your concern about this matter and am glad to be able to refute the allegation made to you about me."[33]

The incident suggested the growing support within the black community for increased activism against segregation. Harris's equivocation concerning the merits of mobilizing black litigants, combined with a firm stance condemning solicitation upon public school property, undoubtedly reflected pressure from white leaders. He specifically acknowledged that the school board was "within its right" to "object to any deliberate interference from outside" with "activities on its campus."[34]

At the same time, Harris was probably aware—given the predominately black middle-class character of his faculty—of the disagreement within the NAACP Branch concerning the suit, editorialized in the *Southern Mediator*. Thus his countenancing of privately approaching black families directly at home was more consistent with ambivalence toward rather than outright opposition to bringing the desegregation suit. Georg recalled that "relatively few children from professional, middle class backgrounds" gathered at the "collection points"; most were "from semiskilled homes." Some parents had to be convinced not to get involved because they were vulnerable to intimidation, such as school board service workers. Ultimately, Georg was undoubtedly correct that the "attempt to test the segregation patterns in January 1956 apparently had the support of large numbers of the Black population. After that support of the NAACP action became a matter of pride. This pride also expressed itself in financial support of the litigation. Once the suit was filed, almost all the money … came from [Little Rock] Blacks."[35]

Still, this heightened black community consciousness was not unqualified. The unwillingness of the branch's two experienced black lawyers to support the idea of a suit once *Brown* II fostered changes in the Blossom plan, undoubtedly involved primarily a disagreement over tactics rather than principle. It nonetheless seemed noteworthy that without Williams—the former branch president who had unwittingly disrupted the branch's informal negotiations with the school board during 1952—the executive committee turned to Georg and Lorch for the initiative in preparing for the suit. Georg's 1960 commentary understated the role in the branch's work of what he later called "a foreign born white." In his letter to me, however, he explained that he, "as chairman of the executive committee … and Dr. Lorch, played a crucial role in the organization of the suit. We did not steer the branch into a direction it would not have followed otherwise. There was a broad consensus behind the decision to challenge the school board's retreat from the original Blossom plan. But in making this decision, the branch followed our advice. The planning for the challenge was directed by me in consultation with Dr. Lorch, Ozell Sutton, Rev. Crenchaw … and the Bates." Subsequent events revealed that there was "clearly broad support within the Black community for this action. On the other hand," he observed, "I do not think that without the organizational work undertaken by myself and Dr. Lorch in the crucial period between December 1955 and January 1956 there would have been a registration attempted at that time or a suit filed."[36]

The Ambivalent Outcome of Defeat

Why did the initiative for bringing the litigation depend so much upon a "foreign born" white? Given the current civil rights historiography's primary concern with black community formation and group consciousness, this is a fair question. After all, the local NAACP's interracial leadership actively promoted challenging the moderate Blossom plan, while for different reasons, neither the branch's own lawyers, the NAACP's national headquarters, nor the city's black, middle-class professionals did so. Yet once the suit was filed local blacks formed a united front, backed up by financial support. At the same time, Little Rock's black voters (apparently including even some members of the local NAACP) helped to elect Faubus in his first reelection primary bid during the spring and summer of 1956, which coincided with the Court challenge to the Blossom Plan. Amid these conflicting currents Georg and Lorch, more so than their black colleagues on the executive committee, were outsiders. Accordingly, they were freer from immediate black community ties to perceive that the retreat of the white moderates in the weaker Blossom plan potentially might be used to foster greater popular support for a new, more activist litigation strategy.[37]

The strategy that the executive board committee agreed upon reflected a change emerging in civil rights activism. In keeping with episodic successes from Scipio Jones to the desegregation of Little Rock's public facilities during the early 1950s, the local NAACP had won some triumphs. But such limited victories did not promote broad-based African-American demand for more assertive claims of racial justice. The desegregation litigation growing out of *Brown*, despite the gradualism inherent in the remedial decree, did, by contrast, foster in the city a more community-based struggle to gain constitutional rights. The switch in position that took place between the two black lawyers and other members of the executive committee following the weakening of the Blossom plan, was consistent with the growing perception—which Georg's idea to organize the litigation around black families demonstrated—that group more than individual action was required after *Brown* II. Thus the mobilization of over thirty families to challenge the multi-school character of the Blossom plan promoted support for desegregation throughout the whole Little Rock black community. This new litigation strategy of 1955/56 confirmed what Julian Bond later said about the civil rights struggle generally. It was, he said, "a great testament to the Constitution's strength. Although ... that code of law had ... been bent and twisted to deny black Americans their rights, it also provided the basic tool used by the movement to win justice." Like so many other members of the civil rights movement, African Americans in Little Rock "knew that segregation was wrong on the basis of the nation's highest law. People were willing ... to fight through the legal system for change, because the Constitution was their ultimate shield."[38]

The tension between gradualism and meaningful justice that *Brown* fostered further altered activist strategy. The accommodation the Blossom Plan made between Jim Crow segregation and token desegregation following *Brown* II, conformed to the distinction Martin Luther King later made between "just laws and ... unjust laws." Thus, he said, "I can urge men to obey the 1954 decision of the Supreme Court because it is morally right, and I can urge them to disobey segregation ordinances because they are morally wrong." The Little Rock branch's "civil disobedience" arose from a direct violation of the Blossom Plan in order to justify federal court litigation, a form of protest King condoned because "as federal courts have consistently affirmed ... it is immoral to urge an individual to withdraw his efforts to gain his basic constitutional rights because the quest precipitates violence. Society must protect the robbed and punish the robber." More broadly, the Little Rock NAACP's community-focused litigation plan was consistent with what later became known as King's nonviolent philosophy.[39]

Contrary to the moderation that characterized Little Rock during the mid-1950s, the desegregation confrontation in Hoxie, Arkansas, revealed the ominous potential for violence. The struggle in the small rural hamlet on the edge of the state's Mississippi Delta region took place over the year 1955/56, the very same period as the Little Rock litigation. Supported by a federal court and the federal government the Hoxie school board's desegregation plan eventually prevailed. The White Citizens Council's resort to systematic intimidation nonetheless portended ill for any desegregation case in Arkansas. Anonymous late-night phone calls, knocks on doors, and a boycott were part of the resistance effort. At rallies inflammatory speeches were commonplace; threats were made repeatedly that "someone might get hurt" unless there were a return to separate schools. One segregationist speaker attacked the Fourteenth Amendment as a fraud, predicting that "blood would run knee-deep all over Arkansas" unless firearms and "grass ropes" were used to keep the "nigger out of the white bedroom." Lynching was a useful device for achieving such a purpose because the "power of government was with the people." Little Rock's vocal segregationist, Amis Guthridge, called the school board a tool of the Supreme Court's "revolutionary plot." He accused the Methodist church of favoring integration and exclaimed that if anyone committed violence against a member of the school board, the FBI would be powerless to intervene. A state-wide segregationist leader, Jim Johnson, discussed the lynching of a black man in Mississippi and predicted "mongrelization" of both white and black races if integration occurred. Also singled out for attack were the University of Arkansas, Harry Ashmore, editor of the *Arkansas Gazette*, and Governor Orval E. Faubus. Guthridge threatened that Faubus's refusal to become involved would lead to political opposition in the 1956 gubernatorial primary campaign. "Pretty soon we're going to tell Faubus he's either for white folks or for the NAACP, and we don't want any smart remarks."[40]

The Hoxie confrontation heightened the racial tensions underlying the Little Rock suit. In preparation for its defense of the Blossom Plan the School Board hired a four-man team of lawyers. Specifically selected to represent a broad range of white-community interests, the lawyers assumed—based upon a misreading of the *Southern Mediator*'s editorial regarding the "disagreement" within the branch—that the NAACP's national office was promoting the desegregation litigation. In addition, the lawyer charged with conducting pretrial depositions of Mrs. Bates and other members of the local branch's executive committee, could not refrain from racist commentary. Local newspapers publicized the exchange. In response, Mrs. Bates issued a statement condemning the "boorish, rude, impertinent, and unethical conduct of counsel employed by the School Board," which was "not an affront against me alone. It is an insult to every Negro. It shows clearly … the determination with which he would relegate us to second-class citizenship." She demanded, but did not receive, a formal apology.[41]

These developments aggravated the public image blacks and whites held as the suit moved toward resolution. Among Little Rock's whites the potential for violence accompanying a more inflammatory racist discourse threatened the interracial moderation that characterized the city's national reputation during the mid-1950s. For the city's blacks, by contrast, these same pressures fostered growing community-wide support for increased activism, despite the ambivalent group consciousness that moderation had engendered.

During the academic year 1956/57 the Iggers spent in Fayetteville, racial tensions in Little Rock persisted. Partially as a result of the inadequate argument that the Dallas-based NAACP lawyer U. S. Tate presented, the branch lost its suit in the federal trial court on 28 August 1956. The outcome was the same upon appeal to the Eighth Circuit in April 1957. Assessing the initial court decision, the *Arkansas Gazette* editorialized that "extremists" both for and against desegregation were "fated" to "attack" the Blossom Plan because it provided "a minimum of integration" spread over a period "that may run as long as 10 years." But despite this "extremist" criticism the *Gazette* observed that the moderate desegregation "program has the support of a considerable majority of the citizens of Little Rock of both races, who accept it as a practical solution to a difficult problem." The paper also generally approved the judicially sanctioned plan because it "takes into account the social problems inherent in any such transition, and the emotional climate in which school officials must function. But it turns away from the futile course of defiance of the legal process ... which [in the form of interposition and racist violence was] being urged across the Deep South." After state and local majorities supported passage of interposition measures in a November 1956 election, a voter coalition of more affluent whites centered in Pulaski Heights and Little Rock's enfranchised African Americans narrowly elected in March 1957 moderate white school board members publicly committed to implementing the token desegregation Blossom Plan. In their campaign the white moderates employed a pragmatic rationale; they exclaimed that what motivated their desegregation program was a simple submission to the constitutional supremacy of federal power.[42]

As the Iggers family departed Arkansas for New Orleans in the late summer of 1957, events moved toward a climax. The white moderates' victories in the *Aaron v. Cooper* case and the school board election in March 1957 encouraged Faubus to maintain an accommodationist stance, acknowledging the constitutionality of school desegregation in the face of the interposition measures advocated by extremists like Jim Johnson. As late as August 1957, Faubus told the *Southern School News* that "Everyone knows that state laws can't supersede federal laws." This embrace of the moderates' minimalist constitutional rationale underlying the Blossom Plan grew out of a political trade with East Arkansas legislators (his tax increase for their interposition laws); and a complex series of secret meetings in the late summer of 1957 involving at different points Faubus, school board members, representatives of the U.S. justice department, an Arkansas federal judge, and, peripherally, some extreme segregationists. But not members of the local NAACP. Nevertheless, one member of the Arkansas NAACP, in a private memorandum on the eve of the crisis, confirmed the view that while Faubus would probably not defend integration and might even promise to delay it legally if that were the "will of the people," the "fact remains that he is not against integration and he is fairly certain that there is no legal means of preventing integration in the long run." Moreover, he would "certainly do everything within his power to keep down violence."[43]

From afar, Georg, like other observers in America and around the world, pondered the unfolding drama. After the crisis broke in September 1957, the Little Rock Nine's courage in the face of racist opposition helped to silence dissension within the city's African American population about Daisey Bates's effective activist leadership. Ironically, black voters in the city and throughout Arkansas continued to vote for Faubus, not only during, but after the crisis from 1957 to 1959. These considerations suggest that Faubus's overriding goal was to shift accountability for enforcing desegregation to federal authorities. Understanding this goal helps to explain why Faubus changed from moderation to demagogic obstruction after August 1957. The usual explanation relies upon the narrow opportunism involved in Faubus's efforts to win a third gubernatorial term in 1958. Nevertheless, throughout the crisis Faubus acknowledged a constitutional obligation to obey "final" federal court orders. In each case, rather than risk a formal contempt charge, he complied. He never formally admitted the established constitutional doctrine that the duty of all elected officials, when confronted with possible or real defiance, was to defend and enforce constitutional rights rather than allow such rights to be subverted. Yet once he could effectively shift direct responsibility for implementing the federal court's desegregation order to federal officials—strikingly symbolized by President Dwight D. Eisenhower's dispatch of combat-ready paratroopers to overcome resistance—he readily did so: Faubus had made a show of defiance and had made it appear that his retreat was being forced by federal authority. He employed this strategy throughout the crisis. As a result, he was the only player in the drama who creatively left himself enough room for maneuver and therefore emerged with unqualified political gain.[44]

The political success this "judicial compliance" strategy brought encouraged Faubus to link his reelection bid in 1958 to federal court tests of new state "interposition" laws. Faubus used these laws to close Little Rock's high schools, even after what seemed the definitive decision from the Supreme Court in *Cooper v. Aaron*, in September 1958. Although that decision favored the African-American litigants by denying the school board's request for a two-and-a-half-year delay, it did not address directly as a matter for the Court's formal decision the constitutionality of interposition and other states' rights measures. Those measures required separate litigation, which ultimately led to lower federal court decisions rejecting the constitutionality of interposition (confirming Faubus's observation from just before the crisis, that no state law superseded a federal law). Meanwhile, the same interracial voting coalition that had maintained the white moderates' influence prior to the crisis reasserted itself, defeating the interposition program Faubus and extreme segregationists used to close the city's schools and "purge" school teachers and officials. What mattered for Faubus, however, was delay. The delay lasted through his 1958 reelection campaign, so it did not really matter that his side ultimately lost in the school board election of May and federal court decisions of June 1959. Nor were there adverse political consequences when Little Rock's newly elected moderate school board surprised him by opening the city high schools early in August 1959 on the basis of token desegregation embodied in the Blossom Plan. The crisis was over.[45]

Conclusion

Seeking meaning in repeated clashes between difference and equality, historians inevitably confront issues of objectivity and involvement. The professional standard to which Georg Iggers held himself and other historians "maintained that objectivity is unattainable in history; the historian can hope for nothing more than plausibility. But plausibility obviously rests not on the arbitrary invention of a historical account but involves rational strategies of determining what in fact is plausible."[46] Georg met the standard he set for himself and others by channeling the force of his German-Jewish immigrant heritage into a powerful and original interpretation of historiography and European intellectual history. His professional discipline was such that he declined to reach outside his field to study what was perhaps his most directly activist contribution to human rights struggle, the Little Rock school desegregation crisis. A historical contextualization of the Iggerses' role in the origins of the crisis hopefully suggests useful interpretive insights about what Little Rock means for America's persistent endeavor to realize its high egalitarian ideals. On a date almost exactly a decade after the Little Rock crisis began, Georg wrote in the *German Conception of History*, "I believe that the dedication is particularly fitting because James Luther Adams, like the best of the men discussed in this volume, has combined scholarly integrity with an active commitment to the great political and ethical problems of the day."[47] Pursuing an understanding of America's quest for equal justice, historians may contemplate with benefit Georg Iggers's dedication.

Notes

The author wishes to thank Professor Georg Iggers for the opportunity to contribute to the "Crossing Boundaries" conference. For financial support, he thanks Dean Kenneth C. Randall of the University of Alabama School of Law, the Law School Foundation, and the Edward Brett Randolph Fund.

1. G. G. Iggers "The Meeting of Two Cultures: a Young Jewish Refugee from Nazi Germany Attends the University of Richmond, 1942–1944" (Stafford Lecture University of Richmond, 5 April 1994); D. A. Gerber, "From Hamburg to Little Rock and Beyond: The Origin's of Georg Iggers's Civil Rights Activism," in *Geschichtswissenschaft vor 2000. Perspektiven der Historiographiegeschichtre, Geschichtstheorie, Sozial- und Kulturgeschichte. Festschrift für Georg G. Iggers zum 65. Geburtstag*, ed. K. Jarausch, J. Rüsen, and H. Schleier (Hagen, 1991), 509–22, reference to commitment at 521. For these and sources noted below, I wish to thank the University of Arkansas at Little Rock Archives (hereafter cited as UALRA) and its staff, including Director Linda Pine and her Assistant John M. Jackson. The full citation to the book is G. G. Iggers, *The German Conception of History: The National Tradition of Historical Thought from Herder to the Present* (Hanover, N.H., 1988).
2. G. C. [*sic*] Iggers, "An Arkansas Professor: The NAACP and the Grass Roots" in *Little Rock, U.S.A.: Materials For Analysis*, ed., Wilson and Jane Cassels Record (San Francisco, 1960), 283–91; Iggers to Freyer, 17 Sept. 1980, UALRA. For the general background, see T. A. Freyer, *The Little Rock Crisis: A Constitutional Interpretation* (Westport, Conn., 1984), and T. A. Freyer, "The Little Rock Crisis Reconsidered, "*Arkansas Historical Quarterly* 56, no. 3 (Autumn 1997): 361–70.
3. Freyer, "The Little Rock Crisis Reconsidered" (see n. 2)
4. See the works cited above in note 1.
5. P. Novick, *That Noble Dream: The "Objectivity Question" and the American Historical Profession* (Cambridge, 1992), as quoted, 365, n. 6.
6. Iggers to Freyer, 17 Sept. 1980, UALRA.
7. Virginia Brady Perschbacher (Director Library Services, Philander Smith College) to Tony Freyer, 7 July 1997, based on *President's Annual Report, 1955–1959*, including 1953/54, 1954/55, 1955/56, 1956/57. Dr. Perschbacher also includes information from Dr. William H. Woods, a 1954 graduate of Philander Smith College, a student of Dr. Iggers, and currently Chair of the Division of Natural and Physical Sciences.
8. Gerber, "From Hamburg to Little Rock and Beyond." See also G. G. Iggers, *The Cult of Authority: The Political Philosophy of the Saint-Simonians: A Chapter in the Intellectual History of Totalitarianism* (The Hague, 1958).
9. "Library Segregation," n.d., UALRA. See also the works by Gerber and Iggers cited above in note 1.
10. Iggers to Freyer, 17 Sept. 1980, UALRA.
11. Little Rock Council On Schools, A Study on Equality under Segregation in the Little Rock Public School System [1952], UALRA.
12. Ibid.
13. Iggers to Freyer, 17 Sept. 1980, UALRA.
14. "School Officials Asked to Study Segregation Breakdown Issue," *Arkansas Gazette* (?), Feb. 1952, UALRA.
15. Iggers to Freyer, 17 Sept. 1980, UALRA. For more on *Brown*, see Freyer, *Little Rock Crisis* and the sources cited therein.
16. Iggers, "NAACP Grass Roots," 287, cited above in n. 2; and n. 11.
17. Iggers to Freyer, 17 Sept. 1980, UALRA.
18. Franz Adler to Georg Iggers, 9 Feb. 1954; Iggers to Adler, 10 May 1954, UALRA.
19. Iggers to Freyer, 17 Sept. 1980, UALRA.

20. Freyer, *Little Rock Crisis*, 63–86.
21. Adler to Iggers, 25 Feb. 1955, UALRA.
22. Freyer, *Little Rock Crisis*, 63–98.
23. Iggers to Freyer, 17 Sept. 1980, UALRA.
24. Iggers, "NAACP Grass Roots," 286, 288. For Williams on the "phoney" Blossom plan, see Lee Lorch to U. Simpson Tate, 7 Dec. 1955, UALRA.
25. Iggers to Freyer, 17 Sept. 1980, UALRA. On Booker and Scipio Jones, see Freyer "Little Rock Reconsidered," 362.
26. All quotes from Iggers to Freyer, 17 Sept. 1980, UALRA, except for reference to "disagreement" in *Southern Mediator*. See Freyer, *Little Rock Crisis*, 49.
27. The sources for this summary of events are Iggers, "NAACP Grass Roots" (see note 2); Iggers to Freyer, 17 Sept. 1980, and Lorch to Tate, 7 Dec. 1955, both in UALRA; and generally Freyer, *Little Rock Crisis*, 41–62.
28. Iggers to Freyer, 17 Sept. 1980, UALRA.
29. Georg G. Iggers to Friends, 10 Jan. 1956, UALRA. The School Board's acceptance of litigation as a device for escaping public blame for a desegregation plan that they favored is central to the logic of the Iggerses' appeal, but not mentioned in either his letter to me or the 1960 essay. The need to assign blame to federal authorities was in fact fundamental to the rationale of many school boards across the South as they moved to comply with *Brown* II; indeed, as I develop below, "blame" was at the heart of the legalistic strategy Governor Faubus and other southern officials pursued after Little Rock.
30. Freyer, *Little Rock Crisis*, 44–45, 50–54.
31. Ibid., 41–59; Iggers to Freyer, 17 Sept. 1980, UALRA.
32. Iggers to Freyer, 17 Sept. 1980, UALRA; Iggers, "NAACP Grass Roots," 289 (see note 2).
33. M. LaFayette Harris to Georg Iggers, 25 Jan. 1956; Georg G. Iggers to President Harris, 25 Jan. 1956, UALRA.
34. Harris to Iggers, 25 Jan. 1956, UALRA.
35. Iggers to Freyer, 17 Sept. 1980, UALRA.
36. Ibid.
37. See the works cited above in note 2.
38. J. Bond, "Introduction," to J. Williams, *Eyes on the Prize: America's Civil Rights Years, 1954–1965* (New York, 1987), xiii-xiv.
39. Martin Luther King Jr., "Letter from Birmingham Jail," 16 April 1963, in M. L. King, Jr., *Why We Can't Wait* (New York, 1964).
40. Freyer, *Little Rock Crisis*, 63–74, phrases, as quoted, at 65.
41. Ibid., 50–54; passage, as quoted, at 54.
42. Ibid., 54–58; passages, as quoted, at 58.
43. Passages quoted in Freyer, "The Little Rock Crisis Reconsidered," 364, 365.
44. Ibid.; Freyer, *Little Rock Crisis*, 87–137.
45. Freyer, "The Little Rock Crisis Reconsidered," 361–70; Freyer, *Little Rock Crisis*, 139–63.
46. Georg G. Iggers, *Historiography in the Twentieth Century: From Scientific Objectivity to the Postmodern Challenge* (Hanover, N.H., 1997), 145.
47. Iggers, *German Conception of History*, xv.

Chapter 10

Activists, Leaders, and Supporters

On the Role of Whites in the National Association for the Advancement of Colored People

Manfred Berg

The struggle for black equality has arguably been the most important political and social movement of twentieth-century American history, but it was not a movement of African Americans only. Although racial discrimination and segregation served the purpose of preserving "white supremacy," numerous white Americans joined the black cause. Their motives were manifold and diverse, ranging from a limited commitment to uphold fundamental legal principles to a sense of compelling civic duty or religious calling. Certainly it is not difficult to comprehend why a young Jewish refugee from Nazi Germany would be appalled by the blatant racism he encountered in the American South. As a student at the University of Richmond in Virginia, Georg Iggers in 1944 became involved in an interracial student organization called the Richmond Intercollegiate Council. Subsequently, he and his wife Wilma, a Jewish refugee from Czechoslovakia, taught at Philander Smith College, a black college in Little Rock, Arkansas, where they joined the local branch of the National Association for the Advancement of Colored People (subsequently referred to as the Association or NAACP). They became instrumental in preparing the lawsuit to desegregate the Little Rock Central High School that in 1957 led to the infamous stand-off between the governor of Arkansas and the federal government of the United States. Later Georg and Wilma Iggers also worked as active members of the NAACP branches of New Orleans and Buffalo, New York.[1]

Grass-Roots Activism and Leadership

The following essay on the role of whites in the NAACP therefore bears an obvious reference to the life of Georg Iggers, but it does not pretend to offer a biographical sketch of his life as a civil rights activist. Instead, it will focus on the more general aspects of the problem of race relations within an interracial civil rights group. It will argue that the successful transition from white to black leadership after the founding of the NAACP and its firm commitment to interracialism were of pivotal importance for the survival and achievement of America's oldest and largest civil rights organization. Given the limitations of space, it will not attempt to present a coherent narrative of race relations within the NAACP from its inception in 1909 to the present.[2] It will also not elaborate on the varieties of motifs that prompted individual whites to join and support the NAACP. Its purpose is to review the role of whites by distinguishing—somewhat arbitrarily—three basic functions in which they have served and aided the Association: grass-roots activists, prominent leaders, and supporters.

Of these three categories, grass-roots activism is by far the most difficult to deal with. Except for the early years, there is very little information on white NAACP members and activists on the local level. True to its integrationist creed that skin-color was irrelevant in the struggle for human rights, the Association did not keep records on the race of its members or on the exact number and proportion of its white membership. Since the founding of the NAACP was basically the work of white neo-abolitionists and social reformers, it is not surprising that several of the early branches were predominantly white. Until 1918, the branch of Boston, Massachusetts, the cradle of abolitionism, not only was the largest NAACP unit, it also had a majority of white members. Its leaders were prominent white citizens with famous names from the abolitionist tradition. The first branch president was Francis Jackson Garrison, the youngest son of William Lloyd Garrison. Successful membership drives in 1918 and 1919, however, brought about 2,000 new members into the branch and reversed its racial make-up. By then, the treasurer of the branch had become worried that too few whites were participating in the Association and proposed that all NAACP units should be committed to strive for at least a 10 percent of white members.[3] In Chicago, white progressives such as Jane Addams and Sophonisba Breckenridge played a prominent, if limited, role in the founding of the local NAACP. Wealthy businessman and philanthropist Julius Rosenwald who has been depicted as a dominating influence on the branch was apparently only marginally involved, according to a recent study of the branch's history.[4]

The NAACP board of directors had advised branches to include white members as early as 1913, but no fixed racial quotas were ever adopted.[5] By 1914 the annual report proudly claimed a black membership of 80 percent to demonstrate that the NAACP had struck firm roots within the black community. In 1920 blacks made up 90 percent of the total membership, according to an estimate by the *Crisis*, the NAACP organ edited by the black intellectual W. E. B. Du Bois.[6] The crucial breakthrough had come during and after World War I, when the high hopes black Americans had associated with the crusade for democracy were bitterly disappointed, and a wave of racist violence swept through America. Between early 1918 and late 1919 membership in the NAACP skyrocketed from 9,000 to 90,000. The number of branches grew from roughly 100 to well above 300 of which one third were located below the Mason-Dixon line.[7] Even if membership figures do not accurately reflect the degree of activism, there can be no question that the NAACP had built a solid base in local black communities. In Boston, a city with a relatively small African-American population of slightly above 16,000, there was one NAACP member for every six black residents at this early peak of numerical strength.[8] Other branches, however, had far more difficulties to attract mass support. In 1916 the Chicago NAACP counted only 275 members and was considered as "dead" by the national office by 1920.[9]

The number and proportion of whites in the local NAACP units and their role as grass-roots activists would have to be determined by a multitude of in-depth local studies that go far beyond the scope of this essay. After 1920 NAACP officials uniformly cited the magic number of an overall 10 percent, when asked to estimate the proportion of white members.[10] It is doubtful as to whether or not integrationism alone accounts for this internal color blindness. As an organization committed to interracialism in its own ranks, the NAACP had to maintain a certain level of white membership. Although this was never publicly admitted, the NAACP leadership might have viewed 10 percent as a minimum that was not to be discredited by any detailed accounts. Still, it is very likely that in states with a small African-American population there were quite a few NAACP branches with a considerably higher share of white members than merely 10 percent.

In the South, however, white NAACP members were rare and endangered birds. The southern branches, which by 1950 accounted for about half of the total membership and 65 percent of all NAACP units, were virtually all black.[11] In the age of white supremacy, the Association's struggle for racial integration and federal protection of black civil rights in the South, made it an utterly radical organization that even the most liberal whites would hardly dare to join. To be sure, there were a number of interracial groups in the South such as the Commission on Interracial Cooperation, the Southern Conference for Human Welfare, the Southern Regional Council, and the various councils of human relations at the local and state levels in which liberal white southerners tried to work for change. These groups and a good number of individuals cooperated with the NAACP on issues such as lynching and abolishing the poll tax. Most white liberals, however, advocated fairness and justice for blacks on the basis of the "separate but equal" doctrine. Fundamental opposition against segregation and unqualified support for the legal, political, and social equality of the races remained confined to a very small and isolated minority.[12] Open membership and activism in the NAACP, moreover, carried grave social and personal risks and was a rare exception. A recent book on the role of white southerners in the civil rights movement during the 1950s and 1960s does not mention a single white NAACP member.[13]

This makes the case of Georg and Wilma Iggers all the more remarkable who were two of the three whites in the Little Rock, Arkansas, branch of the NAACP in the 1950s.[14] But obviously, the Iggerses were not white southerners, and Little Rock, at least prior to the 1957 crisis, was generally regarded as a exceptionally progressive southern city. More detailed research on southern NAACP units would probably yield valuable information on other white members, but this would not alter the overall picture that for all practical purposes the southern NAACP was an all-black organization.

The national leadership of the Association knew perfectly well that its claim to interracialism could not be redeemed in the South and prudently did not make this an issue. Mobilizing support among the black community was obviously difficult enough. There is also no evidence of any efforts to specifically recruit whites in other parts of the country. Although whites were certainly welcome, the claim of the NAACP to represent black Americans was always more important than its racial composition. On occasion, black NAACP leaders even showed some skepticism toward white activists. During the anticommunist anxieties of the early Cold War, white newcomers were sometimes suspected to be communist infiltrators.[15] Also, the NAACP did not approve of the import of white student activists into Mississippi organized by its smaller and more radical rival SNCC, the Student Nonviolent Coordinating Committee, during the Freedom Summer of 1964. When intense rivalries evolved among the various civil rights organizations during the 1960s, the NAACP liked to pride itself of its vast network of black organizers and local branches.[16] At times, the argument became quite nasty. In an early 1965 feud between the Philadelphia NAACP and the local chapter of CORE, the Congress of Racial Equality, the NAACP branch president assailed CORE as being composed of "90 percent insincere, exhibitionist, frustrated, beatnik white intellectuals." Subsequently, the outraged CORE group sued for slander.[17]

Its heavily black membership base notwithstanding, the NAACP faced the charge of being "white controlled," after the radical wing of the civil rights movement, most conspicuously SNCC and CORE, had abandoned the ideal of racial integration and heeded the battle cry of "Black Power." As a matter of fact, the NAACP's low proportion of no more than 10 percent of white members largely spared it from the internal racial tensions that shattered both SNCC and CORE with their much higher numbers of white activists and that eventually led to the expulsion of whites from both groups. White participation in SNCC and CORE became a surrogate issue for the sharp ideological and personal conflicts that led to their demise by the late 1960s. CORE, a largely northern-based organization, had a majority of white members until 1964 and experienced a fatal drain of organizational and financial resources when the white activists were gradually forced out. The NAACP leadership, in contrast, saw to it that anti-white sentiment within the Association was kept in check. An attempt to form an NAACP branch in Tampa, Florida, which wanted to exclude whites from membership was immediately suppressed.[18]

Even more important than the vigilance of the national leadership was the middle-class character of the NAACP membership and local activists. The typical branch official was in his or her forties, had a secure income, mostly from white-collar work, was southern-born and had a strong church affiliation.[19] This social background, and the low proportion of white activists and NAACP officials, prevented the notorious conflicts over educated whites dominating poor blacks from becoming a real issue within the Association. Georg Iggers, for example, has stressed the color blindness of the Little Rock branch, which elected him chairman of both its executive and education committees and even nominated him for the branch presidency—an offer he declined because he believed it unwise for a foreign-born white to head the chapter. This was, to be sure, in the early 1950s when white leadership might have occurred as a natural state of affairs to many southern blacks, but Iggers insists that the whites did not steer the branch into a direction it would not have followed otherwise.[20]

As with the exact number and share of white members, the state of race relations within local NAACP branches during different periods of the Association's history can only be determined by more detailed research. It is unlikely that a picture of undiluted harmony will emerge from such research, but it is incontestable that race relations in the NAACP never deteriorated to the level of outright confrontation and ritualistic purges that helped destroy SNCC and CORE. To some extent, this may have been the result of the centralized leadership structure of the NAACP, which ensured the continued ideological commitment to interracialism and integration. But there is also no evidence that the rank and file membership ever pressed for an all-black organization. By and large, the limited number and role of white activists within the NAACP appears to have been conducive to organizational stability. Certainly, the NAACP was not particularly eager to attract the type of youthful and guilt-ridden idealists whom a CORE member once characterized as "white masochists." Roy Wilkins, the long-time executive director of the Association, liked to scoff at the "white boys and girls" who indulged in "self-reproach" and allowed themselves to be prodded into submission by black radicals playing the race card.[21]

Critics who charged the NAACP with being controlled by whites did not refer to its membership in the first place, but to the influence whites exerted in and on its leadership. As far as the origins of the Association are concerned, this can hardly be contested. The initiative to call the National Negro Conference of May 1909, which is considered the official founding act of the NAACP, came from white social reformers and neo-abolitionists in the wake of the bloody race riots in Springfield, Illinois, which had occurred in the summer of the previous year. Oswald Garrison Villard, grandson of William Lloyd Garrison and editor of the *New York Evening Post*, wrote a "Call" that invited "all the believers in democracy to join in a national conference … for the renewal of the struggle for civil and political liberty." The appeal was published on 9 February 1909, the centennial of Abraham Lincoln's birthday. Among the sixty signers of the "Call," there were fifty-three white persons. The vast majority of the conference participants were white, as were two-thirds of the speakers. The Committee of Forty, which was formed to establish a permanent organization, had a majority of white members and so did the board of directors that was elected after the Association had been incorporated in 1912. The leadership positions of the fledgling organization were almost all filled by whites. Moorfield Storey, a prominent Boston lawyer and former secretary of abolitionist senator Charles Sumner, served as its first president until his death in 1929. The largely ceremonial position of the NAACP president was held by white men until 1975. Oswald Garrison Villard was elected the first chairman of the NAACP board of directors, and also provided office space for the national secretariat in the building of his *Evening Post*. Villard resigned from the chairmanship of the board in 1913, but the first black chairman of the board of directors was elected only in 1935. The first five executive secretaries of the NAACP were white women and men with backgrounds in the progressive movement until the black writer James Weldon Johnson was appointed in 1920. The office of the NAACP treasurer was also held by whites until the 1940s.[22]

The only black person to hold a leadership position in the early Association was W. E. B. Du Bois, the most prominent African-American intellectual who had heeded the call for an interracial civil rights organization after his all-black Niagara movement, founded in 1905, had become defunct. As Director of Publicity and Research and editor of the official NAACP organ, the *Crisis*, Du Bois was also a paid employee of the Association, which led to numerous clashes with the board of directors and the executive secretary. Although these quarrels were ostensibly about Du Bois's neglect of the financial aspects of the *Crisis* and his claim to complete editorial autonomy, race inevitably figured in. Villard, in particular, displayed a good measure of the paternalistic attitudes that had characterized the old abolitionist movement. Executive secretary Mary Childs Nerney, for her part, typified the social reformers who easily lost patience with the objects of their benevolence. Du Bois, on the other hand, was as sensitive as a Geiger counter when it came to the semblance of white condescension, and did not hesitate to charge his antagonists with racism. However, there was a clear understanding on both sides that behind these personal differences loomed the question of race and power. When Villard resigned as chairman of the board of directors in late 1913, Mary White Ovington—a white New York social reformer and one of the initiators of the "Call" who constantly tried to mediate between her friends Du Bois and Villard—saw this as "a confession ... that we cannot work with colored people unless they are our subordinates."[23] This, indeed, was the key question: Did the interracialism of the NAACP extend to blacks exerting authority over whites?

Despite their residual paternalism, the white NAACP founders knew perfectly well that if the Association was to survive and to succeed it had to become a broad-based black organization under black leadership. Not only was Du Bois's prestige as the foremost voice of black protest indispensable, the number and visibility of African-American NAACP leaders had to be increased. The stage for such a transfer of leadership was set in the summer of 1916 at a conference of black leaders called by Villard's successor as chairman of the board of directors, the New York publisher and intellectual Joel Spingarn who also represented the strong Jewish element among the white NAACP founders.[24] The conference not only brought a rapprochement between the NAACP and the followers of the late Booker T. Washington, the leading black accomodationist who had opposed the NAACP as a threat to his own influence with the white liberal elite, it also led to the appointment of James Weldon Johnson as field secretary of the Association. This marked the beginning of the transition to a predominantly black secretariat. When Johnson became the first black executive secretary in 1920, he took over an office in which all responsible positions but one were filled by African Americans.[25] The danger that the NAACP might deteriorate into a debating circle of white philanthropists had been effectively averted.

At the end of its first decade, the board of directors of the NAACP was already made up about equally of black and white members. In a gradual process, the proportion of white NAACP directors steadily declined to 22 percent in the early 1960s and dropped to 12 percent late in the decade, a figure that was roughly commensurate with the share of whites in the overall membership. Even more importantly, after 1920 the power and influence of the black-dominated secretariat had continuously grown vis-à-vis the board of directors, which was no longer capable of leading an expanding organization and limited itself to controlling the work of the national executive staff.[26] For all practical purposes the executive secretary became the real leader of the Association, and Johnson's successors Walter White and Roy Wilkins acquired national prominence during their long-term tenures. Still, the NAACP remained firmly committed to its interracial principles, and white leaders retained visible and significant positions. Villard withdrew from active NAACP work for personal reasons, but Joel Spingarn, his younger brother Arthur, a prominent lawyer, and Mary White Ovington remained in the Association's leadership until the end of their lives.

From the very beginning, the preponderance of white leaders in the early NAACP had provoked criticism. Anti-lynching crusader Ida Wells Barnett, for example, complained about the "patronizing assumptions" of white members in the Chicago branch.[27] The extent and negative consequences of white paternalism, however, should not be exaggerated. In retrospect, it seems incontestable that the social prestige, the financial resources, and the political connections of the white NAACP founders were essential for the survival and the consolidation of the Association. There were no African Americans who could afford to work pro bono as organizers or lawyers, or who could underwrite the deficits of the *Crisis* and the national secretariat. The crucial question was not whether whites had power, but how they used it. During the first three decades of the NAACP's history, when white influence was at its peak, there is no evidence of racial polarization within the organization. Not a single vote by the board of directors was divided along racial lines; no single internal conflict can be reduced to a pattern of whites versus blacks.[28]

Even Du Bois agreed that the NAACP had managed to establish a viable equilibrium between the races. In his autobiography, which was published in 1940 and dedicated to the memory of Joel Spingarn, Du Bois reflected on the basic problem of interracialism. Despite his earlier break with the Association in 1934 over his ideas on the "voluntary separation" of blacks from white society, he advanced a remarkably positive assessment of race relations within the NAACP:

> There was one initial difficulty common to all interracial effort in the United States. Ordinarily the white members of a committee formed of Negroes and whites become dominant. Either by superior training or their influence or their wealth they take charge of the committee, guide it and use the colored membership as their helpers and executive workers in certain directions. Usually if the opposite policy is attempted, if the Negroes attempt to dominate and conduct the committee, the whites become dissatisfied and gradually withdraw. In the NAACP, it was our primary effort to achieve an equality of racial influence without stressing race and without allowing undue predominance to either group. I think we accomplished this for a time to an unusual degree.[29]

The transition from white to black leadership was carried out on a gradual and consensual basis without forcing the white leaders out or breaking the ties with white allies of the liberal establishment. This was no small achievement. It was possible because white leaders basically acted out of a genuine commitment to racial justice and did not seek any personal or political gains from their NAACP work. They were mostly wealthy and influential people without political ambitions in the narrow sense. Besides, working for black rights was hardly an asset in American politics early this century.

The one group of whites that had perhaps the most direct interest in the NAACP's struggle for justice and equality were the Jews who constituted the second major white element of the Association beside members of the New England Protestant elite. Again, any attempt to quantify the presence of Jews in the Association would require meticulous in-depth research at the local level. For the early national leadership, Hasia Diner has stated that "while Jews did not constitute a majority in the upper echelons of the NAACP, they were far out of proportion to their numbers in the population."[30] Presumably, such an overall assessment would also apply to later periods of the civil rights movement. Why then did Jews feel obliged to support the black cause more than other whites?

There are basically two answers to this question that are not mutually exclusive. David Lewis has argued that the established Jews of central European descent, the Spingarn brothers for example, were concerned about the rise of anti-Semitism in the wake of Jewish mass immigration from Eastern Europe just as the established northern black middle class was afraid that the influx of southern black migrants would trigger movements for segregation and disfranchisement in the North. This parallel interest was the cornerstone of the "defensive alliance" between Jews and blacks. Hasia Diner, in contrast, has stressed the general empathy and solidarity of Jewish Americans with an oppressed minority. To the extent that Jewish involvement in the NAACP served Jewish interests, it was in strengthening their ties to the liberal Protestant elite rather than forging an alliance with the relatively powerless black middle class. In any way, Jewish involvement in the NAACP drew on a variety of traditions and motivations, including both empathy and an awareness of parallel interest.[31] Whatever interests whites, Jewish or non-Jewish, may have had to join and support the NAACP, there was never any question that the Association was dedicated to the advancement of black people and that other causes or interests ought to be pursued within different frameworks.

The black leaders of the NAACP, almost exclusively members of the small black middle class with a keen interest in upward mobility and professional opportunity, never lost sight of the key importance of white participation as a source of material support and political legitimacy. Although their power and influence in society at large were vastly uneven, it seems correct to describe the early NAACP leadership as an alliance between white and black elites.[32] This social affinity alone, however, did not assure cooperative race relations. It was necessary that both groups maintained a strong ideological commitment to interracialism, equality before the law, and a color-blind democracy that worked as a safeguard against both white paternalism and black nationalism.

Lawyers and Doctors

Unlike grass-roots activists and prominent leaders, supporters of a movement or an organization need not be fully committed or involved, but give their money, their services or their names to aid a cause. For the purposes of this essay, it appears useful to break down this group into two categories: expert supporters and donors.

Since the NAACP was founded at a time when racism enjoyed a cultural hegemony in American society, the founders of the Association felt compelled to rally expert discourse to counter the "scientific" doctrines of black inferiority. Fittingly, two prominent white scientists opened the National Negro Conference with lectures on race differences and the "Negro Brain." Franz Boas, the foremost American anthropologist, in 1910 wrote a booklet for the NAACP on the race problem from the anthropological point of view and continued to provide the Association with material relevant for the civil rights struggle.[33] More important than scientific information to be used for propaganda purposes, however, were the legal expertise and pro bono services rendered by prominent white lawyers. Since the NAACP had set itself the task "to secure proper legal aid to maintain and defend the colored man's right," litigation formed the backbone of its work.[34] Several of its white leaders were prominent lawyers. NAACP President Moorfield Storey had been a former president of the American Bar Association, and his most important contribution to the NAACP was to prepare the legal briefs for the Supreme Court in cases involving the right to vote and residential segregation. Arthur Spingarn headed the NAACP legal committee from 1913 until 1939, in which year he succeeded his deceased brother Joel as president of the Association.[35] Numerous other famous white lawyers such as Louis Marshall, Clarence Darrow, and Felix Frankfurter sat on the NAACP legal committee or argued important cases.

In the early days of the NAACP, the dominance of prominent white lawyers was both an important asset and inevitable from a practical point of view. By 1910 less than 1 percent of all lawyers in America were black. In the Deep South, the handful of African Americans with legal training faced great difficulties in being admitted to the bar. As a result of racial discrimination in legal education, black lawyers were frequently lacking competence and experience, and in addition faced hostility from white juries and judges. The widespread belief among black people that they needed a white lawyer in order to stand a chance in court was all too often justified.[36] Even the white lawyers working for the NAACP were not always first rate. A good example is Fred Knollenberg, the attorney who represented the NAACP branch of El Paso, Texas, in its litigation against the infamous white primary that excluded blacks from the all-important primary elections of the Democratic Party. Knollenberg was a well-meaning man who enjoyed the confidence of his black clients but committed several serious professional blunders, which made Arthur Spingarn complain about the "unfortunate fact that in choosing a lawyer in a Southern state to undertake causes as unpopular as ours, we have not the same freedom of selection that we should like."[37]

In many highly publicized cases, however, the NAACP was able to secure the services of white lawyers who, according to August Meier and Elliott Rudwick, formed an "elite group" with regard to both their professional reputation and their social standing.[38] Yet despite a number of impressive legal victories won by white NAACP lawyers, there was a growing criticism among local black activists that African Americans were not duly represented in the legal work of the Association. In the litigation against the Texas white primary, such disenchantment led to a serious setback before the Supreme Court in 1935. A group of black lawyers, journalists, and businessmen from Houston, Texas, carried its own lawsuit to the highest court without consulting the Association, which had earlier won two favorable Supreme Court rulings on this matter. The Houston case, however, was poorly prepared and prompted the Court to confirm a resolution of the Texas Democratic Party to bar blacks from voting in its primaries. It took the NAACP another decade to bring new litigation that finally resulted in the Supreme Court's ban of the white primary.[39]

In principle, the NAACP leaders accepted the necessity to shift the responsibility for the Association's legal work to African-American jurists, and white lawyers did not stand in the way of black aspirations. By 1932 half of the members of the legal committee were African Americans. The two black Harvard graduates William Hastie and Charles Houston were diligently building a small elite of black lawyers at the Howard University Law School. In 1935 Houston directed the first NAACP case before the Supreme Court that was handled exclusively by black lawyers, and was subsequently appointed special counsel of the NAACP. Four years later, his famous disciple Thurgood Marshall, who was to become the first black Supreme Court justice in 1967, succeeded Houston in this position, while William Hastie replaced Arthur Spingarn as chairman of the legal committee. Similar to the transition in the Association's leadership at large, the transfer of responsibility from white to black lawyers happened without serious conflict or frictions. The new black legal elite was self-conscious but not hostile toward their white colleagues. Significantly, in 1961 Thurgood Marshall was succeeded as general counsel of the NAACP Legal and Defense Fund by Jack Greenberg, a white man.[40]

As with the exact proportion of white members, it is next to impossible to determine the role of whites as donors to the NAACP in any accurate quantitative sense, especially before the 1960s. It is clear, however, that contributions by white leaders and supporters played a vital role during the first decade. Hasia Diner has documented the donations by wealthy Jewish philanthropists in particular, including, for example, the Chicago-based Rosenwald Fund, established by Julius Rosenwald, the president of Sears, Roebuck. In 1930, the Association received a pledge of $100,000 from the Garland Fund, a foundation initiated by a young idealistic heir with socialist leanings. Due to subsequent differences of opinion over the kind of programs to be supported and the financial difficulties of the fund in the wake of the Great Depression, only $20,000 materialized—enough, however, to underwrite parts of the NAACP's expensive legal programs.[41]

Nevertheless, the importance of external finances for the NAACP must not be exaggerated. As early as 1921, the Association claimed that 90 percent of its funding was derived from membership dues and contributions by blacks, most of them between $1.00 and $5.00.[42] When its membership skyrocketed during World War II to about 400,000, the Association had indeed reached a relatively solid financial base. Between 1940 and 1945 its annual income ballooned from $64,000 to $402,000.[43] According to the most detailed analysis of the external funding of the civil rights movement available, the NAACP was the only major organization that was self-supporting through most of its history. In the early 1950s a mere 5 percent of its total income came from external sources Only when the big corporations and foundations began to fund the civil rights movement on a large scale during the 1960s, did the NAACP become heavily dependent on external money. By 1970, it made up 67 percent of all its income.[44]

Throughout the history of the NAACP, there were always many individual whites who gave money without being accounted for. Georg Iggers, for example, reports that the money to finance the Little Rock school integration case of 1956 came almost entirely from white friends and relatives in the North and Canada.[45] While most of these individual contributions were rather modest, on occasion a big one would also come in. In early 1952 Loula Davis Lasker, a well-to-do Jewish social worker and philanthropist from Texas who wished to remain anonymous, made a donation of $25,000, earmarked for a political action program in the South. The NAACP responded enthusiastically and conducted a well-coordinated voter registration drive in six southern states that played a substantial part in registering about 300,000 additional southern black voters prior to the November elections.[46]

While altruism and solidarity were probably the prevailing motives of most whites who gave money to the NAACP, political opportunism was also not absent. To mention two prominent examples: In the campaign of 1956, Vice President Richard Nixon referred to himself as an "honorary NAACP member" in front of a black audience, apparently because he had once paid an annual membership fee to a California branch and had later made several modest contributions. John F. Kennedy sent a donation after NAACP Executive Secretary Roy Wilkins had attested to him "one of the best voting records on civil rights ... of any Senator in Congress" during his senatorial reelection bid in 1958, but declined to become a member.[47] To be sure, the political support of the Association was not for sale. It was avowedly nonpartisan and supported or opposed candidates only on the basis of their civil rights records, which were meticulously researched and widely publicized among black voters.

Of course, the key issue associated with grants and donations from whites was the question of control and dependency. During the heyday of Black Power in the late 1960s, the stereotype had it that the NAACP was "guided, financed, and controlled by whites." Baseball hero and former NAACP board member Jackie Robinson publicly accused its leaders of being more concerned with gaining money from the Ford Foundation than the respect of young African Americans.[48] However, if the amount of outside funding indicates the extent of white influence, the more radical groups of SNCC and CORE must have been heavily "white controlled" in the mid-1960s, when each of them, although much smaller than the NAACP, received a higher total of external contributions than the Association. In 1964, the external income of the NAACP amounted to $292,738, while SNCC received $631,439 and CORE $694,588.[49] This distribution was dramatically reversed only after the latter groups embraced black separatism in the second half of the decade. Obviously, the NAACP benefited from the desire of the big donors to support the moderate forces within the civil rights movement. But the moderation of the NAACP, that is to say its firm commitment to integration and racial change through the political process, did not have to be bought nor did the Association have to sell its soul to accept money for voter education and civil rights litigation.

Conclusions

Throughout the NAACP's history, the presence and influence of white members, leaders, and supporters time and again prompted black critics to contest its claim to representing African-American interests. When Joel Spingarn in 1914 had attacked Booker T. Washington for his accommodationist approach, Washington's allies within the black press retaliated by pointing to the preponderance of white leaders in the NAACP. Black nationalist Marcus Garvey scoffed at the "National Association for the Advancement of Certain People" because in his view it endeared itself to white society and served the interest of a small black elite. Black Muslim Malcolm X casually dismissed the NAACP as a Jewish organization, because its president Arthur Spingarn was a Jew.[50] Black NAACP leaders, on the other hand, paid back in kind. In the 1920s, Du Bois denounced Garvey as the "most dangerous enemy of the black race," either a "lunatic or a traitor." In the 1960s, Executive Secretary Roy Wilkins condemned Black Power as "a reverse Mississippi, a reverse Hitler, a reverse Ku Klux Klan."[51] Anti-white sentiments, to be sure, also surfaced within the Association, especially in the late 1960. Its first conspicuous showing came in late 1966 when a group of self-declared "Young Turks" tried to oust Walter Reuther from the NAACP board of directors. The powerful president of the United Auto Workers (UAW) had become the symbol for the influence of the liberal white establishment on the Association. The UAW probably gave more funds to the NAACP than all other labor unions combined. Reuther, however, fought back and was handily reelected to the board. At the peak of their strength, the "Turks" could muster the support of roughly one-third of the 1968 annual convention, but failed to commit the NAACP to a program of black separatism. As one member of the board put it, integration remained the goal of the NAACP, "that is the creation of a society where race is irrelevant in human affairs."[52]

At the present time, when many of the more far-reaching hopes associated with the civil rights movement have long since proven elusive, such rhetoric may easily be dismissed as an anachronism. During the 1990s, the NAACP leadership, plagued by financial problems and a dwindling membership, had itself come to believe that it had to embrace black nationalism to make the Association attractive again, especially for young blacks. This strategy reached its low point when in 1993 and 1994 its leaders actively courted favors with Louis Farrakhan and the Nation of Islam (NOI), graciously ignoring the NOI's rabid racism and anti-Semitism. When the Association even failed to protest a violently anti-white and anti-Semitic hate speech by one of Farrakhan's lieutenants, Georg Iggers protested this lack of principle and historical awareness, citing his lifelong record of NAACP activism and membership.[53] In the meantime, the leadership crisis of the Association appears to have been resolved. In 1995 the newly elected chairwoman of the board of directors Myrlie Evers-Williams, widow of NAACP martyr Medgar Evers, and the new NAACP Executive Director Kweisi Mfume, a former leader of the Congressional Black Caucus, both promised to restore the credibility of the Association and its ties to its traditional white allies.[54]

Even if whites no longer play prominent roles in the NAACP, its history of interracialism is an important legacy in times of troubled race relations. The NAACP's historical mission of inclusion, fairness and justice for all Americans has traditionally struck a sympathetic chord with many white Americans and appears as relevant as ever. The misleading dichotomy of "black self-determination" versus "white control" obscures several remarkable historical achievements that this essay has attempted to recover: While whites created a national organizational framework, the NAACP simultaneously developed a black grass-roots network committed to protest racial discrimination. Despite some internal racial tensions, a polarization between black and white was avoided. The transfer of leadership was not characterized by bitter power struggles. White leaders realized that blacks had to take charge, and black leaders managed to take charge without ritualistic purges. As a black-based, but interracial organization the NAACP survived and to a remarkable extent also succeeded in its struggle against racial discrimination.

Notes

1. Georg Iggers to Tony Freyer, 17 Sept. 1980, and to Rev. Dr. Benjamin F. Chavis, Jr., then executive director of the NAACP, 9 Feb. 1994. Both letters are in the possession of the author courtesy of Georg Iggers.
2. The historiography on the NAACP is surprisingly wanting. At present, no synthesis of its history is available. The brief introduction by J. L. Harris, *History and Achievement of the NAACP* (New York, 1992), is of no value for serious historical inquiry. See instead A. Meier and J. H. Bracey, "The NAACP as a Reform Movement, 1909–1965: 'To reach the conscience of America,'" *Journal of Southern History* 59 (1993): 3–30. There are several monographs dealing with specific NAACP policies during limited periods of its history. For example, see R. L. Zangrando, *The NAACP Crusade against Lynching, 1909–1950* (Philadelphia, 1980); M. V. Tushnet, *The NAACP's Legal Strategy against Segregated Education, 1925–1950* (Chapel Hill, N.C., 1987). The author has recently published a study on the NAACP's struggle for black voting rights from its founding to the present under the title *The Ticket to Freedom: Die NAACP und das Wahlrecht der Afro-Amerikaner* (Frankfurt a.M., 2000), which also offers a broader political history of the Association. An English language translation is planned.
3. On the Boston NAACP branch during its first decade, see M. R. Schneider, *Boston Confronts Jim Crow 1890–1920* (Boston, 1997), 133–59.
4. C. R. Reed, *The Chicago NAACP and the Rise of Black Professional Leadership, 1910–1966* (Bloomington, Ind., 1997), 17–43, esp. 24–25. See also idem, "Organized Racial Reform during the Progressive Era: The Chicago NAACP, 1910–1920," *Michigan Historical Review* 14 (1988): 75–99.
5. C. F. Kellogg, *NAACP: A History of the National Association for the Advancement of Colored People, 1909–1920* (Baltimore, Md., 1967), 118. Kellogg's book is the most comprehensive account of the NAACP's founding and first decade.
6. *NAACP Annual Report 1914* (New York, 1914); *The Crisis: A Journal of the Darker Races* (hereafter cited as *Crisis*), March 1920, 243.
7. These figures are based on a memorandum of 15 June 1954 that traces the development of membership figures and the number of branches from 1912 to 1950. The memorandum was prepared by R. Williams for Gloster Current, the NAACP director of branches. See Records of the National Association for the Advancement of Colored People, Library of Congress, Manuscript Division, Washington, D.C., Part II, Series A, Box 202 (hereafter quoted as: NAACP II A 202.
8. Schneider, *Boston Confronts Jim Crow*, 158.
9. Reed, "Organized Racial Reform during the Progressive Era," 93.
10. For example, see the interviews with Lucille Black, long-time membership secretary of the NAACP, and Gloster Current, long-time director of branches. Ralph J. Bunche Oral History Project, Moorland-Spingarn Research Center, Howard University, Washington, D.C. (hereafter cited as: RJB), interviews nos. 70 and 167.
11. According to an estimate by the director of branches Gloster Current, quoted in R. Gavins, "The NAACP in North Carolina during the Age of Segregation," in *New Directions in Civil Rights Studies*, ed. A. L. Robinson and P. Sullivan (Charlottesville, Va., 1991), 105–25, 105.
12. On the varieties of racial dissent by white southerners in the age of white supremacy see M. Sosna, *In Search of the Silent South: Southern Liberals and the Race Issue* (New York, 1977); A. P. Dunbar, *Against the Grain: Southern Radicals and Prophets, 1929–1959* (Charlottesville, Va., 1981); J. Egerton, *Speak Now Against the Day: The Generation Before the Civil Rights Movement in the South* (Chapel Hill, N.C., 1994); D. L. Chappell, *Inside Agitators: White Southerners in the Civil Rights Movement* (Baltimore, Md., 1994); P. Sullivan, *Days of Hope: Race and Democracy in the New Deal Era* (Chapel Hill, N.C., and London, 1996).

13. Chappell, *Inside Agitators*. In fact, Chappell's book seems mistitled, because it largely deals with the attitudes of racial moderates in the South during the 1950s and 1960s and gives very little information on southern whites who actively participated in the civil rights movement.
14. Iggers to Freyer, 17 Sept. 1980, cited above, n. 1.
15. The background for this were attempts by the Communist Party to take over several branches in California and the Northeast. See the letter by Acting Executive Secretary Roy Wilkins to Wilson C. Record, 21 Dec. 1949, NAACP II A 202. The NAACP leaders never openly exposed the race of the alleged infiltrators, but it is clear from the sources that the suspects were mostly white. For example, see the material on the Richmond, California, and San Francisco branches in the late 1940s, NAACP II C 18. The anticommunism of the NAACP is discussed more thoroughly in my book cited above, n. 2.
16. For example, see the reports "NAACP Summer Projects," 17 and 23 July 1965, NAACP III A 268, as well as the speech by NAACP voter registration activist W. C. Patton, 5 Oct. 1967, NAACP IV A 62.
17. See the article "Picketing Threat By CORE Hit" in the *Philadelphia Inquirer*, 6 Jan. 1965, a copy in NAACP III A 202, as well as the letter from James O. Williams to Roy Wilkins, 7 Jan. 1965, and Wilkins's reply of 12 Jan. 1965, ibid.
18. On the expulsion of whites from SNCC and CORE, see C. Carson, *In Struggle: SNCC and the Black Awakening of the 1960s*, 2nd ed. (Cambridge, Mass., 1995), 236–43; A. Meier and E. Rudwick, *CORE: A Study in the Civil Rights Movement, 1942–1968* (Urbana, Ill., 1975), 379–93, 415–20. See also E. Rudwick and A. Meier, "Integration vs. Separatism: The NAACP and CORE Face Challenge from Within," in *Along the Color Line: Explorations in the Black Experience*, ed. A. Meier and E. Rudwick (Urbana, Ill., and Chicago, 1976), 238–263. I have dealt elsewhere with the response of the NAACP to the "Black Power" challenge in detail. See M. Berg, "Black Power: The National Association for the Advancement of Colored People and the Resurgence of Black Nationalism during the 1960s," in *The American Nation—National Identity—Nationalism*, ed. K. Krakau (Münster, 1997), 235–62. On the Tampa branch, see the interview with Gloster Current, RJB, no. 167.
19. On the social profile of NAACP branch officers, see the memorandum from Daniel Wright to Gloster Current, "A Study of the NAACP Branch Presidents, Secretaries and Treasurers," 30 Oct. 1967, NAACP IV C 55.
20. Iggers to Freyer, 17 Sept. 1980, cited above, n. 1.
21. Meier and Rudwick, *CORE*, 383. See also Wilkins's syndicated weekly newspaper column of 23 Sept. 1963 entitled "The New Left Conference," copy in Roy Wilkins Papers, Library of Congress, Manuscript Division, Washington, D.C., Box 39.
22. The story of the founding of the NAACP has been told many times. See Kellogg, *NAACP*, esp. 9–30, as well as the appendices to Kellogg's book for a list of the signers, members of the Committee of Forty and the board of directors, and the names of all leading NAACP officials during the first decade, ibid., 297–308. See also *Proceedings of the National Negro Conference 1909* (New York, 1969). On Moorfield Storey, see W. B. Hixson, Jr., *Moorfield Storey and the Abolitionist Tradition* (New York, 1972). For further details, see O. G. Villard, *Fighting Years: Memoirs of A Liberal Editor* (New York, 1939), and J. W. Johnson, *Along this Way: The Autobiography of James Weldon Johnson*, 3rd ed. (New York, 1990).
23. Quoted in Kellogg, *NAACP*, 96. On Ovington's long-time work for the NAACP, see her autobiography M. W. Ovington, *The Walls Came Tumbling Down: The Autobiography of Mary White Ovington* (New York, 1970). On Du Bois's work as editor of the *Crisis* and his quarrels with the board of directors, see D. L. Lewis, *W. E. B. Du Bois: Biography of a Race, 1868–1919* (New York, 1993), 408–24, 466–500.
24. On Spingarn see B. J. Ross, *J. E. Spingarn and the Rise of the NAACP, 1911–1939* (New York, 1972), 47–48. See also Johnson, *Along this Way*, 308–310.
25. Ovington, *The Walls Came Tumbling Down*, 176.

26. E. Rudwick and A. Meier, "The Rise of the Black Secretariat in the NAACP, 1909–1935," in *Along the Color Line*, ed. Meier and Rudwick, 94–127. On the racial composition of the board of directors see idem, "Integration vs. Separatism," 257, and Ross, *Spingarn and the Rise of the NAACP*, 52.
27. Reed, "Organized Racial Reform in Chicago," 82.
28. Ross, *Spingarn and the Rise of the NAACP*, 52–58.
29. W. E. B. Du Bois, *Dusk of Dawn: A Essay Toward An Autobiography of A Race Concept*, 3rd ed. (New Brunswick, N.J., and London, 1984), 227.
30. On the role of Jews in the NAACP, see H. Diner, *In the Almost Promised Land: American Jews and Blacks, 1915–1935*, 2nd ed. (Baltimore. Md., 1995), 118–54, esp. 122.
31. Ibid. See also D. L. Lewis, "Parallels and Divergences: Afro-American and Jewish Elites from 1910 to the Early 1930s," *Journal of American History* 71 (1984/85): 543–64.
32. Ross, *Spingarn and the Rise of the NAACP*, 53.
33. L. Farrand, "Race Differentiation—Race Characteristics," in *Proceedings of the National Negro Conference 1909*, 14–21; B. G. Wilder, "The Brain of the American Negro," ibid., 22–66. On Boas, see Diner, *In the Almost Promised Land*, 142–49.
34. *Crisis* (May 1911), 25. The legal work and strategies of the NAACP have been analyzed in a number of works. For example, see M. V. Tushnet, *The NAACP's Legal Strategy*, and R. C. Cortner, *A Mob Intent on Death: The NAACP and the Arkansas Riot Cases* (Middletown, Conn., 1988).
35. Hixson, *Moorfield Storey*, 134–45, as well as the interview with Arthur Spingarn, RJB no. 165.
36. A. Meier and E. Rudwick, "Attorneys Black and White: A Case Study of Race Relations within the NAACP," in *Along the Color Line*, ed. Meier and Rudwick, 128–73, esp. 130–36.
37. Arthur Spingarn to Nathan Margold of 16 Oct. 1930, Arthur Spingarn Papers, Library of Congress, Manuscript Division, Washington, D.C., Box 33.
38. Meier and Rudwick, "Attorneys Black and White," 133.
39. On the struggle against the white primary see D. C. Hine, *Black Victory: The Rise and Fall of the White Primary in Texas* (New York, 1979), esp. 167–72. The 1935 case was *Grovey v. Townsend*, 295 U.S. 45 (1935).
40. Meier and Rudwick, "Attorneys Black and White," 147–154. On Houston and Marshall, see G. R. McNeil, *Groundwork: Charles Hamilton Houston and the Struggle for Civil Rights* (Philadelphia, 1983); M. V. Tushnet, *Making Civil Rights Law: Thurgood Marshall and the Supreme Court, 1936–1961* (New York and Oxford, 1994); J. Greenberg, *Crusaders in the Court: How a Dedicated Band of Lawyers Fought for the Civil Rights Revolution* (New York, 1994), 292–98.
41. Diner, *In the Almost Promised Land*, 124–28. On relations with the Garland Fund, see Tushnet, *The NAACP's Legal Strategy*, 2–8, 13–20.
42. *Crisis*, Jan. 1921, 105.
43. Membership figures according to a memorandum dated 15 June 1954, NAACP II A 202. See also *NAACP Annual Reports 1940 to 1945* (New York, 1940–45).
44. See H. H. Haines, *Black Radicals and the Civil Rights Mainstream, 1954–1970* (Knoxville, Tenn., 1988), esp. 93–94.
45. Iggers to Freyer, 17 Sept. 1980, cited above, n. 1.
46. On the Lasker donation, see NAACP II A 477, folder entitled "Lasker Fund Reports." These records yield no information on Lasker's possible motives. On Lasker, see *Who's Who in America?* (Chicago, 1950–51), 1569. On the increase of black registration, see the reports by NAACP Director of Public Relations Henry Lee Moon to NAACP Executive Secretary Walter White, 20 Aug. 1952 and 4 May 1953, NAACP II A 452.
47. On Nixon's NAACP membership, see Roy Wilkins to Gertrude Gorman, 9 Oct. 1956, and to Cynthia Hubbard, 22 Oct. 1956, NAACP III A 239. On Kennedy, see Wilkins to Herbert Tucker of the Massachusetts Citizens Committee for Minority Rights, 16 Oct. 1958, as well as Kennedy's letters to Wilkins, 28 Oct. 1956, and Kivie Kaplan, 22 June 1959, all in NAACP III A 176.

48. C. Stone, *Black Political Power in America* (Indianapolis, Ind., and New York, 1968), 9, as well as J. Robinson, "Taking off on the NAACP," *Amsterdam News*, 14 Jan. 1967, copy in NAACP IV A 79.
49. Haines, *Black Radicals*, 84, table 8.
50. Kellogg, *NAACP*, 128. See the quote from Garvey in L. W. Levine, "Marcus Garvey and the Politics of Revitalization," in *Black Leaders of the Twentieth Century*, ed. J. H. Franklin and A. Meier (Urbana, Ill., and Chicago, 1982), 105–37, quote at 133–34. The quote from Malcolm X comes from a 1963 *New York Times* story that is reprinted in G. Samuels, "Two Ways: Black Muslim and NAACP," in *Black Protest in the Sixties*, ed. A. Meier, J. Bracey and E. Rudwick (New York, 1991), 37–45, 40.
51. Du Bois, "Marcus Garvey, " *Crisis*, Jan. 1921, 112–15; idem, "A Lunatic or a Traitor?" ibid., *Crisis*, May 1924, 8–9. For the text of Wilkins's speech at the NAACP annual convention of July 1966, see an unidentified newspaper clipping, NAACP IV A 16.
52. See the Young Turk's "Open letter to the Convention Delegates," 12 July 1967, NAACP IV A 12, as well as "The NAACP's Young Turk Movement," n.d., sent as a memorandum of 4 March 1968, by Gloster Current to Roy Wilkins, NAACP IV A 80. See also the interview with Young Turk leader Celes King, RJB#420, as well as Rudwick and Meier, "Integration v. Separatism," 254–57. On Reuther, see N. Lichtenstein, *The Most Dangerous Man in Detroit: Walter Reuther and the Fate of American Labor* (New York, 1995), 315–16, as well as Edward B. Muse to Roy Wilkins, 9 July 1968, NAACP IV A 80 (quote).
53. See "Excerpts from remarks by Khalid Abdul Mohammad, Nation of Islam National Spokesman, at Kean Collge, New Jersey, Nov. 29, 1993," leaflet by the Anti-Defamation League of B'nai 'Brith; and Georg Iggers to NAACP Executive Director Rev. Dr. Benjamin F. Chavis, 9 Feb. 1994, in possession of the author courtesy of Georg Iggers.
54. L. Goldstein, "On NAACP Agenda: A Capital Trip," *Washington Post*, 20 Feb. 1995; M. Fletcher and K. Merida, "Mfume Is Chosen to Lead NAACP," ibid., 10 Dec. 1995.

PART FOUR

HISTORIOGRAPHICAL REFLECTIONS ON DIFFERENCE AND EQUALITY

Chapter 11

CROSSING BORDERS IN AMERICAN CIVIL RIGHTS HISTORIOGRAPHY

Tony A. Freyer

Assessing American civil rights historiography tests the boundary between objectivity and involvement. C. Vann Woodward, the great historian of race relations and the American south, traversed the borderline in his classic treatment, *The Strange Career of Jim Crow*. In successive editions of a work first published in 1955, Woodward revised the interpretation of how and why the South's Jim Crow racial apartheid system emerged, prospered, and collapsed from the late-nineteenth century to the 1970s.[1] While Woodward's interpretive vision was dynamic, his underlying purpose remained constant: he sought to articulate a view of the past that would serve liberal democratic reform in the present.[2] Over the decades since *Strange Career* first appeared, civil rights historiography followed a similar interpretive course. Almost uniformly, historians approached the civil rights struggle in a spirit advocating racial justice. The substantive focus, however, underwent a significant change. By the 1990s the prevailing historiography was weary of subjects involving outcomes won through judicial action, including the Supreme Court's historic decision of *Brown v. Board of Education* (1954), which formally overturned the constitutional basis of Jim Crow established in *Plessy v. Ferguson* (1896). Instead, historians argued that African-American consciousness-raising and community formation shaped the triumphs achieved through the nonviolent mass protest movement identified with Martin Luther King, Jr.[3] Although King himself recognized that appropriate judicial action facilitated his peaceful protest strategy, historians have neglected this in their studies of seemingly unequivocal victories resulting from black community solidarity.[4]

The following discussion attempts to show that civil rights historiography may benefit from a renewed interest in the institutional dynamics of social struggle. Throughout, I use as a reference point the Little Rock school desegregation crisis of 1957 and its equivocal resolution following the Supreme Court's decision of *Cooper v. Aaron* (1958).[5] The first section considers how Woodward's trust in gradualism advocated by southern white liberals, articulated in an early edition of *Strange Career*, influenced subsequent historiography. I begin by contrasting Woodward's hopeful assessment with the ultimately more prescient view Georg G. Iggers expressed about the time, based on his personal experience during the origins of the Little Rock crisis. The second section suggests the usefulness of considering how judicial institutions influenced the contradictory protest strategies both African Americans and segregationists pursued. The third section suggests further that liberal macroeconomic labor policies instituted during the New Deal and the federal government's Cold War propaganda campaign provided incentives for civil rights activists such as Martin Luther King, Jr., to incorporate a federal litigation strategy into their nonviolent protests. The final section draws together the preceding themes to argue that the Little Rock crisis—particularly the degree to which it grew out of federal litigation strategies employed for opposing purposes by pro-segregationists and African Americans alike—could be reconciled with the prevailing civil rights historiography of the 1990s.

Gradualism and Its Discontents

Shortly after the Little Rock crisis ended, Georg G. Iggers published an assessment that rejected that gradualism was inevitable. His documentary essay of 1960 argued that the dramatic confrontation that began in late August 1957 originated from the local NAACP branch's successful effort to mobilize black-community support against the weakening of the Little Rock School Board's initially progressive school desegregation plan that followed *Brown*. Accordingly, he asserted, "I find it difficult to escape the conclusion that the crisis ... was not the result of premature integration but the breakdown of authority and the weakness of a false sort of gradualism." The Little Rock School Board believed that, "by progressively weakening its own plan and by emphasizing its own reluctance to follow the Supreme Court's [Brown] decision it would make the bitter pill more palatable." This accommodationist strategy, however, "actually helped to consolidate extremist opposition."[6] Iggers's perception that gradualism encouraged southern white massive resistance suggested an understanding of the interplay between diverse motivations of different groups within the local white and African-American communities, and their relation to wider American society and institutions, which anticipated the future course of civil rights historiography. Even so, by the 1990s the dominant historiographical interpretation emphasized white and African-American community dynamics and group consciousness, but neglected the more ambiguous outcomes like those in the Little Rock crisis.[7]

America's leading southern historian, by contrast, endorsed gradualism. Beginning in the 1930s, C. Vann Woodward articulated a brilliant revisionist account of southern history. Earlier historians of the South had accepted the premise that slavery, its racialist roots, and their influence upon the emergence and life of the Jim Crow apartheid system represented a historical process of institutional and cultural continuity. Through an ingenious reevaluation of the so-called New South era that followed the Civil War and Reconstruction, however, Woodward argued convincingly that Jim Crow had arisen from historical discontinuity. Thus, Woodward believed, during the first postbellum generation the potential for creating a genuine liberal-democracy embracing southern whites and African Americans was real. Moreover, the "strange career of Jim Crow" had submerged but not destroyed the South's liberal democratic tendencies. As a result, Woodward embraced the virtues of gradualism. He suggested that "Negroes have already shown new capacities for leadership that have surprised their friends as well as their opponents. In the long run, it may be that their own resources will prove decisive in the contest." Still, he believed that the initiative for bringing about the "eventual doom of segregation in American life" lay primarily with a new generation of southerners—"in the long run ... [which] implies 'gradualism.'" Unlike the failure of the first Reconstruction following the Civil War, he postulated, the gradual progress that characterized the second Reconstruction emerging during the 1950s in places such as Little Rock "would seem to promise more enduring results."[8]

American historian David M. Potter examined Woodward's underlying impulse. Woodward, Potter said, was certain that history was "a key which the past gives us for guidance in confronting the problems of the present. But the difficulty with this concept lies in the dilemma: can history retain its integrity even while partaking of public ... uses in our encounters with current issues?" Potter conceded that as more empirical data revealed the shortcomings of Woodward's reassessment of Jim Crow, he revised his revisionist account. The "urgency of Woodward's desire to find answers in the past which would aid in the quest for solution of the problems of the present," had led him to contend, Potter continued, that if "historically ... legalized segregation was relatively a new phenomenon, and that promises of equality were a century old, it might be easier to induce people to abandon segregation and to accord equality to Negroes." Yet, Potter observed, "[s]ince Woodward himself later modified or even changed his position on both these matters, it seems reasonable to suppose that the tension between his devotion to liberal goals and his devotion to historical realism distorted his image of the past, at least for a time and to a limited degree."[9]

Woodward had always acknowledged that African Americans could shape their own destiny. His recognition that blacks possessed an independent initiative was consistent with the black community, group-identity studies that focused upon an approach to activism represented by Martin Luther King, Jr. This slant on black activism emerged, however, from Woodward's primary concern with gradualism as the only realistic course southern whites would follow in giving up a social order based on terror, legally mandated racial discrimination, and second-class citizenship. The causal dynamics of class, culture, race, and politics underpinning this gradualism thus facilitated studies of the indigenous sources of resistance within black communities. The underlying assumption was that the national NAACP's judicially centered strategy identified with *Brown* and public school desegregation had resulted in little more than tokenism. The shift to mass protests that King immortalized in the Montgomery bus boycott and the Selma voting rights march culminated, by contrast, in significant legislative outcomes like the Civil Rights Act of 1964 and the Voting Rights Act of 1965.[10]

Still, the historiographical motivation for examining these significant and clear-cut victories did not question Woodward's emphasis upon gradualism. By the 1970s the prevailing view among commentators was that such politically astute southern leaders as Orval Faubus and George Wallace had successfully manipulated litigation outcomes to impede the cause of racial justice.[11] This assessment affirmed the view of northern "[c]ivil-rights activists … [who] tended to label white people in positions of power in the South not as 'moderates' or 'segregationists' but as 'smart segs' or 'dumb segs.' By the late fifties … smart segs, realizing that the courts had gradually rendered [southern white] massive resistance useless as a strategy for avoiding desegregation, concentrated instead on delaying tactics in the courts and the sort of anti-integration laws that usually avoided the word 'Negro' or 'race.'" Leaders like Birmingham, Alabama's public safety commissioner, Bull Conner, by contrast, were said to be "dumb segs."[12] Conner earned the less flattering epithet because his subordinates deployed fire hoses and police dogs against peacefully demonstrating African American children. The commissioner's error was not merely the brutality itself, but that he carried it out before a media that transmitted the images across America and around the world. Even so, the emphasis upon white southern leaders left the dominant impression that desegregation litigation had achieved nothing but gradual, limited compliance with *Brown*. As a result, a historiographical study of the civil rights movement published in 1991 said little about public school desegregation, suggesting that it was a settled issue no longer requiring attention: the article did not even mention the nine black children's courageous stand at Little Rock Central High School. The essay focused instead on works about the growth of African-American group identity within local communities or protest organizations from the 1930s to the 1970s, particularly the rise of the civil rights movement identified with Martin Luther King's leadership.[13]

The historiographical interpretation that separated activism from litigation had several noteworthy shortcomings. First, it failed to recognize that judicial action significantly influenced even "clear-cut" victories like the Montgomery bus boycott and the Selma voting rights march. Mark Tushnet's incisive study of Thurgood Marshall and the NAACP Legal Defense Fund observed that by 1955, the year following the first *Brown* decision, when Rosa Park's refusal to move to the back of the bus sparked the historic Montgomery boycott, "the legal issues raised by Jim Crow ordinances [mandating racially segregated seating on public transportation] were not difficult, but it took a Supreme Court decision to end bus segregation in Montgomery." More particularly, the Supreme Court upheld the federal trial court's earlier decision "without even hearing argument." Thus it was judicial action that brought the Montgomery bus boycott to an end. "Despite the Court's role in the outcome," Tushnet nonetheless concludes, "the most important part of the Montgomery story, to the African-American community and to the nation as a whole, was the boycott itself, not the litigation. The boycott, stimulated by the community's sense that Jim Crow laws were wrong and unconstitutional, provided the context in which a new set of leaders come to the fore [especially Martin Luther King]."[14] Within a decade, King and other "new leaders" employed judicial action—in conjunction with the more conspicuous strategy of nonviolent protest—to bring about passage of the Civil Rights Act of 1964 and the Voting Rights Act of 1965. The dominant historiographical interpretation largely ignored, however, this strategic use of litigation.[15]

Neglecting litigation as integral to civil rights protest minimized that protest's most conspicuous triumph: the defeat of institutionalized racial inequality. I have noted elsewhere that King, Julian Bond, and others acknowledged how central was judicial sanction of constitutional rights to overturning the Jim Crow apartheid system.[16] The pursuit of favorable litigation outcomes before sympathetic lower federal court judges such as Alabama's Frank Johnson and Richard Rives represented a strategic choice aimed at raising the most effective possible challenge to every facet of institutional oppression segregation represented. Since most southern federal judges acted haltingly until the Supreme Court specifically settled a given desegregation issue, the civil rights protesters' reliance upon the few activist federal judges was instrumental to the success of the nonviolent, passive resistance campaign. Taylor Branch's and David J. Garrow's monumental studies of King and the civil rights movement note the pivotal role Judge Johnson, especially, played in the Montgomery boycott, the Freedom Rides, and the Selma voting rights march.[17] Johnson, Rives, and the small number of other pro-desegregation judicial activists were thus part of the context within which, according to Branch, the civil rights movement "institutionalize[d] its major gains.... Legal segregation was doomed. Negroes no longer were invisible, nor were those of normal capacity viewed as statistical freaks."[18]

Dismissing court action as essential to the defeat of Jim Crow also suggested that gradualism was inevitable. Woodward's hope that, following *Brown*, southern white liberals possessed sufficient strength to overturn segregation sustained his faith in gradualism. Iggers perceived, however, that southern white moderates appealed to gradualism in order to justify token desegregation enforced by federal authority. Southern elected officials grasped the strategic advantage implicit in this gradualist rationale. Used in conjunction with states' rights and surrogate racist images, it enabled Faubus, Wallace, and many others to shift to federal authorities not only the legal and political responsibility and accountability—but also the blame—for implementing desegregation. Thus gradualism was itself a rhetorical device employed to legitimate explicit political goals. Significantly, civil rights activists never accepted that gradualism was the only practical route to bringing about meaningful change. Marshall and the Legal Defense Fund systematically challenged the constitutional and legal claims underpinning "southern massive resistance," and ultimately won. King and other civil rights activists incorporated this judicial action into a broader nonviolent protest campaign to gain enduring victories over institutionalized racial injustice.[19]

The Little Rock Crisis: A Test Case

To be sure, recent civil rights scholarship that questioned the impact of *Brown* also accepted Woodward's analytical framework. Focusing upon the importance of the southern white backlash to *Brown*, the first conspicuous example of which was Little Rock, Michael Klarman's central contribution is the well-documented argument that determining *Brown*'s significance required consideration of the "relative contribution to racial change of *Brown* as compared with the plethora of social, political, economic and other forces." Employing a comparative, multicausal analysis, this recent work revised the standard view of *Brown*'s short-term impact, arguing that the decision was a catalyst not only of massive resistance, but more particularly that "*Brown* both significantly exacerbated the level of … violence and rendered officially sanctioned suppression politically profitable." This argument relies upon incisive treatments of the pivotal confrontations in such places as Montgomery and Selma.[20] As with Woodward, however, southern whites and the pressures driving gradualism are the catalyst for change.

In what follows I outline why I think this emphasis is misplaced. Indeed, some historians suggested that a criticism of gradualism was more prophetic than Woodward's trust in it. In this connection several points deserve attention. First, given the recent prevalence of community studies focusing on black group-identity formation as a precondition for the success of the mass nonviolent protest strategy, it is important to understand the extent to which, as Iggers's essay of 1960 pointed out, that Little Rock's long history of black activism prepared it for a similar strategy.[21] Thus, unlike the civil rights historiography that prevailed by the 1990s, the popular television series, *Eyes on the Prize*, and accompanying book did give ample play to Little Rock and depicted the crisis there as arising from local community protests that were part of the larger struggle, shaping and shaped by national institutions and events.[22] Second, it is important to understand, as Michael Belknap has argued concerning much of the civil rights struggle as a whole, federal authorities "evaded an obligation" to prosecute white "troublemakers" and "unreliable" state officials who "deprive[d] blacks of rights guaranteed them by the United States Constitution."[23] The government's refusal to support these rights, except in the most extreme cases, also supports David Goldfield's conclusion that in the early civil rights confrontations in the 1950s, "blacks found themselves alone," and white moderates only responded "belatedly, primarily to hold down losses (economic and political) rather than to facilitate meaningful change."[24]

King perceived, moreover, that federal litigation could overcome gradualism. Appropriate federal judicial action was integral to the campaign of nonviolent, passive resistance; state court litigation, however, worked against civil disobedience. Thus in his 1963 "Letter From the Birmingham Jail" King said that "I can urge men to obey the 1954 decision of the Supreme Court because it is morally right, and I can urge them to disobey segregation ordinances because they are morally wrong." Federal judges such as Frank Johnson recognized the difference, King stated, because "as federal courts have consistently affirmed ... it is immoral to urge an individual to withdraw his efforts to gain his constitutional rights because the quest precipitates violence. Society must protect the robbed and punish the robber."[25] In the Montgomery bus boycott King noted the practical distinction between federal and state judicial action. "Our local [Alabama] judges, it seems, succumb to whims and caprices of local custom in deciding cases like ours. In the federal courts, a judge is appointed and doesn't have to worry about being reelected. God grant them the moral courage and integrity to interpret the Constitution in its true meaning." Nine years later King shaped his protest strategy around the expectation that Judge Johnson's court order would aid the successful outcome of the Selma voting rights march. It was reported at the time that King described Johnson as "a man of great honor, [who] gave true meaning to the word justice."[26]

Accordingly, King criticized the gradualist strategy of "legalism" that southern white leaders employed to further their massive resistance. African Americans "must not get involved in legalism [and] needless fights in lower [state] courts." This was "exactly what the white man wants the Negro to do. Then he can draw out the fights.... Our job now is implementation [of the full constitutional spirit and substance of the

Brown decision].... We must move on to mass action ... in every community in the South, keeping in mind that civil disobedience to local laws is civil obedience to national laws."[27] Prominent leaders of the NAACP in New York clearly disagreed with King. Nevertheless, as Mark Tushnet noted, concerning the interplay in the Montgomery bus boycott between litigation and peaceful mass protest, successful federal judicial action against the segregation laws "unified the African-American community and, ironically, divided the white community's leadership." Overall, Montgomery "illuminate[d] the changing context of civil rights litigation" emerging after 1955.[28]

Even so, Adam Fairclough asks: Was the Little Rock crisis a success or failure for the NAACP? The answer consistent with Woodward's focus and that of the community studies is that "Little Rock helped the Civil Rights movement only in the negative sense of illustrating the futility of [court-centered, activist] legalism, thereby encouraging a trend toward direct action that began with the Montgomery bus boycott [of 1955–56] but only became widespread with the student sit-in movement of 1960." Fairclough argues, however, that "such a conclusion would be wrong." He suggests that the litigation strategy like that which the Little Rock NAACP pursued before and during the crisis was a form of "activism" growing out of *Brown* and the new role it gave federal courts. The "success" of such "non-violent direct action" as "[s]it-ins, freedom rides, and demonstrations occurred at a time when the federal judiciary was increasingly sympathetic to the goals and methods of the civil rights movement." Thus the "NAACP's great achievement" was that in Little Rock and elsewhere its "legalistic strategy undermine[d] the legal foundations of segregation," paving the way for larger civil rights triumphs.[29]

Historiographically, the arguments by Belknap, Goldfield, and Fairclough are consistent with Iggers's participant-observer assessment, which first set me thinking along lines that departed from Woodward. Eventually, I arrived at a view that focused on the symbolic and operational importance of the legalistic strategies that Little Rock's NAACP and Faubus each pursued. While socio-political isolation strengthened African Americans' independence and solidarity, it also facilitated Faubus's strategy of maneuver. Through the summer and fall of 1957, Faubus realized that the city's white moderates and the Eisenhower administration were unwilling to accept responsibility for enforcing desegregation, except on the basis of a minimal obligation to obey federal court orders. Meanwhile, the advocacy of conflicting constitutional principles—equal protection of the laws and states' rights—by black activists and segregationists both politicized and obscured the moderates' and the president's claims of federal supremacy. At the same time, local NAACP activists observed privately that racism did not motivate Faubus, a view reinforced by continued black support for him at the polls. Faubus's strategy of maneuver aimed above all at shifting accountability for desegregation to others, particularly federal authorities. Faubus shrewdly gained popular credit for resistance without suffering a direct legal or political penalty. One of the broader implications of this is that in Little Rock as elsewhere, racism, persistent and damaging as it is, did not take, at least in public, the blatant form advocated by extreme segregationists. Instead, Faubus, like public officials elsewhere, articulated surrogate racial images, emphasizing preservation of peace, public order, states' rights, freedom of choice for white people, and so forth. Despite that evasiveness and despite Faubus's victories, and the victories of numerous governors who followed in his footsteps, African Americans won considerable ground through their own claims of constitutional rights.[30]

As Iggers's assessment long ago suggested, for blacks the fruits of this legalist strategy were nonetheless mixed. King's sanction of activist litigation as a form of civil disobedience recognized this same tension.[31] Similarly, Ernest Green, the oldest of the Little Rock Nine looking back after thirty years, observed that "the thing integration demonstrated is that, as you challenge the system, it doesn't stop with schools. It extends to include all other arrangements and relationships. Once you open Pandora's box and let the genie out, you can't put the genie back in."[32] The genie was that finally, nearly a hundred years after the establishment of the constitutional principle of federal protection of minority rights in the Fourteenth Amendment, continued violation of minority rights would bring disorder and, under the right circumstances, federal compulsion. Yet because successful defense of these rights became synonymous with compulsion, progress was likely to be limited and ambiguous. Thus the Little Rock crisis demonstrated that it is not so much the attainment of but the striving for the ideal of equal justice that keeps the ideal alive.[33]

Among whites the legalist strategy also had, again as Iggers had suggested, an ambiguous outcome. The level of violence associated with southern massive resistance was arguably greater than it might have been, largely because southern public officials from Faubus on, and for a long time federal authorities as well, created a law-enforcement vacuum. State officials' defense of states' rights and the federal government's prolonged deference to local authority, moreover, legitimated opposition. Public authority's equivocal response to *Brown* thus made suppression of or indifference to the civil rights movement politically rewarding because state officials, and to a lesser degree federal officials, could gain political capital by blaming the need for change on the Supreme Court and federal judges.[34] The most successful practitioner of the "blaming" strategy was ultimately Alabama's governor, George Wallace, whose primary object of attack often was, indeed, Alabama's federal judge Frank Johnson. The Eisenhower and Kennedy administrations did not formally pursue such a strategy, but their uneven support of the federal courts forced judges such as Johnson to decide between independent action and maintaining the status quo. Had Johnson and his activist colleagues not taken an independent course, the political advantages of resistance or delay may have been diminished, but the status quo would have persisted even longer than it did.[35] Thus legalism was a central strategy that African American and white leaders pursued to achieve contrary civil rights outcomes.

The Economic and International Context

New Deal liberal macroeconomic policies influenced the recourse to legalism during the civil rights struggle. The historiographical tradition represented by Woodward and the community-consciousness studies assumed that the South's civil rights conflict grew out of a historical process in which economic, cultural, and ideological discontinuity shaped future outcomes. According to this tradition legal and constitutional institutions and values reflected a changing South as dependent variables.[36] An argument emphasizing the centrality of legalistic strategy to the process of change contends, however, that legal and constitutional institutions constitute as well as mirror society's development; these institutions may be examined, then, as independent variables.[37] Economic historian Gavin Wright employs such a constitutive institutionalism to argue that the New Deal's nondiscriminatory labor policies of the 1930s were a precondition for the civil rights movement's triumph. One of Wright's case-study examples is, indeed, Little Rock.[38]

Wright suggested how the New Deal institutional regime transformed the South. White southerners' declining dominance over African-American labor that New Deal liberalism fostered provided incentives for both resisting and accommodating the end of Jim Crow. Blue-collar and lower middle-class southern whites faced increased market and sociocultural competition with African Americans; hence, these whites provided the rank and file for the extreme segregationists' campaign of racist violence and disorder. Wealthier white business and civic groups generally benefited, however, from the larger macro-economic transformation New Deal liberalism brought about; and so they were the chief advocates of gradualism and tokenism based on deference to the supremacy of federal constitutional authority symbolized by the Supreme Court and the *Brown* decision. The legal strategy employed by successful leaders such as Faubus and Wallace effectively exploited these ambivalent political and racist dynamics within the institutional parameters imposed by uneven federal executive and judicial action.[39] As Iggers's brief commentary on Little Rock revealed, African Americans also did not initially agree concerning how best to challenge the South's apartheid system. Those African Americans possessing a stake in the macroeconomic factors undermining Jim Crow favored gradualism, while others belonging to local organizations such as the NAACP urged varying degrees of activism. Again, it was a flexible legal strategy incorporating court litigation and peaceful disobedience sanctioned by appeals to the Constitution as higher law, which united both groups in common cause. During the mid-1960s a more violent black nationalism emerged that denied this strategy altogether, but its impact on civil rights policy was largely indirect.[40]

Mary L. Dudziak approaches American civil rights constitutionalism and Cold War foreign relations in terms of their institutional autonomy. The Cold War's initial decades coincided with the dissolution of European colonial empires and the triumph of indigenous African, Asian, Middle Eastern and Latin American national identities. In the ensuing propaganda war between the United States and communist regimes, America's political and constitutional sanction of the South's Jim Crow apartheid system undermined the legitimacy of the "Free World's" assertion that it stood for democratic ideals. Since Jim Crow was truly antidemocratic, communist propagandists could rebut their American counterparts without lying. Dudziak and other scholars have explored the federal government's growing defense of civil rights from the late 1940s to the mid-1960s as a Cold War, foreign-policy strategy. According to Dudziak, moreover, the Little Rock crisis was a turning point in the propaganda battle.[41] Although token desegregation resulted from *Cooper v. Aaron*, the Supreme Court's vigorous affirmation of *Brown* in that decision received overwhelming favorable attention throughout Latin America, Asia, Africa, the Middle East, and Western Europe. "From the perspective of President Eisenhower, the core interests at stake in Little Rock had more to do with federal authority and foreign affairs than with racial equality," Dudziak argues persuasively. "To the extent that safeguarding the image of America was behind Eisenhower's involvement, he got what he needed with *Cooper v. Aaron*. At this juncture, the Cold War imperative could be addressed largely through formal pronouncements about the law. More substantive social change would await another day."[42]

Dudziak's internationalizing perspective refocused Klarman's critique of *Brown*. Klarman locates *Brown* within the "dramatic transformation in American racial attitudes spawned by World War II." Because this transformation was a precondition for *Brown*, Klarman contends that the causal importance of the decision has been exaggerated. Nevertheless, Klarman concedes, that at least outside the South, Americans attained a heightened consciousness that racist ideologies and egalitarian democracy were inconsistent. Dudziak's emphasis upon the federal government's use of *Brown* and *Cooper* as effective Cold War propaganda reasserts the instrumental significance of the Supreme Court's desegregation decisions. Approached in this light, Klarman's own version of institutional dynamics resonates with the autonomy of politics Dudziak suggests, although in America the pervasive reliance upon judicial conflict resolution was culturally distinctive. Accordingly, Klarman writes, "most of the Court's famous individual rights decisions of the past half century [following World War II] involve either the Justices seizing upon a dominant national consensus and imposing it on resisting outliers or intervening on an issue where the nation is narrowly divided and awarding victory to one side...." In either case, Klarman observes, the "racial views of culturally elite [Supreme Court] Justices in 1954 (the year of *Brown*) probably were more similar to those of the general population in 1954 than to those of the cultural elite in 1896 (the year of *Plessy*)."[43]

The interplay between institutional autonomy and foreign affairs also was central to African-American activist consciousness. During World War II, Gunnar Myrdal's influential study of segregation exposed the inconsistency between Jim Crow and American democracy. Thurgood Marshall of the NAACP Legal Defense Fund stated, accordingly, that "[a]t the present time all eyes are focused on democracy in the United States and it seems the fate of democracy depends on the United States. The true test of democracy is the equality of rights and privileges granted all citizens which is measured by the protection given minority groups." As the Cold War began, an NAACP member attacking segregated eating places in the nation's capital in 1948 exclaimed to a federal official, "I know our enemies abroad use such facts to discredit our democratic way of life."[44]

McCarthyism fueled criticism that civil rights activists were themselves dupes or even agents of the communist conspiracy. Leaders such as Marshall and Martin Luther King countered such assaults by linking their litigation campaign or passive resistance to the advocacy of an American democratic faith that espoused the equality of the Declaration of Independence and the Constitution's sanction of minority rights. King proved to be particularly effective at defending the struggle for equal justice by denying the evils of communism. In a public address before Chicago business leaders prior to the march on Washington in 1963 he said, "I believe that one of the weaknesses of communism" was Lenin's advocacy of deception and aggression. "And this is where nonviolence breaks with communism or any other system that would argue that the end justifies the means, for in the long run the end is pre-existent in the means, and the means represents the ideal in the making and the end in process."[45]

Former Legal Defense Fund lawyer Derrick Bell contended that King's anticommunist pronouncements had a larger meaning. Directly or indirectly, King established a convergence between the African-American civil rights struggle and the majority of white Americans who favored democracy and constitutionally sanctioned minority rights but also feared communism and the Cold War.[46] This rhetorical strategy aligned African Americans with the dominant liberal consensus, while it politically isolated the South's segregation system as aiding the communists' anti-American propaganda campaign. Clearly, Marshall and King realized, anticommunist appeals would positively influence presidential administrations fighting the Cold War propaganda battle.[47] At the same time, the strategy tapped into segments of white and African-American liberal public opinion that identified the nation's democratic resistance to communism with postwar anticolonialism. During the time of the Little Rock crisis King told supporters privately that colonialism and racial segregation were essentially the same form of oppression. Comparing the American civil rights struggle to African independence movements, he said further: "The oppressor never voluntarily gives freedom to the oppressed.... Privileged classes never give up their privileges without strong resistance.... Freedom comes only through persistent revolt, through persistent agitation, through persistently rising up against the system of evil." On another public occasion he told Kenyan leader Tom Mboya: "I am absolutely convinced that there is no basic difference between colonialism and segregation. They are both based on a contempt for life, and a tragic doctrine of white supremacy. So our struggles are not only similar; they are in a real sense one."[48]

Thus George M. Fredrickson's incisive comparative assessment of racial conflict in the American South and South Africa is most suggestive. Unlike the African National Congress's struggle against the apartheid system entrenched under an exploitive state controlled by a white minority, the "American protesters faced a divided, fragmented, and uncertain governmental opposition. The most important division among whites that the [civil rights] movement was able to exploit was between northerners who lacked a regional commitment to legalized segregation and southerners who believed that Jim Crow was central to their way of life." According to Fredrickson, then, the civil rights movement's triumph "stemmed ultimately from its ability to get the federal government on its side and to utilize the U.S. Constitution against the outmoded states' rights philosophy of the southern segregationists. When King proclaimed that 'civil disobedience to local laws is civil obedience to national laws,' he exploited a tactical advantage the South African resisters did not possess."[49] Cold war imperatives linking the American white majority's fear of communism to anticolonialism thus strengthened the institutional and political autonomy of the legalistic strategies white segregationist and African-American civil rights leaders pursued; the uneven liberal economic transformation that was slowly transforming the South reinforced further this autonomy.

Toward a New Historiographical Interpretation

Recent studies of the Little Rock crisis are consistent with an interpretation linking uneven macroeconomic transformation, Cold War discourse, and constitutive legalism. In September 1997 a scholarly symposium was held in the Arkansas capital in conjunction with President Bill Clinton's commemoration of the fortieth anniversary of the Little Rock crisis.

Contributions to the symposium, in addition to those by Adam Fairclough and myself, included studies assessing the significance of the crisis for international relations (Azza Salama Layton and Richard H. King), black activism (John A. Kirk), religion (Mark Newman), the media (Allison Graham), gender (Elizabeth Jacoway), white social-class relations (C. Fred Williams), and the South's massive resistance (Tony Badger).[50] For direct interpretive purposes only Fairclough's use of legalism approximates what I would call a constitutive theory. Nevertheless, most of the contributors offer new evidence revealing the shaping influence of legal and constitutional institutions.[51] Jacoway demonstrated how a group of the city's white, upper-middle-class women helped to liberate themselves from southern gender stereotypes as they joined in the struggle to achieve racial justice. Adolphine Fletcher Terry and the Women's Emergency Committee, in conjunction with a campaign pushed by the Little Rock Chamber of Commerce rallied moderate white and black voters to win a special recall election on 25 May 1959, ending de facto segregationist control of the school board. Each white moderate organization employed the same pragmatic rationale for their campaign that the school board had relied on when publicizing the desegregation plan prior to the crisis: the constitutional supremacy of federal power. Jacoway presents this legalism as a tactical device; considered within the economic transformation and Cold War framework sketched above, however, legalism's institutional autonomy shaped rather than merely reflected social change.[52]

Social class conflict strengthened the instrumental force of legalistic and constitutional discourse. Williams argues that it was Little Rock's white "working-class" citizens' anger at the elite, upper-class "Cadillac Crowd" who dominated the school board, which drove popular resistance to the desegregation plan. Thus, for Williams the "Crisis at Central High was a form of social protest in the mold of the Boston Tea Party. Race may have been the triggering mechanism, but this rise of massive resistance in the capital city was fundamentally an expression of class conflict." Yet Williams emphasizes in turn that it was the political life that Faubus gave to class-based anger that was ultimately most important. This affirmation of the linkage between white working-class consciousness and political defiance indirectly recognizes that symbolically as well as operationally, legal-constitutionalism represented by *Brown*, the Supreme Court, and the federal government channeled political activism. Thus, Williams concludes, "Not only did … [Faubus] stand against the symbolic intrusive actions of the federal government, but he also showed his opposition to the local elite when its decision-makers defied the popular will. For many white working-class Little Rockians, Faubus became one of their own by his action at Central High." In conjunction with uneven economic transformation and Cold War ideological conflict, then, social class tension may be said to have intensified the impact of the legalistic-constitutional discourse all sides employed in Little Rock.[53]

Religious consciousness within a divided white Protestant community also diverged in its advocacy of legal constitutionalism. Soon after the Little Rock crisis erupted, informed contemporaries observed that local white churches were not united concerning the racial conflict. Newman's study entitled "The Arkansas Baptist Convention and Desegregation, 1954–1968" revealed both the character of the split and its political significance.[54] Within Little Rock and across the state "[s]ome … prominent pastors and a few denominational officials, were [according to Newman] progressives who believed that the Bible did not support racial segregation." A greater minority were "hard-liners who claimed that selected biblical verses of 'proof-texts' demonstrated that God had been the author of segregation. The majority of Southern Baptists in the state were moderate segregationists who held that the Bible neither supported nor opposed segregation."[55] Those whom Newman designates as progressives contributed to the 20 percent of Arkansas whites who, in a 1956 survey, favored desegregation.[56] The religious justification that came to be shared by the majority of the state's white Protestants accepted desegregation only out of deference to a legal-constitutional discourse that included the Cold War imperative. Shortly after the 101st Airborne arrived to quell the white mob on 25 September 1957, an editorial in the moderate *Arkansas Baptist* stated: "Jesus would not be a part of any crowd committing acts of violence in resistance to duly constituted law and order. He taught His disciples to be law abiding and to respect those in authority." A subsequent editorial warned readers that the disorder supported by Baptists advocating extreme segregationist views threatened both the immediate religious and larger Cold War reach of the church's missionary efforts: "The cause of missions and of democracy [in the struggle against communism] have suffered inestimably from the 'Little Rock' incident."[57]

Kirk's well-researched article in the Fortieth Anniversary symposium chronicles in rich detail how long-standing and deep was the Little Rock black community's resistance to Jim Crow. Most importantly he reveals that during the decade preceding the crisis, black activists were not united.[58] He confirms that the local "NAACP's move from the periphery to the center of black community politics during the years after the *Brown* decision was the most significant development in black activism in Arkansas." This was the case until the local branch leadership overcame internal opposition to mount the litigation against the school desegregation plan that culminated in *Cooper v. Aaron*. Kirk's valuable contribution is to locate the litigation strategy within the history of the state's and the city's black activism. Kirk's chief source for his thesis is Iggers's essay from 1960, but he does not connect it to the wider socio-religious, political, and Cold War context that the legal-constitutional strategy reflected.[59]

Three other contributors to the symposium follow a similar course. Layton's probing piece entitled "International Pressure and the U.S. Government's Response to Little Rock" adds invaluable detail to Dudziak's study. Layton is particularly good at showing that the interaction between the Cold War propaganda battle and anticolonialism encouraged Martin Luther King's appeals to American blacks. Looking back from 1963 King explained that the "American Negro … realized … that by [then] … more than thirty-four African nations had risen from colonial bondage. The Negro saw black statesmen voting on vital issues in the United Nations and knew that in many cities of his own land he was not permitted to take that significant walk to the ballot box." Layton thus argues that "a strong causal relationship" existed between the civil rights movement and the Cold War; Dudziak nonetheless goes farther to show how a strategy of legal-constitutional discourse limited change.[60]

Badger's excellent study of Arkansas moderates' role in making the Southern Manifesto of 1956, was similarly open to qualification. Nationally recognized Arkansas moderates Senator William J. Fulbright and Congressman Brooks Hays, along with most of their southern colleagues in the U.S. Senate and House, joined in signing the Manifesto, which employed states' rights theory to claim that *Brown* was unconstitutional. The document advocated any and all "lawful" resistance; just what that meant, however, was left vague. Ultimately, the moderation represented by Fulbright and Hays played into the hands of Faubus, who switched back and forth between espousing a moderate and extreme segregationist agenda. According to Badger's apt characterization: "Faubus's moderate strategy in 1956 was predicated on the notion that concessions to segregationist pressure would enable moderates like himself to stay in office and defuse the extremist threat. Instead, he found that in a battle where one side is prepared to mount a righteous crusade to defy the Supreme Court and the other wants to keep quiet, the extremists were going to win." Badger notes correctly that the political consequence of this moderation was that it was "difficult to try to convince people that there was no alternative to obeying the law of the land when leading politicians in the state were proclaiming that there was an alternative."[61] The argument ignores, however, the ample evidence which shows that Faubus and white moderates generally employed a legal-constitutional discourse *strategically* to impel federal enforcement of federal court orders. This neglect in turn closes off consideration of how the NAACP's and the president's pursuit of a similar strategy guided the course of change along constricted channels.[62]

The image of the media and the civil rights struggle also leaves the legal-constitutional strategy unexamined. Graham locates the press reports of the Little Rock crisis within the northern media's broad characterization of the South during the 1950s and 1960s. She challenges as superficial the contention that "those first flickering transmissions from Little Rock must have sparked a traumatic shift in consciousness for people south of the Mason-Dixon Line. To see oneself—really see oneself—as others do, to become aware of oneself as an image: such was the legacy of television's intervention in the region's racial crisis, according to TV's early defenders." Graham expertly dissects this assertion, arguing persuasively that the media's impact on the nation's sectional consciousness was ambivalent. Under the influence of conflicting commercial and public-spirited motivations the northern media presented a stereotypical South identified with the Gothic violence of *The Birth of a Nation*, the impoverished desperation of Depression era *Tobacco Road*, the deplorable romantic racism of *Gone With the Wind*, and the "harmless" yet principled "hillbilly" of *The Andy Griffith Show*. These mixed impressions presented African Americans as dignified, dependent victims and most white southerners as "ignorant." Print and TV journalists in turn transmitted these stereotypes in their reports of civil rights struggles. Graham's most valuable contribution, however, is to suggest that for white southerners the result of this media-constructed projection was not "self-loathing" but anger, resentment, and "a sense of national marginalization," which "'to a large extent ... galvanize[d] the white opposition.'" Graham does not consider the larger meaning of this important insight for the NAACP's litigation strategy, King's campaign of civil disobedience, and the federal government's Cold War propaganda battle: that they are profoundly interconnected is nonetheless apparent.[63]

The Fortieth Anniversary Symposium also included an evaluation of the Little Rock commentary written by Hannah Arendt. During the confrontation in the fall of 1957, Arendt wrote a short essay entitled "Reflections on Little Rock," which *Dissent* published in 1959. Symposium contributor Richard H. King considered the meaning Arendt's views had for the American civil rights struggle. At one level, King explains how Arendt's arguments about the relations and distinctions among public, social, and private spheres led her to oppose federally enforced school desegregation. On another level, he shows how Arendt's belief that her own German-Jewish experience and that of southern blacks were, for analytical purposes, complementary, resulted in her misunderstanding the distinctively American racial and institutional character of the civil rights struggle that Little Rock epitomized. Finally, King makes clear that, notwithstanding Arendt's failure to grasp the divergence between America's racial dilemma and the Jewish history of oppression in Europe, "she did suggest new and different ways to think about issues of race and education, the relationship of the political to the social, and the responsibility of parents for children, without sharing in the conventional wisdom of either the liberals or the segregationists."[64]

Conclusion

The critique of Arendt's "Reflections" accentuates the irony Iggers's Little Rock commentary represented for civil rights historiography. Following an interpretive tradition identified with C. Vann Woodward, recent civil rights studies placed Little Rock outside their purview. Employing a more institutionally oriented approach to the nation's struggle against racial injustice, other recent scholarship has revealed—like Iggers's personal experience—the community-consciousness dimensions of the crisis and its origins. Iggers explained his civil rights activism as an outgrowth of his German-Jewish background; in light of the evidence presented here, that heritage led him to a realistic and perceptive appraisal of the dilemma racial discrimination posed for southern life and American democracy. According to King, the "sentiments" Arendt expressed in her essay also "grew out of her experience as an educated, middle-class European Jew, which she then imposed on the realities of post-Emancipation black southern life." But Arendt failed to understand, in the words of Ralph Ellison, that a black person in the American South had to "face the terror and contain his fear and anger precisely because he is a Negro American." King observes that "[t]o Ellison the ritual of Little Rock was necessary for southern black students and best seen as a form of group strengthening rather than [as Arendt had argued] a form of group humiliation."[65] Having lived and worked in the southern black community of Little Rock, Iggers was better prepared than Arendt to grasp Ellison's insight, despite the common immigrant heritage both shared. The historiographical interpretation argued in this essay viewed strengthened African-American self-consciousness as an important result of nonviolent protests fought through mass political activism and the courts. The practical amelioration of institutional and societal discrimination may have been continually contested, but it opened the way to eventually attaining the ideal of equal justice.

Notes

In this essay no attempt is made to explore whether Georg Iggers's involvement in the origins of the Little Rock crisis—near the beginning of his academic career—influenced his significant contributions to the study of historiography and European intellectual history. For what I hope are some suggestive thoughts on the question, see my other contribution included in this volume. The author would like to thank Dean Kenneth C. Randall, The University of Alabama Law School Foundation, and the Edward Brett Randolph Fund for their support of his involvement in this project.

1. Woodward's influential work remained continually in print from its initial publication by Oxford University Press in 1955. The first revised edition appeared as an Oxford University Press paperback in 1957; Oxford published the second and third revised editions in 1966 and 1974, respectively. Woodward delivered the original work in 1954 as a series of lectures at the University of Virginia.
2. D. M. Potter, "C. Vann Woodward and the Uses of History," in D. E. Fehrenbacher, ed., *History and Society: Essays of David M. Potter* (New York, 1973), 136–79.

3. S. F. Lawson, "Freedom Then, Freedom Now: The Historiography of the Civil Rights Movement," *American Historical Review* 96 (1991): 456–71.
4. Ibid. Compare D. J. Garrow, *Bearing the Cross: Martin Luther King, Jr., and the Southern Christian Leadership Conference* (New York, 1986), 91–92; T. Branch, *Parting the Waters: America in the King Years 1954–63* (New York, 1989), 435, 469, 542; J. Bass, *Taming the Storm: The Life and Times of Judge Frank M. Johnson, Jr., and the South's Fight over Civil Rights* (New York, 1993), 109, 248; and, above all, Martin Luther King, Jr., "Letter from Birmingham Jail," 16 Apr. 1963, in M. L. King, Jr., *Why We Can't Wait* (New York, 1964).
5. For an overview of civil rights historiography, including its relation to the Little Rock crisis, see D. L. Chappell, "Editor's Introduction" to the "Special Issue: 40th Anniversary of the Little Rock School Crisis," *The Arkansas Historical Quarterly* 56 (1997): ix–xvi. In the same volume see also T. A. Freyer, "The Little Rock Crisis Reconsidered," 361–70. A monographic study of the Little Rock Crisis is T. Freyer, *The Little Rock Crisis: A Constitutional Interpretation* (Westport, Conn., 1984).
6. G. C. [sic] Iggers, "An Arkansas Professor: The NAACP and the Grass Roots," in W. and J. C. Record, eds., *Little Rock, U.S.A.: Materials For Analysis* (San Francisco, 1960), 283–91, quotes at 286, 288, 289.
7. See the works cited above in notes 4 and 5.
8. C. V. Woodward, *Strange Career of Jim Crow* (1957 edition), quotes at 175, 178–79. See also notes 3 and 4.
9. Quotes from Potter, "Woodward and the Uses of History," 172, 178.
10. See the works cited in notes 1, 3, and 5.
11. Chappell, "Editor's Introduction" (see note 5).
12. C. Trillin, "Remembrance of Moderates Past," *The New Yorker*, 21 Mar. 1977, quotes at 85, 86.
13. See the works cited above in note 3.
14. M. V. Tushnet, *Making Civil Rights Law: Thurgood Marshall and the Supreme Court, 1936–1961* (New York, 1994), 304–5.
15. See the works cited above in notes 3 and 4.
16. In this volume, see Freyer, "Objectivity and Involvement: Georg G. Iggers and Writing the History of the Little Rock School Crisis," especially notes 38 and 39.
17. See the works cited above in notes 3 and 4.
18. Branch, *Parting the Waters*, 922.
19. Compare the sources quoted in notes 4, 5, and 14.
20. M. J. Klarman, "Brown, Racial Change, and the Civil Rights Movement," *Virginia Law Review* 80 (1994): 185.
21. See the works cited above in notes 6 and 16.
22. J. Williams, *Eyes on the Prize: America's Civil Rights Years, 1954–1965* (New York, 1987), 91–119.
23. Quote from M. R. Belknap, *Federal Law and Southern Order: Racial Violence and Constitutional Conflict in the Post-Brown South* (Athens, Ga., 1987), 52.
24. D. R. Goldfield, *Black, White, and Southern: Race Relations and Southern Culture, 1940 to Present* (Baton Rouge, La., 1991), 106.
25. King, "Letter from Birmingham Jail," *Why We Can't Wait* (see note 4).
26. King, as quoted in Bass, *Taming the Storm*, 109, 248,
27. King, as quoted in Garrow, *Bearing the Cross*, 91–92.
28. Tushnet, *Making Civil Rights Law*, 303, 305.
29. A. Fairclough, "The Little Rock Crisis: Success or Failure for the NAACP?" *Arkansas Historical Quarterly* 56, No. 3 (Autumn 1997): 373, 375.
30. See the works cited above in notes 5, 6, and 16.
31. Compare the works cited above in notes 11, 25, 26, 27, and 29.
32. E. Green, "Don't Let Them See You Cry," *Parade Magazine*, 16 Feb. 1992.
33. Freyer, "The Little Rock Crisis Reconsidered." See also Goldfield, *Black, White, and Southern*, 87–198, and Fairclough, "The Little Rock Crisis," 371–75.

34. See the works cited above in notes 20, 23, and 31.
35. T. Freyer and T. Dixon, *Democracy and Judicial Independence: A History of The Federal Courts in Alabama, 1820–1894* (Brooklyn, N. Y., 1995), 215–56. See also the works cited in note 33.
36. See the works cited above in notes 1 and 2.
37. See note 33.
38. G. Wright, *Old South, New South: Revolutions in the Southern Economy Since the Civil War* (New York, 1986), 239–74.
39. Ibid. See also the works cited in notes 1, 11, 20, 22, and 24.
40. See the works cited above in notes 6, 16, 31, and 32.
41. M. L. Dudziak, "The Little Rock Crisis and Foreign Affairs: Race, Resistance, and the Image of American Democracy," *Southern California Law Review* 70 (1997): 1641–1716; A. S. Layton "International Pressure and the U.S. Government's Response to Little Rock," *The Arkansas Historical Quarterly* 56 (1997): 257–72.
42. Quotes from Dudziak, "Little Rock Crisis and Foreign Affairs" (see note 41), 1715–16.
43. M. J. Klarman, "What's So Great About Constitutionalism?" *Northwestern University Law Review* 93 (1998): 192.
44. Tushnet, *Making Civil Rights Law*, 128.
45. For Marshall and McCarthyism, see Tushnet, *Making Civil Rights Law*, 128, 295–96. For the quote from King, see Branch, *Parting the Waters*, 871.
46. D. Bell, Jr., "Brown and the Interest-Convergence Dilemma," *Harvard Law Review* 93 (1980): 518–33. See also Klarman, "What's So Great About Constitutionalism?" 188–89.
47. See the works cited in notes 41 and 45.
48. King, as quoted in Garrow, *Bearing the Cross*, 91, 118.
49. G. M. Fredrickson, *The Comparative Imagination: On the History of Racism, Nationalism, and Social Movements* (Berkeley, Calif., 1997), 183–84.
50. See note 5.
51. See note 29.
52. E. Jacoway, "Down from the Pedestal: Gender and Regional Culture in a Ladylike Assault on the Southern Way of Life," *The Arkansas Historical Quarterly* 56 (1997): 345–52, 355.
53. C. F. Williams, "Class: The Central Issue in the Little Rock School Crisis," *The Arkansas Historical Quarterly* 56 (1997): 341–44.
54. M. Newman, "The Arkansas Baptist State Convention and Desegregation, 1954–1968," *The Arkansas Historical Quarterly* 56 (1997): 294–313.
55. Ibid., 295–96.
56. Ibid., 295.
57. Ibid., as quoted, 303.
58. J. A. Kirk, "The Little Rock Crisis and Postwar Black Activism in Arkansas," *The Arkansas Historical Quarterly* 56 (1997): 273–93.
59. Ibid., quoted at 288. For the references to Iggers, see 288–91.
60. Ibid., 257–72. King, as quoted, 272, and Layton, quoted passage, 272, supra, note 5. For Dudziak, see above n. 41.
61. T. Badger, "'The Forerunner of Our Opposition': Arkansas and the Southern Manifesto of 1956," *The Arkansas Historical Quarterly* 56 (1997): 353–60, quote at 360.
62. See the works cited above in notes 47–51.
63. A. Graham, "Remapping Dogpatch: Northern Media on the Southern Circuit," *The Arkansas Historical Quarterly* 56 (1997): 334–340, quotes at 334–35, 340.
64. R. H. King, "American Dilemmas, European Experiences," *The Arkansas Historical Quarterly* 56 (1997): 314–33, quote at 333.
65. Ibid., King and Ellison, as quoted, at 325.

Chapter 12

OBJECTIVITY AND INVOLVEMENT

Writing the History of German Historiography

Georg G. Iggers

In February 1971, a few days after the German edition of my *The German Conception of History*[1] appeared, I received a letter from Thomas Nipperdey,[2] who later wrote a masterful history of Germany from 1800 to 1918[3] in which he defended aspects of the German past against its postwar critics.[4] Nipperdey criticized my approach. The history of German historiography, he suggested in his letter to me, must be written not in terms of a critique of the ideological assumptions of the historians, but of their contributions to historical scholarship. The underlying assumption of his letter, which he developed more fully in his later theoretical essays,[5] is that the historian must and can aim at objectivity free of ideology. My position was that while scholarship could not be reduced to ideology, scholarship, and particularly that of the German historical school, could not be understood without the political and philosophic presuppositions that affected it. In brief I took a stand between the objectivism, attributed to Ranke and more recently championed by G. E. Elton,[6] which maintained that the historian using critical methods of inquiry could impartially recapture the past "as it actually was [*wie es eigentlich gewesen*]," and the relativism of Hayden White[7] or Frank Ankersmit,[8] which argued that every historical account is essentially fictional.

Believing that historical scholarship does not operate in a vacuum, but is deeply shaped by the milieu in which it originates, and that personal experiences also play a role, I shall introduce a brief autobiographical note and relate how I arrived at my evaluation of German historiography. The fact that I was born in Germany in late 1926, spent almost six years of my childhood under the Nazi regime, and was able to emigrate to the United States in October 1938, a few weeks before the November pogrom, the so-called *Reichskristallnacht*, contributed to my occupation with the

German political and intellectual traditions. The encounter with Nazism shaped my commitment to political democracy and my subsequent involvement in the United States in the struggle for racial equality.[9] My training as a historian was unconventional. I came to history from literature and philosophy. After a B.A. in Romance Languages and an A.M. in German literature, I spent a year studying philosophy and sociology at the New School for Social Research and returned to the University of Chicago to complete a doctorate in nineteenth-century European intellectual history under the interdisciplinary Committee on the History of Culture with a particular focus on the impact of philosophies of history on political thought.

At this point I knew relatively little about the German historical discipline. A study I began on the decline of the idea of progress[10] turned into an examination of the historicist tradition. I began with a careful reading of Ranke who had been viewed in the literature as the founder of history as a rigorous professional discipline at the German universities that aimed at impartiality and objectivity through the critical examination of sources. Not only the German historians built on this ideal of an impartial, objective historiography but so did historians all over the world as historical studies there too underwent professionalization.

The image I had gathered from my studies in Chicago and other readings in the American literature was that of a hyperpositivistic scholar, strictly following a documentary method. In addition to Ranke, I began to read interpretations of his method and outlook as they appeared in the German and the American literature in the last third of the nineteenth century. The result was an article in 1962 in *History and Theory* on "The Image of Ranke in German and American Historical Thought."[11] Two very different interpretations of Ranke appeared side by side, in America that of a craftsman untroubled by philosophical and political ideas, in Germany that of a historian deeply steeped in German idealist philosophy. From there I proceeded to Ranke's theoretical essays, the "Great Powers," "The Political Dialogue," and the various introductions to his great works and to his lecture courses.[12]

What struck me was the central role that a metaphysics of history occupied in these essays. Ranke took issue with Hegel whose schematic view of historical development he rejected. Instead he insisted that the historian must concentrate on the uniqueness of every historical situation and the openness of the course of history. The latter, he stressed, "cannot be defined or put in abstract terms" but only be directly "observed."[13] Yet he accepted Hegel's conviction that the state not only forms the central historical institution, but at the same time embodies "thoughts of God."[14] For him as for Hegel, the state constituted an "ethical reality" governed by its own principles of growth. Like Hegel he subordinated the needs of "civil society" to the power political (*machtpolitische*) interests of the state. For the ultimate arbitrator, he agrees with Hegel, is war. As he notes in the

"Political Dialogue": "But seriously, you will be able to name few significant wars for which it could not be proved that genuine moral energy achieved the final victory."[15] While in his famous statement on the idea of progress he notes: "Every epoch is equally immediate to God,"[16] he in fact stresses that some epochs are less historical than others, that in fact the Chinese and the Indians have no history,[17] and that there is divine guidance in history, the hidden "hand of God."[18] He stresses the need of the historian to be "impartial," but is convinced that this impartiality reveals the "objective" tendencies in history that justify the existing order of things and in Burkean manner repudiates any attempts to remodel this order.[19]

Turning then to his great historical works, I found that they were profoundly shaped by these metahistorical and political assumptions. Ranke's popularity in his time rested as much or more on his ability to write, i.e., to narrate well, than on his careful scholarship. In fact, his works are much freer of annotation than such eighteenth-century historical classics as Gibbon's *Decline and Fall of the Roman Empire*. The similarities of Ranke's histories to the realistic historical novels of the nineteenth century have been noted.[20] Moreover, there is a very uncritical aspect to his use of documents. Ranke wants to write a history based on primary sources, as he does in his use of the reports of the Venetian ambassadors;[21] but he takes these reports very largely on face value not asking to what extent they reflect the viewpoints of the ambassadors or their desire to report what is expected of them.

When I wrote the Ranke chapter in *The German Conception of History*, I was very much aware that ideas cannot be isolated from the political culture in which they occur. But I did not yet place sufficient stress on the broader institutional framework of historical studies of which Fritz Ringer's book on the German academic profession[22] and Wolfgang Weber's study of the recruitment of professors of history from 1800 to 1970[23] made me aware. In my book I traced a continuity in the basic political and philosophic assumptions of the German historical profession from Ranke until the mid-1960s, when the tradition of the historical study and teaching that rested on these assumptions was for the first time seriously questioned in Germany.[24] An ideological shift took place among the historians who followed Ranke. Ranke was in many ways still a man of the old regime, a European in outlook concerned with the system of the great powers, who devoted as much time to the history of France, England, Serbia, and the papacy as to that of Germany. He was a staunch monarchist who distrusted even limited constitutional government. The next generation of historians often labeled as "the Prussian School" were fervent German nationalists and in a peculiar way liberals.[25]

Three ideas played a key role in the conception of history of the German historical school until its dissolution in the 1960s. The first was a peculiar fusion of authoritarianism and constitutionalism as it characterized the German Empire forged by Bismarck. Its advocates firmly opposed the parliamentarization of Germany, although a minority wing, including Friedrich Meinecke and Ernst Troeltsch favored concessions in that direction and after 1918 reluctantly supported the Weimar Republic. They all favored a policy of German expansion in Central Europe and overseas although again the moderate wing around Meinecke, Troeltsch, and Max Weber after 1917 counseled caution. And they almost to a man—Otto Hintze was the notable exception—opposed any attempt to introduce concepts and methods of social analysis into historical studies. When at the turn of the century generally in the world, in France,[26] the United States,[27] and even Imperial Russia,[28] historians began increasingly to turn to social and cultural history, the German historians almost to a man—I am saying "to a man" because there were no women historians—including Meinecke as editor of the *Historische Zeitschrift*, resisted Karl Lamprecht's attempt to write a culturally oriented history of Germany, which admittedly suffered from a certain muddle-headedness and sloppy research, and suspected him unjustly of subversive political and even Marxist sympathies.[29] The result was that German historical studies, which had enjoyed a tremendous reputation internationally, remained stagnant until well after World War II and became increasingly irrelevant in a world in which new approaches to history were explored.

After 1918 the majority of the German historians, again excluding a minority of moderates such as Meinecke, passionately opposed the Weimar Republic. I do not claim in my book that there is a direct line between their historiography and the Nazis. The Nazis were much too populist for the conservative historians. But the latter agreed on so many points with the Nazis, the need to replace Weimar democracy with a strong authoritarian government, the restoration of Germany as a major world power, German expansion to the East, and the dislike of Jews, that almost all of them were able to continue their work without great difficulty under the Nazis.[30] They learned little from the German defeat in 1945. In constructing the story of a German resistance against Hitler consisting primarily of aristocrats, officers, and church leaders, they interpreted Nazism as an outgrowth of a Western movement of mass democracy with few roots in German traditions.[31]

Nevertheless, by the 1920s there were two orientations in historical and historiographical thought and writing at the margins of the profession to whom the established school of academic history seemed outdated. One, democratically oriented, turned to sociological models, including those of Max Weber and Karl Marx, to introduce greater analytical rigor into historical inquiry. All of the historians associated with this orientation, including such younger scholars such as Eckart Kehr, Hans Rosenberg, Gustav Mayer, Hajo Holborn, and Hedwig Hintze, were driven into emigration after 1933.[32] The other group, on the radical right, sought an alternative to the conservatism of the academic establishment by moving the focus away from high politics and elites to the *Volk* understood in biological terms.

History appeared to them as relentless racial conflict.[33] Having cleansed themselves of Nazi phraseology, they established themselves in the early years of the Federal Republic as founders of a new social history of the industrial age.[34]

The great reputation that the German historians enjoyed well into the twentieth century rested in large part on their claim to professionalism, which was admired and imitated elsewhere. Professionalism was identified with *Verwissenschaftlichung*, the process by which history became a science. Since Ranke German historians had understood history as a *Geisteswissenschaft*, a cultural science dealing with the human spirit, and stressed that the task of the historian was to understand (*verstehen*) the uniqueness and meaning of historical situations and the diversity and openness of history. The abstract explanatory models of the generalizing sciences had no place in history and were to be avoided as ahistorical. Yet they shared with other *Wissenschaftler* the insistence on impartial inquiry guided by strict methodological guidelines, the results of which are capable of being examined by other scholars equally committed to this logic of inquiry. In this sense they considered themselves to be scientific and objective. Yet they failed adequately to take into account the extent to which historical studies, or for that matter all science, takes place within the framework of culture, society, and politics. This is very apparent in the history of German historical scholarship. Ideology and scholarship are closely interwoven. The scholarly ethos calls for impartiality and objectivity. Yet I am struck how closely the new professional scholarship was accompanied by ultranationalism, not only in Germany but also in the other countries where the German model was imitated in the process of professionalization.

The German historical profession reflects the political and intellectual conditions of the post-Napoleonic world in which it emerged, a society aware of the deep changes that had been wrought but which sought a balance between modernity and continuity, constitutionalism and authority, seeking always to maintain social stability. It must be remembered that when we normally speak of the German historical school we think of the Protestant historians at the predominantly North German universities.[35] We proceed too easily with the notion that professional historiography was secular. As we saw already in the case of Ranke, it integrated Lutheran religious beliefs into its conception of history. These beliefs pervaded historical thought and writing well into the twentieth century, clearly to Friedrich Meinecke and Gerhard Ritter. John Moses[36] has pointed out that a Lutheran conception of the two realms permeated Protestant German political culture, freed the state from the standards of normal morality, and demanded the firm obedience of the Christian to the state. Hegel, Ranke, Droysen, Treitschke, and Meinecke all stood in this tradition. From this there derived in World War I the notion of specific German "Ideas of 1914," which embodied a conception of freedom distinct from the revolutionary "Ideas of 1789."[37] There was no place in this religion for a critical attitude toward the established authorities as there was in the dissenting churches in the Anglo-American world.

American, British, and French historians, even in World War I,[38] admired the academic freedom, or *Lehrfreiheit*, that the German historical profession supposedly enjoyed, which enabled them to express their scholarly opinions freely. In fact there was relatively little diversity of opinion among the historians at the German universities. On one level German professors did enjoy greater self-determination than their American colleagues generally and their British colleagues outside Oxbridge. Trustees and administrators in the English speaking world interfered much more directly with the affairs of the universities and colleges, including appointments and even teaching content,[39] than did the state ministries in Germany where matters of internal control were left largely to the professoriate. So, although the universities in Germany were state institutions, or perhaps because they were, the German professoriate suffered much less external interference than their Anglo-American colleagues. But the mechanisms of recruitment guaranteed a much greater degree of consensus than was the case in the latter countries. A small elite of full professors, or *Ordinarien*, controlled the affairs of the history institutes like feudal lords and prevented persons of differing opinions, religious orientation, or political outlook from being admitted to university teaching.[40] Thus persons who were not Protestants or did not share in the "national liberal" consensus were effectively excluded.[41] At the same time there was direct government interference, as in the case of the *Lex Arons* of 1898, which barred Social Democrats from teaching at Prussian universities.[42] The case of the liberal historian, Veit Valentin, who in 1917 lost his *venia legendi*, the right to teach at a university, because of his moderate views on the war, is an example of the limitations of academic freedom.[43] In America, to be sure, many more professors lost their positions during World War I than in Germany, partly also because greater diversity of opinion existed at the American universities. The firm hold of the conservative professoriate over the historical profession remained unbroken in Germany until a new and more critical generation took their places in the late 1960s and 1970s.

The German Conception of History appeared in German in 1971 at the point when a new generation of historians educated after 1945 reexamined German political traditions and the role that German historiography occupied in these traditions. I neither then nor now have maintained that historical scholarship can be reduced to ideology, but I did maintain that ideological assumptions and political convictions colored the scholarship of the German profession. In the current debate between relativists such as Hayden White and Frank Ankersmit who have maintained that history is indistinguishable from literature and fiction, that "the best grounds for choosing one perspective on history rather than another are ultimately aesthetic or moral rather than epistemological,"[44] and those like Richard Evans[45] who defend the role of the historian to reconstruct the past honestly, I have sided with the latter.[46] The questions that historians or social scientist ask reflect their cognitive interests. As soon as we proceed from a narrow reconstitution of the past to an attempt to place these facts into a meaningful context, elements of perspective enter. Thus there can be very different accounts of, let's say, the French Revolution or the Nazi rise to power. However, these accounts are not purely arbitrary but involve both an empirical factual basis and challengeable procedures of logical reasoning that enter into the production of these accounts. It is never possible to establish with finality "wie es eigentlich gewesen" because of the complexity of historical subject matters, which require a diversity of perspectives to understand them, but it is often possible to establish "*wie es nicht gewesen*," or how it did not happen. In this sense historical studies represent an ongoing dialog involving a consensus on what constitutes rational inquiry. The fault of the tradition of academic historical scholarship that I examined in my book was that in its claim to scientific authority it declined to recognize the ideological elements that colored its findings. It used or misused the ethos of professionalism to buttress its political program. And this program, while it did not directly lead to Nazism, gave scientific respectability to an antidemocratic ideology that substantially contributed to the collapse of democracy in Germany and the reign of terror that followed.

By the 1970s the monopoly of the German conception of history was broken. I myself felt great sympathy for historians of the new critical school who occupied themselves with the question how Nazism could come to power in Germany and sought answers in German history.[47] They pointed at the uneven modernization of Germany since the mid-nineteenth century in which older predemocratic institutions and attitudes persisted to a much greater extent than in other Western industrial countries.[48] In recent years this so-called *Sonderwegsthese* has been challenged by historians such as Thomas Nipperdey on the right[49] and Geoff Eley and David Blackbourn on the left[50] who have argued that Germany's development did not differ fundamentally from that of other Western countries. I agree that there is no norm by which modernization can be measured but still believe that the thesis of the persistent illiberalism[51] in industrializing Germany has a good deal of validity.

I have also followed closely the critiques of the German past in the historiography of the former GDR, but found them disappointing. As I have pointed out in my writings on GDR historiography,[52] historians in the German Democratic Republic (GDR), proceeding from Marxist hypotheses, made important contributions in a large number of fields from the history of the two world wars to the history of everyday life. Yet the attempts to analyze the German past, and the road that led to Nazism, tended largely to be schematic and superficial, less Marxist than nationalistic and opportunistic. GDR historians in the 1980s reinterpreted German history from Luther via Frederick II to Bismarck to provide legitimation for the authoritarian regime of the GDR.[53] In doing so they were much less aware than critical West German historians of the autocratic and *völkisch* aspects of the nineteenth-century German nationalist movement.

This essay should not be understood as a rejection of scholarly approaches but rather as a warning against an overly uncritical view of what constitutes scholarship and science and against the apotheosis of professionalism. Every history presupposes a set of political, moral, and aesthetic values. The historian should be aware of his perspective and at the same remain intellectually honest. The distinction between history and propaganda must be stricter than it was in the classical German tradition. My own commitment is frankly to a socially just democratic society. For that reason the ideology of the German classical tradition with its defense of privilege and its justification of collective violence was abhorrent to me. At the same time, I remain firmly committed to history as an ongoing dialog among persons who despite widely differing values and outlooks are willing to communicate along lines that do not distort historical evidence.

Notes

1. G. G. Iggers, *The German Concept of History: The National Tradition of Historical Thought from Herder to the Present* (Middletown, Conn., 1968).
2. Thomas Nipperdey to Georg G. Iggers, 15 Feb. 1971.
3. T. Nipperdey, *Deutsche Geschichte 1800–1866* (Munich, 1983), and *Deutsche Geschichte 1866–1918*, 2 vols. (Munich, 1993).
4. See also T. Nipperdey, "Wehlers 'Kaiserreich'. Eine kritische Auseinandersetzung," *Geschichte und Gesellschaft* 1 (1975): 539–60.
5. T. Nipperdey, *Gesellschaft, Kultur, Theorie. Gesammelte Aufsätze* (Göttingen, 1976).
6. G. R. Elton, *The Practice of History* (Sydney, 1967).
7. In this respect, see H. V. White, *Metahistory: The Historical Imagination in Nineteenth-Century Europe* (Baltimore, Md., 1973); *Tropes of Discourse: Essays in Cultural Criticism* (Baltimore, Md., 1978); *The Content of the Form: Narrative Discourse and Historical Representation* (Baltimore, Md., 1987); "Historical Emplotment and the Problem of Truth" in *Probing the Limits of Representation: Nazism and the Final Solution*, ed. S. Friedländer (Cambridge, Mass., 1992), 37–53.
8. F. R. Ankersmit, *History and Tropology: The Rise and Fall of Metaphor* (Berkeley, Calif., 1994).
9. See D. Gerber, "From Hamburg to Little Rock and Beyond: The Origins of Georg G. Iggers's Civil Rights Activism" in *Geschichtswissenschaft vor 2000. Perspektiven der Historiographiegeschichtre, Geschichtstheorie, Sozial- und Kulturgeschichte. Festschrift für Georg G. Iggers zum 65. Geburtstag*, ed. K. Jarausch, J. Rüsen, and H. Schleier (Hagen, 1991), 509–22.
10. See G. G. Iggers, "The Idea of Progress in Recent Philosophy of History," *Journal of Modern History* 30 (1958): 215–26, as well as "The Idea of Progress: A Critical Reassessment," *American Historical Review* 71 (1965–66): 1–17.
11. *History and Theory* (1962): 17–40.

12. L. von Ranke, *The Theory and Practice of History*, ed. G. G. Iggers and K. von Moltke (Indianapolis, 1973).
13. "The Great Powers," ibid., 100.
14. "A Dialogue on Politics," ibid., 119.
15. Ibid., 117.
16. "On Progress in History," ibid., 53.
17. "On the Character of Historical Science," ibid., 18. 46. On India, see "On the Character of Historical Science," ibid., 34.
18. Ranke, "Preface to the First Edition of Histories of the Latin and German Nations," ibid., 138.
19. See Ranke, "On the Character of Historical Science," ibid., 41–43. See also "Über die Verwandtschaft und den Unterschied der Historie und der Politik" in L. von Ranke, *Sämtliche Werke*, 54 vols. (Leipzig, 1873–90), 24: 280–293.
20. See H. White, *Metahistory*, as well as L. Gossman, *Between History and Literature* (Cambridge, Mass., 1990).
21. See G. Benzoni, "Ranke's Favorite Source: The Venetian Relazioni," in *Leopold von Ranke and the Shaping of the Historical Discipline*, ed. G. G. Iggers and J. M. Powell (Syracuse, N.Y., 1990), 45–57.
22. F. K. Ringer, *The Decline of the German Mandarins: The German Academic Community, 1890–1933* (Cambridge, Mass., 1969).
23. W. Weber, *Priester der Klio. Historisch-sozialwissenschaftliche Studien zur Herkunft und Karriere deutscher Historiker und zur Geschichte der Geschichtswissenschaft 1800–1970* (Frankfurt a.M., 1984).
24. See Wehler's "Einleitung" to E. Kehr, *Der Primat der Innenpolitik*, ed. H.-U. Wehler (Berlin, 1965); W. J. Mommsen, *Geschichtswissenschaft jenseits des Historismus* (Düsseldorf, 1971).
25. See R. Southard, *Droysen and the Prussian School of History* (Lexington, Ky., 1995).
26. See P. Burke, *The French Historical Revolution: The Annales School, 1929–1989* (London, 1990).
27. R. Hofstadter, *Progressive Historians: Turner, Beard, Parrington* (New York, 1968); E. Breisach, *American Progressive History: An Experiment in Modernization* (Chicago, 1993).
28. See T. Bohn, *Russische Geschichtswissenschaft von 1880 bis 1905. Pavel N. Miljukov und die Moskauer Schule* (Cologne, 1998).
29. The best study of Lamprecht is R. Chickering, *Karl Lamprecht: A German Academic Life (1856–1915)* (Atlantic Highlands, N.J., 1993).
30. See K. F. Werner, *Das NS-Geschichtsbild und die deutsche Geschichtswissenschaft* (Stuttgart, 1967); H. Heiber, *Walter Frank und sein Reichsinstitut für Geschichte des Neuen Deutschland* (Stuttgart, 1966); K. Schönwalder, *Historiker und Politik. Geschichtswissenschaft im Nationalsozialismus* (Frankfurt a.M., 1992); P. Schöttler, ed., *Geschichtsschreibung als Legitimationswissenschaft 1918–1945* (Frankfurt a.M., 1997). Apologetic and in my opinion wrong is U. Wolf, *Litteris et Patria. Das Janusgesicht der Historie* (Stuttgart, 1996).
31. H. Rothfels, *The German Opposition to Hitler* (London, 1961); G. Ritter, *Carl Goerdeler und die deutsche Widerstandsbewegung* (Stuttgart, 1954).
32. See P. T. Walther, "Von Meinecke bis Beard? Die nach 1933 in die USA emigrierten deutschen Neuhistoriker," (Ph.D. diss., State University of New York at Buffalo, 1989. See also G. G. Iggers, "Die deutschen Historiker in der Emigration" in *Geschichtswissenschaft in Deutschland*, ed. B. Faulenbach (Munich, 1974), 97–111, 181–83.
33. See W. Oberkrome, *Volksgeschichte. Methodologische Innovationen und völkische Ideologisierung in der deutschen Geschichtswissenschaft 1918–1945* (Göttingen, 1993); W. Schulze, *Deutsche Geschichtswissenschaft nach 1945* (Munich, 1989), chap. 16; Schöttler, *Geschichtsschreibung als Legitimationswissenshaft*. On the nationalism and opposition to democracy of German historians in the Weimar Republic, see B. Faulenbach, *Ideologie des deutschen Weges. Die deutsche Geschichte in der Historiographie zwischen Kaiserreich und Nationalsozialismus* (Munich, 1980). On the proximity of established historians to the Nazis, see Schönwalder, *Historiker und Politik, passim*.

34. See Schulze, *Deutsche Geschichtswissenschaft*, chap. 16.
35. On the distinction between Protestant and Catholic historiographical traditions in Germany, see K. C. Cramer, "The Lamentations of Germany: The Historiography of the Thirty Years' War, 1790–1890" (Ph.D. dissertation, Harvard University, 1998).
36. J. A. Moses, "The British and the German Churches and the Perception of War," *War and Society* 5 (1987): 23–41.
37. See Ringer, *Decline of German Mandarins*, 180–99.
38. For a comparative international perspective, see G. G. Iggers, "Historians Confronted With the War," paper delivered at the conference "European Intellectuals and the War," Trento, Italy, 4–6 November 1998, and published in V. Calì, G. Corni, and G. Ferrandi, eds., *Intellettuali e Grande guerra* (Bologna, 2000).
39. For the United States, see R. Hofstadter and W. P. Metzger, *The Development of Academic Freedom in the United States* (New York, 1955); C. S. Gruber, *Mars and Minerva: World War I and the Use of Higher Learning in America* (Baton Rouge, La., 1975); P. Novick, *That Noble Dream: The "Objectivity Question" and the American Historical Profession* (Cambridge, 1988), chap. 5. On Great Britain, see S, Wallace, *War and the Image of Germany: British Academics, 1914–1918* (Edinburgh, 1988) with a special chapter "Historians and the War," 58–73.
40. See Weber, *Priester der Klio* (n. 23).
41. See G. G. Iggers, "Academic Anti-Semitism in Germany 1870–1933. A Comparative International Perspective," *Tel Aviver Jahrbuch für deutsche Geschichte* 27 (1998): 473–89. On Catholics, see also N. Hammerstein, *Antisemitismus und deutsche Universitäten 1871–1933* (Frankfurt a.M., 1995).
42. See Ringer, *Decline of German Mandarins*, 141–42.
43. On the Valentin case, see H. Cymorek, *Georg von Below und die deutsche Geschichtswissenschaft um 1900* (Stuttgart, 1998), 263–267; F. Fehrenbach, "Veit Valentin," in *Deutsche Historiker*, ed. H.-U. Wehler, vol. 1 (Göttingen, 1971), 69–87; Ringer, *Decline of German Mandarins*, 56–57; Hans Schleier, *Die bürgerliche Geschichtsschreibung der Weimarer Republik* (Berlin, 1975), 346–98.
44. White, *Metahistory*, xii.
45. R. J. Evans, *In Defence of History* (London, 1997).
46. G. G. Iggers, *Historiography in the Twentieth Century: From Scientific Objectivity to the Postmodern Challenge* (Hanover, N.H., 1997).
47. See G. G. Iggers, *New Directions in European Historiography* (Middletown, Conn., 1975), as well as Iggers's "Introduction" to G. G. Iggers, ed., *The Social History of Politics: Critical Perspectives in West German Historical Writing Since 1945* (Leamington Spa, 1985). 1–48.
48. H.-U. Wehler, *The German Empire, 1871–1918* (Leamington Spa, 1985).
49. Nipperdey, *Deutsche Geschichte 1866–1918.*
50. G. Eley and D. Blackbourn, *The Peculiarities of German History: Bourgeois Culture in 19th-Century Germany* (Oxford, 1984).
51. F. Stern, *Failure of Illiberalism: Essays on the Political Culture of Modern Germany* (New York, 1972).
52. G. G. Iggers, ed., *Marxist Historiography in Transformation: East German Social History in the 1980s* (New York, 1981).
53. See J. H. Brinks, *Die Geschichtswissenschaft auf dem Weg zur deutschen Einheit. Luther, Friedrich II und Bismarck als Paradigmen politischen Wandels* (Frankfurt a.M., 1992).

Chapter 13

RESHAPING THE WORLD

Historiography from a Universal Perspective

Eckhardt Fuchs

With the publication in 1968 of his book *The German Conception of History*, Georg Iggers belonged to those American historians who introduced a new, critical view of the nineteenth-century German historiographical tradition.[1] The main point of this new approach was to show the political, ideological, and philosophical assumptions of German historiography within the context of modern German history. It revealed that despite the idea of objectivity, history was often written for national and political interests: the burgeoning *Geschichtswissenschaft*, or historical science, offered a scientifically authenticated and authorized historical narrative that helped to create a national myth, which placed one's own nation and political system at the center of history.

Iggers and numerous German historians afterwards have pointed out the deficiencies of German national historiography, which are rooted in the epistemology of historicism, or *Historismus*. They also have shown that the process of professionalization and scientification of historiography in the course of the nineteenth century was characterized by a loss of certain elements that shaped the historiography of the Enlightenment. One of these elements was world or universal history. In taking up Iggers's approach, in this essay I will look at the German tradition of world history, a topic that has been dealt with only marginally in the research on the history of historicism. I will sketch a general outline of German world historiography and show that it was shaped by ideological assumptions just as was the writing of Germany's national history. Referring to the most recent debates on world history, I will discuss in the second part of this essay the problem of how to write a transcultural history of historiography.

Writing World History in Germany

The writing of world and universal history was a central part of Enlightenment historiography, and Voltaire belonged to its leading figures. In his *Essay sur les moeurs et l'esprit des nations et sur les principaux faits de l'histoire depuis Charlemagne jusqu'à Louis XIII* (1756), Voltaire broke radically with the medieval eschatological world-view. German historians of this era, such as Isaak Iselin, Johann Christoph Gatterer, August Ludwig Schlözer, and Friedrich Schiller—to name just a few—followed Voltaire, whose essay on the spirit of nations was translated into German between 1760 and 1762. Thus a secularized historical world-view that included non-European cultures replaced the biblical *historia sacra* of the "four world empires."[2] The world historians based their histories of mankind on travel reports, linked historical with anthropological and ethnological data, and rejected the traditional historiography as a history of kings and dynasties.[3] Johann Gottfried Herder's concept of world history was the most ambitious attempt because he took the position that every culture deserved an equal place in human history. He saw the ideal for other cultures neither in the enlightened civilization of Europe nor in a progressive process of perfectibility. He rather emphasized the singularity of other peoples and a cultural diversity that could not be understood with European normative concepts and teleology.[4]

However, it soon became obvious that a gulf was developing between enlightened universalism and the belief in the superiority of one's own civilization. The idea of the difference between primitive and civilized peoples—or more accurately the inferiority of other cultures to Indo-European ones—can be traced back to the Enlightenment, as exemplified by Christoph Meiners's *Grundriß der Geschichte der Menschheit* published in 1785.[5] In general, the process of scientification in the nineteenth century encouraged a geographic narrowing of its subject matter. In abandoning Herder's and Immanuel Kant's ideas on universal history, the Eurocentric claim for representing human civilization found its philosophical justification in Hegel's *Vorlesungen über die Philosophie der Geschichte* and its historiographical foundation in Leopold von Ranke's *Weltgeschichte*.[6] In the course of the nineteenth century, European history was elevated to the level of a world history in which the Other simply faded away. It was this invention of Europe, of its unified history and culture since classical Greece, which caused certain peoples and societies to be excluded from world history.[7] This Eurocentrism was by no means a product of Europe but of a few, domineering European nations of the early modern and modern periods.[8]

The universalization of European historical thought in the nineteenth century coincided with a nationalistic and Eurocentric historiography that barely took non-European peoples into account or, with the exception of the classical civilizations, condemned them as "stagnant" or "without history." There was an unbreakable connection between modernity, the modern historical discipline, and Eurocentrism. This Eurocentrism found its initial historiographic expression in the European national histories. Non-European history became the domain of other disciplines, from folklore, anthropology, and ethnology to archaeology and American studies. Oriental studies would soon dominate, but their primary objective was not history but to decipher and compare non-European languages.[9] But even if knowledge about the world was mostly obtained in the context of colonialism and imperialism, and non-Western history was interpreted through a Euro-American perspective, a tradition of world history existed at the margins of the profession.

World history itself played a minor role in German historiography for most of the nineteenth century. Early world histories, such as the ones by Friedrich Christoph Schlosser and Carl von Rotteck, were written in the universalist tradition of Enlightenment and, in Schlosser's case, were based on Kant's philosophy of history.[10] Except for Ranke who published his *Weltgeschichte* in nine volumes in the 1880s, world history was written on the periphery or outside of historical scholarship.[11] In these works world history did not mean the universal history of mankind but the history of cultivated peoples that is embedded in the state. "What existed before the stage of culture," as Georg Weber stated, "is excluded from the scope of the historian's research."[12] His *Allgemeine Weltgeschichte*, the first volume of which appeared in 1857, as well as another collection by the same title, the first volume of which was published by Ferdinand Justin, Julius von Pflugk-Harttung, and others in 1884, were aimed primarily at a popular audience to educate the German *Bildungsbürger* and were not considered historical research even if they were based on academic scholarship.[13]

With the exception of Ranke, professional historians did not show much interest in world history. In his second edition of 1882, which appeared at the same time as Ranke's opus, Weber regretted that "the present moment is not a good moment to take the path to the stronghold of universal historical science."[14] And as Ottokar Lorenz noted four years later: "Among scholars the history of mankind has long died out. It is searching in vain for an advocate who could undertake its defense from a thorough knowledge of the material. In this respect the development of historiography has completely diverged from [the path set by] Schlosser. No one any longer claims to be a universal historian."[15]

Two decades later the situation changed. Around the turn of the century professional historians turned to world history.[16] On the one hand historical events, such as the Taiping Rebellion and civil war in China, the mutiny and great revolt in India from 1857 to 1859, the Civil War in the United States, the reformation of Russia after 1861, the war of 1864 to 1870 in Paraguay, the Meiji Revolution in Japan, to name just a few, drew attention to the fact that there was a real general development of the world, a "real world history" as Dietrich Schäfer put it, or to quote Helmolt, a representative whose ideas differed diametrically from those held by Schäfer, "the world is small."[17] World history became relevant for the imperial politics of the great powers, and the colonial empires needed knowledge about their colonized people.[18] On the other hand, new archaeological, ethnological and anthropological discoveries supplied the historians with many new historical facts about the history of the so-called primitive peoples and non-Western societies.

However, the world histories of professional historians became even more limited than the preceding world histories with their assumption of a universal spread of Occidental-Christian culture. As early as 1864 Georg Weber stated in the introductory remarks of his *Weltgeschichte*, "that the German people more than any other is called upon to give world history its real shape and formation. Its position in the middle of Europe, its striving for universal education, its inherent cosmopolitan tendencies, which also applies the standard of humanity, justice, and philanthropy to the strange and hostile, makes it appear as if it is specially qualified to act as the guardian and custodian of historical treasures."[19] This statement indicates a shift from a world history written from the Enlightenment perspective of a universal mankind and Ranke's European view of world history to the perception of the world through the German eye that occurred in the course of nineteenth-century German historiography.

Around the turn of the century, professional historians such as Dietrich Schäfer and Hans Delbrück published world histories that were founded on political aspects of the state (*Machtstaatgedanken*) and served imperialistic aims of the German Empire.[20] They not only confined world history to the history of the cultured peoples of Europe as Ranke did, but moved Germany to the center of human history. Although Ranke's *Deutsche Geschichte im Zeitalter der Reformation* belonged to his most important works, he was more a historian of European history who had nothing in common with the Borussian historiography à la Heinrich von Treitschke or with a nationalistic view, such as Schäfer's. Whereas for Ranke German history was part of European history, Treitschke emphasized the "mass aristocracy of the white man," and Schäfer placed, as Weber did before, the German people on top of European and human civilization.[21] Even after World War I, Schäfer wrote in the preface of his *Weltgeschichte* that "there is no nation that is able to achieve more for mankind [than the German nation] provided that it regains its freedom to act, a freedom that has been taken from it not just because of the jealousy, power hunger, and restfulness of its enemies but also because of its own political and national immaturity."[22]

Although Theodor Lindner, a student of Ranke's and a professor at the University of Halle, called for the integration of non-Western cultures in his philosophy of history, he did not overcome the Eurocentric perspective. In his *Weltgeschichte seit der Völkerwanderung*, the first volume of which appeared in 1901, Lindner distinguished between three relevant groups in world history: the Mongolian, the Semitic, and the Indo-Germanic. In his racist view, the latter one adapted best. Lindner saw the characteristics of this Indo-Germanic group in its "individualism, that striving of the individual for sustaining the right of his own personality within the community as a whole as well as its propensity for the supernatural. This particular talent of the Indo-Germans explains why their history, so rich in change, has finally led them to world power."[23] He nevertheless went beyond Ranke and the German nationalist historians in trying to apply the historicist theory of historical writing to non-European cultures.[24]

The nationalistic view of German historians becomes also evident if one looks at their attitude toward the newly established international historical congresses. The inaugural congress of 1898 was held under the banner of traditional European diplomatic history, but eight sessions of the following congress in Paris 1900 bore the motto of comparative historiography.[25] In his evaluation of the inaugural historical congress of 1898, Georg von Below had urged that the endeavor be continued, although he expected nothing more from these international meetings than personal contacts and presentations, which hardly permitted any real progress for (national) historiography.[26] He was no exception; resistance to international congresses was voiced by other German historians as well. The proposal of French historians at the 1903 congress of historical science in Rome that the next meeting be held in Berlin in 1908 met with little sympathy from historians there. Supporters of the idea included Adolf von Harnack, probably the most ardent scientific internationalist in Germany, classical philologist Ulrich von Wilamowitz-Moellendorf, and legal historian Otto von Gierke. Others, however, complained that such a congress would bear little scientific fruit. Their argument was probably not entirely unjustified judging from the results of the preceding congresses. The influence of political and national conflicts on historiography, stated the skeptics, left little room for consensus in the scientific discussion.

Not only the German but the majority of European historians followed a nationalistic and Eurocentric orientation. A look at the participants (see the following table) and subjects of the first historical congresses reveals that non-European historiography was a marginal phenomenon. Non-European issues were discussed only in the section on comparative legal history, in which numerous missionaries and colonialists participated. Legal history was regarded as a political tool of European colonial policy, for example, in the training of colonial officials.[27] Overall, however, as Pasquale Villari emphasized in his inaugural address at the Rome congress, the congresses were oriented toward a concept of history that went beyond traditional methodology, allowing national-centered historiography to be placed in a broader context of world history. It went without saying, however, that this was restricted to Europeans.[28]

TABLE 1: Participants of First Historical Congresses[29]

	Registered Participants			
Congresses	Africa	Asia/ Australia	Latin America	Total Participants
The Hague 1898	1	3	1	360
1. Paris 1900	3	5/1	18	864
2. Rome 1903	7	3/1	3	2,060
3. Berlin 1908	7	5	1	1,042
4. London 1913	-	–	–	680
5. Brussels 1923	5	8	–	999

In 1908 in Berlin, a section on the history of the Orient was added to the program for the first time. In 1913 in London, it was expanded to "Oriental History with Egyptology." However, even these two congresses had a strongly national orientation biased toward the host country. Nevertheless, in England, the leading colonial power, the Section on Modern History had a subsection dealing with colonial policies of the major European powers and the United States. The Section on Related and Auxiliary Sciences had a subsection on Ethnology, Historical Geography, Topography, and Local History, in which nine papers on non-European subjects were given.[30] However, no non-European scholars spoke in these sections either. Overall, scholars from outside Europe or North America rarely participated in the congresses.

One might explain this nationalism and Eurocentrism among historians with a general Zeitgeist in the imperial age. Although not as nationalistic as the majority of professional historians, for most German scholars, from Otto Hintze and Ernst Troeltsch to Max Weber, the universalistic conception of world history was rooted in Euro-American culture. However, there was a subversive discourse in Germany. A few cultural historians, such as Karl Lamprecht and Kurt Breysig, as well as outsiders of the academic circles, such as Hans Helmolt, opposed the one-sided political history of historicism and tried to introduce a non-nationalistic world history.[31]

Helmolt rejected the Eurocentric world-view and called for the incorporation of all people, even the ones "without history" into a general world history. For him, Ranke's world history signaled a regression in historical scholarship.[32] Helmolt's scheme was not based on historical chronology or the development of various stages but on ethno-geographical criteria, and he denied the notion of historical progress and the existence of historical laws. His history of the world began with America and the Pacific Ocean, continued with Oceania, the Indian Ocean, and West Asia, before he moved on to the Mediterranean and southeastern Europe. The last volumes dealt with the Germans and Romans, Western Europe, and the Atlantic Ocean. Since for him it was not possible to separate nature from history, geography becomes the basis for world history. Referring to Adolf Bastian and Friedrich Ratzel, Helmolt tried to link history with comparative psychology of peoples (*vergleichende Völkerpsychologie*).[33]

Aside from Karl Lamprecht and his socio-psychological theory of *Kulturzeitalter*, or cultural epochs, that he applied not only to his German history but also to his conception of universal history,[34] the most prominent historian who conducted universal history before World War I was Kurt Breysig, a professor in Berlin. He developed the concept of an evolutionary universal history in *Der Stufenbau und die Gesetze der Weltgeschichte*, which was published in 1905. Based on the idea of the unity of humanity, he stated that world history is a sequence of conditions or phases that are equal for all peoples but are passed through in different times.[35] In the first volume of his *Geschichte der Menschheit* from 1907 Breysig elaborated his thesis that the contemporary primitive peoples reflect the original stage of the so-called cultural peoples. On occasion of the international congress of historical sciences in Berlin in 1908, Breysig gave a talk on "Über Ziele und Wege einer vergleichenden weltgeschichtlichen Forschung," where he finally introduced an evolutionary model of history based on universal comparison.[36] Following the example of Lamprecht, who had established a separate department for cultural and universal history at the Historical Seminar in Leipzig in 1905—which became the independent "Institute for Cultural and Universal History" in 1909—Breysig suggested the establishment of an interdisciplinary institute for comparative historical research in Berlin.

But he had already gone too far and his idea faced a strong resistance among historians. It is not surprising that a few years after the German methodological controversy, or *Methodenstreit*, which had ended with the defeat of Lamprecht's cultural history by the (mostly Berlin) historicists in 1899, Breysig's ideas and works were rejected by his colleagues in the Berlin faculty. Their in some ways justified critique addressed Breysig's construction of historical laws, the renunciation of empirical work, and the exceedingly broad scope of his approach.[37] Behind this rejection, on the other hand, lay ideological prejudices that had already shaped the debates on Buckle's historical approach in the 1860s and 1870s and which erupted again during the Lamprecht controversy in the 1890s.[38] But by and large, on the other hand, it was the historicist tradition, with its focus on individuality in history and its centrality of foreign policy, that reduced universal history to the political history of European powers and banished alternative approaches from the discipline. The exclusion of "primitive peoples" from history served not only the political purpose of cultural superiority and colonial imperialism. It must also be seen as the attempt to close off the historical discipline from other disciplines such as anthropology, ethnology, and the social sciences, which professional historians viewed as a major threat.[39] In this respect German historiography did not open up to innovative tendencies that were developed in France and the United States.[40]

A quick look back at world histories in the twentieth century reveals that until the 1970s the Eurocentric picture has changed little since the time of Leopold von Ranke. Even if early twentieth-century philosophers of history and historians tried to develop a more professional world historiography that abandoned the nation-state as the theoretical framework to gain a broader approach to history, most of them nevertheless emphasized the superiority of European history and culture. But early writers such as Oswald Spengler and Arnold J. Toynbee established concepts of large and complex civilizations that inspired historians while establishing world history as a subdiscipline beginning in the 1960s.

The growing interest in world and global history after World War II was caused by the emergence of two superpowers and the Cold War. In the United States a modernization analysis defined by economics, interpreted Western democracies—and especially the United States—as a universal model of development that would prevent young nations from joining the communist block. "Western Civilization," an introductory course for history students at American universities, was actually world history with the ideological and political mission to put the United States at the top of historical development. The Soviet Union, in the meantime, tried to establish a narrative on world history whose high point was communist society.[41] The creation of a Marxist-Leninist world history as the theoretical foundation for historical research and the general framework for education became the basis for communist ideology.[42]

In Germany, it was not the status of a superpower but rather the attempt to come to terms with the nationalistic historiography after 1945 and to regain its European intellectual heritage that led to a growing interest in world history in the 1960s. Therefore, from Hans Freyer to Karl Jaspers and Alfred Heuß the Eurocentric view of world history in the vein of Ranke, Jacob Burckhardt, and Ernst Troeltsch prevailed over the German-centered view of Schäfer and Delbrück. The title of Freyer's book *Weltgeschichte Europas* shows that Troeltsch's phrase "For us there exists only a universal history of European culture" was still the dominant credo after 1945.[43]

Without a doubt, world history in the cold war period was every bit as political and ideological as it was in nineteenth-century historiography. However, over the last two decades this has drastically changed. More recent debates on world history and postcolonialism, especially in the United States, have not only challenged the Eurocentrism in Western historiography but have also led to the emergence of world history as a subdiscipline with its own institutions, such as institutes, journals, associations, and congresses. Even if Eurocentrism still remains the main determinant of modern historiography to the present day, the existence of new paradoxes such as localism vs. globalism, cultural homogeneity vs. heterogeneity, and denationalization vs. ethnocentrism, leads to new challenges for historical science. These are manifested primarily in a critique of universalized Eurocentrism and, therefore, in the concept of Western modernity.

It is no longer possible to ignore the non-Western voices that are questioning this Eurocentrism and demanding reinterpretations of history that take non-European peoples into account. Edward W. Said's book *Orientalism*, which appeared in 1978 and subjected European orientalism to a thorough critique, was doubtless a significant catalyst and turning point in this regard.[44] This book has led to an intensive debate and postcolonial critique of orientalism[45]—a critique that, on the one hand, "delegitimized and disempowered colonial knowledge at a historical time when direct political hegemony was waning, revealing societies and discourses hidden by imperial historiography and literary products."[46] On the other hand, it led to a blanket condemnation of Europe and indiscriminate stereotyping of the historical process. It is not surprising, therefore, that calls have been heard recently for "de-occidentalizing" the West, whereby the "occidentalism" of Said and his supporters is seen as an epistemological category that homogenizes and dehistoricizes the West regardless of historical variations and contexts, and conceives the West solely in terms of colonial power and hegemony. The "occidentalization of the imperial other" in this regard produces just as vacuous and generalized a version of intellectual history as does "orientalization of the colonial other."[47]

The vehement discussion in recent years among North American and Western European historians regarding the theoretical and methodological principles of the discipline has remained confined to this cultural region without casting so much as a glance beyond the borders of Europe. It is a discussion summed up by such key words as linguistic turn, cultural history, and the end of history. Aside from "world" historians[48] and those few specialists in African and Asian history, historians have missed a debate conducted under the heading of decolonialism by non-Western historians and representatives of other disciplines, the main objective of which has been to deconstruct and replace the Eurocentric picture of history presented by present-day historiography. For these scholars, history is not ending but only just beginning, and they draw upon European theoretical concepts from the traditional social sciences or contemporary postmodern philosophy.[49]

The debate on "post-colonialism" that has been taking place since the early 1990s, particularly among non-Western intellectuals teaching at American universities, reflects the search for an epistemological concept that can be used for postmodern recording and interpretation of current global political, economic, and cultural processes in the present day, i.e., following decolonization.[50] The 'post-colonial' marks a critical interruption into the entire grand historiographical narrative—which, in liberal historiography and Weberian historical sociology, as much as in the dominant traditions of Western Marxism, gave this global dimension a subordinate presence in a story that could essentially be told from within its

European parameters."[51] The prefix "post" thus has both a chronological and an epistemological dimension. The critics of postcolonial discourse point to the cultural self-reflection of these intellectuals and the antifoundational basis of their culturalism, which excludes the analysis of real global capitalism and its mechanisms. However, the end of European colonial rule and the increasingly interwoven global networks caused Eurocentrism to be called into question from both sides.

Historiography from a Universal Perspective

The historiographical tradition of world history, especially its political and ideological assumption, of German (and European) historiography before World War I has not garnered much attention up to now.[52] It is not surprising that the ethnocentric perspective of modern European historiography also applies to the history of historiography. In Germany in particular, Iggers's book has inspired extensive research over the last two decades on the history of German historical science since the eighteenth century.[53] The focus has been on the historiography of the Enlightenment and the development of Historismus as the view of history under which the study of history in Germany "became scientific," i.e., became an academic discipline, over the course of the nineteenth century.

For all their different interpretations, German historians of historiography had in common an approach to historicism that analyzes it from a purely German perspective while emphasizing its universality and its leading role in the institutionalization and professionalization of nineteenth-century historical science. As a component of the modernization wave, the historicist understanding of science was elevated to a guiding paradigm. A look at the international Western literature shows that research outside Germany on the history of historiography had also been written primarily from a national perspective.[54] Syntheses describe only the European development and do not include other cultures.[55] Nevertheless, the historiographical traditions of non-Western societies have enjoyed a rising attention in recent years.[56]

One might ask if the present emergence of world history and the debates on postcolonialism and globalization might lead to similar tendencies in the field of historiography.[57] Taking world history and the history of historiography of the past two centuries into account, the question arises whether there can be a historiography—and, thereby a history of historiography—based on the theoretical, methodological, and terminological concepts of modern history but not Eurocentric. The practice of using European historiography as a reference point is hardly a renunciation of Eurocentrism if the questions asked by non-European historiography are European questions, and if the chronological concepts are based on modern European history. There is no doubt that we need to critically examine the Western scientific model, its epistemological basis, and the resulting institutional structure of science.

This means, first of all, giving up the idea that German historicism and the associated institutional forms for historiography have global significance per se and are a *conditio sine qua* for the development of historical science outside of Europe. The most recent research has focused on a broader approach. The transcultural comparison of historiography and historical thinking has shown that one can hardly speak, as has been done before, of a global adoption of the "German model," that is, of a "universal triumphal procession"[58] of historicism. Its reception outside Germany was too diverse and heterogeneous, as a number of bilateral comparisons indicate.[59]

The idea of a transcultural history of historiography raises general epistemological and methodological problems. Neither the inclusion of the "Other" in history nor the rejection of Eurocentric teleology automatically means surrendering Eurocentrism, especially if one assumes that, by virtue of the dominance of its conceptions of space and time, it has become a fundamental component of global thought and thus a deciding principle of historiography in India, the Arab world, etc. If Eurocentrism is inextricably linked to modernity, then the rejection of Eurocentrism must also entail surrendering concepts of modern provenance. Ultimately, this means giving up the concept of history as a science.

Georg Iggers suggests an answer to this challenge. He asks how history can become a scientific discipline that avoids subjectivism and relativism and guarantees certain epistemological standards that allow general, meaningful, and true statements about historical facts or events, instead of an arbitrary interpretation. For him the answer is the critical self-recognition of every historian that specific cognitive interests and—less obvious and very often unconscious—values are reflected in his or her work, leading to different interpretations and perspectives of history. Pure objectivity is unattainable, for the historian can only reach a certain plausibility. But consensus dictates that any historical inquiry must be based on rational thinking and logical reasoning in order to consider a diversity of perspectives. Communication based on the ethic of "honesty" is for Iggers a way to overcome epistemological limits of modern historical writing. He sees, therefore, "history as an ongoing dialog among persons who despite widely differing values and outlooks are willing to communicate along lines which do not distort historical evidence."[60] Referring to Max Weber's differentiation between value judgments (*Werturteile*) and value relations (*Wertbeziehungen*),[61] Iggers rejects the former and stresses the various value relations of historians who can only communicate because of a mutual acceptance of differences based on rationality and intersubjectivity. But even if we agree on a specific set of historical methods and acknowledge a diversity of perspectives of the same historical fact, all of which are valid, the questions remain who then decides which account is closer to the "historical truth" and more probable in the "scientific" sense, and who establishes the modes of rationality and logic.

Since history has always been and still is a discipline that has a direct impact on the public sphere and its institutional boundaries, there will be hierarchies that exclude or oppress certain approaches.The ongoing dialog on equal terms, as Iggers suggests, faces the problem of mutual (mis)understanding and seems to remain, at least as long as the historical profession is structured as it is, an ideal. This concept contains problems of the contemporary historical profession that Weber could not deal with and Iggers left open in his text: Who defines dialogue? Who is included and excluded? What is the epistemological basis of communication? Can we communicate with other persons if we do not understand their concepts and terms or do not share their epistemological assumptions? How do we communicate with people from other cultures who have felt oppressed by a political system, Western values, a Eurocentric view, and scientific standards that we take for granted? In my view, such a dialogue has been a form of power that is based on the Western dominance on the one hand, and the structure of the existing historical institutions on the other hand, institutions that have not changed since the nineteenth century. If we reject the relativistic radicalism of postmodern approaches regarding the epistemological foundations of the historical profession, then how can we overcome the limitations of the historical profession in order to make a dialogue possible?[62]

These epistemological problems are not easy to solve. From the methodological perspective I suggest two ways for a world history of historiography: first, the transcultural comparison, and second, the concept of transcultural transfer. Comparing the different developments of historiography in various cultures, we are faced with the question of how the triad of industrialization, modernization, and historicization, which was decisive in the development of modern academic historiography in Europe, is also valid, albeit with a different chronology, for Asia, Africa, and Latin America. This includes the problem whether other factors such as indigenous cultural traditions, national identity, or the colonialism-independence dichotomy played a more decisive role in those places. In general there is no simple answer to this question.It can be said, however, that historiography in the past two centuries was initially constituted as national historiography, either in the context of formation of independent nations or in connection with a movement for independence from colonial oppression.

There is a twofold dilemma of a transcultural comparison. First, it is the problem of the parameters. Jörn Rüsen suggests to look for the most general, anthropologically defined common denominators of historical consciousness as theoretical basis for the comparison. In doing so, he tries to develop a theory of transcultural historical science above and beyond any kind of ethnocentrism by defining the various (historical) cultures as a combination of elements that are present in all cultures. However, his attempt to establish a general periodization of historiography is based on the process of modernity and Max Weber's theory of universal rationalization and disenchantment.[63]

The second dilemma of the transcultural comparison is that, on the one hand, it requires to perform a history of historiography from a universal perspective that disregards a national (European) model in favor of an approach that looks for specific processes of adoption, rejection, and mediation of historical knowledge. On the other hand, there is always "a *politics* of historical comparison" behind "the method of historical comparison," as Chris Lorenz has stated in a recent essay.[64] In our case, it becomes apparent that a transcultural comparison is not possible without reference to European historical science. European concepts of history and science have conquered the world, and historians in India, China, Japan, and elsewhere have adopted some of the modern institutions and epistemological standards of Europe. The spread of European cultural, political, and economic dominion around the globe led to the foundation of specific institutions of "cultural imperialism" that influenced and shaped the historical consciousness of other cultures. On the one hand, it could not, however, completely control it because especially popular, nonacademic history on the local level deprived these institutions of Eurocentric hegemony. On the other hand, the political elites often used Western forms of institutions and modes of historical research to legitimate their own rule.

Therefore, considering the complex phenomenon of the "Europeanization of the world,"[65] a transcultural history of historiography cannot stop with structural comparison but must also be a relational history. Such an approach considers the transfer of ideas and institutions, mutual perceptions and apperceptions, and institutional connections between Europe and local historical knowledge in other cultures. A group of French scholars has introduced the concept of "cultural transfer" for the Franco-German relations as a social-historical approach that does not mean a transfer of "culture" but a transfer between cultures. Such an approach focuses mainly on the channels of transfers, their mediums, and the use of the transferred knowledge from a specific social and cultural system to another.[66]

In terms of the history of historiography this concept of "cultural transfer" can help to show the ways in which historical writings both shape and are shaped in the course of cultural encounters, and what happens to a historical paradigm when it is introduced into another culture. This can be a direct or an indirect import.[67] An adaptation depends not only on the concrete political and cultural conditions in the importing culture, but also on the status of development of the discipline in question. Interdisciplinary boundaries may make the difference between adoption and rejection of foreign influences. In addition, certain views of science are not static, but are subject to change over time.[68] The extent and speed of introduction of Western thought depended to a significant extent on the strength of a culture's own scientific and cultural traditions. In principle, one may say that the import of scientific paradigms altered the indigenous tradition and generated new concepts. However, such imports functioned only through certain channels that actively engaged in or supported the import of ideas and/or institutions.[69]

It was not uncommon for the import to be a conscious process, for example in Japan, where certain scientific concepts, technologies, and institutions were adopted from the countries in which their development was most advanced.[70] For historiography, this was to a large extent Germany. It is not surprising, for example, that Japan brought in a German historian to promote professional historical science.[71] Thus, even before the turn of the century, the Japanese Historical Association and the Office of Historiography were established as professional associations based on the European model. At the same time, this was no straightforward adoption of Western models, because those models came into contact with existing traditional concepts. This amalgamation process led to "overlapping," through which traditional ideas were elevated in a new national concept.[72]

Conclusion

Taking up Iggers's ideas of critical self-reflection and (transcultural) communication, I suggest a "soft" Eurocentrism as a basis for a world history of historiography, namely a Eurocentrism that is conscious of its ideological, political, economic, and cultural foundation. Only with this kind of self-consciousness regarding the historicity and epistemological limits of his/her view of history and the world can the historian open the door to non-European and transcultural perspectives that will allow him/her to stop seeing Europe as the center of the world.

Moreover, only this kind of self-reflection will permit him to question his own theoretical and methodological assumptions. One could use Dipesh Chakrabarty's term and refer to this as "provincializing Europe."[73] If modernity is historicized and thus no longer interpreted as a universal valid project, it opens the door for competing narratives of history. This competition will lead to new conceptions of history beyond a nationally bound historiography, which might result, in turn, in certain structural changes to the institutions of historical production. Thus, instead of radically rejecting modern Eurocentric historiography, it should be opened up to competition with a variety of other models, leading to a critique and modification of the European myth.

European, or more accurately occidental, historiography must be understood as *one* form of historical thinking among others rather than as the model of historical science having the universal claim to truth. To the extent that such a historiography critically reflects upon (but not necessarily discards) the scientific and ideological corset of modernity, it will be able to free itself from Eurocentrism and become literally postmodern. Thus, it is not a matter of automatically rejecting European concepts, but of rejecting their hegemonic dominance. Such an undertaking must not be content with merely showing how various cultural perspectives can be articulated and synthesized in a world history. It must also show how the necessary egalitarian communication across cultural boundaries can be achieved. The prerequisite for this is knowledge and acceptance of different conceptions of history and historiography, and, therewith, acknowledgment of intercultural differences without hegemonic claims.

Notes

1. G. G. Iggers, *The German Conception of History: The National Tradition of Historical Thought from Herder to the Present* (Middletown, Conn., 1968).
2. In this respect, see, I. Iselin, *Philosophische Muthmaßungen über die Geschichte der Menschheit*, 2 vols. (Frankfurt and Leipzig, 1764); J. C. Gatterer, *Abriß der Universalhistorie in ihrem ganzen Umfange* (Göttingen, 1773); A. L. Schlözer, *Vorstellung seiner Universal-Historie*, 2 vols. (Göttingen and Gotha, 1772–73); F. Schiller, "Was heißt und zu welchem Ende studiert man Universalgeschichte?" [1789], in *Schillers Werke. Nationalausgabe*, ed. K.-H. Hahn (Weimar, 1970), 17: 359–76. For general information, J. Osterhammel, "Neue Welten in der europäischen Geschichtsschreibung (ca. 1500–1800)," *Geschichtsdiskurs*, ed. in W. Küttler, J. Rüsen, and E. Schulin, vol. 2: *Anfänge modernen historischen Denkens* (Frankfurt a.M., 1994), 202–15; H. W. Blanke and D. Fleischer, eds., *Theoretiker der deutschen Aufklärungshistorie*, 2 vols. (Stuttgart and Bad Cannstadt, 1990); P. H. Reill, *The German Enlightenment and the Rise of Historicism* (Berkeley, Calif., Los Angeles, and London, 1975).
3. M. Harbsmeier, "World Histories before Domestication: Writing Universal Histories, Histories of Mankind and World Histories in 18th-Century Germany," *Culture and History* 5 (1989): 93–131.
4. J. G. Herder, *Ideen zur Philosophie der Geschichte der Menschheit* [1784–91], in *Werke in zehn Bänden*, ed. M. Bollacker, vol. 6 (Frankfurt a.M., 1989). From a philosophical perspective, see I. Kant, "Idee zu einer allgemeinen Geschichte in weltbürgerlicher Absicht [1784]," in *Kants gesammelte Schriften*, ed. Prussian Academy of Sciences, vol. 8 (Berlin, Leipzig, 1923), 15–31.
5. C. Meiners, *Grundriß der Geschichte der Menschheit* (Lemgo, 1785).
6. G. F. W. Hegel, *Vorlesungen über die Philosophie der Geschichte*, in *Werkausgabe*, vol. 12 (Frankfurt a.M., 1970); L. v. Ranke, *Weltgeschichte*, 9 vols. (Leipzig, 1889). On both men, see E. Schulin, *Die weltgeschichtliche Erfassung des Orients bei Hegel und Ranke* (Göttingen, 1958), and "Universal History and National History, Mainly in the Lectures of Leopold von Ranke," in *Leopold von Ranke and the Shaping of the Historical Discipline*, ed. G. G. Iggers and J. M. Powell (Syracuse, N.Y., 1990), 70–81, as well as G. Masur, *Rankes Begriff der Weltgeschichte* (Munich and Berlin, 1926), and the essays in W. J. Mommsen, ed., *Leopold von Ranke und die moderne Geschichtswissenschaft* (Stuttgart, 1988).

7. For German historiography, see A. Pigulla, *China in der deutschen Weltgeschichtsschreibung vom 18. bis zum 20. Jahrhundert* (Wiesbaden, 1996); C. Marx, *'Völker ohne Schrift und Geschichte'. Zur historischen Erfassung des vorkolonialen Schwarzafrika in der deutschen Forschung des 19. und frühen 20. Jahrhunderts* (Stuttgart, 1988); J. Osterhammel, "'Peoples Without History' in British and German Historical Thought," in *British and German Historiography: Traditions and Transfers*, ed. B. Stuchtey and P. Wende (Oxford, 2000).
8. A. Dirlik, "History Without a Center? Reflections on Eurocentrism," in *Across Cultural Borders: Historiography in a Global Perspective*, ed. E. Fuchs and B. Stuchtey (Cambridge, forthcoming). On the explanations of the myth of European superiority, see J. M. Blaut, *The Colonizer's Model of the World: Geographical Diffusionism and Eurocentric History* (New York and London, 1993), and most recently A. G. Frank, *ReOrient: Global Economy in the Asian Age* (Berkeley, Calif., Los Angeles, and London, 1998).
9. See T. Philipp, "Geschichtswissenschaft und die Geschichte des Nahen Ostens," *Saeculum* 45 (1994): 166–78; A. Hourani, *Islam in European Thought* (Cambridge, 1991), chap. 1. In general, see J. Osterhammel, "Vorbemerkung: Westliches Wissen und die Geschichte nichteuropäischer Zivilisationen," in *Geschichtsdiskurs*, vol. 4: *Krisenbewußtsein, Katastrophenerfahrungen und Innovationen 1880–1945*, ed. W. Küttler, J. Rüsen, and E. Schulin (Frankfurt a.M., 1997), 307–13; J. Fück, *Die arabischen Studien in Europa bis in den Anfang des 20. Jahrhunderts* (Leipzig, 1955).
10. F. C. Schlosser, *Weltgeschichte in zusammenhängender Erzählung*, 4 vols. (Frankfurt a.M., 1815–41); idem, *Weltgeschichte für das deutsche Volk*, 19 vols. (Frankfurt a.M., 1844–57); C. v. Rotteck, *Allgemeine Geschichte vom Anfang der historischen Kenntniß bis auf unsere Zeiten. Für denkende Geschichtsfreunde*, 11 vols. (Freiburg, 1813–18).
11. Examples for world histories written by amateurs in the mid-nineteenth century for a general audience are E. A. Schmidt, *Grundriß der Weltgeschichte für Gymnasien und andere höhere Lehranstalten zum Selbstunterricht für Gebildete*, 2nd ed. (Berlin, 1835); G. Struve, *Weltgeschichte*, 2nd ed. (New York, 1853); J. G. Kutzner, *Die Weltgeschichte in zusammenhängenden Einzelbildern nach schul- und volkspädagogischen Grundsätzen für Volkslehranstalten und zur Selbstbelehrung für Jedermann aus dem Volke* (Berlin, 1858).
12. G. Weber, *Geschichte des Morgenlandes. Nach dem neuesten Stande der orientalischen Geschichtswissenschaft bearbeitet* (Leipzig, 1882), 16f. Weber's "Allgemeine Weltgeschichte" was published in 19 volumes between 1857 and 1881.
13. See T. Flathe, G. F. Hertzberg, F. Justi, J. v. Pflugk-Harttung, and M. Philippson, eds., *Allgemeine Weltgeschichte*, vol. 1 (Berlin, 1884). Pflugk-Harttung later became the editor of the Ullstein *Weltgeschichte*. See J. v. Pflugk-Harttung, ed., *Weltgeschichte. Die Entwicklung der Menschheit in Staat und Gesellschaft, in Kultur und Geistesleben*, 6 vols. (Berlin, 1910). These volumes differ from other editions, such as those by Wilhelm Oncken cited in n. 14, and the German-centered world histories, since there is a link between the different volumes, whereas some of the authors—such as Karl Lamprecht with his socio-psychological and nomothetic concept, Ernst Haeckel with his idea of the unity of all knowledge, and the sinologist and Ranke student August Conrady, with his cultural methodology—offer a different historical approach.
14. G. Weber, "Vorrede zur ersten Auflage," in idem, *Geschichte des Morgenlandes*, xvi. In addition to Ranke's world history, in 1885 the first volume of an "Allgemeine Geschichte in Einzeldarstellungen" was published under the editorship of Wilhelm Oncken. This collaborative project undertaken by professional historians was, nevertheless, no comprehensive world history. It was published in forty-five volumes between 1878 and 1893.
15. Quoted in R. Wittram, *Das Interesse an der Geschichte. Zwölf Vorlesungen über Fragen des zeitgenössischen Geschichtsverständnisses* (Göttingen, 1958), 128.
16. I cannot address the tradition of world history outside Germany at this point. For France, see E. Lavisse and A. Rambaud, eds., *Histoire Générale du IVe siècle à nos jours*, 12 vols. (Paris, 1893–1901). For England, see A. W. Ward, G. W. Prothero, and S. Leathes, eds., *The Cambridge Modern History*, 13 vols. (Cambridge, 1904–1912).

17. D. Schäfer, *Weltgeschichte der Neuzeit*, 11th ed., vol. 1 (Berlin, 1922), 3. The first edition was published in 1907. See also H. F. Helmolt, "Gegenstand und Ziel einer Weltgeschichte," in *Weltgeschichte*, ed. H. F. Helmolt, 9 vols. (Leipzig and Vienna, 1899), vol. 1, 4.
18. See F. Meinecke, "Gedanken über Welt- und Universalgeschiche" [1942], in idem, *Zur Theorie und Philosophie der Geschichte*, ed. E. Kessel (Stuttgart, 1959), 141.
19. Weber, *Weltgeschichte*, XIII.
20. H. Delbrück, *Weltgeschichte. Vorlesungen, gehalten an der Universität Berlin 1896/1920. Erster Teil: Das Altertum* (Berlin, 1924), 10. A critique of this position can be found in F. Wagner, "Die Europazentrik des klassischen deutschen Geschichtsbildes und ihre Problematik," *Saeculum* 14 (1963): 44.
21. H. v. Treitschke, *Politik. Vorlesungen gehalten an der Universität zu Berlin*, ed. M. Cornicelius (Leipzig, 1897), vol. 1, 121.
22. D. Schäfer, "Vorwort zur neunten Auflage" [1919], in idem, *Weltgeschichte*, vii.
23. T. Lindner, *Weltgeschichte seit der Völkerwanderung* (Stuttgart, 1901), vol. 1, vi; idem, *Geschichtsphilosophie. Einleitung zu einer Weltgeschichte seit der Völkerwanderung* (Stuttgart, 1901). On Lindner, see B. Mütter, *Die Geschichtswissenschaft in Münster zwischen Aufklärung und Historismus unter besonderer Berücksichtigung der historischen Disziplin an der münsterischen Hochschule* (Münster, 1980), 208ff.
24. Pigulla, *China*, 244. Pigulla analyzes Linder's concept of world history from the latter's perspective on Chinese history.
25. See *Exposition Universelle Internationale de 1900. Congrès International d'Histoire Comparée. Tenu à Paris du 23 au 28 Juillet 1900. Procès-Verbaux Sommaires* (Paris, 1901). The sessions were General and Diplomatic History; History of Institutions and Law; Comparative History of Social Economy; History of Religious Affairs; History of Sciences; History of Literature; History of the Arts of Design; and History of Music. On the history of the international historical congresses, see K. D. Erdmann, *Die Ökumene der Historiker. Geschichte der Internationalen Historikerkongresse und des Comité International des Sciences Historiques* (Göttingen, 1987).
26. See G.v.B. [Georg v. Below], "Vermischtes," *Historische Zeitschrift* 82 (1899): 185–87, here 186.
27. *Annales internationales d'histoire. Congrès de Paris 1900*, vol. 2 (Paris, 1900).
28. See *Atti del Congresso Internazionale die Scienze Storiche (Roma, 1–9 Aprile 1903)*, vol. 1: *Parte Generale* (Rome, 1907), 97ff.
29. The compilation is based on data in Erdmann, *Ökumene der Historiker*, 468ff. The first international congress took place in The Hague in 1898. However, the official counting starts with the congress in Paris.
30. See *International Congress of Historical Studies. London, April 3rd to 9th, 1913. Pamphlet C. List of Readers*, 16, 22.
31. Helmolt was the student of the geographer Friedrich Ratzel and of Lamprecht but could not further his career as a historian because of the *Methodenstreit*. Working as an editor, he began to edit a world history in 1899 that was oriented toward ethnology, psychology, and geography. See Helmolt, *Weltgeschichte*.
32. Helmolt, "Gegenstand und Ziel," 15.
33. Idem, VI, 19f.
34. K. Lamprecht, "Zur universalgeschichtlichen Methodenbildung" [1909], in H. Schleier, *Karl Lamprecht. Alternative zu Ranke. Schriften zur Geschichtstheorie* (Leipzig, 1988), 374–404; idem, "Universalgeschichtliche Probleme," in idem, *Moderne Geschichtswissenschaft: Fünf Vorträge* (Freiburg i.Br., 1905), 103–30. On Lamprecht's concept of world history, see R. Chickering, "Karl Lamprechts Konzeption einer Weltgeschichte," *Archiv für Kulturgeschichte* 73 (1991): 437–52.
35. K. Breysig, *Der Stufenbau und die Gesetze der Weltgeschichte* (Stuttgart and Berlin 1927).
36. K. Breysig, *Die Geschichte der Menschheit: Die Völker ewiger Urzeit. Die Amerikaner des Nordwestens und des Nordens* (Berlin, 1907). On Breysig's concept of universal history, see B v. Brocke, *Kurt Breysig. Geschichtswissenschaft zwischen Historismus und Soziologie* (Lübeck and Hamburg, 1971), 268ff.

37. Brocke, *Breysig*, 87ff.
38. On Buckle and his reception in Germany, see E. Fuchs, *Henry Thomas Buckle. Geschichtsschreibung und Positivismus in England und Deutschland* (Leipzig, 1994). For recent publication on Lamprecht and the *Methodenstreit*, see R. Chickering, *Karl Lamprecht: A German Academic Life* (Atlantic Highlands, N.J., 1993); L. Schorn-Schütte, *Karl Lamprecht. Kulturgeschichtsschreibung zwischen Wissenschaft und Politik* (Göttingen, 1984); and Brocke, *Breysig*, 62ff.
39. See A. Zimmerman, "Geschichtslose und schriftlose Völker in Spreeathen. Anthropologie als Kritik der Geschichtswissenschaft im Kaiserreich," *Zeitschrift für Geschichtswissenschaft* 47 (1999): 197–210. Historians who favored an interdisciplinary approach, such as Helmolt, therefore faced wide rejection.
40. L. Raphael, "Historikerkontroversen im Spannungsfeld zwischen Berufshabitus, Fächerkonkurrenz und sozialen Deutungsmustern: Lamprecht-Streit und französischer Methodenstreit der Jahrhundertwende in vergleichender Perspektive," *Historische Zeitschrift* 251 (1990): 325–63; idem, "Die 'Neue Geschichte' – Umbrüche und Neue Wege der Geschichtsschreibung in internationaler Perspektive (1880–1940)," in *Beschichtsdiskurs*, ed. W. Küttler, J. Rüsen, and E. Schulin, vol. 4: *Krisenbewußtsein, Katastrophenerfahrung und Innovationen 1880–1915* (Frankfurt a.M., 1997), 51–89. See also G. G. Iggers, "The 'Methodenstreit' in International Perspective: The Reorientation of Historical Studies at the Turn from the Nineteenth to the Twentieth Century," *Storial della Storiografia* 6 (1984): 21–32.
41. For an excellent overview of the American tradition of world history in the twentieth century, see J. H. Bentley, "Shapes of World History in Twentieth-Century Scholarship," in *Essays on Global and Comparative History* (Washington, D.C., 1996).
42. In this respect, see the Soviet world history that was published in ten volumes under the title *Vsemirnaja Istorija* between 1955 and 1965.
43. In this respect, see H. Freyer, *Weltgeschichte Europas* (Wiesbaden, 1948), and E. Troeltsch, *Der Historismus und seine Probleme I: Das logische Problem der Geschichtsphilosophie*, in *Gesammelte Schriften*, vol. 3 (Tübingen, 1922), 710. On the critique of this tradition, see F. Hampl, "Universalhistorische Betrachtungsweise als Problem und Aufgabe. Ihre Bedeutung in Theorie und Praxis der modernen Geschichtswissenschaft," in idem, *Geschichte als Kritische Wissenschaft*, vol. 1: *Theorie der Geschichtswissenschaft und Universalgeschichte*, ed. I. Weiler (Darmstadt, 1975), 132–81; and P. Rassow, "Nationalgeschichte und Universalgeschichte," *Geschichte in Wissenschaft und Unterricht* 2 (1951): 513–21.
44. E. W. Said, *Orientalism* (London, 1978).
45. See J. Lütt, N. Brechmann, C. Hinz, and I. Kurz, "Die Orientalismus-Debatte im Vergleich: Verlauf, Kritik, Schwerpunkte im indischen und arabischen Kontext," in *Gesellschaften im Vergleich. Forschungen aus Sozial- und Geschichtswissenschaften*, ed. H. Kaelble and J. Schriewer (Frankfurt a.M., 1998), 511–67. With respect to Said, see R. Inden, *Imagining India* (Oxford, 1990). Further German voices in the orientalism debate are U. Freitag, "The Critique of Orientalism," in *Companion to Historiography*, ed. M. Bentley (London and New York, 1997), 620–38; and J. Osterhammel, "Edward W. Said und die 'Orientalismus'-Debatte. Ein Rückblick," *Asien-Afrika-Lateinamerika* 25 (1997): 597–607.
46. L. I. Rudolph and S. H. Rudolph, "Occidentalism and Orientalism: Perspectives on Legal Pluralism," in *Cultures of Scholarship*, ed. S. C. Humphreys (Ann Arbor, Mich., 1997), 222.
47. Ibid., 223, 229. Among others, see C. Xiaomei, *Occidentalism as a Counter-Discourse in Post-Mao China* (New York, 1995); J. G. Carrier, ed., *Occidentalism: Images of the West* (Oxford, 1995); O. P. Kejariwal, *The Asiatic Society of Bengal and the Discovery of India's Past, 1784–1838* (New Delhi and Oxford, 1999); W. Halbfass, *India and Europe: An Essay in Understanding* (Boulder, Colo., 1997).
48. See, among others, P. Pomper, R. H. Elphick, and R. T. Vann, eds., *World History: Ideologies, Structures, and Identities* (Oxford, 1998).

49. See D. Chakrabarty, "Postcoloniality and the Artifice of History: Who Speaks for 'Indian' Pasts?" *Representations* 37 (1992): 2. He also addresses the paradox that non-Western thinkers use European social theories developed in ignorance of non-European cultures to analyze their own society.
50. Among others, see I. Chambers and L. Curti, eds., *The Post-Colonial Question: Common Skies, Divided Horizons* (London and New York, 1996); C. A. Breckenridge and P. Van der Veer, eds., *Orientalism and the Postcolonial Predicament: Perspectives on South Asia* (Philadelphia, 1993); P. Chatterjee, *The Nation and its Fragments: Colonial and Postcolonial Histories* (Princeton, N.J., 1993); G. Prakash, ed., *After Colonialism: Imperial Histories and Postcolonial Displacements* (Princeton, N.J., 1995); G. Prakash, "Writing Post-Orientalist Histories of the Third World: Indian Historiography is Good to Think," in *Colonialism and Culture*, N. B. Dirks (Ann Arbor, Mich., 1992).
51. S. Hall, "When was 'The Post-Colonial'? Thinking at the Limit," in *The Post-Colonial Question*, ed. Chambers and Curti, 250.
52. The research on Lamprecht is rather an exception. See also W. Goetz, "Weltgeschichte," *Archiv für Kulturgeschichte* 24 (1933/34): 273–303; Wagner, "Die Europazentrik"; J. Vogt, *Wege zum historischen Universum. Von Ranke bis Toynbee* (Stuttgart, 1961); A. Randa, ed., *Mensch und Weltgeschichte. Zur Geschichte der Universalgeschichtsschreibung* (Salzburg and Munich, 1969); E. Schulin, "Einleitung," in *Universalgeschichte*, ed. E. Schulin (Cologne, 1975), 11–65; idem, "Universalgeschichtsschreibung im zwanzigsten Jahrhundert," in *Traditionskritik und Rekonstruktionsversuch. Studien zur Entwicklung von Geschichtswissenschaft und historischem Denken* (Göttingen, 1979), 163–202; B. Mütter, "Grenzen der weltgeschichtlichen Perspektive in der deutschen Geschichtsschreibung vom Zeitalter der Aufklärung bis zur Epoche des Imperialismus: Das Beispiel Lateinamerika," in *Geschichtsbewußtsein und Universalgeschichte. Das Zeitalter der Entdeckungen und Eroberungen in Geschichtsschreibung, Unterricht und Öffentlichkeit*, ed. W. Fürnrohr (Braunschweig, 1992), 45–72.
53. From the now immense body of literature, see O. G. Oexle and J. Rüsen, eds., *Historismus in den Kulturwissenschaften. Geschichtskonzepte, historische Einschätzungen, Grundlagenprobleme* (Cologne, Weimar, and Vienna, 1996); G. Scholtz, ed., *Historismus am Ende des 20. Jahrhunderts: Eine internationale Diskussion* (Berlin, 1996); O. G. Oexle, *Geschichtswissenschaft im Zeichen des Historismus: Studien zu Problemgeschichten der Moderne* (Göttingen, 1996); F. R. Ankersmit, "Historicism: An Attempt at Synthesis," *History and Theory* 34 (1995): 143–61, including the discussion between Ankersmit and Iggers, ibid., 162–73; F. Jaeger and J. Rüsen, *Geschichte des Historismus* (Munich, 1992); A. Wittkau, *Historismus* (Göttingen, 1992). A critical overview can be found in I. Veit-Brause, "Eine Disziplin rekonstruiert ihre Geschichte: Geschichte der Geschichtswissenschaft in den 90er Jahren (I)," *Neue Politische Literatur* 43 (1998): 36–66.
54. Among more recent publications, see P. den Boer, *History as a Profession: The Study of History in France (1818–1914)* (Princeton, N.J., 1998); E. Breisach, *American Progressive History: An Experiment in Modernization* (Chicago and London, 1993); P. Burke, *The French Historical Revolution: The Annales School 1929–1989* (London, 1990); C. Parker, *The English Historical Tradition since 1850* (Edinburgh, 1990); P. Novick, *That Noble Dream: The "Objectivity Question" and the American Historical Profession* (Cambridge, 1988).
55. G. G. Iggers, *Historiography in the Twentieth Century: From Scientific Objectivity to the Postmodern Challenge* (Hanover, N.H., and London, 1997); C. Simon, *Historiographie. Eine Einführung* (Stuttgart, 1996); G. Thuillier and J, Tulard, *Les Ecoles Historiques* (Paris, 1990); E. Breisach, *Historiography: Ancient, Medieval, and Modern* (Chicago, 1983); C.-O. Carbonell, *L'Historiographie* (Paris, 1981). An overview is to be found in E. Schulin, "Synthesen der Historiographiegeschichte," in *Geschichtswissenschaft vor 2000. Festschrift für Georg G. Iggers zum 65. Geburtstag*, ed. K. H. Jarausch, J. Rüsen, and H. Schleier (Hagen, 1991), 151–63. Exceptions to this include Bentley, *Companion*, and the essays in *Storia della Storiografia* 5 (1984), which resulted from a congress organized by the Commission Internationale d'Histoire de l'Historiographie in Montpellier in 1983

on the subject of "L'Historiographie dans le monde à la fin du XIXe et au début du XXe siècle." The German journal *Saeculum*, particularly the volumes for 1987, 1994, and 1995, should also be mentioned positively in this regard, as should the annual journal for non-European history, *Periplus*.

56. For India, see D. Rothermund, "Nationale und regionale Geschichtsschreibung in Indien," *Periplus* 3 (1993): 75–82. For Japan, see C. Gluck, "The People in History: Recent Trends in Japanese Historiography," *Journal of Asian Studies* 38 (1978): 25–50; B. Martin, "Deutsche Geschichtswissenschaft als Instrument nationaler Selbstfindung in Japan," in *Universalgeschichte und Nationalgeschichten*, ed. G. Hübinger, J. Osterhammel, and E. Pelzer (Freiburg i.Br., 1994), 209–29. For Africa, see C. Neale, *Writing "Independent" History: African Historiography, 1960–1980* (Westport, Conn., 1985). For China, *Using the Past to Serve the Present: Historiography and Politics in Contemporary China* (Armonk, 1993).
57. The following paragraphs are based on my essay "Provincializing Europe: Historiography as a Transcultural Concept," in *Across Cultural Borders*, ed. Fuchs and Stuchtey.
58. See U. Muhlack, *Geschichtswissenschaft im Humanismus und in der Aufklärung. Die Vorgeschichte des Historismus* (Munich, 1991), 10.
59. P. Schöttler, "Das 'Annales-Paradigma' und die deutsche Historiographie (1929–1939). Ein deutsch-französischer Wissenschaftstransfer," in *Nationale Grenzen und internationaler Austausch. Studien zum Kultur- und Wissenschaftstransfer in Europa*, ed. L. Jordan and B. Kortländer (Tübingen, 1995), 200–220; Raphael, "Historikerkontroversen"; Fuchs, *Buckle*; M. Jokipii, "Über deutsche Einflüsse auf die finnische Geschichtsschreibung am Ende des 19. Jahrhunderts," *Wissenschaftliche Beiträge der Ernst Moritz Arndt-Universität Greifswald* (1990): 73–86; M. Vakarii, "Die Tradition der finnischen Geschichtsschreibung und Karl Lamprecht," *Storia della Storiografia* 6 (1984): 33–43; A. F. Grabski, "Z Zagadnien Stosunkow Polsko-Niemieckich w Zakresie Historiografii Drugiej Polowy XIX w.," *Kwartalnik Historii Nauki I Techniki* 29 (1984): 323–44; J. Krasuski et al., eds., *Stosunki Polsko-Niemieckie w Historiografii*, Part 2: *Studia z Dziejow Historiografi Polskiej I Niemieckie* (Posen, 1984); G. G. Iggers, "Geschichtswissenschaft und Sozialgeschichtsschreibung 1890–1914," in *Marxistische Typisierung und idealtypische Methode in der Geschichtswissenschaft*, ed. W. Küttler (Berlin, 1986), 234–44; L. Schorn-Schütte, "Karl Lamprecht und die internationale Geschichtswissenschaft an der Jahrhundertwende," *Archiv für Kulturgeschichte* 67 (1985): 417–64; E. Schulin, "German 'Geistesgeschichte,' American 'Intellectual History,' and French 'Histoire des mentalités' since 1900: A Comparison," *History of European Ideas* 1 (1981): 195–214.
60. See G. G. Iggers, "Objectivity and Involvement: Writing the History of German Historiography" in this volume.
61. Whereas for Max Weber the value judgment should not be a part of scientific investigation because its normative statements reach beyond the limits of an empirical science, value relations are entirely valid, because they mean that the research is guided by norms and interests and therefore selective and subjective. This definition, however, does not lead to a pure subjectivism because the research interests are determined by general norms of the time and an intersubjective validity. Since they underlie a steady change, the knowledge permanently changes as well. See Max Weber, *Gesammelte Aufsätze zur Wissenschaftslehre*, 2nd ed. (Tübingen, 1951), 146–214; 475–526, 566–97.
62. See M. Brocker and H. H. Nau, eds., *Ethnozentrismus. Möglichkeiten und Grenzen des interkulturellen Dialogs* (Darmstadt, 1997). On actual theoretical problems of historical writing, see R. E. Berkhofer, Jr., *Beyond the Great Story: History as Text and Discourse* (Cambridge, 1997).
63. J. Rüsen, "Some Theoretical Approaches to Intercultural Comparative Historiography," *History and Theory* 35 (1996): 5–22; and *idem*, "Einleitung: Geschichtsdenken im interkulturellen Diskurs," in *Westliches Geschichtsdenken. Eine interkulturelle Debatte*, ed. J. Rüsen (Göttingen, 1999), 13–28.
64. C. Lorenz, "Comparative Historiography: Problems and Perspectives," *History and Theory* 38 (1999): 39.

65. G. Klingenstein et al., eds., *Europäisierung der Erde? Studien zur Einwirkung Europas auf die außereuropäische Welt* (Vienna, 1980).
66. M. Espagne and M. Werner, "Deutsch-französischer Kulturtransfer als Forschungsgegenstand. Eine Problemskizze," in idem, eds., *Transferts. Les relations interculturelles dans l'espace franco-allemand (XVIIIe et XIXe siècle)* (Paris, 1988), 11–34; idem, "Deutsch-Französischer Kulturtransfer im 18. und 19. Jahrhundert. Zu einem neuen interdisziplinaeren Forschungsprogramm des C.N.R.S.," *Francia* 13 (1985): 502–10; idem, "La construction d'une référence culturelle allemande en France. Genèse et histoire," *Annales* 42 (1987): 969–92. See also J. Paulmann, "Internationaler Vergleich und interkultureller Transfer. Zwei Forschungsansätze zur europäischen Geschichte des 18. bis 20. Jahrhunderts," *Historische Zeitschrift* 267 (1998): 649–85.
67. Nakayama refers, for example, to a case in which the Dutch version of a German anatomy textbook was introduced for use in Japanese medicine. See S. Nakayama, *Academic and Scientific Traditions in China, Japan, and the West* (Tokyo, 1984), 199. Osterhammel points to four criteria on which the export of science, and thus cultural contact in general, depend: the quality of indigenous traditions, their specific condition at the time of the cultural contact, the manner of transmission and presentation of Western knowledge, and the political and cultural context. See Osterhammel, *Westliches Wissen*, 308. On important proposals for a theory of cultural relations, see idem, "Kulturelle Grenzen in der Expansion Europas," *Saeculum* 46 (1995): 101–38.
68. For example, the term "science" in Japan had a philosophical dimension when translated as *kyuri* during the Edo period; when translated as *kagaku* (specialized science) during the Meiji period, it was restricted to nonphilosophical, technical disciplines. For further information, see Nakayama, *Academic and Scientific Traditions*, 208f.
69. See the case study by W. Schwentker, *Max Weber in Japan. Eine Untersuchung zur Wirkungsgeschichte 1905–1995* (Tübingen, 1997).
70. Nakayama, *Academic and Scientific Traditions*, 219.
71. Ludwig Rieß, for example, was called to the Imperial University in Tokyo in 1887 to help establish a historical institute. See W. Schwentker, "Zwischen Weltaneignung und Selbstdeutungszwang. Entwicklungstendenzen der Geschichtswissenschaft in Japan 1860–1945," in *Geschichtsdiskurs*, ed. Küttler, Rüsen, and Schulin, vol. 4, 344ff.; M. Mehl, *Eine Vergangenheit für die japanische Nation. Die Entstehung des historischen Forschungsinstituts Tokyo daigaku Shiryo hensanjo (1869–1895)* (Frankfurt a.M., Berlin, Berne, New York, Paris, and Vienna, 1992), 158ff.
72. On the influence of Western science in Japan, see E. Pauer, "Japanischer Geist – weltliche Technik. Zur Rezeption westlicher Technologie in Japan," *Saeculum* 38 (1987): 19–51, and I. Hiroshi, "British Influence on Modern Japanese Historiography," *Saeculum* 38 (1987): 99–112. On Japanese world history, see S. Conrad, "World History, Japanese Style: Reading the Japanese Past Through a European Lens," *Storia della Storiografia* 35 (1999): 97–112.
73. See Chakrabarty, *Postcoloniality and the Artifice of History*, 20. While Chakrabarty assumes that this concept is impossible within existing institutional limits, I believe that substantive and institutional changes are interwoven processes that occur more or less simultaneously. In this respect, see also J. Osterhammel, "Transkulturell vergleichende Geschichtswissenschaft," in *Geschichte im Vergleich*, ed. H.-G. Haupt and J. Kocka (Frankfurt a.M., 1996), 271–313. On the dichotomy of tradition and modernity, see K. Hafez, ed., *Der Islam und der Westen. Anstiftung zum Dialog* (Frankfurt a.M., 1997).

Contributors

Werner T. Angress is Professor Emeritus of History at the State University of New York at Stony Brook. He emigrated from Germany in 1937 and came to the United States in 1939, where he served in the U. S. Army during World War II. He is the author of several books, most notably *The Stillborn Revolution: The Communist Bid for Power in Germany* (1963) and *Between Fear and Hope: Jewish Youth in the Third Reich* (1988).

Klaus J. Bade teaches modern history at the University of Osnabrück. He is a member of the board of the Institute for Migration Research and Intercultural Studies (IMIS) at Osnabrück and has published extensively on colonial, social, and political history as well as on population and migration issues in the past and present.

Ronald H. Bayor is Professor of History at Georgia Tech University in Atlanta, and is editor of the *Journal of American Ethnic History*. His *Race and the Shaping of Twentieth-Century Atlanta* (1996) received an outstanding book award from the Gustavus Myers Center for the Study of Human Rights in North America, while a collection of essays co-edited with Timothy J. Meagher under the title *The New York Irish* (1996) was winner of the Donnelly Prize for the best book in history from the American Conference for Irish Studies.

Manfred Berg teaches history at the John F. Kennedy Institute for North American Studies of the Free University of Berlin. He previously served as a research fellow at the German Historical Institute in Washington, D.C., and is a specialist on the history of the civil rights movement in the United States. His latest book is *The Ticket to Freedom: Die NAACP und das Wahlrecht der Afroamerikaner* (2000).

Tony A. Freyer is University Research Professor of History at Law at the University of Alabama in Tuscaloosa. He has authored or co-authored nine books, including *The Little Rock Crisis* (1984), *Justice Hugo Black and Modern America* 1990), and, with Frank M. Johnson, *Defending Constitutional Rights (Studies in the Legal History of the South)* (2001).

Eckhardt Fuchs is currently a postdoctoral research fellow at the Max Planck Institute for the History of Science in Berlin. From 1996 to 2000 he was a research fellow at the German Historical Institute in Washington, D.C. His main field of research is American and European intellectual history in the nineteenth and twentieth centuries as well as the history of scientific internationalism.

Michael Hänel is currently finishing his doctoral thesis on Ernst Cassirer's philosophy of history at the Max Planck Institute for History in Göttingen, where he has studied history, philosophy, and political science. His publications include a forthcoming essay, "Problemgeschichte als Forschung. Die Erbschaft des Neukantianismus," in O. G. Oexle, ed., *Das Problem der Problemgeschichte 1880–1932* (2001).

Georg G. Iggers is Professor Emeritus of History at the State University of New York at Buffalo. He is author of *The German Conception of History: The National Tradition of Historical Thought from Herder to the Present* (1968), *The Social History of Politics: Critical Perspectives in West German Historical Writing Since 1945* (1986), and, most recently, *Historiography in the Twentieth Century: From Scientific Objectivity to the Postmodern Challenge* (1997).

Konrad H. Jarausch is Lurcy Professor of European Civilization at the University of North Carolina at Chapel Hill and co-director of the Zentrum für Zeithistorische Forschung in Potsdam, Germany. He is author of more than a dozen books on different aspects of modern German history, including *The Unfree Professions: German Lawyers, Teachers, and Engineers, 1900–1950* (1990) and *The Rush to German Unity* (1994), and is most recently co-editor of *Dictatorship as Experience: Towards a Social-Cultural History of the GDR* (1999).

Larry Eugene Jones is Professor of History at Canisius College in Buffalo, New York. He is the author of *German Liberalism and the Dissolution of the Weimar Party System, 1918–1933* (1988), and has co-edited several collections of essays, including *In Search of a Liberal Germany: Studies in the History of German Liberalism from 1789 to the Present* (1990) with Konrad H. Jarausch, and *Between Reform, Reaction, and Resistance: Studies in the History of German Conservatism from 1789 to the Present* (1993) with James N. Retallack.

Trude Maurer is a lecturer in East European and Modern History at the University of Göttingen and has been a visiting professor at the Universities of Göttingen, Cologne, and Jena, and the Humboldt University of Berlin. Her publications include *Ostjuden in Deutschland 1918–1933* (1986), *Die Entwicklung der jüdischen Minderheit in Deutschland 1780–1933* (1992), and *Hochschullehrer im Zarenreich. Ein Beitrag zur russischen Sozial- und Bildungsgeschichte* (1998).

Patricia Mazón is Assistant Professor of History at the State University of New York at Buffalo. Her publications include "Fräulein Doktor: Literary Images of the First Female University Students in Fin-de-Siècle Germany," in *Women in German Yearbook* (2000), and "Germania Triumphant: The Niederwald National Monument and the Liberal Moment in Imperial Germany," in *German History* (2000). She is currently preparing a book-length manuscript entitled "Intellectual She-Monsters: The Admission of Women to German Universities, 1865–1914" for publication.

Supriya Mukherjee is an Adjunct Professor of History at the University of Memphis. She studied at the University of Buffalo, where she complete a doctoral thesis on the German psychologist and philosopher William Stern. Her research interests include the history of education and psychology during the Second Empire and Weimar Republic. She is currently writing on homosexuality in the German youth movement as portrayed by pedagogical psychologists in imperial Germany.

Jochen Oltmer is Assistant Professor of Modern History at the University of Osnabrück and serves as a board member on the Institute for Migration Research and Intercultural Studies at Osnabrück. His most recent publications include a collection of essays co-edited with Klaus J. Bade entitled *Aussiedler. Deutsche Einwanderer aus Osteuropa* (1999) and *Migration als Gefahr. Transnationale Migration und Wanderungspolitik in der Weimarer Republik* (2001).

www.ingramcontent.com/pod-product-compliance
Lightning Source LLC
Chambersburg PA
CBHW060031030426
42334CB00019B/2274

* 9 7 8 1 5 7 1 8 1 3 0 6 0 *